HAIG'S ENEMY

Crown Prince Rupprecht of Bavaria

HAIG'S ENEMY

JONATHAN BOFF

*Crown Prince Rupprecht
and Germany's War on
the Western Front*

OXFORD
UNIVERSITY PRESS

OXFORD
UNIVERSITY PRESS

Great Clarendon Street, Oxford, OX2 6DP,
United Kingdom

Oxford University Press is a department of the University of Oxford.
It furthers the University's objective of excellence in research, scholarship,
and education by publishing worldwide. Oxford is a registered trade mark of
Oxford University Press in the UK and in certain other countries

Published in the United States of America by Oxford University Press
198 Madison Avenue, New York, NY 10016, United States of America

British Library Cataloguing in Publication Data
Data available

Library of Congress Control Number: 2017953093

ISBN 978-0-19-967046-8

Printed in Great Britain by
Clays Ltd, St Ives plc

Acknowledgements

I could not have completed this book without the help and support of too many people to list here. I am immensely grateful, first, for the encouragement and support, moral and practical, that I have received from friends and colleagues both at the University of Birmingham and within the history community more broadly. The generosity I have encountered has been inspiring. Nick Crowson, Elaine Fulton, Sabine Lee, and Corey Ross helped create the space for me to research this book, and my fellow foot-soldiers in the War Studies trenches, past and present, kindly took up the teaching slack. Pete Gray has been a good friend and a sage mentor to whose wisdom I owe much. Members of the Centre for War Studies, most notably John Bourne, have offered inspiration and education in equal measure at our seminars. I am grateful to the participants at a range of seminars and conferences to whom I have presented aspects of this work over the years, for their comments and suggestions; and to those who took part in the 2014 and 2016 British Army staff rides to the Western Front, from whom I learnt much. I am especially grateful to Holger Afflerbach, Tony Cowan, Robert Foley, Markus Pöhlmann, Christian Stachelbeck, and Dave Zabecki, all of whom shared their expertise in the history of the German military with a generosity and patience which was humbling to this novice. My students, inevitably, have taught me the most: I thank them for that and for turning a job into a joy.

Special thanks to Professors David French, David Stevenson, and Sir Hew Strachan, who have been especially supportive in multiple ways, most of them beyond the call of duty.

Without the help of archivists, not much history would get written. I am grateful to the staffs of the following archives and libraries: in Britain, the British Library, Imperial War Museum, London Library, National Archives, and National Army Museum; in Germany, the Bundesarchiv-Militärarchiv in Freiburg im Breisgau, and, in Munich, the Bayerische Staatsbibliothek and Bayerisches Hauptstaatsarchiv, both Abteilung IV (Kriegsarchiv) and

Abteilung III (Geheimes Hausarchiv). Special thanks at the last of these to Dr Gerhard Immler, a prince among archivists, and the very patient Herr Leipnitz.

Thanks to Barbara Taylor once again for her excellent maps. Others who helped me in specific ways are thanked at the appropriate place in the Notes.

Several friends were kind enough to read drafts: thank you to Holger Afflerbach, Tony Cowan, Aimée Fox, Sabine Lee, Corey Ross, Gary Sheffield, Andy Simpson, and to the anonymous readers for Oxford University Press. Thank you for the keen attention to detail you brought to the task and for saving me from howlers. This is a better book for your insights and suggestions: the shortcomings that remain are my fault.

Luciana O'Flaherty first approached me about publishing with Oxford University Press, and I am grateful to her, Matthew Cotton, Martha Cunneen, Carrie Hickman, Kizzy Taylor-Richelieu, and the whole team there for their encouragement, patience, tact, and efficiency. Thanks also to Sally Evans-Darby for the speed and accuracy of her copy-editing.

When it briefly looked as though this project might be derailed, the professionalism and skill of Andy Chukwuemuka, Diana Holdright, Susan Horsewood-Lee, and the staff of the Cromwell Hospital kept it on track. I owe them more than I can say.

Friends and family have tolerated the absences, both physical and mental, of a distracted author with good humour and patience which I didn't always deserve. This applies especially to my wife, Yuko. This book is hers as much as mine: I might never have started it, and certainly couldn't have finished it, without her love and encouragement. It is dedicated to her, and to my godchildren, Phoebe, Jack, Tom, James, and Luke, with love.

Contents

List of Illustrations

List of Maps

Maps

BR	British	XXXXX □ Army Group	
Bav	Bavarian	XXXX □ Army	
FR	French	XXX □ Corps	
ANZAC	Australian and New Zealand Army Corps	XX □ Division	
AUS	Australian	□ German	
CAN	Canadian	⊠ Infantry	
Gds	Guards	◢ Cavalry	
NZ	New Zealand		
Res	Reserve	**(-)** Elements of unit	
Ter	Territorial		
▪▪▪▪▪▪	Railways		
•••••••	Canals		

1. General Key for All Maps

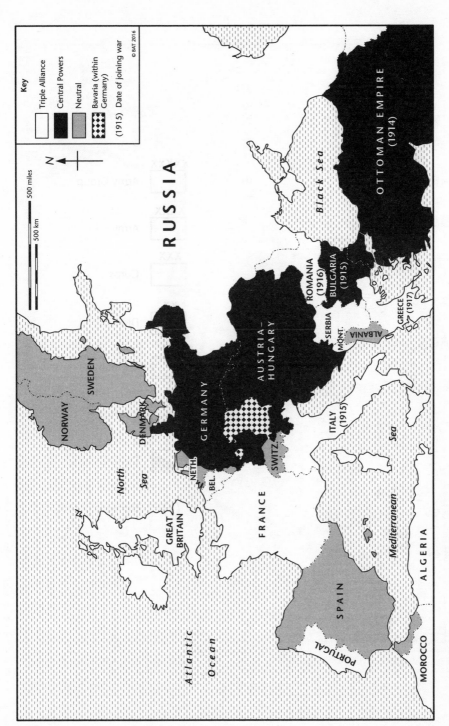

2. Europe and the Contending Alliances, 1914

Key

Triple Alliance
Central Powers
Neutral
Bavaria (within Germany)

(1915) Date of joining war

N

500 miles
500 km

RUSSIA

Atlantic Ocean

GREAT BRITAIN

North Sea

NORWAY

SWEDEN

DENMARK

NETH.

BEL.

GERMANY

FRANCE

SWITZ.

AUSTRIA–HUNGARY

ITALY (1915)

SERBIA

MONT.

ALBANIA

GREECE (1917)

ROMANIA (1916)

BULGARIA (1915)

Black Sea

OTTOMAN EMPIRE (1914)

SPAIN

PORTUGAL

Mediterranean Sea

MOROCCO

ALGERIA

3. The Western Front, 1914–18

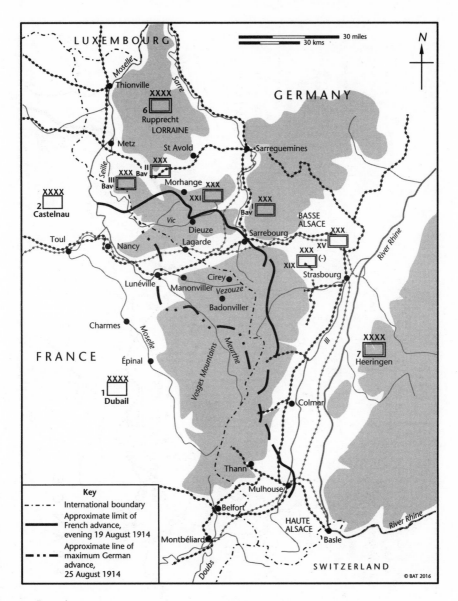

 contains the following labels:

LUXEMBOURG

Moselle

Thionville

Sorre

GERMANY

XXXX
6
Rupprecht
LORRAINE

Metz

St Avold

Sarreguemines

XXX
II

XXX Bav

III
Bav

Morhange

XXX
XXI

Vic

XXX
Bav

BASSE
ALSACE

XXXX
2
Castelnau

Seille

Toul

Nancy

Dieuze

Lagarde

Sarrebourg

XXX
XV

XXX (-)
XIX

Strasbourg

River Rhine

Lunéville

Cirey

Manonviller

Vezouze

Badonviller

Charmes

Moselle

FRANCE

Épinal

Vosges Mountains

Meurthe

III

XXXX
7
Heeringen

XXXX
1
Dubail

Colmar

Thann

Mulhouse

Belfort

HAUTE
ALSACE

River Rhine

Montbéliard

Basle

SWITZERLAND

Doubs

30 miles
30 kms

N

© BAT 2016

Key

–·–·– International boundary

——— Approximate limit of
French advance,
evening 19 August 1914

–··–··– Approximate line of
maximum German
advance,
25 August 1914

4. Lorraine 1914

5. Somme 1914

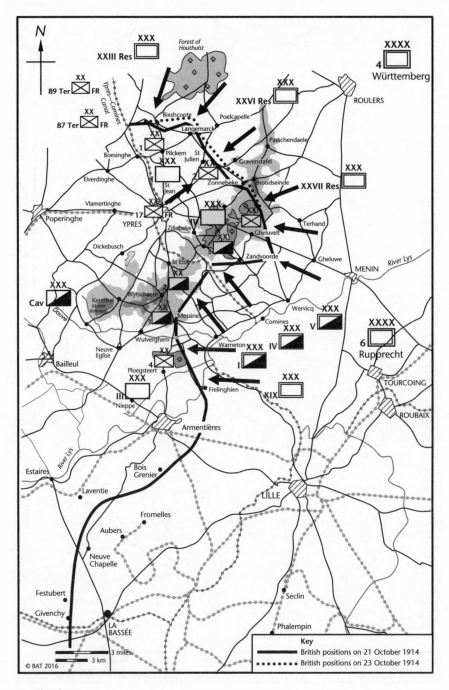

6. Flanders 1914

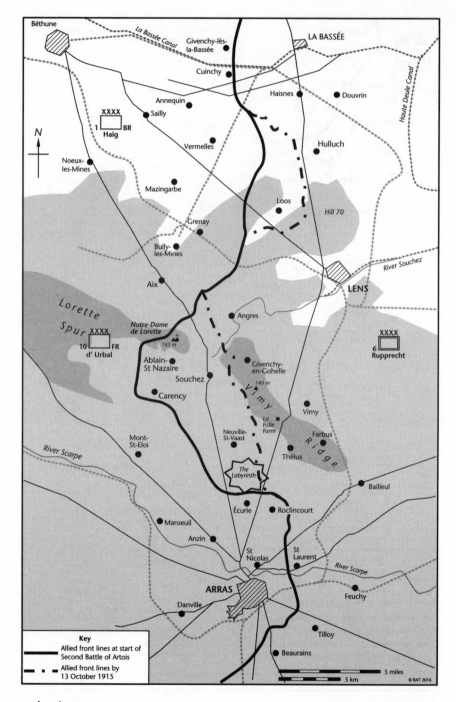

Béthune

La Bassée Canal

Givenchy-lès-
la-Bassée

LA BASSÉE

Cuinchy

Haisnes

Douvrin

Annequin

Sailly

XXXX
1 [ ] BR
Haig

Vermelles

Hulluch

N

Noeux-
les-Mines

Mazingarbe

Loos

Hill 70

Haute Deule Canal

Grenay

Bully-
les-Mines

Aix

River Souchez

LENS

Lorette

Spur

XXXX
10 [ ] FR
d' Urbal

Notre-Dame
de Lorette
165 m

Angres

Ablain-
St Nazaire

Souchez

Carency

Givenchy-
en-Gohelle

140 m

V i m y

XXXX
6 [ ]
Rupprecht

Vimy

La
Folie
Farm

Farbus

Mont-
St-Eloi

Neuville-
St-Vaast

Thélus

R i d g e

River Scarpe

The
Labyrinth

Bailleul

Maroeuil

Écurie

Roclincourt

Anzin

St
Nicolas

St
Laurent

River Scarpe

ARRAS

Feuchy

Danville

Tilloy

Beaurains

Key

⎯⎯ Allied front lines at start of
Second Battle of Artois

–·–·– Allied front lines by
13 October 1915

5 miles

5 km

© BAT 2016

7. Artois 1915

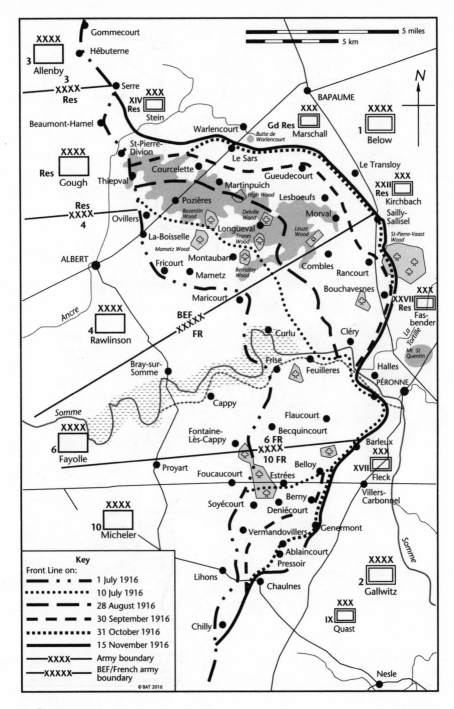

Key

Front Line on:

▬ · ▬ · ▬	1 July 1916
• • • • • •	10 July 1916
▬ ▬ ▬	28 August 1916
▬ ▬ ▬	30 September 1916
▪▪▪▪▪▪	31 October 1916
▬▬▬▬	15 November 1916
—XXXX—	Army boundary
—XXXXX—	BEF/French army boundary

© BAT 2016

8. Somme 1916

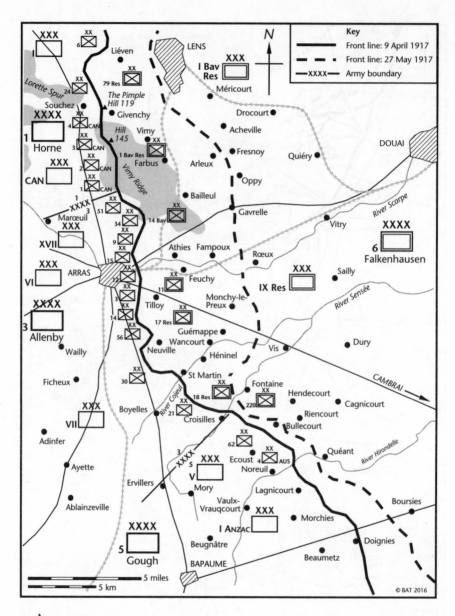

Key

——	Front line: 9 April 1917
----	Front line: 27 May 1917
XXXX	Army boundary

N

I
XXX

6
XX

Liéven

LENS

I Bav Res
XXX

Méricourt

Lorette Spur

24
XX

79 Res
XX

The Pimple
Hill 119

Drocourt

Souchez

Givenchy

Acheville

DOUAI

1
XXXX

Horne

4 CAN
XX

Hill 145

Vimy

Fresnoy

Quiéry

3 CAN
XX

1 Bav Res
XX

Farbus

Arleux

CAN
XXX

2 CAN
XX

Oppy

1 CAN
XX

Bailleul

1
XXXX
3

51
XX

XX

14 Bav
XX

Gavrelle

Vitry

River Scarpe

Marœuil

34
XX

6
XXXX

XVII
XXX

9
XX

Athies Fampoux

Rœux

Sailly

Falkenhausen

15
XX

VI
XXX

ARRAS

12
XX

Feuchy

IX Res
XXX

River Sensée

3
XX

11
XX

Monchy-le-Preux

3
XXXX

Tilloy

14
XX

17 Res
XX

Dury

Allenby

56
XX

Guémappe
Wancourt

Vis

Wailly

Neuville

Héninel

CAMBRAI

Ficheux

St Martin

Fontaine

30
XX

18 Res
XX

220
XX

Hendecourt

Cagnicourt

VII
XXX

Boyelles

River Cojeul

21
XX

Croisilles

Riencourt

Bullecourt

Quéant

River Hirondelle

Adinfer

62
XX

Ayette

3
XXXX
5

V
XXX

Ecoust
Noreuil

4
XX AUS

Ervillers

Mory

Lagnicourt

Boursies

Ablainzeville

Vaulx-Vraucourt

XXX

Morchies

Doignies

5
XXXX

Gough

Beugnâtre

I Anzac
XXX

BAPAUME

Beaumetz

5 miles

5 km

© BAT 2016

9. Arras 1917

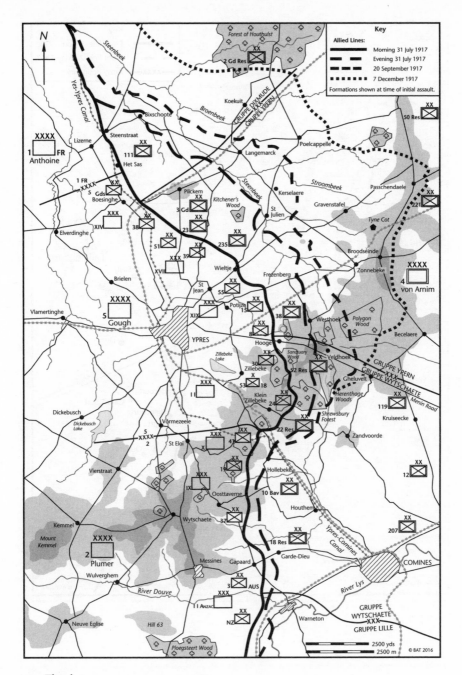

Key

Allied Lines:

— — — Morning 31 July 1917

— — — Evening 31 July 1917

— — — 20 September 1917

••••••• 7 December 1917

Formations shown at time of initial assault.

10. Flanders 1917

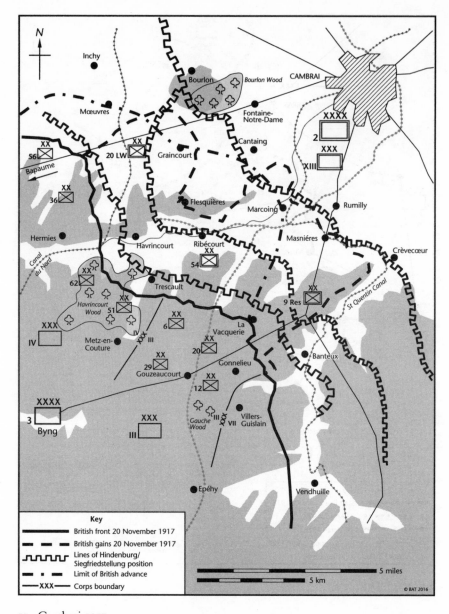

Key

```
━━━━━━━━  British front 20 November 1917
─ ─ ─ ─ ─  British gains 20 November 1917
ᴖᴖᴖᴖᴖᴖ  Lines of Hindenburg/
          Siegfriedstellung position
─ ·— ·— ·  Limit of British advance
──XXX──  Corps boundary
```

5 miles

5 km

© BAT 2016

11. Cambrai 1917

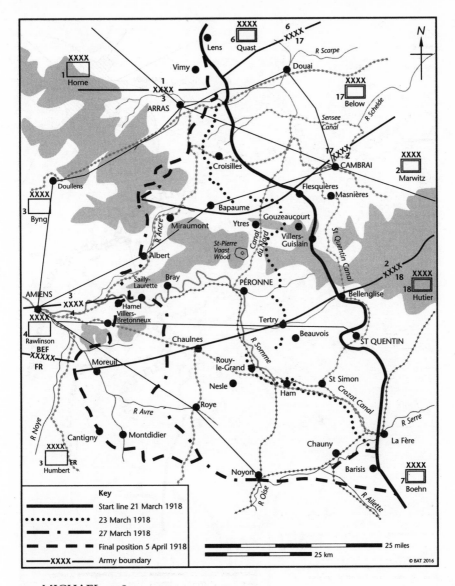

Key

————————	Start line 21 March 1918
••••••••••••	23 March 1918
—·—·—·—·—	27 March 1918
— — — — —	Final position 5 April 1918
—XXXX—	Army boundary

25 miles

25 km

© BAT 2016

12. MICHAEL 1918

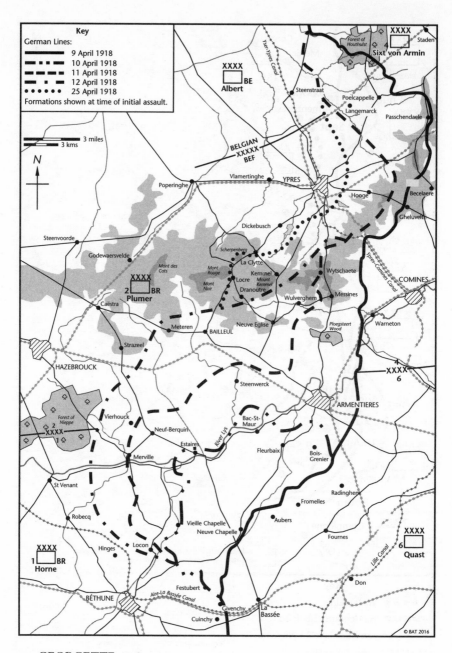

Key

German Lines:

———— 9 April 1918
—·—·— 10 April 1918
—■—■— 11 April 1918
—·—·— 12 April 1918
••••• 25 April 1918

Formations shown at time of initial assault.

3 miles
3 kms

N

XXXX
Sixt von Armin 4

Staden

Forest of Houthulst

XXXX
BE
Albert

Steenstraat

Poelcappelle

Langemarck

Passchendaele

BELGIAN
XXXXX
BEF

Vlamertinghe

YPRES

Hooge

Becelaere

Poperinghe

Gheluvelt

Dickebusch

Scherpenberg

Steenvoorde

La Clytte

Wytschaete

COMINES

Godewaersvelde

Mont des Cats

Mont Rouge

Kemmel

Mount Kemmel

Locre

Messines

XXXX
2 Plumer BR

Mont Noir

Dranoutre

Wulverghem

Caëstra

Meteren

Neuve Eglise

Ploegsteert Wood

Warneton

Strazeel

BAILLEUL

XXXX
4 6

HAZEBROUCK

Steenwerck

ARMENTIERES

Vierhouck

Bac-St-Maur

XXXX
2

Forest of Nieppe

Neuf-Berquin

Estaires

River Lys

Fleurbaix

Bois-Grenier

Merville

St Venant

Radinghem

Fromelles

Robecq

Vieille Chapelle

Aubers

Neuve Chapelle

Fournes

XXXX
1 BR
Horne

Hinges

Locon

XXXX
6 Quast

Don

Festubert

BÉTHUNE

Aire-La Bassée Canal

Givenchy

La Bassée

Lille Canal

Cuinchy

© BAT 2016

13. GEORGETTE 1918

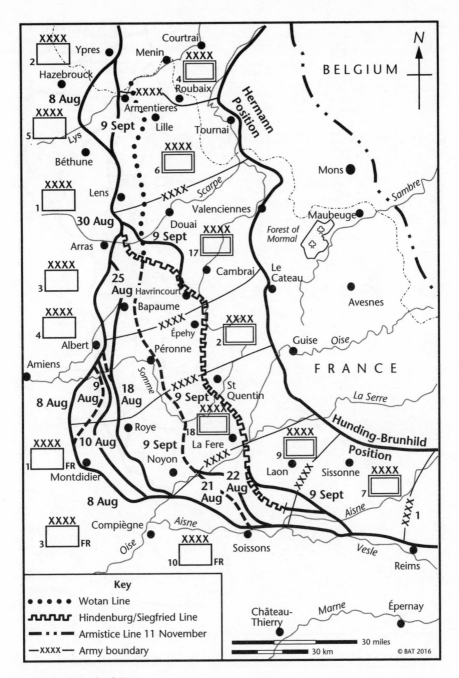

14. The Hundred Days

Introduction

Crown Prince Rupprecht of Bavaria first came alive for me a few years ago. I was working on a book about the last few months of the war on the Western Front and had gone to Munich to explore the archives of the Bavarian army. These somehow escaped the Second World War firebombs which destroyed many of the Prussian records and as a result constitute one of the best sources for information on the German army during the First World War. On the last day of my trip, as I was idly flicking through a folder of apparently random documents, one sheet of paper caught my eye. It was a passport, issued by the Dutch embassy in German-occupied Brussels, allowing the Marquis de Villalobar and his party to enter the Netherlands on 12 November 1918. What was it doing in the personal files of Crown Prince Rupprecht of Bavaria?

I already knew a little about Rupprecht. I knew, for instance, that he served as one of Germany's most senior generals between 1914 and 1918 and spent most of the war fighting against the 'tommies' of the British Expeditionary Force (BEF), leading the German Sixth Army, and later an army group of one and a half million men, in famous battles such as Ypres, the Somme, and Passchendaele.[1] It was Rupprecht's men who launched Germany's last-gasp offensives in March 1918, and when they failed it was his army group that felt much of the weight of Allied counter-attacks during the so-called 'Hundred Days' campaign in August–November 1918. Rupprecht's closest British counterpart and most consistent enemy was probably Sir Douglas Haig. Like Rupprecht, Haig rose to command an army group: the BEF; and everywhere Haig and the BEF turned from October 1914 on, Rupprecht and his men were in the way. A good parallel from the Second World War might be the mythical rivalry between Bernard Montgomery and Erwin Rommel, although Haig and Rupprecht, who never met and were in no sense personal rivals, would have despised any propaganda of personality of that kind. What did the Marquis de Villalobar have to do with Rupprecht, though, and why was he travelling to neutral Holland the day after the Armistice had been signed?

In the early days of November 1918 Germany was in double crisis. At home, Socialist agitators were whipping up revolution, pushing crowned heads from their thrones and seizing power. Among those deposed were Kaiser Wilhelm II and Rupprecht's father, King Ludwig III of Bavaria. At the front, the famed discipline of the German army was breaking down after a series of heavy battlefield defeats. Some units were already setting up Russian-style soldiers' councils ('soviets'). The people of Brussels, where Rupprecht had his headquarters, cowered behind locked doors as gangs of drunken German soldiers rampaged through the streets, looting and worse wherever they could. Rupprecht's life might be in danger. Less than four months before, after all, Bolsheviks had pitilessly murdered the Russian Tsar and his entire family. The Spanish ambassador to Belgium, Rodrigo Marqués de Villalobar, came to Rupprecht's rescue. He offered sanctuary in the embassy and made arrangements to smuggle him, disguised as plain Mr Landsberg, to safety in the Netherlands. That was what the passport was for and that explained why it had found its way to the archive in Munich.[2]

Answering one question, however, raised others. How was the proud heir to an ancient throne, a man of consequence in Germany and across Europe, a field marshal who had led hundreds of thousands of men in battle, reduced to skulking across borders under cover of darkness and a false name? This is the first question this book seeks to answer. It offers the first biography of Crown Prince Rupprecht in English, concentrating on his military career. He has had several German biographers but they have tended not to be specialists in the history of warfare. Only a couple of scholarly articles in German have addressed this aspect of his career before now.[3] As we will see, the human story is a fascinating, moving, and possibly tragic one. It also, however, raises important questions with broader ramifications than the purely individual. Studying Rupprecht's military career allows us to interrogate and challenge several of the preconceptions we have about the First World War and about modernity itself.[4]

We can, for instance, see the war from a new perspective if we look through Rupprecht's eyes. Too often we have been told the story of the Western Front from the British point of view alone.[5] The French, and even the Germans, often fade into the background or even out of the picture altogether. This book aims to help correct this distortion and to give the proper weight to all three armies, enabling us to understand the war in a more balanced way.

We can also explore important questions about the war. One of the key ones is: why did Germany lose the First World War? Inevitably, a range of factors played a part. Germany did not lose the First World War only because her army was defeated on the Western Front. Events on other fronts and at home, some of which had little or nothing to do with Rupprecht, played a part in determining the outcome. So there are limits to what studying him can tell us. For instance, his contribution to grand strategy, the level of war where politicians set overall aims and allocate resources, was, as we shall see, limited. He did, however, know all the key decision-makers and was extremely well informed. Consequently, he is a useful source of information about the direction of the war. We will see that the German leadership made strategic mistakes at every stage. Few historians would disagree with that. The more interesting question is: why?

Rupprecht himself spent the war fighting on the Western Front, working at the operational level of war. This is where generals construct and fight campaigns, design and sequence battles, allocate resources and manage reserves to achieve the mission they have been set by the strategists. Below the level of operations lies that of tactics, where soldiers fight their battles. Get the tactics right, and you win battles. Get the operational art right, and you win campaigns. Get the strategy right, too, and you win wars. The Western Front was one campaign of a larger war and for both sides winning there was necessary, even if it was not sufficient, for victory. Control of France and Belgium was precisely what many thought they were fighting for in the first place and it was here that both sides deployed their most powerful forces. The focus of this book, therefore, is on the operational level of war on the Western Front, where seeing events through Rupprecht's eyes can be very helpful.

This is an aspect of Germany's war which historians have tended to neglect, concentrating instead either on the view of the supreme com-mander or of the individual soldier in the trench.[6] Germany has even less of a tradition of operational military history than British academia.[7] In neither English nor German has any historian yet followed a single senior German general, and the formations he commanded, through the whole war as this book does. Doing so shows how the German military reacted to the stresses of conflict and the need for rapid and sometimes radical change. Many mili-tary historians tend to assume that the German army of the first half of the

twentieth century was highly skilled tactically, largely because it operated a
flexible system of command known as Auftragstaktik ('mission command')
which delegated authority and ensured that the man best placed to make
any decision was the one issuing the orders. Other strengths included high
levels of training and motivation. However misguided or downright evil the
purposes to which the army was put, they argue, it constituted a fine tech-
nical instrument. Here I challenge that interpretation and suggest that the
German army of 1914–18 had structural weaknesses and conceptual shortcomings which inhibited innovation, distorted decision-making, and
eventually helped destroy it. Some of those weaknesses were unique to the
military, but others carried over from broader German society.[8] Studying
armies as institutions in their own right is interesting but when, as in the
two world wars, they are mass citizen forces, they open a window onto
society as a whole which allows analysis of the military to take on wider
significance.

If historians have sometimes overlooked the operational art of the German
army, the same cannot be said of the BEF, which has been studied under the
finest of microscopes. One of the most influential and persistent myths in
history, first sketched out by Winston Churchill and David Lloyd George and
enthusiastically developed and promulgated by Basil Liddell Hart and others,
is that which sees the Western Front primarily in terms of British failure.[9]
The traditional narrative assumes that what went wrong on the Western
Front did so because the generals were too stupid, or the army too hide-
bound, to adjust to the modern reality of barbed wire and the machine gun.
The commemorations of the war's centenary have repeated the stereotypes
encapsulated in *Oh! What a Lovely War* and *Blackadder* more often than they
have challenged them, showing how deeply seared into the public con-
sciousness this myth is. The gulf between popular perceptions of the war and
recent academic research has never been wider, because since the 1980s a
generation of British and Commonwealth military historians have been
mining the archives to revise that traditional view. They have dissected almost
every aspect of the BEF in minute detail and argue that its leaders were not,
on the whole, fatheads and knaves who never learnt a thing. Instead, the
British army did remarkably well to overcome the immense challenges it
faced and adapt to radical change in the most trying conditions, by marrying
the best civilian expertise with military know-how to climb a metaphorical
'learning curve', until by 1918 it was capable of fighting the toughest army in
the world toe-to-toe—and beating it.[10]

The 'learning curve' idea captures the central truth that the British army of 1918 was certainly more effective than it had been even a year or two previously. It is not without problems, however, largely stemming from exploring the BEF in isolation without sufficient comparative research into the French and German armies. This is understandable given the mass of detail involved in the study of just one army, much less three, even before taking into account the language barrier. Nonetheless, this risks making British learning look exceptional. Also, it can exaggerate the British achievement by ascribing too much of the BEF's success to its learning curve and taking insufficient account of any deterioration in the German army. One of my core contentions here is that it is a mistake to see the war as a one-sided (British) struggle to learn a new way of fighting and break the stalemate. Although the front was deadlocked for much of the war, it was so only because there was a continuous dynamic of push and pull, measure and counter-measure, between the two sides. This produced a deceptively stable equilibrium. This book argues that the battlefield defeat of the German army in 1918 was at least as much the result of the Germans getting worse as it was of the British getting better. It therefore challenges us to revise our views of the BEF, which was neither a collection of 'butchers and bunglers' nor an institution made up exclusively of forward-thinking quick learners, but somewhere between the two.

So, Rupprecht's war enables us to see the war and the armies which fought it in a fresh way. It also prompts us to think again about the relationship between the First World War, modernity, and the agency of the individual. One of the things that first attracted me to Rupprecht was that he seemed to stand for a generation which was destroyed by the events of 1914–18. By the time the war finished, his eldest son and many of his friends were dead. He had lost his throne and, instead of leading a triumphant homecoming parade, he sneaked back into Bavaria incognito. The threat of trial for war crimes hung over his head for years. Never again would he enjoy true power or influence. Throughout the 1920s and 1930s he watched as political violence convulsed his fatherland. Under Hitler, he lost his home, his family, and nearly his life. Like the cosmopolitan aristocrats of central Europe so vividly evoked in Patrick Leigh Fermor's travel books, Rupprecht can be seen as one of the many relics of a bygone age swept away by the tsunami of modernity.[11] How far does such a romantic picture correspond to reality, though?

Seeing Rupprecht as a victim fits neatly into popular perceptions of both the First World War and modernity itself. Most of us first encounter the war at school, through poets such as Wilfred Owen and Siegfried Sassoon. The worm's-eye view they offer inevitably drains meaning from the existence of the soldiers they depict. Unable to discern the larger patterns which make sense of their lives—and deaths—of course the war seems bewildering and futile. These poets were keen to reject what they saw as the twee conservative pastoralism of Edwardian Britain and so they eagerly highlighted the impersonal, the mechanical, and the modern in ways which have further influenced our view of the war. In Owen's poem, the Western Front is where, amid the monstrous clamour of modern industrial warfare, 'doomed youth' are herded to their deaths with all the passivity of cattle. Similarly, it is a mark of the insignificance of the individual in *All Quiet on the Western Front* that the novel's ironic title derives from the official bulletin issued on the day its everyman hero dies. In other self-consciously modern depictions of the war, such as C. R. W. Nevinson's painting 'La Mitrailleuse', soldiers have lost their humanity altogether. Flesh and steel fuse into war-fighting machines. The fact that we concentrate our commemorations today on memorials to those who were killed, not those who survived, only reinforces the victimhood motif. Also, to view the participants as victims rather than agents has the advantage of being psychologically easier on us.[12] The victimhood we ascribe to the soldiers of the First World War is, therefore, multi-faceted: it combines inevitable and pointless death with a sense of alienation from a modern world increasingly dominated by the machine, where humans have shrunk to insignificance and have no control over their own destiny. For all the efforts of some historians to correct it, this perception of the ordinary soldier as victim remains firmly dug in.[13]

Even if it is correct that 'the soldier in the trenches can be characterized as the victim of modern warfare *par excellence*', does that apply equally to all? Were there active subjects, as well as passive objects, on the First World War battlefield? To whom can we ascribe moral responsibility?[14] Was Rupprecht entirely caught up by forces he could neither understand nor control? Did he conform to the romantic stereotype? Or was what happened to him the consequence of his own decisions?[15]

The sources this book draws on are mostly new to an English-speaking audience. I have worked through a range of archival collections, primarily in Germany. First, Crown Prince Rupprecht kept a war diary, which is preserved in the Bavarian Household Privy Archive in Munich. It extends to 4,197 handwritten pages and was mainly put together as the war went on. There are two exceptions: he reconstructed the first few months of 1914 from notes over the following winter, and he also had to re-write the last week of the war, having burned the original pages before going on the run. This manuscript diary is full of detail, not only about what was going on in his sector but also about the wider war. The entry for a typical day, 1 October 1917, for example, covers: his tactical and logistical situation (one page); an intelligence report concerning a recent top-level Anglo-French meeting to discuss offensive plans (another page); diplomatic developments (one page); and the domestic situations in Britain, France, Russia, and the United States of America (nearly six pages). During the 1920s Rupprecht's generalship in August and September 1914 attracted criticism in the early volumes of the German official history. The retired staff officers at the Reichsarchiv in Potsdam who were compiling it blamed errors he made for the failure of the Schlieffen Plan. To put his side in the long-running controversy which ensued, Rupprecht decided to publish a version of his diaries. He asked some of his former staff officers to read and check the manuscript, which was then edited down to a quarter of its original length and published in three volumes in 1929. Much of the material cut out was repetitive or, like the sometimes lengthy domestic and foreign press summaries Rupprecht used to write up, not relevant. On the whole, the published diary maintains the sense of the original closely, although on occasion Rupprecht was unable to resist tweaking it to make himself look better, as we shall see. He also toned down, or left out completely, some of his criticisms of individuals. Some historians have drawn on the published diary, but few have bothered with the manuscript version, or with other unpublished papers including Rupprecht's correspondence with his family, friends, and politicians.[16]

Another major source was the official records of the formations Rupprecht led: Sixth Army and Army Group Crown Prince Rupprecht. These are held in the Bavarian State War Archive, also in Munich, and cover most aspects of both day-to-day operations and longer-range policy in considerable detail.[17] They relate not only to Bavarian formations but also to all those under his command, so they give us a broad view across the German army. The after-action reports compiled by units at all levels after battle, in an effort to learn lessons for next time, proved particularly valuable. These papers were supplemented by other official documents from the federal military archives in Freiburg-im-Breisgau, where any surviving records from Potsdam are stored, along with other private papers belonging to Rupprecht's associates and subordinates. Published primary sources include the fourteen-volume German official history, *Der Weltkrieg*, the Bavarian official history, *Die Bayern im Großen Kriege 1914–1918*, the series of battle monographs compiled by the Reichsarchiv between the wars, German regimental histories and officers' memoirs, and, of course, the voluminous French and British official histories.[18]

This book is divided into five Parts. The first four tell the story of Rupprecht's war from the beginning through to the end. Seeing the Western Front through German eyes in this way invites us to review existing, largely British, narratives of the battles fought there. We will discover, for instance, that battles which loom large in British military history sometimes hardly even feature as footnotes in the German equivalent. This also enables us to explore some of the broader themes already mentioned. Prominent among these is how the character of warfare evolved and the different armies adapted to change. Many chapters conclude with a section on this strand. Another recurring theme is the nature of command on the First World War battlefield. Such themes help explain both the war's outcome and the underlying strengths and weaknesses of the forces fighting it. The fifth and final Part assesses Rupprecht as military commander and political actor and offers answers to some of the questions raised in this Introduction. An Appendix on military terminology seeks to guide readers who want help telling the difference between a corporal and a colonel or a company and a corps.

The war which emerges from this book is one of radical and dynamic change where the ability to out-think your enemy was just as important as being able to out-muscle him. It took both sides time and immense effort to adapt to the new ways of war, not least because every time they came close to an answer, the enemy changed the question. Eventually, however, the German army was dragged down by its inherent weaknesses and fell behind in the race to adapt. The results were disastrous. Sometimes Rupprecht and his colleagues were constrained in the choices they could make, but the decisions they took were nonetheless too often poor. The First World War was not just a war of bodies and a war of machines: it was a war of brains, too. The Germans lost all three.

PART I

To War 1914

I

Rupprecht's Road to War

Prince Rupprecht Maria Luitpold Ferdinand was born in Munich shortly before nine o'clock on the morning of 18 May 1869.[1] He was the newest member of the Wittelsbachs, the dynasty which had ruled Bavaria for nearly 700 years. Rupprecht was the first of thirteen children born to Prince Ludwig and his wife, the Habsburg Princess Maria Therese. Rupprecht was related to most of the crowned heads of Catholic Europe: not only the Habsburgs but also the Braganzas, the house of Luxembourg, and even the Stuarts. Indeed, some saw his mother as the rightful Stuart heir, tracing her ancestry back to Charles I. When Rupprecht visited London for Queen Victoria's diamond jubilee in 1897, members of the Jacobite Order of the White Rose tried to pay homage to him as the future King Robert I and IV. Rupprecht never took this claim seriously, but his very name had a Stuart link: King Charles I's nephew and famous cavalry commander during the English Civil War, Prince Rupert of the Rhine, was a Wittelsbach ancestor.

Rupprecht was not born to the throne. The King of Bavaria in 1869 was his great-uncle, Ludwig II. Just twenty-three years old, he appeared perfectly vigorous and there seemed no reason why he should not live long and build a family of his own. In fact, however, Ludwig's enthusiasms lay elsewhere. He was Richard Wagner's patron and was more interested in building fairy-tale castles than in continuing the royal line. The towers of his castle at Neuschwanstein later inspired Walt Disney. Known as 'Mad King Ludwig', he died in murky circumstances in 1886, childless and unmarried. His brother Otto succeeded to the throne. Unfortunately, while there was room for doubt about Ludwig's mental health, there was none in Otto's case. He was indisputably insane. He had already been locked away for years and remained so until he eventually died in 1916. The uncle of Otto and Ludwig, and grandfather of Rupprecht, Prince Luitpold became the real ruler of

Bavaria as regent. When he died, in 1912, Rupprecht's father took over, finally setting Otto aside and declaring himself King Ludwig III the next year. Thus, at the age of forty-four, Rupprecht became heir to the throne and acquired the title by which he was known for the rest of his life: Crown Prince of Bavaria.

The throne which Rupprecht should one day inherit was a constitutional, rather than absolute, monarchy. The King was supposed to stand above politics and rule by consensus with his government and the two houses of the Bavarian parliament, the Landtag. In reality, he wielded considerable power. Although from 1906 the Lower House was elected by universal male suffrage, the King dominated the Upper House, appointed and dismissed the government at will, and dominated policy.[2] The biggest constraint on Bavarian royal power was external, rather than internal. In 1871 Bavaria became part of the new imperial Germany. She was now just the second state among many, lying far behind Prussia in importance. Of the total German population, over 60 per cent were Prussian, while only a little over 10 per cent came from Bavaria. Prussia had the power to veto constitutional change on her own whereas Bavaria could only do the same by building a broad coalition of the smaller states. That said, the government in Munich retained considerable powers and rights, including control over direct taxation. In peacetime it remained responsible for raising and running its own army. Officers pledged allegiance to the Bavarian King, rather than the German Kaiser. The army, however, was built on Prussian lines and in the event of war the Kaiser would become Supreme War Lord of all the German armies. Most crucially of all, the decision to declare war belonged to the Kaiser alone.

The first half of Rupprecht's life saw dramatic change for all Germany, with rapid population growth, a rush to the cities, and huge industrial expansion. Bavaria was affected too, but differences in the patterns of growth and development across the new country exacerbated pre-existing regional tensions. For example, although the population of Munich grew six-fold between 1850 and 1910, towns such as Essen in the Ruhr expanded more than thirty times over. Bavaria remained the least urban of the major German states, and invested less in industry and scientific research. Overall, Bavaria could not match the pace of growth in the north. In 1870, the population of Bavaria had been 4.8 million. By 1910, it had increased by 40 per cent, to 6.9 million. This was huge growth in a short period, but remained well below the German average of 60 per cent.

Bavaria retained deep cultural roots in its agrarian past. Seventy per cent of the population was Catholic, with 28 per cent Protestant. In Prussia, the religious proportions were almost exactly reversed. At the risk of generalization, Bavaria remained relatively agricultural, Catholic, and conservative even as Germany as a whole was becoming increasingly urban, Protestant, and socially progressive. Even her conservatism, founded in the values of the smallholder farmer, was very different from the Junker- and industrialist-dominated conservatism of the imperial ruling class. All these differences, new and old, created fault-lines which divided Bavaria and Prussia. Even in peacetime, the relationship between the two was not always easy. Prussians tended to treat Bavarians with condescension, while the latter were prickly about anything which seemed to be eroding their rights and privileges. As we shall see, wartime only made these tensions worse.[3]

Rupprecht later complained that his childhood was a strict one and to modern eyes his upbringing seems indeed to have been harsh. It is not clear that it was particularly so by the royal standards of the time, however. As a young child he saw his parents only at mealtimes, had lessons daily from eight a.m. until five p.m., and was frequently beaten, both by his short-tempered father and by his tutor. In the finest tradition of German royalty, his relationship with his father remained difficult throughout his life. It is perhaps telling also that he reacted against the religious atmosphere of home in later life: at least as a young man his Catholicism did not go much beyond observing the proprieties. At thirteen he became the first member of the Bavarian royal family to be educated at a public school. He graduated from high school in 1886 and was commissioned into the Regiment of Foot Guards. He later also spent time serving in artillery and cavalry regiments. He seems to have enjoyed to the full the relative freedom of life in the sub-alterns' mess, as well as the perks of being a young royal prince. Alongside his military duties he spent several terms studying at universities in Munich and Berlin. He also began his public career. For instance, he attended Kaiser Wilhelm I's funeral in March 1888.

When fully grown, Rupprecht was rather taller than average, at five feet ten inches. He took immaculate care over his appearance and carried himself with the upright bearing of the natural athlete. In his youth he had enjoyed swimming and skating and throughout his life remained a devotee of physical exercise and gymnastics. Well into middle age he could sit down on the ground and get up again without using his hands or arms. He was a keen sportsman, in the old, aristocratic sense: nothing so vulgar or English as team games for him. Instead he enjoyed game birds and hunting, both in the Alps and abroad. In India he killed a tiger from the back of a moving elephant with his second shot. Like most members of the upper classes of the time, he rode often. Even during wartime, a daily ride remained part of his exercise regime.[4]

In 1891, while serving in the 1st Heavy Cavalry Regiment, Rupprecht began going to lectures at the Bavarian War College (Kriegsakademie), where officers hoping to join the elite General Staff underwent three years of intensive training. He attended some of the classes but was excused the strenuous exams. The aim, after all, was not to produce a professional staff officer, but to teach him command and leadership. In 1893 he was promoted to command a squadron as Captain (Rittmeister). He rose rapidly through the ranks until in 1900 he was promoted to Major-General (Generalmajor) in charge of the 7th Infantry Brigade at Bamberg. In 1904, as a Lieutenant-General (Generalleutnant) he became General Officer Commanding (GOC) the 1st Division and soon thereafter took over the 1st Bavarian Corps. He was promoted to full General (General der Infanterie) in 1906. He seems to have taken his military duties seriously and to have been a respected and able commander of men.

Away from his military career, Rupprecht was well travelled. Italy proved a special and enduring love. He went there almost every year of his adult life. He knew most of Europe well but had also journeyed extensively around the Mediterranean and Middle East, Asia, and America. He even wrote travel books. Some of his travel, of course, was for royal business. For example, in 1911 he attended the coronation of King George V, writing to an artist friend:

> Time and again I admired the English race and its unique culture. The celebrations were great, but also absolutely exhausting. It is extraordinary how England is on the one hand so modern yet on the other so exceedingly con-servative. I wished you could see the coronation in Westminster Abbey with me, the picture was so artistic, a real symphony of colours.[5]

He was a man of culture and taste. Although his reading was 'intense and critical' and he enjoyed music (but not Wagner), his passion was for art. He earned a reputation as a connoisseur and many of his friends were artists or collectors. His first enthusiasm was for the Italian Renaissance, but he was a keen patron also of modern artists.

His private life can only be described as tragic. After a playboy youth, Rupprecht decided that, once he passed his thirtieth birthday, it was time to settle down. In the course of 1899 he began to court his twenty-year-old cousin, Marie-Gabriele. She was receptive enough but her parents were less convinced. When they sent her off on a trip to Verona and Florence with an aunt, Rupprecht pursued her. Travelling under a pseudonym, he somehow managed to get past the chaperone, proposed, and was accepted. After a furious family row, Rupprecht finally secured the approval of his father and grandfather and the couple were married on 10 July 1900 in the court chapel of the Residenz, the old royal palace in Munich.

As far as we can tell, the marriage seems to have been a love match. Of five babies, however, one was still-born and another two died in infancy. Marie-Gabriele died in 1912, aged just thirty-four. Rupprecht was left alone with their two boys and his career as a soldier. He threw himself into his work with redoubled energy. In 1913 he became a Colonel-General (Generaloberst) and commander designate of the largely Bavarian-manned Sixth Army in the event of war.

On 28 June 1914 Archduke Franz Ferdinand, heir to the thrones of Austria-Hungary, was assassinated in Sarajevo. Since he had close family ties with members of the Bavarian royal family, and had visited them only two months previously, the news came as a great shock in Munich. Over the weeks that followed, crisis mounted as the powers of Europe jostled for power and prestige. The Bavarian royal family and government played a passive role as onlookers. Although they had good contacts in both Berlin and Vienna, and remained well informed throughout, they made no attempt to rein in Germany's reckless brinkmanship during the July crisis. The sympathies of King Ludwig III and his Austrian queen lay, unsurprisingly, with Vienna and Berlin and in early July Bavaria intervened to block an attempt by the state of Württemberg to question the handling of the crisis in the federal Upper House foreign affairs committee.

By the last week of July passions were starting to run high across Europe. Outside the royal palace, crowds gathered to sing patriotic hymns and shout slogans against the Serbs and Russians. The royal family had to go out onto their balcony again and again to wave to the crowd. The atmosphere on the streets grew feverish. Enemy agents were rumoured to be poisoning the reservoirs; air raids were expected any minute; every woman in the street might be a cross-dressing spy. The mob harassed anyone who looked foreign or in any other way suspicious and threw stones through the windows of the Serbian consulate.[6] When Austria-Hungary declared war on Serbia on 28 July, the Munich mob cheered. The next day all officers of the Bavarian army were ordered to return to their units. In this jittery environment, Rupprecht later noted, 'one was entirely aware of the seriousness of the situation but also fully confident and believed, that, given how things had turned out, it was best to appear utterly determined'.[7]

At five o'clock in the afternoon of 1 August 1914, Kaiser Wilhelm II sat down at his desk, carved, ironically, from the timbers of Nelson's *Victory*. The Chancellor, Theobald von Bethmann Hollweg, handed him the order that would mobilize the German army and set the world at war. The Kaiser and his advisers had discussed war time and again over the previous few days. The time for thinking and talking was now past. He did not consult Bavaria or other princely states. He did not need their agreement. The Kaiser was Supreme War Lord of their armies, too. Wilhelm, with a flourish, signed the mobilization order. As soon as the news reached Munich, Ludwig III issued the proclamations which sent Bavarian soldiers scurrying to their depots to report for duty. Reservists returned to the colours, drew their equipment, and filled the ranks up to war establishment. Everything had been planned for and prepared, and within hours the first trains began to roll, carrying the army to the frontier.[8]

2

The Battle of the Frontiers

Rupprecht set up Sixth Army headquarters in the luxurious surroundings of the Hotel Bayerischer Hof in Munich. His staff began to organize the myriad details involved in moving 220,000 men to war, working under the chief of staff, Konrad Krafft von Dellmensingen.[1] Ever since 1813, each field commander had been assigned a chief of staff. In theory, the division of labour between commander and chief of staff was clear. As one of the leading historians of the German army, Robert M. Citino, has put it, 'the chief of staff was not a co-commander, a surrogate commander or even a vice-commander. He was simply a highly trained officer...who could give sound advice.... The army or corps commander still had a great deal of leeway in deciding how to proceed. Although he was ultimately responsible for making the decision, a wise commander also listened carefully to the advice of his chief of staff.' In practice, however, things were not always so simple. Conflicting views existed of the responsibilities of chief of staff and army commander. When the thirty-three-year-old Crown Prince Wilhelm of Prussia was given command of Fifth Army, for instance, the Kaiser told him to do whatever his chief of staff advised. The Chief of the General Staff, Helmuth von Moltke the Younger, who was also present, hurried to correct the Kaiser. He told the young prince:'never forget that the Army Commander is and remains the responsible head. The Chief of Staff has to advise, and now—God be with you!' The relationship between army commander and chief of staff was ambiguous and fluid and much depended on the personalities involved.[2]

Major-General Konrad Krafft von Dellmensingen was fifty-two years old and the Chief of the Bavarian General Staff when he was sent to work alongside Rupprecht. This was a surprise appointment, the result of a mixture of politics and luck. Originally, the Prussian Lieutenant-General Konstantin Schmidt von Knobelsdorff was pencilled in as Sixth Army chief of staff, with Krafft down to work with the Prussian Colonel-General Eichhorn at Fifth Army. Eichhorn, however, was not fit to take the field after a riding accident. Crown Prince Wilhelm was promoted to take his place, despite his youth and inexperience: he had never commanded anything larger than a division. Clearly, he would need considerable support. Schmidt von Knobelsdorf was the obvious man to step in. Not only was he the most senior member of the General Staff after Moltke, but he had been teaching Wilhelm tactics and operations at the Kriegsakademie and knew him well. Teaming Schmidt with Wilhelm would also avoid the awkwardness of the heir to the empire taking instructions from a Bavarian. So Moltke swapped Schmidt and Krafft over. Rupprecht was not only glad to have a Bavarian colleague, but knew Krafft personally from their time together at the Munich Kriegsakademie and respected him as a 'smart and energetic man'. The two forged and maintained a close bond from the start. The next three most senior staff officers were also Bavarians Rupprecht knew, the rest being a mix of Bavarians and Prussians.[3]

Indeed, four of the five army corps which comprised Sixth Army were made up of Bavarian troops. The other was Prussian. Each corps fielded two divisions of about 18,000 men each. In addition, there was a Bavarian cavalry division, plus a brigade of older Landwehr troops to guard the lines of communication. Rupprecht's orders were to set up his headquarters in St Avold, east of Metz in German Lorraine. He was to take overall command of the whole German left wing, including Seventh Army to his south in Alsace. Under the famous Schlieffen Plan, designed by Moltke's predecessor, most of the German army would swing through Belgium and across northern France. Meanwhile, Rupprecht and the left flank were to tie down as many French troops as possible until the German right had outflanked and defeated them. In this way Schlieffen and Moltke planned to knock France out of the war within weeks, freeing up troops to shift east against Russia. Specifically:

> The mission of the overall commander [of the left wing] is to advance towards the Moselle between Frouard and the Meurthe...to tie down the French troops concentrated there and prevent them being transferred away to the French left wing.

> If the French for their part attack between Metz and the Vosges in superior strength, this mission may become impossible. In the case that it becomes necessary for the parts of our army in the Reichsland [Alsace-Lorraine] to withdraw, they should so direct their movements as to prevent the left flank of the main German forces being threatened....

Should Sixth and Seventh Armies not encounter superior French forces, then
the possibility arises of operations by Sixth Army...past Metz or to the south
on the left bank of the Moselle.[4]

Rupprecht claimed in his diary that he knew neither his order of battle nor
his mission until the deployment orders arrived on 2 August. This may have
been true in the very narrow sense that he may not have seen his specific
orders in advance. It is less plausible that he knew nothing at all. The composition of Sixth Army, its area of operations, and its mission had all been
fixed for nearly ten years. Staff rides and wargames had examined many
aspects of the plan. Bavarian officers had been closely involved in exercises
practising operations in Lorraine. Even French intelligence had managed to
obtain a copy of Germany's plans. It hardly seems likely that Rupprecht knew
nothing, therefore. From later comments in his diary, where Rupprecht dis-
cusses deviations from the Schlieffen Plan, he was clearly aware of its outline.
He had also taken part in a mobilization exercise in Berlin in January 1914,
where further intentions must have been discussed. In fact, during that exercise Moltke specifically briefed Rupprecht on the most controversial aspect
of the whole Schlieffen Plan: the violation of Belgian neutrality. Rupprecht
may have been playing down his foreknowledge to understate his involvement in an aggressive war plan which ultimately failed.[5]

The first few days of August saw a flurry of staff activity as the Bavarian
War Ministry and Sixth Army headquarters toiled to build up the army
and get it moving. The peacetime strength of the Bavarian army was 4,089
officers and 83,125 other ranks. It suddenly expanded nearly five times, to
a total of nearly 416,000 men. Two-thirds of these constituted the field
army, with the rest remaining in reserve at home. To deploy these men
where they were supposed to go, the authorities commandeered some
5,500 locomotives and moved 285,000 carriages and wagons in the first
two weeks of the war. We can begin to imagine the scale and complexity
of the task facing Rupprecht's staff if we remember that a single army corps
would occupy 140 trains or fill nearly 65 kilometres of road. Each corps
required 130 tons of food and fodder per day, just to survive. Sixth Army
had five such corps, as well as other attached units, all of whom had to get
to the right place at the right time.[6]

While Krafft oversaw this administration, he also took the lead in drawing
up detailed plans for the first campaign. He suggested that the best way to tie
down the French would be to seize the initiative and go on the offensive,

rather than wait for the enemy to move first. Rupprecht wholeheartedly agreed. The news that the British had joined the war worried Krafft little: 'We'll easily deal with them, too.' Rupprecht was not so sure: 'You don't know the English', he replied.[7] Rupprecht found this period of preparation stressful and had trouble sleeping. The febrile atmosphere in Munich did not help. The weather was oppressively hot and the night-time streets were noisy, with crowds singing patriotic songs and hymns. He was relieved to be on the move at last when, in the evening of 7 August, he tucked his two sons up in bed, drove to the station, and boarded his train for the Western Front.[8]

Nearly thirty-six hours later, just before eight in the morning of Sunday 9 August, Rupprecht and his staff disembarked at St Avold. A grimy industrial and garrison town some 50 kilometres east of Metz, it is today in France. In 1914 it was German, in the part of Lorraine annexed in 1871 after the Franco-Prussian War. As he got down from his train, Rupprecht received news of the first casualties. Two German officers had cracked up and shot themselves. The war had already begun to extract its blood price.[9]

Figure 2.1. Rupprecht with his two sons before the war

Of greater military significance were reports of early combat. Cavalry skirmishes along the border on 5–6 August had been followed by a major French move down in Alsace. General Auguste Dubail's French First Army sent General Louis Bonneau across the border to seize Mulhouse. This Bonneau did on 8 August. French joy at this propaganda success was short-lived. The German Seventh Army under Colonel-General Josias von Heeringen was responsible for the area from Strasbourg to the Swiss frontier. It soon bundled the French out again and within forty-eight hours the French were back where they had begun. Bonneau became the first of many French generals in 1914 to be sacked by the commander-in-chief, General Joseph Joffre.

On 10 August, Heeringen formally came under Rupprecht's command. To delegate responsibility for the left wing to a local commander in this way was a sensible plan. Communications were expected to be difficult, which would make it hard for Moltke to control everything from Army Supreme Command (Oberste Heeresleitung: OHL). Telephones and radios were scarce and both were liable to interception; on the other hand, given the distances involved, face-to-face liaison was time-consuming and tricky.[10] No formal command mechanism such as a separate Army Group headquarters had been planned for, however, and the whole arrangement was jury-rigged. Already stretched Sixth Army staff were simply expected to take on more work. Nor had the two headquarters practised working together. Rupprecht thought this a fatal mistake. Although the two armies exchanged liaison officers, coordination remained poor. Strained relations between the commanders did not help. Rupprecht thought Heeringen 'extremely nervous'. Heeringen, on the other hand, a decorated veteran of 1870 who had served as Prussian War Minister and was nearly twenty years older than Rupprecht, felt that he was the senior of the two army commanders on the left wing and resented being subordinated. The use of a similar arrangement on the German right wing proved disastrous on the River Marne in September.[11]

Elements of Sixth Army began to probe forwards. Near the border, sharp, small-scale engagements took place at Lagarde (11 August) and Badonviller (12–13 August). The former was a neat combined arms fight, where infantry, artillery, and cavalry worked together well to take the village and nearly 1,500 prisoners. Losses, however, were heavy. At one point, about 1,000 Bavarian Uhlans charged, lances couched, downhill and into the village. Cavalry on horseback immediately proved extremely vulnerable to modern rifle fire: nearly a quarter of the men were lost. Badonviller was a more confused affair. Here, combined arms cooperation broke down. The Bavarian

Foot Guards, desperate to prove their courage, refused to wait for artillery support. Charging across 400 metres of open ground, the regiment lost twenty-one officers and 398 men to capture a town of little account. Rupprecht was angry at this bravado: 'How often during peacetime exercises did I tell people not to charge until much closer to the enemy!'[12]

The main campaign opened on 14 August. In a thrust designed to synchronize with the first Russian offensive into East Prussia, the French Second and First Armies, under Generals Noël de Castelnau and Auguste Dubail respectively, pushed across the frontier, heading north-east towards Morhange and Sarrebourg. The French army is often criticized for tactical naivety in the early battles of 1914. The impression we have is of white-gloved officers, deeply indoctrinated in the cult of the offensive, repeatedly leading red-trousered infantry forwards to ineluctable death, pitting fixed bayonets, heartbreaking élan, and flying tricolours against machine-guns. There certainly were events like that. Two French infantry regiments were ripped to shreds by Bavarian firepower when they tried to capture the town of Cirey with a bayonet charge across 2,000 metres of mainly open ground, for example. More generally, however, it was not the recklessness, but the caution, of the French attack which was remarkable. Despite generally only light opposition, Castelnau insisted on 'a methodical organization of the advance', with 'painstaking artillery preparation' before any infantry assault; all ground taken was to be carefully consolidated in case of enemy counter-attack. Meanwhile the Germans withdrew as planned, hoping to suck the French forward into the trap.[13]

At first the Germans thought the Lorraine attack marked the main enemy effort. Strategic intelligence suggested that as many as eighteen of the twenty-two active corps in the French army were involved. Only after three days of combat did Sixth Army correctly identify that the enemy was only half that strong. Collating intelligence in mobile warfare was never easy: terrain and enemy cavalry got in the way and it was often hard to tell the difference between active and reserve formations. These factors made it difficult to estimate the enemy's true strength. The Germans also had a problem of interpretation, however. They thought the Lorraine offensive was Joffre's main effort primarily because that was what they wanted to believe. The idea of a major French drive to regain Alsace and Lorraine played too neatly into what the Germans dreamt their enemy would do.[14]

The French were advancing 'so extremely slowly and methodically'— only 5–8 kilometres per day—that Sixth Army was beginning to think the chances of springing a trap were slight. The realization that they were facing only a subsidiary attack reinforced Rupprecht and Krafft's feeling that the best way to tie hostile forces in Lorraine was to attack, not defend. They had been pushing OHL to approve an offensive for days but now they stepped up the pressure. In a series of telephone calls and face-to-face meetings between 16 and 18 August, with a shifting cast of OHL characters including the chief of operations, Lieutenant-Colonel Tappen, the head of the Political Section, Lieutenant-Colonel von Dommes, and the Quartermaster General, Lieutenant-General von Stein, Rupprecht pushed vehemently for permission to attack. He was growing frustrated at OHL not giving him a free hand to carry out his mission. One encounter, with Dommes on 17 August, grew so heated that Dommes forgot his sword and helmet in his hurry to get away. Finally, during the afternoon of 18 August, Krafft spoke again with Stein, who told him that OHL would not forbid an attack, that Sixth Army must do what it considered right, and 'you must bear the responsibility'. They decided that Sixth and Seventh Armies would attack. The date they chose was 20 August.[15]

By the early morning of that day, the French had pushed up to 30 kilometres across the border. Dubail's men were in Sarrebourg, preparing to drive on the heights north-east of the town. Castelnau, buoyed by the apparent ease of his army's advance, discarded his earlier caution on 18 August and called for 'all possible vigour and speed' and 'the energy and élan of all'. Despite this encouragement, only Ferdinand Foch's XX Corps, the famous 'Iron Corps', made much progress on 19 August. Crossing the plain of the River Seille, they arrived in front of a steep ridge. On the heights above perched the small town of Morhange. Foch, despite orders from Castelnau to wait, decided to storm this ridge at six o'clock on the morning of 20 August.[16]

At five o'clock, as 'the sun rose blood red above the ground haze', Foch's men began forming up. Suddenly, German shells from gun positions on the high ground rained down among them. Bavarian infantry swept down the slopes. 'Our troops, in their enthusiasm, attacked with flags flying', wrote Rupprecht. Never again would they do so, but on 20 August, with surprise on their side, the Germans swept all before them. XX Corps held up relatively well but the rest of the French Second Army collapsed. Within just ninety minutes the Bavarians swarmed across the valley and overran the French artillery lines. Further east, on the French First Army front, the pattern was slightly different. French morning attacks around Sarrebourg were shot to pieces by German defenders dug in on the hills, who then counter-attacked in the afternoon. Here, too, the French fell back in disorder. Some French units lost half their strength. German losses were also heavy, how-ever: one Bavarian division lost nearly half (45 per cent) of its men.[17]

Within forty-eight hours the French armies lost everything they had gained in nearly a week and were back where they had started on 14 August. Joffre had to shelve plans to transfer a corps from Nancy up to the north. The first major engagement of the war had resulted, as the French official history admitted, in 'a serious defeat'. Moltke wept at the news of Rupprecht's success. The Kaiser awarded Rupprecht the Iron Cross both Second and First Class.[18]

On 22 August the Germans won another major victory, crushing French forces in the Ardennes and adding to the general euphoria. Rupprecht and Krafft thought that they had done enough damage to the French that their mission in Alsace-Lorraine was complete. It was time now to stand pat there and send men north to join the main attack on the right. When Krafft sug-gested this to Tappen over the telephone in the afternoon of 22 August, however, Tappen asked him to hold on the line while he went off to consult the Chief of the General Staff. When he came back, Moltke's answer was so surprising that Rupprecht later asked for it to be repeated in writing. Rather than redeploying northwards, Sixth Army was to exploit success in the south, with a drive on Epinal. They were to try and cut off the 120,000–150,000 Frenchmen still thought to be in the Vosges Mountains. Rupprecht was worried that such a move risked stretching Sixth Army very thin and leav-ing its flank exposed to attack from Nancy.

OHL had misjudged events on the German left flank. Communications had broken down in the hilly terrain and the French had retreated so fast that the Germans had lost contact. The situation was not as healthy as it seemed: the defence had buckled but not broken. Both French armies had caught their breath and reorganized and they were now securely established behind tough defences along the imposing heights of the Grand Couronné de Nancy. From up there they could watch every move the Germans made on the broad plain below. The French also still held Fort Manonviller, behind the German lines. This blocked communications and only surren-dered after several days of bombardment by monstrous Krupp 420-mm howitzers. By that time, Sixth Army was already tiring and the swing south had slowed. The French appeared to be slipping out of the trap in the Vosges. OHL, as always, pushed for greater speed, but Moltke seemed increasingly out of touch. Rupprecht complained in his diary that OHL 'under-estimates the difficulties of the pursuit. The Kaiser thinks it's sufficient to lead the cavalry through!' A request to send troops to help Crown Prince Wilhelm's Fifth Army west of Metz further irritated him. Not only was he already juggling several missions, but he felt Wilhelm was making his own difficulties by handling his forces poorly.[19]

It soon became impossible for Rupprecht to help Wilhelm, in any event. In the early morning of 25 August reports arrived of a major French attack out of Nancy, into Sixth Army's right wing. Here the commander of III Bavarian Corps, Lieutenant-General Ludwig von Gebsattel, had been ordered to sit on the defensive, well out of range of the French heavy guns in Nancy, and cover Rupprecht's flank. Gebsattel, however, decided that the best way to execute his mission was to ignore his orders and attack. A series of savage encounter battles ensued. Gebsattel's men advanced 'as if they were on manoeuvres with live ammunition. The full seriousness of the war had so far come home to few. By the evening of that day some had certainly become acquainted with its full weight.' French artillery fire overwhelmed the German attackers, who fell back in disarray. As rumours of the setback spread through the streets of Lunéville, panic broke out. Shots were fired and nineteen civilians killed. In all, seventy houses were burnt down. A member of Rupprecht's staff, Major Rudolf von Xylander, wrote that 'it is incredible how a victorious army can be reduced in so short a time to such a state by one single reverse. The nerves of our troops, who have been fighting bravely for several days without a break, are simply overstretched.' It was not just the Germans who made battlefield mistakes that day. Men of General Émile Fayolle's 70th Division attacked Hoéville at seven o'clock in the morning. Fayolle described the result as a 'catastrophe': there had been no reconnaissance, no artillery preparation, and too many men were sent forwards in the battle line. Four thousand men were lost. 'It's crazy', he concluded. Nonetheless, as the day went on, the scale of the French threat grew. By the evening of a 'dramatic and critical day', during which Rupprecht had not been able to leave his operations room even for a moment, it seemed that this was another of Joffre's big pushes.[20]

At nine o'clock, a liaison officer arrived from OHL with new orders to turn west and drive through the Charmes gap between Toul and Epinal. Rupprecht was now to join hands with Fifth Army behind Toul. This unrealistic order was followed next morning by another: Sixth Army was to attack the fortifications north and east of Nancy. This difficult task would require significant heavy artillery and thus take time to prepare. Rupprecht was getting increasingly frustrated: 'despite the detailed reports we send them, OHL seems not to see the real picture and to be possessed by unfounded optimism'.[21] There was no way Rupprecht could execute these grandiose and conflicting orders. Instead, Sixth and Seventh Armies both went onto the defensive. The infantry of both sides had fought themselves to a standstill. The guns, however, still killed. French artillery observers seemed remarkably efficient. If even a single German was spotted in the open, shells rained around him. The only response was to dig. Trenches, dugouts, barbed wire: all the diabolical architecture that was to define the Western Front made its first appearance here in Lorraine. As yet it remained improvised and ad hoc but, already, trench warfare had begun.

3

The End of the Campaign
in Lorraine

The first sign that something was wrong was a telegram from home, late
in the evening of 26 August. It told Rupprecht that his elder son,
Luitpold, was seriously ill. The boy's condition deteriorated rapidly. At one
o'clock the next afternoon, the doctors diagnosed the 'Swedish disease':
polio. Little more than an hour later came the shattering news that Luitpold
had died. He was just thirteen years old. Rupprecht had now lost his whole
family except for nine-year-old Albrecht. Even in an age more accustomed
to children dying young than our own, and for a man with the stiffest of
public upper lips, this was a cruel blow. Rupprecht tried to be stoic: 'there is
no time to grieve, there's too much to do. Work is my consolation.' He told
his father that 'duty requires action, not grief'. When Major-General Karl
von Wenninger saw him, however, he thought 'the poor man looked dreadful', crushed by the dual burden of news from home and the stress of the
campaign. Luitpold was buried in Munich, with his father still far away.[1]

On the battlefield, both sides launched local attacks and the artillery
continued to roar, but the front settled into an uneasy stalemate with little
change in the overall situation. On 1 September the French began withdrawing into their fortifications around Nancy, trading space for time and
allowing Joffre to pull troops out and send them to his threatened northern
flank. Seven divisions had left Alsace-Lorraine by 2 September, some of them
in time to take part in the Battle of the Marne. This was precisely what the
Germans feared most. Although Oberste Heeresleitung (OHL) continued
to press Rupprecht to keep attacking to forestall such a transfer, disagreement continued about how best to proceed. Poor intelligence and these
disputes hindered decision-making. OHL wanted Sixth Army to break
through the Charmes Gap and cross the River Moselle. Rupprecht, however,

thought this impossible until Nancy had been neutralized, which would require siege guns and time to prepare. On 30 August the Bavarian military representative at OHL, Wenninger, had just returned from a visit to Rupprecht when Moltke ambushed him as he walked into headquarters. 'You were with Sixth Army: when are they finally going to attack?' Moltke barked. Wenninger explained that enemy artillery fire was intense, losses had been heavy, and the men were very tired: some units had been in action constantly for nineteen days. Moltke had no sympathy: 'That's the same for the other armies too, yet they attack!' In any case, he said, 'Sixth Army's casualties were in many cases unnecessary. The units run into enemy artillery fire. That must cease!' Moltke stalked back into his office, hardly waiting to hear Wenninger's reply.[2]

While Tappen and Moltke continued to push for the drive into the Charmes Gap, others at OHL took a different line. Major Max Bauer, for instance, the OHL heavy artillery expert, agreed that it was important to take Nancy first and promised to find siege guns to do so. Sixth Army heard what it wanted to hear from the babel of voices and began work on plans for capturing Nancy. Krafft managed to overcome the nerves of his staff officers and corps commanders, reeling from casualties as high as 50 per cent in just two weeks, and organize an attack on the Grand Couronné for the night of 4/5 September.[3]

Sixth Army hoped that a night attack would maximize surprise and reduce the impact of enemy firepower. Unfortunately, the sky was clear and the moon full, so the attackers were easy to spot. The experience of the 14th Bavarian Infantry Regiment (5th Bavarian Infantry Division), attacking the village of Réméréville, a dozen kilometres east of Nancy, was typical. Two battalions advanced an hour before midnight, each deployed with four companies abreast, covered by a few skirmishers. Meanwhile, artillery bombarded the village. After about an hour, with the attackers still 500 metres short of the buildings, the French detected them. The Bavarians tried to charge, but were forced to the ground by heavy fire from well-dug-in defenders to the front and left flank and the assault soon foundered. Attempts to clear the French from woods on the flank failed. Losses were mounting. Nearly all the officers were killed or wounded and, around three a.m., order broke down completely. Even when the Bavarians shelled the village with a couple of field guns firing over open sights, the situation remained dangerous. Further reinforcements in the shape of a battalion of light infantry (Jäger) did not help much and the French finally evacuated the village only around noon. Casualties had been brutal: the Bavarians lost 750 men, or probably about half their strength, including the two commanding officers.[4]

The German attack on Nancy made little progress elsewhere, either. OHL now seemed to be losing interest in Lorraine. On 5 September Tappen told Krafft to send two corps to the German right flank in the north. Sixth Army had never thought its task easy but now, it seemed, OHL was going to make it harder. Rupprecht and Krafft felt they were being hamstrung but their protests were ignored. From OHL's perspective, the quick results hoped for had not materialized and Moltke now had much bigger problems than Nancy or the *amour-propre* of the Bavarian crown prince. On 5 September the Battle of the Marne began with a French drive into the extreme-right flank of the German army, followed the next day by an offensive by over a million Entente soldiers from Verdun all the way to Paris. On 9 September, the Germans began to withdraw, only eventually stopping 60 kilometres back along the River Aisne. Moltke's attempt to knock France out of the war with a single deadly blow had failed.[5]

The situation on the Marne, and the increasing difficulties of Crown Prince Wilhelm around Verdun, threatened to draw further resources away from Sixth Army. When Rupprecht was told to give up further ammunition and divisions, he drove at once to OHL in Luxembourg to complain. There he met Moltke who 'impressed me as a sick, broken man. His tall body was hunched and he seemed extremely haggard.' The whole interview struck Rupprecht as surreal: 'Moltke went on to say things I didn't properly under-stand. He spoke of a new mission for me and stared at me wide-eyed.' To Rupprecht's surprise, Moltke agreed that the attack on Nancy could continue after all, on condition that the heavy guns be given up in a week at most. Surprise soon turned to even greater confusion, however. Even while Rupprecht had been motoring to Luxembourg that morning, an OHL staff officer arrived at Sixth Army bearing new written instructions. All forces in Alsace-Lorraine were to go on the defensive. Active formations were to disengage, reorganize, and prepare to be moved by train to northern France, leaving the front held by second-class units. This was the new mission Moltke had spoken so cryptically about. He probably had not realized that Rupprecht knew nothing of it. When Sixth Army asked whether it was to follow the verbal instructions to attack, or the written ones to disengage, it finally received an unambiguous and clear answer: the latter.[6]

On 10 September, Rupprecht's men began pulling out of the front line. Three days later the first men left for Belgium. On 17 September, Rupprecht

handed over the Lorraine command to General von Falkenhausen, who
established a defence line more or less along the old frontier. And there, for
the next four years, the front lines sat.

Losses on both sides had been heavy. Of every eight German soldiers
who arrived in Lorraine at the beginning of the war, approximately three
became casualties and one died. In front-line combat infantry, who bore the
brunt of the fighting, the proportion of casualties was inevitably higher.
Some units lost as much as 60 per cent of their infantry strength. French
losses are harder to pin down but were probably similar.[7]

Neither side had much to show for these losses. The front lines settled
pretty much along the 1914 border. No crucial resources or strategic positions
changed hands. That was not the point, however. Neither army had fought
there for such reasons. In the minds of both Joffre and Moltke, this had
always been a secondary theatre. The aim of both armies in Alsace-Lorraine
was primarily to tie down the enemy while they won the war elsewhere.
Neither side got what it wanted, though. Both German and French troops
were able to slip away and bolster the defence in the north at critical
moments that autumn. The only decisive battle fought in the west in 1914 was
the defeat of Germany's attempt to overrun France. The Marne was not the
battle which won the war. But it did ensure that France would not lose it.

Before we leave Lorraine and explore the events of autumn of 1914, we
need to address the issue of war crimes. John Horne and Alan Kramer have
demonstrated that, within days of the war's outbreak, civilians as well as
soldiers were suffering its violence. German soldiers massacred townsfolk at
Dinant and Tamines and destroyed the ancient library at Louvain. Men
under Rupprecht's command in Alsace-Lorraine also committed atrocities.
For example, after the bloody capture of Badonviller on 12 August, they
accused the villagers of helping the French army. Bavarian troops burned
down houses, knocked down the church tower from which partisans,
known as franc-tireurs, had supposedly been sniping, and killed ten villagers,
including the wife of the mayor. On 20 August, men of Sixth Army attacked
and took Nomény. During confused street fighting in the town, they came
under fire. Blaming the civilian population, they torched the town and shot
forty-six inhabitants dead as they fled the flames. Two more were fatally
wounded, while another seven suffocated as they cowered in their cellars.
Four days later, other German soldiers came under fire in Gerbéviller. They
burned down the village and killed sixty inhabitants, some of them in two
mass executions. Another incident took place at Lunéville on 25 August.

As Bavarian troops retreated through the town in confusion, shooting broke out. Major Berthold Schenk von Stauffenberg took sixty hostages and nineteen civilians were killed. Some seventy houses were destroyed.[8]

These atrocities were not isolated incidents but part of a widespread pattern. In August–September 1914 across Belgium and France there were 129 incidents involving the summary execution of ten or more civilians. About half of all the regiments in the German army, from every corner of the Reich, were implicated. Probably some 6,500 civilians were killed. Nearly a thousand of them were French, the rest Belgian. Many thousands of homes were destroyed. In some cases, senior officers took the lead in committing war crimes. For instance, Major-General Stenger, a brigade commander at the Battle of Sarrebourg on 20 August, the next morning ordered some of his officers to kill all their wounded French prisoners. Five days later he repeated a similar order, this time in writing. More notably, on 12 August Moltke himself ordered that anyone not in uniform resisting the German advance was to be shot at once. This level of direct involvement was rare, however. More often, as Isabel Hull explains, ordinary soldiers or very junior officers carried out the atrocities. More senior officers got involved only when they chose either to ignore or to approve such acts, or indeed to systematize them, as Moltke did.[9]

Rupprecht's involvement in atrocities was, it seems, limited, but he cannot escape all blame. Although he was number 33 on the French post-war list of 890 wanted war criminals, his case never came to trial. One of the charges was that he had been responsible for the 'methodically organized' crimes committed by units under his command in occupied territory in August–September 1914. Evidence that he was personally culpable is thin. No order survives to link him to the killing of civilians or the burning of houses. The most accurate accusation was that he had been present on 22 August when Dieuze was pillaged. Ten houses were set on fire and the mayor and local *curé* were shot. Even if it cannot be proved that Rupprecht had blood on his own hands, however, we have already seen that men under his command did. Perpetrators were not disciplined and indeed some, such as Stenger, were soon promoted. The failure of the Crown Prince properly to investigate, much less take decisive action against, those implicated must rank at least as a sin of omission. Whatever the stresses on him, and even if it was not his finger on the metaphorical trigger, we cannot absolve him of, at a minimum, moral responsibility for the crimes committed under his command.[10]

To judge those who have long been dead by modern ethical standards achieves little beyond stoking the fires of our own self-righteousness. It is more interesting to try and understand why they did what they did than to condemn or praise them for it. Untangling Rupprecht's attitude to what we call atrocities is tricky. He became more sensitive to criticism on this score after the failed Leipzig War Crimes Trials of the early 1920s. Consequently, his published diary differs in intriguing ways from the wartime evidence he left. For instance, Rupprecht mentioned the Dieuze episode in his published diary, but not in the manuscript version. Presumably by 1929 he felt he needed to counter French allegations. According to him, after shots were fired during the night he permitted a house-to-house search. Fifteen French soldiers were hauled out of hiding places around the village. The civilians were, therefore, he implied, far from innocent of war crimes themselves and reprisals were well deserved. He said nothing of executions, however.[11]

Rupprecht's attitude to Dieuze specifically, and the use of violence against civilians generally, was moulded by three factors. First, it reflected how German officers conventionally interpreted the laws of war at this time. Soldiers, they thought, possessed ample latitude to override even the established law of the Hague Conventions (1899 and 1907) if military necessity demanded it. As Isabel Hull has demonstrated, this view of military law had diverged radically from that of the liberal European states for decades. Both British and French officers were taught that suspected partisans must be tried and could not be shot out of hand, whereas we have already seen that Moltke's stated policy was the opposite. When Rupprecht's men shot French civilians, they could argue that they were only following the orders of the Chief of the General Staff. This attitude to law was a sub-set of the second factor: the broader ethos of the German army. This idolized the objective of annihilating the enemy. All other considerations were secondary. Civilians, therefore, were at best instruments and more likely obstacles. The expectation that civilian franc-tireurs would oppose the German advance, as they had during the Franco-Prussian War of 1870–1, found in such a military culture rich soil in which to flourish. German soldiers saw snipers behind every bush and shutter, largely because they expected to. The third factor, the particular pressures of the 1914 campaign, ratcheted up the level of violence further. The whole design of the German campaign depended on rapid movement and the ruthless destruction of resistance. Without speed, the Schlieffen Plan was nothing. If the demanding timetable was to be met, opposition must be crushed at once. There was no time for niceties such as trials of enemy civilians.[12]

So, Rupprecht probably saw little wrong with most of the violence his troops visited on the local population. He did retain some sense of proportion, however. There were limits to what he thought acceptable. For instance, he criticized some of the house-burning carried out by Bavarian troops on 20–1 August as unjustified. More generally, Rupprecht was publicly frustrated by the continued burning of French villages. He tried to reduce or stop the practice. On 24 August, for instance, he issued an Order of the Day:

> Wanton destruction of enemy property of any kind, whether belonging to military or civilian authorities or to private citizens, is unworthy of the German soldier.
>
> Necessary searches of offices of enemy military or civilian powers for secret material or weapons must be carried out thoroughly and energetically but should restrict themselves to the objects of the search.
>
> It is the absolute duty of each commander to maintain, even using the harshest measures, the renowned discipline and good name of the German soldier at all times, even under the most difficult circumstances.
>
> Even if the enemy is guilty of allowing outrages, this in no way justifies German soldiers following suit.
>
> Further, German soldiers should continue their victories and spread fear and terror only through their determination for victory, not through other means.

Presumably from concern that they might not be obeyed, these orders were repeated on 29 August and 9 September, with a similar Order of the Day issued on 19 September, as Sixth Army redeployed to France, and again on 2 October. Arson became increasingly subject to formal process, with the last of the series ordering that whole villages could only be burned down by order of OHL or an Army commander, while the authorization of Corps HQ must be sought for any partial destructions.[13]

Rupprecht issued these high-profile orders from four main concerns, which were more pragmatic than ethical or legal. First, burning a village took time and damaged food and shelter which might be needed one day. Second, it was a punishment which hurt innocent and guilty alike and left the population homeless and jobless 'which is definitely not in our interest'. Third, it risked undermining army discipline and might provoke the locals to riot. Fourth, he had the breadth of vision to see that not everyone shared the German military's interpretation of law and that the enemy was likely to pick up on anything that looked like an atrocity and use it in propaganda. Many others lacked the imagination to see this. Even civilian statesmen in the Foreign Office or Chancellery either followed the military line or knew that it was futile to attempt to intervene. After all, the Kaiser himself had long used the most bloodthirsty of language against his enemies. Rupprecht was proved right. The Entente shouted quick and loud about German atrocities in Belgium and France. Perhaps the German authorities failed to investigate war crimes because they wanted to avoid giving their enemies ammunition for further propaganda. Equally, however, they may well have expected that victory would simply solve the problem for them.[14]

Once Sixth Army moved to Picardy and the River Somme, it operated in a less densely populated landscape from which much of the population had already fled. As a result, there were fewer opportunities for friction with the civilian population. The number and scale of atrocities against civilians soon fell away. The fighting, however, only grew harder.

4

The First Battle of the Somme

On Friday 18 September 1914, Rupprecht and Krafft travelled up to their new headquarters at Namur in Belgium. On the way, they stopped at Oberste Heeresleitung (OHL) to discuss their mission with Moltke's replacement as Chief of the General Staff, the War Minister, Erich von Falkenhayn. Moltke had been sacked after the Marne but for propaganda purposes the news had not yet been made public. Awkwardly, Moltke was present at the meeting. Rupprecht found him 'considerably calmer' than the last time they had met. To Krafft, however, Moltke seemed 'very shy, he hardly said a word to us: not even hello or goodbye'. Falkenhayn explained that a series of attacks were underway all along the line to pin the French army in place, while Rupprecht and Sixth Army were to swing around the open flank north of the River Oise and land the decisive blow. To begin with, Rupprecht would have at his disposal XXI Corps together with I and II Bavarian Corps. After 23 September, XIV Reserve Corps, largely recruited from the industrial areas of Baden, would join them. Not all the troops were yet in place, though. Rear area communications remained sketchy. The bridges over the River Meuse at Namur had not yet been repaired so four whole German armies would have to rely on a single railway line via Brussels. Most troops would have to get off their trains at Namur and march the 160 kilometres to the area of operations around St Quentin. The question was whether Sixth Army had a few days to wait, concentrate, and strike in strength; or must advance as soon as possible with whatever was to hand. Rupprecht and Krafft preferred the first option. Falkenhayn insisted they throw troops in as they arrived, for two reasons. First, there were already signs of French pressure on General Alexander von Kluck's First Army on the right of the German line. The open flank there must be protected as soon as possible. Second, he under-estimated enemy resilience and exaggerated German strength. One more push and the French, Falkenhayn thought, would collapse.[1]

Such intelligence estimates were based on little more than guesswork. In mid-September, the Germans had little clue where enemy units were, never mind how strong or ready to fight they were. Indeed, they were having trouble keeping track of their own men. For instance, three of the cavalry divisions supposed to be reconnoitring the open right flank had completely disappeared. Communications had advanced little since the days of Frederick the Great or Julius Caesar: wireless sets were too bulky and scarce to be used below army level at best; it was impossible to build out telephone networks quickly enough to keep up with the rapidly moving troops; pigeons were no use for any but the shortest communications. The best way to send a complex message remained to send a man with it, for all that he might get captured, killed, or simply lost. In any case, the German cavalry had suffered heavy losses and lost the initiative to the stronger and more cohesive French. Poor weather prevented aerial reconnaissance from filling the gap.[2]

Joffre was playing the same game as Falkenhayn. He also was shifting formations north to try to outflank his enemy. Even as Rupprecht headed for that open flank, so did the Frenchmen of his old adversary Castelnau's Second Army. Joffre had the advantage of an intact rail system which enabled units to be unloaded close to the action, while the Germans had to make long approach marches from railheads in the rear. Thus, while French units could transfer from Lorraine to the new battlefields in five or six days, it took the Germans nine. This extra speed was sufficient to allow the French to block German outflanking manoeuvres but not great enough to allow their own moves to succeed. Instead, time and again the same pattern played out over the next few weeks. One side or the other would advance, trying to get around the enemy flank. At first, they would encounter only light opposition, mainly from cavalry and artillery. Soon, however, enemy resistance consolidated, the weight of fire increased, and it became ever harder to push forward until eventually the attackers went to ground and began to dig themselves in, while to their north, the process began again. The fighting between Rupprecht and Castelnau in September and October 1914, in what we might call the First Battle of the Somme, neatly shows how that process unfolded. It also introduces place names which later played an ill-starred role in British military history.[3]

The first elements of Sixth Army went into action on 23 September. Advancing south-west from St Quentin, XXI Corps clashed with French units coming up from Montdidier. Over the next few days they fought their way forward north of Roye, suffering heavy casualties as they did so.

Rupprecht sent I Bavarian Corps to block any French attack from Amiens by seizing Péronne and the crossings over the River Somme and occupying the Flaucourt Plateau on the left bank of the Somme. In the face of fierce French attacks these Bavarians became increasingly bogged down around Lihons. On 25 September, therefore, Rupprecht ordered his II Bavarian Army Corps to attack along the right bank of the Somme, working around the enemy from the north. Two divisions of cavalry were to march on Albert to protect the infantry's flank. Meanwhile XIV Reserve Corps was to march on Bapaume from Cambrai.

II Bavarian Corps attacked north of the Somme, fighting its way forward in the face of toughening resistance from French Territorial troops, through Morval to Maricourt and Ginchy. Rupprecht was keen to exploit this success and push the enemy back beyond Amiens. While cavalry probed to the south of Arras, he ordered XIV Reserve Corps to advance through Bapaume on Albert while II Bavarian Corps, pivoting on its left, wheeled right towards the line of the Somme. With the rest of Sixth Army apparently stuck, if victory were to be won anywhere, it could only be north of the Somme. Unfortunately, not everything went according to plan. Attempts to work forward under cover of darkness to storm the defences early next morning only left the attackers horribly exposed in the open when the sun rose on 26 September. Tired troops advanced only slowly and, although the Germans made some progress and captured Mametz Wood, for example, the front was beginning to congeal once more. XIV Reserve Corps, commanded by Lieutenant-General von Stein, one of Schlieffen's closest disciples and until very recently Moltke's deputy at OHL, came in for particular criticism. According to Krafft's diary, Stein was 'very soft even compared with his extremely soft troops—the Badeners have done poorly in the whole campaign right from the start—one can detect the social-democrat taint!' Stein and Rupprecht had an awkward interview the next day.[4]

Rupprecht remained determined to get across the river, turn the French flank, and deliver the longed-for decisive victory. On 28 September XIV Reserve Corps closed up to the River Ancre, with German cavalry occupying Thiepval. From here they could watch French troops moving around the houses of Beaumont, Hamel, and Serre on the other side of the valley. Further enemy forces were reported in Arras and Douai. The next day II Bavarian Corps occupied Fricourt after a night of fighting from house to house, at one point using a searchlight to provide illumination. The French defenders turned out to be from the élite XX Corps, the same 'Iron Corps' which had covered the retreat from Morhange under General Foch five weeks previously. Meanwhile, Rupprecht went to watch units of XIV Reserve Corps fighting in the outskirts of Albert from the windmill at Pozières. He could clearly see the golden Madonna atop the basilica in Albert and watched an artillery duel between a German howitzer battery and what they thought were British horse artillery. It felt, he later wrote, as though the Germans were no longer the ones doing the outflanking. Others felt an ominous shift in the psychological balance between the two sides. One German colonel noted that

> the enemy had changed too. The battles in Lorraine had given our troops a feeling of superiority. They received an extremely rude shock when they had to accept near Maricourt that the French, even though they were from the same corps that we had brushed aside in Lorraine, had changed. They were tough, daring and self-confident. The Miracle of the Marne had so raised the morale of the French that the order to withdraw must be regarded as a crime against all things German. Against such an opponent [our] ill-prepared, unco-ordinated and over-hasty minor attacks were dashed to pieces.[5]

As it became ever clearer that the enemy would not be beaten on the Somme, Rupprecht's attention began to drift north. He handed command of his units south of the river over to General Fritz von Below and began work to capture Arras. The situation there remained obscure. He had little idea of the likely strength of opposition. Consequently, he turned down a proposal for a night-time coup de main to seize Arras. Instead, he ordered a pincer attack. On 1 October IV Corps was to march up from Bapaume and the south while I Bavarian Reserve Corps swung through Douai and approached Arras from the east. The Prussians of IV Corps, however, found their way blocked by both French territorials and élite mountain troops of the Chasseurs Alpins. At Douai, the Bavarians faced only light opposition and took the town easily, but they, too, were not moving quickly enough. Resistance grew the next day and progress remained sticky. Rupprecht was becoming impatient. He drafted a sharply worded order telling units to report back at once if they failed to reach their objectives and reminding cavalry that they must bypass enemy concentrations, rather than stop at the first sight of them. On reflection, however, he decided not to send it, largely from fear of upsetting his Prussian subordinates: 'if I were a Prussian, I wouldn't have thought twice'.[6]

The real problem, however, was that the troops were getting increasingly worn out. Krafft wrote in his diary: 'The men see "fortifications" everywhere.

One cannot hide the fact that the offensive spirit has declined since the sad time in Lorraine. But it is the same amongst the troops of the other armies. Everyone has his limit. The troops have had too much asked of them.' Each of the Bavarian corps had now lost between 7,000 and 9,000 men since the start of the war. Some divisions were down to just 5,000 men. 'The sad truth', Krafft noted, was that it was proving impossible to dislodge entrenched defenders with field artillery and tired infantry alone. Only if heavy guns were brought up and a set-piece attack developed was it possible to make progress. The cavalry were a particular problem. Their staff officers blamed slow progress on the difficult industrial terrain. Reports to Krafft, however, suggested that the real problem was sybaritic officers who were unused to the rigours of campaigning and would not leave their baggage behind.[7]

Rupprecht did not want to get sucked into large-scale street fighting. So he continued to try to surround Arras before entering the town. To the north, I Bavarian Reserve Corps drove back the French defenders and occupied Vimy Ridge and Souchez late on 4 October. In the south, the Guard Corps struggled forward. At one stage aerial reconnaissance reported that the French were pulling out. Attempts by Rupprecht to take advantage of this, however, collapsed when his troops met renewed strong opposition. In fact, Castelnau had been on the brink of a large-scale retreat but he was overruled by the new commander of all French forces north of the River Oise, his former subordinate, Ferdinand Foch. General Foch forbade any further trade-off of space for time. Instead his men were to hold firm everywhere and, if possible, counter-attack to regain the initiative. One such counter-attack threatened the northern flank of the Bavarians scrapping their way westward along the ridge of Notre Dame de Lorette on 5–6 October. Other French forces were reported to be detraining further north again, at La Bassée. At the same time, strong enemy counter-attacks halted German progress south of Arras. Rupprecht threw the newly arrived XIV Corps into the gap between Lens and Lille on 8 October. They encountered heavy opposition around and north of Loos. Again, progress was less than hoped. The same day, a major French assault south of the Somme forced the extreme left wing of Sixth Army to postpone a large-scale breakthrough attempt it had been preparing. That night the over-extended I Bavarian Reserve Corps came under severe French pressure. Fighting in Carency was heavy and forced the Germans onto the defensive. They had to abandon thoughts of further advances between Arras and Notre Dame de Lorette for now.

The difficulties facing the German army were multiplying. Ammunition supply, for example, was becoming an ever greater challenge. By 9 October Sixth Army had enough shells for just one more day of battle. Stalemate set in around Arras. General von Fasbender, the commander of I Bavarian Reserve Corps, summed up the difficulties he faced: he was advancing against a strongly entrenched enemy. His troops were exhausted and he lacked heavy artillery support. How he was to take the four villages next in his way, he knew not.[8] The capture of La Bassée on 11 October, and Lille the next day, extended the line further northwards, but progress was becoming ever slower and harder. Even the cavalry was encountering more solid enemy resistance. Most significant of all in the long term, on 12 October they exchanged shots with British troops around Estaires and Merville. Yet again, it was clear, attempts to outflank the enemy had failed and Sixth Army was ordered onto the defensive. The battle for Arras was over—for now.

5

To Ypres

Still the search for an open flank went on. The eyes of both Falkenhayn and Joffre now turned to Flanders, the last free space on the map. Once again, they pulled troops out of the trenches in stalemated sectors, loaded them onto trains, and sent them north. Antwerp finally surrendered on 12 October, freeing up further German units to advance towards the French frontier.

On 14 October Oberste Heeresleitung (OHL) ordered Sixth Army to stand on the defensive for the moment, holding a line from Menin through Armentières and La Bassée and then on south. Falkenhayn hoped that this would tempt the British and French to try to overlap him in Flanders. He then planned to strike them in the flank using a new Fourth Army. This comprised four newly raised reserve corps under Duke Albrecht of Württemberg and was forming up near Brussels. Falkenhayn had read his enemy perfectly: Field Marshal Sir John French was already directing the British Expeditionary Force (BEF) eastwards through the gap between La Bassée and the sea. The harder the British pushed Rupprecht's right wing back, the further they would be sticking their head into the noose. If, on the other hand, the BEF awoke to the threat from Albrecht and turned north-east to face him, then Sixth Army would be able to break through at Arras, drive west and north, and split the enemy in two. Either way, Albrecht and Rupprecht would surround and destroy the Entente forces in northern France.

Rupprecht did not think much of this plan. 'The mission we've been given', he grumbled, 'is analogous to what we had at the beginning of the campaign and it remains as questionable as before whether the enemy will run into the trap. *This return to Schlieffen's ideas, under very different circumstances, seems to me very dubious.* We're ceding the initiative completely to the enemy.' It was all very well for Falkenhayn to tell Rupprecht to break through at Arras, but he gave no clue as to how this might be achieved.

Rupprecht dismissed the orders as '*a purely amateurish view of the situation!*'
He would have preferred to attack with his right wing, cross the River Lys,
and occupy the high ground south and east of Ypres. This offered better
positions in which to await Fourth Army, which could not arrive before
21 October at the earliest. Krafft had similar concerns. Further, the defensive
line Falkenhayn had chosen possessed only poor fields of fire and, at 40 kilometres, was very long for the manpower available. Even the strongest corps
was at less than half strength and some were much worse off.[1]

Rupprecht's subordinate commanders, such as the GOC IV Corps,
General Friedrich Sixt von Armin, were very worried about their ability to
break through at Arras. Sixt suggested complaining to OHL, but Rupprecht
advised against: this was OHL's idea and therefore its responsibility. In fact,
Falkenhayn told Rupprecht and Krafft not to be too restricted by these
orders. They were to take any chances that came along. While the prince
welcomed the apparent freedom of action this gave him, Krafft was more
cynical. He saw this as Falkenhayn's way of shifting blame if anything went
wrong: 'this fully lived up to the scheming character of this man!' In the
event, Falkenhayn's plan nearly worked. It also led to the First Battle of
Ypres, one of the most famous battles of British military history.[2]

Over the week beginning 13 October, the British clashed with Rupprecht's
men for the first time. One British corps advanced only hesitantly and made little progress towards La Bassée. Further north, the British had better success. By
17 October they had overcome light opposition to capture Armentières and
the next day they gained a foothold on the Pérenchies Ridge. From here they
could look down on Lille, less than 8 kilometres away. Meanwhile, British
and French troops moved through Ypres and took up position on the
crescent of gentle ridges east of the town. Sir Douglas Haig's I Corps was
concentrating to the west, ready to advance despite intelligence warning of
a growing German threat. The BEF seemed to be playing so neatly into
German hands that Rupprecht found its movements hard to comprehend.[3]

Rupprecht first encountered British troops for himself in the courtyard of
Douai town hall. He was struck by their soldierly bearing, especially relative
to the dirty and ill-disciplined French. He intervened to stop the guards
'requisitioning' the excellent 'British warm' overcoats. Tactically, he found them
less impressive: at La Bassée on 14 October 'the English blundered forwards
in columns and suffered heavy losses to artillery'. Nonetheless, the British,
together with the French Chasseurs Alpins, were the toughest opponents his
men faced.[4] On 19 October Rupprecht issued an order of the day to his men:

Soldiers of Sixth Army!

We now have the fortune to be facing British troops on our front, troops of the nation which, consumed by age-old jealousy, has been working to encircle us with a ring of foes and throttle us. So, when you go forwards against this enemy, make sure you make him pay for his malevolent treachery and the heavy sacrifices he has caused us. Show him that the Germans cannot be wiped out of world history so easily! Show him that with a specially German thrashing! Here is the enemy who, more than any other, stands in the way of a return to peace!

Onwards!

Rupprecht, Crown Prince of Bavaria[5]

This order provoked outrage in the London press. The *Daily Mail* interpreted it as a call to 'Annihilate the English'. A leader in *The Times* quoted it as another example of deep-seated German Anglophobia. This order, together with another a week later which described the British as 'our most hated foe', ensured that the London newspapers gave Rupprecht a reputation for intransigence and bloodthirstiness which proved hard to shift. The *Daily Mail* took to calling him 'Bloody Rupprecht' or 'Rupprecht the Bloody'. In May 1915 British newspapers gleefully reported allegations that Bavarian soldiers had murdered British prisoners on Rupprecht's express orders, depicting him as the Super-Hun.[6]

The new German Fourth Army came down through Roulers and began to press the French and British east of Ypres. Albrecht's men showed their enthusiasm and inexperience by often advancing without waiting for proper artillery support. Consequently, they suffered heavy losses and made slow progress, even against only light opposition. On 20 October Rupprecht ordered his men between Armentières and La Bassée to attack, trying to split the BEF and drive some of the British into the pocket Fourth Army was creating. Over the next twenty-four hours Sixth Army pushed the British back off the Pérenchies and Aubers ridges, regaining most of the ground recently lost. On 22 October, however, the German offensive stalled. The two sides dug in south of Armentières, their trenches just 100 metres apart. Rupprecht was annoyed by the performance of his men and worried how well Fourth Army would get on. Albrecht's troops, he feared, were poorly trained and led by rather old, retired, or reserve officers. How effective would they be in full-scale combat?[7]

He soon had an answer. On 21 October, east and north of Ypres, Albrecht's men ran straight into the advancing French cavalry and Haig's

British I Corps. The British quickly dug themselves in wherever they were. Albrecht's attacks on Ypres the next day were bravely carried out but poorly coordinated. They gained little ground for heavy loss. Over the next two days his inexperienced reserve troops struggled to make progress in the teeth of hostile fire. These were the battles which gave rise to the later myth of the Langemarck *Kindermord*, the 'massacre of the innocents', which supposedly saw battalions of student volunteers sacrifice themselves for Germany, marching to their deaths singing 'Deutschland, Deutschland über Alles'.[8]

Fourth Army's slow progress was beginning to make OHL nervous. Albrecht was apparently stuck east of Gheluvelt on the Menin Road: he seemed unable to dislodge British cavalry from the Messines Ridge. To the north, the Belgian army was holding the line of the River Yser all the way to the sea. South of the River Lys, Sixth Army was doing rather better. It had pushed the British back some 5 kilometres on a 15-kilometre front. Horace Smith-Dorrien's II Corps, in particular, was feeling the strain, although fresh men of the Indian Corps were now starting to join the especially ferocious fighting around Neuve Chapelle. Nonetheless, Falkenhayn's first attempt to encircle the BEF had yielded little and his frustration and friction mounted. To maintain what momentum he had near Ypres, he first stripped divisions from Second Army and set them marching north. Then he told Krafft that he intended to form an independent new command of some six divisions under General Max von Fabeck to attack into the gap from Ploegsteert to Gheluvelt, between Sixth and Fourth Armies.

When Falkenhayn began requisitioning Rupprecht's divisions for Fabeck's command, however, the Crown Prince objected violently. He argued that this would disrupt his promising attack south of the Lys. In fact, however, progress there had begun to slow and Rupprecht was simply expressing general anger. First, OHL was humiliating him by countermanding the order he had just issued, which called for a continued energetic offensive. Second, the scale of his command was being eroded. Third, he had heard that Falkenhayn was being disrespectful about him behind his back. Lastly, he resented a clumsy attempt to 'bribe' him with an offer of the Grand Cross of the Iron Cross. If OHL tried to take more of his men, he resolved to drive to see the Kaiser:

> Either I command the army, or I resign. This cannot go on. Falkenhayn lets himself be influenced by every Chinese whisper and jumps to conclusions which are in every way damaging, which weaken the offensive spirit of the

men and undermine their trust in their superiors. *If only Falkenhayn would be replaced by Colonel-General von Bülow or one of the senior generals.* On the one hand army commands are kept too much in the dark about the general situation, on the other OHL interferes in their business, instead of contenting itself, in the manner of the great Moltke, with issuing general directives and leaving the armies to carry out the missions they've been assigned.[9]

A showdown was only averted when Falkenhayn put Fabeck's task force nominally under Rupprecht's command.

In reality, however, Sixth Army's control over Fabeck was limited. It was Fabeck, his chief of staff, Lieutenant-Colonel Fritz von Loßberg, and Falkenhayn together who planned the next major attack for 30 October. 'Only later, when the attack got more and more bogged down, did General Falkenhayn once again involve the [Army HQ] in command.' Having beaten off British and French counter-attacks from 25 to 28 October, Falkenhayn's scheme involved Fourth Army crossing the Yser and bypassing Ypres to the north while Fabeck swung south of the town. The two pincers would then link up, surrounding part of the BEF. This was a much more limited objective than in Falkenhayn's earlier attacks. His ambitions had previously encompassed destroying all the enemy in northern France and Flanders. Partly, this was because many of Fabeck's units were weak. For instance, the battalions of II Bavarian Corps were only 500–700 men strong.[10]

The German attack in the north stalled almost at once when the Belgians opened the sluices in the dykes, allowing the sea in and flooding the land from Dixmuide to the coast. To the south, Fabeck's men drove to within just 5 kilometres of Ypres itself, although he thought the attack could have achieved more if units had cared less for their flanks and pushed on more aggressively. Rupprecht noted that 'we seemed to have forgotten how to fight on the move, how to outflank the enemy and how to stop him out-flanking us by deploying in echelon—everything we learnt on staff rides and the manoeuvre grounds'.[11]

The next day, 31 October 1914, proved one of the most dramatic of the BEF's war. It is most famous for the actions around Gheluvelt on the Menin Road, where German troops, including Adolf Hitler's regiment, captured the village and tore a hole in the British line. The situation was only restored by a brave charge by the 2nd Battalion Worcestershire Regiment across 1,000 metres of open ground. This recaptured Gheluvelt Chateau, halted the German advance, and bought time for the situation to be recovered. Important fighting also went on further south. Fabeck's main attack aimed to seize the Messines Ridge and drive westwards on the high ground at Mount Kemmel which dominated the whole salient. Success was only partial, however. Bavarian soldiers seized but lost Wytschaete, while troops from Württemberg gained no more than a foothold in Messines in the face of opposition from, among others, the 'London Scottish' (1st/14th Battalion, London Regiment), the first British Territorial soldiers to see significant action. Heavy fighting continued along the Menin Road and on the Messines Ridge over the next few days. It 'had almost the savagery of the Middle Ages'. By 2 November the lines had stabilized once more. Fabeck's men held Wytschaete and Messines but were unable to push further ahead. Rupprecht watched the action from his battle headquarters at Linselles, accompanied by Kaiser Wilhelm II and the famous Swedish explorer, Sven Hedin. Meanwhile, his men launched local attacks further south, designed to pin French forces in place and prevent reinforcements being sent north. Among the few gains made was the chapel of Notre Dame de Lorette, captured on 2 November.[12]

In Flanders, the fighting was intense everywhere. It often occurred at close quarters. In Ploegsteert Wood, for instance, the two sides were only thirty paces apart. Casualties were heavy. The Germans probably lost 80,000 men in Flanders between the middle of October and beginning of November. On 3 November, their heavy artillery, now ranged on three sides of Ypres, began to bombard the town. Among the buildings destroyed, controversially, was the beautiful medieval Cloth Hall. In his diary, Rupprecht tried to argue that the guns were targeting the railway station and claimed he gave orders to preserve the Cloth Hall. This seems disingenuous. The station and Cloth Hall were only 400 metres apart. The destruction of the Cloth Hall may not have been intended, but the possibility must have been anticipated.[13]

After 3 November, the tempo of operations slowed somewhat, although local actions remained frequent and sharp. For example, the British launched eight counter-attacks on the factory in Ploegsteert Wood, five of them during the night of 9/10 November alone. Generally, though, the weather was wet and both sides were running short of artillery ammunition. Sir Douglas Haig had so few shells that he sent a third of his guns to the rear. Even so, on 5 November he had to ration the remaining field guns to twenty rounds each daily. On the German side, too, all immediately available stocks of field artillery ammunition had been expended. By 9 November, half Fabeck's heavy artillery was unable to fire.[14]

Between 3 and 10 November the Germans contented themselves with pinning the Entente forces in place while they concentrated fresh forces for a new attack. By now Falkenhayn had given up hope of a war-winning victory on the Western Front, but he remained keen for some kind of morale-boosting local success. He formed another ad hoc task force under General von Linsingen, including a new composite corps, led by General Plettenberg and incorporating units of the Prussian Guard. Their mission was to drive up the Menin Road at Gheluvelt. Fourth Army would lend support on the right; Fabeck and Sixth Army on the left. When front-line commanders objected that ammunition was short and their men tired while enemy defences were strong, OHL offered little sympathy: 'Command knows the problems very well: they must be overcome.'[15]

Again, coordination was poor. Fourth Army attacked on 10 November, taking Dixmuide and gaining some ground near Bixschoote and Langemarck. Plettenberg and Linsingen, however, postponed their assault by twenty-four hours to allow extra time for reconnaissance. They advanced on 11 November. The best known incident of the day was the attack of the Prussian Guard north of the Menin Road. This briefly broke the British line near Polygon Wood before stalling under heavy fire. Again a brave counter-attack restored the situation, this time by the 2nd Battalion Oxfordshire and Buckinghamshire Light Infantry. Fourth Army was apparently exhausted and unable to provide much support. Units were down to between a third and a half of establishment and Albrecht's request for reinforcements elicited a curt 'no' from Falkenhayn. Much of Sixth Army seems hardly to have attacked at all.[16]

The next day, Falkenhayn told a meeting of the chiefs of staff of each army that, after a few more days' work to capture Ypres, the army in the west would dig in on the defensive for the winter. This would free up troops to be sent east, where Austro-Hungarian demands for reinforcement were becoming daily shriller. When Falkenhayn suggested another attack on 13 November, both Sixth and Fourth armies argued that their forces were too weak to continue. Each corps of Sixth Army was down to about one-quarter of its August strength. On 17 November Albrecht formally suspended offensive operations. The following day, OHL ordered Sixth Army to take six divisions out of the line to be transferred to the Eastern Front. As the German official history explained, this 'meant in reality, even if the words did not really say so, the suspension of all offensive operations in the west, forced partly by the exhaustion of the troops and lack of ammunition, partly by the need to intervene in the east with strong forces'. Formal orders to go

Figure 5.1. Rupprecht setting out for a morning ride

over to the defensive followed on 25 November. Within days, eight divisions had been sent to the Eastern Front, almost all of them from Flanders.[17]

Casualty figures are never easy to nail down, but in Flanders they were certainly heavy. According to the British official history, the BEF lost 58,155 men.[18] The French and Belgians had casualties of 50,000–85,000 and 18,000–19,000 respectively, while the Germans probably lost some 134,300 men, of whom 19,600 were killed. It seems conservative to suggest Rupprecht's army lost about 50,000 men overall between La Bassée and Ypres. Around a quarter of a million men on both sides were probably killed, wounded, or captured in this first clash in Flanders.[19]

The First Battle of Ypres was a tactical and strategic draw. A draw was enough, however, to confirm the verdict of the Marne: Germany would not conquer France in 1914. The grandiose schemes of envelopment which both sides came up with had collapsed as Flanders filled with troops and room for manoeuvre disappeared. In the encounter battle that ensued, neither army was initially able to batter a way through the rapidly petrifying front. Increasingly, the fighting took on the character of desperate Entente defence against German thrusts, until eventually the attackers were worn out and forced to give up. The Entente defence held partly because they did at least three things right. First, Anglo-French cooperation was better than it had ever been before in 1914 or would be again until 1918. Liaison was excellent and reserves were promptly sent where they were needed, regardless of nationality. Second, the defence itself was boldly and skilfully handled. With Ypres close behind and reserves scanty, the more the defenders could hold in place, rather than give ground and allow the battle to open up to manoeuvre, the better. When the Germans broke in, as a rule, aggressive counter-attacks proved effective at re-establishing the front. Third, when combat broke down into small-unit actions, as it often did, individual junior officers and other ranks fought bravely.

The Germans also did several things wrong, however. At the tactical and operational levels, as Krafft admitted in his diary, they had attacked on too narrow a front, in insufficient strength, and without enough artillery support. The troops were over-tired. Lack of ammunition was critical: no-one had anticipated how fast modern warfare would eat through supplies. Falkenhayn erred in changing the place of main effort and axis of his attacks three times. Heavy losses in junior officers hit the combat effectiveness of the infantry, who became too reliant on the artillery clearing the way for them. Exhausted staffs and units, often thrown together in ad hoc task forces, struggled properly to coordinate their attacks.[20]

There was a more fundamental problem of intelligence and analysis at work, too. The British official historian, James Edmonds, believed that German intelligence overestimated the strength of Entente reserves and that this contributed to excessive caution by the attackers. Douglas Haig went further: he believed that the Germans' nerve had failed just as they stood on the threshold of victory on 31 October. If only they had pushed on, Ypres might have been theirs. The real mistake which cost the Germans the Battle of Ypres involved under-estimating Entente strength, however, not exaggerating it, and it was made on 15 September. When Falkenhayn and Tappen decided, even with their tired and weakened forces, to resume the offensive after the retreat from the Marne, they set their army on the road to Flanders, to frustration and failure, and to the hospitals and graveyards. By the end of the First Battle of Ypres, Bavaria alone had suffered casualties of about 100,000 men, nearly half of those who had marched away in August.[21]

Before we leave 1914, let us consider in more detail how the combatant armies responded to the shock of the new warfare. The first issue they faced was how to manoeuvre tactically in the face of twentieth-century firepower.

The idea that the impact of modern weaponry came as a complete shock has long been discredited. Militaries had obsessively studied the wars of the previous two generations and knew full well that quick-firing artillery, machine-guns, and rapid smokeless rifle fire might make it harder for infantry to attack and seize ground. Nonetheless, the evidence of the Russo-Japanese and other wars seemed to demonstrate that attackers could still overcome the defence. All they needed to do was to adopt more open formations, combine their own firepower intelligently with movement, and, most importantly, win the battle of wills. With enough courage and skill, any attacker could triumph.[22]

So, when commanders on both sides began to find their infantry having trouble manoeuvring on the battlefield and getting pinned down by enemy fire, their first response was a form of denial. After all, they thought, this was a problem they had fully anticipated and trained their troops to overcome. If attacks were nevertheless breaking down, then one of three things must be true. Perhaps the defensive had indeed become invincible. Maybe they had trained their troops badly. Or, the troops were failing to follow their training. The generals could hardly accept that the first two possibilities could be true. Therefore, the attackers' tactics must be faulty. Thus, as we saw in Chapter 2, the heavy casualties suffered by the Bavarian Foot Guards at Badonviller (12–13 August) were seen as the result of impetuous officers ordering their men to charge prematurely and contrary to their training. Likewise, the failed French attack on Cirey (15 August) was blamed on the poor tactics of a single divisional commander. It was easier to blame individuals than accept that problems might be systemic and hard to resolve. No-one ascribed failure to commanders' shortcomings more enthusiastically than Joffre, who sacked generals liberally. The idea that individuals had fallen short of training standards remained a recurring theme in both French and German explanations of defeat throughout the rest of 1914. For example, a Sixth Army lessons-learnt report of 1 October listed seventeen detailed areas for improvement but at the top of the list still featured that staple of peacetime doctrine and exercises: artillery–infantry coordination.[23]

Discerning observers, however, were beginning to realize that they had been under-estimating the strength of the defensive. They saw that they were going to have to change their approach and pay firepower more respect. The French General Dubail suggested overturning some of the principles of peacetime training. He argued for more night manoeuvres to offset enemy firepower. Greater use should be made of counter-battery fire, even if that meant less direct support for the infantry. On the German side, the failure to capture Maricourt on 27 September showed Krafft that field artillery was useless against a dug-in enemy and it was heavy artillery which was required in much greater quantities. Falkenhayn soon revised pre-war artillery principles in the light of the new circumstances. He suggested new approaches including more use of indirect fire directed by forward observers and guns engaging less by line-of-sight.[24]

Both sides soon realized that, in addition to the tactical difficulties, there were operational problems at work, too. Joffre thought the French army was trying to do too much at once. It was dispersing effort when it should be concentrating it. Rather than launching a series of feeble attacks up and down the line, it would be better to proceed more methodically, focus effort, and capture one objective after another. This would gradually wear down the enemy until he broke. On the German side, Rupprecht still saw operations in more traditional terms. He had not yet realized that million-man armies could not manoeuvre in the old way anymore. The space available was too narrow; even the most improvised trench defences were awkward obstacles; and the defender could always use the railways to plug gaps in his line faster than the attacker could open them. Krafft's view was closer to Joffre's, having already identified that the central problem of the Western Front was the operational one of how to create and maintain momentum. On 22 October he wrote that:

> the operations are unfortunately beginning to stagnate once more.... It is quite clear that what is not accomplished in the first rush can never be achieved on the second, third or subsequent days. The enemy has learnt too well to dig himself in quickly so that the struggle becomes an exhausting local battle from village to village and hamlet to hamlet which after a few days drains away into complete stasis.

This showed a good grasp of the character of the new warfare and the problems it posed, even if he had no solution to propose as yet.[25]

In the early days of the war the way both sides learned had been fairly informal. Sixth Army's initial deployment orders had included instructions to pass on any lessons learnt as quickly as possible. Early in the war, if this happened at all it often did so either verbally or in hastily scribbled notes which have not survived. Thus, for example, we know from Rupprecht's diary that on 29 August he verbally ordered all corps to imitate the relatively successful methods of III Bavarian Corps, waiting for heavy artillery support before attacking fortifications and deploying in depth when on the defensive. His men were to garrison the front line only thinly, to provide a security screen, while most of the strength was held in reserve ready to counter-attack enemy advances. Some of these ideas were reflected in the first formal lessons-learnt report which survives in the Munich archives, submitted on 31 August.[26]

Over the course of autumn 1914, learning became increasingly formal and developed into a process. Once the front solidified, the German army began systematically collecting lessons-learnt reports. On 11 December Sixth Army told all of its corps to submit theirs by January. These were not just about what had gone wrong. They were also to include examples of good practice to be emulated. Thus, on 26 December Rupprecht sent all his corps commanders a report on a successful local action to seize British positions at Festubert, stressing the importance of careful preparation and 'exemplary tactical execution'. Captured enemy documents containing tactical hints were translated and distributed. On 27 November, for example, Sixth Army intelligence circulated the British 7th Division's after-action report. Enemy actions were also analysed closely. A report written by an observer with the German 89th Grenadier Regiment on French attack tactics between 21 and 25 December 1914 was passed up to First Army and thence to OHL, who distributed it back down to all army headquarters in the west on 4 January 1915. Sixth Army sent it on down to its subordinate commands three days later. In other words, within two weeks the whole German army had been informed of the latest French tactics. One of the most important functions of the General Staff was to collate such reports and sift them for valuable lessons to disseminate and incorporate into doctrine for both training and fighting.[27]

French army learning displayed the same mix of formal and informal methods. After-action reports became increasingly important. Within forty-eight hours of a local attack by French VIII Corps on 8 November, for instance, the army commander had read and was commenting on their report. This approach was supplemented by liaison officers attached to each army who reported back to French supreme headquarters (Grand Quartier Général: GQG), as well as all manner of unofficial friend-to-friend or colleague-to-colleague communication. Thus, on 9 November GQG issued two doctrine notes on how best to use artillery. These were explicitly designed to spread experience from other sectors of the front. In the much smaller BEF, informal transmission of lessons learnt was easier, but, as we have already seen in the case of the 7th Division's after-action report, formal approaches were also gaining ground.[28]

All three armies, therefore, after an uncertain start, had quickly appreci-
ated the need for radical change if they were to survive on the Western
Front battlefield. They had begun to develop a three-dimensional approach
to managing change. First, they used pre-existing informal networks to
disseminate best practice, as they always had. In addition, however, they had
begun to develop coherent processes to capture and distribute lessons from
their operations. This second dimension worked vertically. Typically, information was passed up from the bottom of the chain of command to the top,
where new ideas and doctrine were formulated and passed back down to
the men at the front. There was also, however, a third dimension, working
horizontally, where experience from one unit or sector was distributed
around the army, normally mediated by OHL or GQG. The scale and
complexity of these learning processes, still in their infancy in the winter of
1914/15, would grow as the war went on.[29]

PART II

The Anvil 1915–16

6

A Difficult Winter

L ooking back now, the Western Front campaign of 1914 was clearly decisive. But it had not been conclusive. Germany's failure to break Entente resistance, first on the Marne and then in Flanders, doomed her to the long war she knew she could not afford. At the time, however, remarkably few members of the German high command were prepared to accept this. Falkenhayn was one of those who could. He was unable now to imagine how to gain a decisive victory either in the congested and fortified west or among the huge expanses of the east. Therefore, he could see no military solution to Germany's problem. On 18 November he told Chancellor Bethmann Hollweg that they must seek a diplomatic way out of their predicament. Negotiations should begin with Russia. Remove her from the war, he suggested, and France might sue for peace. Even if the French fought on, the resources freed up from the east would enable Germany to win in the west.

This approach seemed unduly pessimistic at the headquarters for the Eastern Front, known as OberOst. Here, the two ambitious and capable officers who had already masterminded a string of victories, Field Marshal Paul von Hindenburg and Lieutenant-General Erich Ludendorff, felt that the German army could still win the war. A series of successful manoeuvre battles could yet crush Russia and enable Germany to turn west. To win the necessary victories, however, fresh troops and ammunition would be crucial. Any new formations raised, they argued, should be sent to them. This fed into the existing strategic debate within the highest reaches of the German command. It also, however, formed part of a power struggle. Ludendorff and Hindenburg were trying to bring down Falkenhayn, a man they detested, and seize control of the army. Falkenhayn was relatively junior and not much liked in the army anyway; his handling of the Battle of Ypres had generated concern; and the idea of a compromise peace was anathema to most of the German army.

Consequently, the OberOst fronde recruited an impressive list of supporters. Generals commanding armies, such as Karl von Einem, Duke Albrecht of Württemberg, Bülow, Gallwitz, and Crown Prince Rupprecht, were quick to sign up. Rupprecht in particular had never been confident that Falkenhayn was the right man for the job. His doubts had grown over the autumn as victory kept slipping out of reach. Falkenhayn's manner was sarcastic and boorish and Rupprecht resented what he saw as unwarranted interference in his own command. In fact, the three most senior heirs to German thrones—Rupprecht, Albrecht, and Crown Prince Wilhelm himself—all came out against Falkenhayn. Moltke and Bethmann Hollweg both suggested sacking him. Even the Kaiserin (Empress) Augusta Victoria wrote to her husband urging change. When Wilhelm II refused to move, Hindenburg threatened to resign if Falkenhayn did not go. The Kaiser was infuriated by this insubordinate ultimatum. Hindenburg, however, was too popular to sack, so Wilhelm reached a compromise. Falkenhayn would keep his position as chief of staff but lose responsibility for the War Ministry. Wilhelm II compensated him with a promotion but four new recently raised army corps were to be sent east.

This leadership crisis made it clear that Falkenhayn had lost the confidence of the army. From now on, he would be entirely dependent on the Kaiser's support, with important consequences for the exercise of command in the German army to which we shall return. It also showed Hindenburg that he could challenge the Kaiser's authority and survive. The reinforcements took part in the Second Battle of the Masurian Lakes, fought between 7 and 22 February. This proved, as Falkenhayn had worried, indecisive.[1]

As 1914 faded away on the Western Front, the tempo of fighting dropped. Both sides struggled to reorganize themselves. The Entente powers tidied up their jumbled units in Flanders, with the French taking responsibility for much of the Ypres Salient. The British Expeditionary Force (BEF), meanwhile, side-stepped south and took over 35 kilometres of line from Wytschaete down to Givenchy, near the La Bassée Canal. In the German army, Rupprecht was given command of an ad hoc Army Group covering the sector from the sea to the River Oise. He had Fourth, Sixth, and Second Armies under his control. Heeringen took over First, Seventh, and Third Armies in the centre and Crown Prince Wilhelm had charge of Fifth Army around Verdun and the left wing all the way to

Switzerland. With action over the winter likely to be fairly local in scale, these Army Groups were designed to allow any reinforcements needed to be shifted from one army to another without requiring Oberste Heeresleitung (OHL) to get involved. It is not clear how thoroughly this idea was followed through, however. As in August 1914, no provision was made for any dedicated Army Group headquarters and this ad hoc arrangement was unwound in early March, at least partly because better weather increased the chances of larger operations again.[2]

Across Belgium and France, men dug. They deepened the scrapes hurriedly scrabbled away under enemy fire, linking them up into rudimentary trench systems protected in front with barbed wire. The war was rapidly taking on the character of a siege, Rupprecht noted with resignation. His army was stripped of men. He had to send five divisions to the Eastern Front and was left covering a 120-kilometre sector with fewer than one infantryman per metre of front line, much thinner than pre-war rules of thumb allotted. Reserves and ammunition were scarce. The weather was rainy and cold and conditions for the soldiers in the line quickly became abysmal. By 11 December, for instance, the trenches at St Eloi on the south side of the Ypres Salient were up to a metre deep in water. Even on 'dry' land, men sank up to their ankles in mud with every step they took.[3]

For all the rain and mud, the end of the battles for Ypres did not mean the fighting was finished. Far from it. Despite the general exhaustion, a series of sharp and sometimes bloody actions followed as both sides struggled to gain some kind of edge over their enemy. They patrolled, raided, and launched local attacks to straighten the lines or gain points of tactical value. They struggled for physical features, such as higher ground, but also for psychological dominance. It was important to show the enemy who was boss. Men fought also to try out new tactics or weapons, to keep up offensive spirit and avoid lethargy, as well as out of ambition or the spirit of competition. On some occasions, no doubt, they fought just for something to do. The result was a low rumble of near-continual small-scale but often deadly operations.[4]

In the middle of December, the level of violence stepped up. Between 14 and 16 December, French and British troops began probing Rupprecht's positions on the south side of the Ypres Salient. They made little progress. The mud was thick and the German defences remained intact. At first these attacks gave 'the impression they were undertaken reluctantly and only for the sake of doing something', and indeed the British effort was half-hearted

by design. Nonetheless, losses were sometimes heavy. In front of their positions the 3rd Bavarian Division counted 350 French bodies, having lost
between eighty and ninety men themselves. By 16 December, however,
something more serious seemed underway. French probes were growing in
aggression and purpose. Rupprecht reckoned that in fact the enemy was
trying, but failing, to carry out a single coordinated attack. When prisoners
of war were brought in, they confirmed that a full-scale attack had indeed
been ordered. This was merely one of a number of attacks taking place all
along the front, part of a much bigger plan for major offensives in both
Artois and Champagne. Joffre's intention was to take advantage of German
troop withdrawals for the Eastern Front to drive in the shoulders of the
German salient that bulged towards Noyon.[5]

On 17 December, French Tenth Army in Artois launched a major operation
to clear the Notre Dame de Lorette Spur and capture Vimy Ridge. Resources
were scarce. One French division possessed just fifteen pairs of wire-cutters
when they needed 100. Problems in coordination and lack of artillery
resulted in attacks being made piecemeal and on narrow fronts. The German
defenders of XIV Corps quickly regained any trenches lost on Notre Dame
de Lorette and the French made little progress. Within two days the attack
had been suspended. After a patch of poor weather, the French tried again
on 27 December, with no more success. Again the offensive was suspended.
Even now, the intention was to try again. Only a further fortnight of bad
weather finally killed off the idea. For paltry gains, the French had suffered
heavy losses. At no point were the German defenders unduly stretched. The
units on the spot were quite capable of containing the French assaults on
their own, without calling for help from Sixth Army.[6]

Rather than Lorette and Vimy, it was the heavy fighting between
Givenchy-lès-La-Bassée and Festubert which appears to have captured
Rupprecht's attention. Here, on 20 December, men of the German 14th
Infantry Division attacked and defeated units of the Indian Corps, capturing Givenchy and nearly 800 prisoners. Rupprecht heard that Indian troops
at Festubert had run away when the attack began, throwing away their
weapons. Soon afterwards, General Haig's I Corps was brought in to replace
the Indians, who were thoroughly worn out after two long and bloody
months in the trenches.[7]

Also on 20 December, the French General Fernand de Langle de Cary
launched the operation which became known as the First Battle of
Champagne. The fighting here was long and brutal. It dragged on until

20 March. The French lost nearly 100,000 casualties and, again, had little or nothing to show for the sacrifice. Meanwhile, smaller-scale fighting continued on the Sixth Army front. It was a rare day which saw no action at all. Some local truces did take place on Christmas Day, of course. In popular myth these truces were all about swapping cigarettes and playing football. The reality was normally grimmer and more pressing. Much of Christmas Day was spent clearing corpses from the battlefield. Inevitably there was some fraternization and there were occasional recurrences over the next few days. There is even some evidence of French and German soldiers shaking hands in No Man's Land up on top of the Lorette Spur. This ridge, 150 metres high, which dominates Vimy Ridge, Lens, and the Douai Plain, was one of the most hotly contested places on the entire Western Front. It was the scene of near constant and intense close-quarters fighting throughout 1914 and 1915. The trenches were always within shouting distance of each other and often nearer. Any truce up here could not last long. Artillery fire soon broke it up. Especially heavy fighting took place at Lorette on 27 December, 15–24 January, 3–8 March, and again on 15–21 March.[8]

Other hotspots throughout the late winter of 1914/15 were at Écurie, north of Arras, and at two places on the BEF front: the Cuinchy-Givenchy area either side of the La Bassée Canal and near St Eloi, south of Ypres. Trench fighting, however harsh, was inevitably not as bloody as mobile warfare had been. Sixth Army casualties in December were less than half the monthly average in August to November. In 1914, Sixth Army lost, on average, 37,630 men per month in combat. In December 1914 the number of casualties fell by more than half to 15,799. Sickness rates, however, remained high. No fewer than one in ten of Sixth Army's total strength reported sick in December 1914. Illness was a consequence of the armies still learning how to live in the trenches. The primitive trenches offered only poor protection from bad weather and sanitation arrangements were as yet only rudimentary. Learning how to live in such conditions was an immense challenge for all the combatants. For many, this first winter in the trenches was the most miserable of them all.[9]

With the approach of spring the ground began to dry out and planning for larger-scale operations could begin. With the Germans busy in Poland, it was clear to all that the initiative on the Western Front lay with Marshal Joffre and Sir John French. Rumours of British amphibious landings in Flanders had come to nothing, but German intelligence knew that Canadian troops were already arriving in France and thought fresh divisions of Kitchener's

New Armies were, too. What they did not know was that British formations which had been promised to the BEF in France were now being diverted to the Mediterranean for the Dardanelles expedition. This prevented Sir John French from taking over more of the line as Joffre requested. Out of frustration, and to show that the British were doing something to help, he ordered an attack at Neuve Chapelle for 10 March 1915. An advance there would have the benefit of enabling his men to move out of the waterlogged valley of the River Lys and up onto the higher and drier La Bassée-Aubers Ridge. If they could do that, not only would they no longer be overlooked by the enemy, but in turn British observers would be able to see all the way to Lille.[10]

The Battle of Neuve Chapelle has always enjoyed a prominent place in the history of the BEF. The British official history, for instance, dedicates eighty pages to it: a lot for a fight which lasted three days and involved just four British divisions. The German official history, in contrast, devotes only two. Neuve Chapelle attracts attention from Commonwealth historians for four reasons. It marked the first time during the war that the British army launched a major set-piece offensive against a dug-in enemy. It was, therefore, a landmark in trench warfare, for the British at least. Second, it demonstrated that it was possible to break in to the enemy's fortifications. In retrospect lessons can be discerned from Neuve Chapelle which would prove important in the long run, even if they were not universally accepted in the near term. Third, it greatly influenced British planning over the rest of the war. Lastly, it was relatively successful, certainly compared with most of the other British battles of 1915.[11]

The British attack at Neuve Chapelle surprised Rupprecht. His attention had been further north, overseeing plans for an attack at St Eloi. Rain had prevented German aerial reconnaissance, so he received no prior warning. The first reports to reach Sixth Army headquarters in the morning of 10 March spoke of two attacks: one at Givenchy, another at Neuve Chapelle. The former, carried out by the British 2nd Division, failed badly. British artillery failed to cut the wire and the defences remained largely intact. When the assaulting battalions went over the top, German machine-guns cut them down in No Man's Land. The Givenchy attack, though, was only one of several attempted diversions designed to conceal the main effort. This was made by the IV and Indian Corps on the village of Neuve Chapelle itself. General Sir Douglas Haig was in overall command.

The German positions here were weak. First, they lay in a salient. The British could fire in on them from almost three sides. Second, since the water table was less than a metre below the surface, the front-line trench was largely built up with a breastwork of sandbags, a metre and a half high and nearly 2 metres thick. A double row of barbed wire between 2 and 5 metres deep ran in front. The village itself was in ruins but not especially fortified. Further back from the front ran the old British 'Smith-Dorrien Trench' of October 1914. This had not been maintained and was largely waterlogged. A thousand metres behind, the Germans had built a line of concrete machine-gun nests. These were spaced some 800 metres apart. They were to serve as support points in case the enemy broke through the front-line defences. The commanders on the ground had asked for permission to link up these strongpoints with a continuous trench. Their requests had been refused, however, on the grounds that the front-line defenders would not fight as hard if they knew a second line lay behind them.[12]

The British launched the first assault with three brigades on a 2,000-metre front. They only had enough shells for a short and sharp bombardment. So, after 276 field, and sixty-four heavy, guns had dropped 3,000 shells on the German defences in just thirty-five minutes, the infantry would attack. Zero Hour was set at five past eight in the morning. Everything depended on the guns. Where they had sufficient time to register their fire properly, they cleared much of the barbed wire, knocked down large stretches of the breastwork and also silenced the German artillery. In these sectors the British infantry advanced swiftly. They overran five of the eight German companies in the front line and swept through the village. A protective barrage to the east of Neuve Chapelle prevented the intervention of German reserves. After a little over three hours the British had captured the German front line and broken into their defences. Rawlinson wanted the men of his IV Corps to advance on towards Aubers Ridge. Three major problems arose, though. First, the assault units were predictably disordered. They needed to reorganize before they could push on. Second, they had outrun their telephone wires and could only be contacted by runner. Inexperienced staffs under-estimated how difficult this could be on the lethal and disorientating First World War battlefield. In fact, Rawlinson's orders never got through to the front brigades. Nonetheless, some of these moved forward again on their own initiative, only to be hit by shells from their own artillery, which was aiming at the German strongpoints. Third, German reserves had managed to throw together a defensive position around the machine-gun casemates. Thinly manned and sketchy as it was, it more than sufficed to contain the uncoordinated attacks that were all the British could manage before darkness fell.

The British had mixed views on what they had achieved on 10 March. Some, like Rawlinson, were delighted to have captured 748 prisoners and penetrated 1,200 metres on a front about 4 kilometres wide. As he wrote in his diary: 'We have had a grand day—our plans succeeded admirably... Douglas Haig is certainly pleased and we have received the congratulations of Sir John French.' Others, including Haig himself, were more downbeat, convinced that Rawlinson had missed the chance to do more.[13]

From the German reaction, it is clear that they took this attack seriously. As soon as General von Claer, commanding the defenders from VII Corps, heard that Neuve Chapelle was lost, he asked Sixth Army headquarters for reinforcements. Rupprecht sent more than a division of infantry and four heavy artillery batteries to his aid on 10 March. The next day, when a captured copy of Haig's orders showed the full scale of the British attack, Rupprecht despatched another seven battalions. On 10 March the British had outnumbered the Germans by forty-eight battalions to twelve. Within twenty-four hours they faced thirty-two. The Germans had also strengthened their defences overnight, piling up breastworks and wire along much of their new line.

Although Rawlinson and Haig were keen to see a further advance on 11 March, communication difficulties continued to make coordinated attacks tricky. Moreover, visibility was poor and the artillery had been unable properly to register their fall of shot. The consequence was weak or non-existent artillery preparation, piecemeal British attacks, and 'a fiasco'. No progress was made. Attacking units were swept away by machine-gun fire as soon as they went over the top. The commanding officer of at least one battalion refused to order his men to waste their lives. By mid-afternoon the artillery fire was dying away. In the morning, Rupprecht had been able to hear only a continuous roar from the guns. Now he could pick out individual shots.[14]

Rupprecht was close enough to hear well because he was visiting Claer's headquarters at Marquillies, 9 kilometres from the fighting. Here he could avoid repeated jittery telephone calls from Falkenhayn and OHL.[15] More importantly, he could review VII Corps' plans for an attack to win back Neuve Chapelle on 12 March. Rupprecht suggested to Claer that there was too little time for proper artillery preparation. Perhaps a further twenty-four hours' delay was called for? Claer disagreed. He argued that another day would give the British time to dig in more firmly. In any case, to prepare a full set-piece attack properly would take weeks. There was no point in waiting for all the heavy artillery reserves in transit: there were not enough suitable observation posts for him to use them all, anyway. Rupprecht, somewhat reluctantly, approved Claer's plan. He clearly did not want to interfere with decisions made by the man on the spot. In Krafft's opinion, this was a mistake and Claer should have been ordered to wait.[16]

Rupprecht and Krafft were right to be worried. After a thirty-minute artillery bombardment, Claer's attack went in at six a.m. on 12 March. His infantry found that the guns had largely missed the defences. Vickers machine-guns scythed swathes in the attacking units, which hesitated and then fell back. Within two hours, the assault was abandoned. On 13 March Rupprecht noted the British were bringing up wire and seemed to be consolidating the positions they already held, rather than gearing up to attack again. Indeed, late on 12 March, Haig had ordered Rawlinson to suspend the attack. The battle for Neuve Chapelle was over.[17]

The British had eliminated an enemy bulge into their lines and demonstrated that, with careful preparation and sufficiently accurate and heavy artillery preparation, they could break into the enemy's fortifications. The battle proved that the scale of any assault must be proportional to, and determined by, the amount of heavy artillery on hand and the availability of ammunition. In three days Haig had used up seventeen days' worth of total UK shell production. The battle had also shown, however, that the difficult bit was how to follow up a break-in. Rawlinson seems to have understood that he had been wrong to carry on hammering away with increasingly disorganized forces against ever stronger defences on 11 and 12 March. Instead, from now on he argued for a policy of 'bite and hold', seizing a small piece of the enemy's position and defeating the inevitable counterattack. Some historians have seen in this limited-objective 'bite-and-hold' approach a genuine operational alternative to the search for that elusive breakthrough. Consequently, Neuve Chapelle appears to mark an important stage on the British army's 'learning curve'. As we shall see, however, if any conceptual advance had indeed been made, it was far from fully accepted and internalized, even by Rawlinson, much less by Haig or the rest of the BEF. Practice lagged even further behind.[18]

The Germans were learning lessons, too. Neuve Chapelle got right to the heart of the two core doctrinal debates about how to mount the defensive. First, should the defence be rigid and forward, or elastic and in depth? The former aimed to stop the attacker dead, ideally literally so, in No Man's

Land, while the latter absorbed pressure, falling back until, exhausted and extended, he could be counter-attacked and defeated. Second, should the defenders counter-attack to win back lost ground and, if so, when? To begin with, on 11 November 1914, Falkenhayn had laid down as a basic principle that 'to guarantee holding our position, the front line must be held with all resources'.[19]

This principle, embodied in the catchphrase 'Was gewonnen ist, muß unbedingt gehalten werden' ('What's been won, must be held at all costs'), was the foundation upon which the whole German approach to the defensive was built in late 1914 and the early months of 1915. This came through in a series of orders and memoranda issued by both Sixth Army and OHL. Nonetheless, where there was a danger the enemy might break through, a second line should also be prepared. Quite how this second line might fit in to any scheme of defence provoked debate. When Rupprecht and others expressed concern that the front-line garrison might be less steady if they knew there was a second line behind them, Falkenhayn reiterated that any fall-back position was no more than a contingency measure. He had no intention of mounting a more flexible defence unless he absolutely had to. He repeated that it was crucial to hold the front line as firmly as possible. The failure of the French winter offensives in Artois and Champagne seemed to vindicate this principle.[20]

Rupprecht thought that at Neuve Chapelle VII Corps had left too many men in the front line where they were vulnerable to enemy artillery and could be overrun. Once the front line was lost, it had been a mistake to defend as far forward as Claer's men did. Rather than digging in along the line of the blockhouses, it would have been better to conduct the main resistance further back, up on Aubers Ridge itself. Here reserves could more easily assemble for a decisive counter-attack. In fact, the more Rupprecht thought about it, the more he felt Neuve Chapelle was an unimportant village not worth retaking. Not only had Claer counter-attacked too soon, but he had probably erred in counter-attacking at all. It would have been better to preserve strength and launch a set-piece attack in his own time. It was obvious that the 12 March counter-attack had failed for want of preparation.[21]

OHL's comments on Sixth Army's battle report found fault with VII Corps' execution of its counter-attack and blamed Rupprecht for not having forbidden it, to his predictable annoyance. Otherwise, however, Falkenhayn seemed fairly happy with the outcome. It was and is hard to avoid the conclusion that the British had little to show for their efforts. BEF casualties were 583 officers and 12,309 other ranks. The British official history estimated similar losses for the Germans, but they were probably lower. The German official history estimated casualties of 'almost 10,000 men' and Rupprecht's diary and Sixth Army records suggest a final total around 8,500. Whatever the true figure, Aubers Ridge remained out of reach and unfinished business for the British.[22]

7

A Successful Spring

The war in the East devoured men remorselessly through the early months of 1915. The reinforcements combed out from the Western Front after Ypres had proved unable to shatter the Russians at the Second Battle of the Masurian Lakes (7–22 February). Any German progress was undercut by repeated Austro-Hungarian defeats. On 23 March the great fortress at Przemyśl surrendered to the Russians, its garrison of over 120,000 men heading into captivity. The Habsburg regime seemed on the brink of military collapse. More German troops were desperately needed. Where, however, could they be found? The field army was already consuming 180,000 replacements per month. The answer was to reduce existing divisions from four regiments to three and top up the remaining regiments with fresh replacements so that overall rifle strength remained the same. Simultaneously, field artillery batteries were cut from six guns to four. The infantry and artillery freed up in this way were then formed into fourteen new, but experienced, divisions.[1]

There still remained nowhere in the west to employ these forces to any purpose. Between February and April Falkenhayn solicited proposals for offensives from some of the staff. The responses he received all required unrealistic amounts of manpower and heavy artillery. Krafft, for instance, suggested attacking with fifteen new army corps on a 25-kilometre front either side of Arras, supported by nearly 200 heavy batteries. Such an operation would have dwarfed even the Battle of Verdun a year later. Indeed, not until March 1918 could the Germans concentrate so much artillery for a major assault. It is unclear whether Krafft was setting the bar so high on purpose to imply that an attack was out of the question.[2]

Falkenhayn was already convinced that 'we won't see a war of movement now again. It's just trench warfare. We cannot make a breakthrough, because then the enemy can breakthrough somewhere else.' Rupprecht's response when Falkenhayn said this was brutally direct: 'if that's your view then we must get a peace as soon as possible and at any price'. Rupprecht had already begun to show signs of pessimism at the end of November. He had warned Krafft then that the weight of enemy manpower, especially from the British Empire, now meant they were in for a long war. Unless they could restore mobility, the Entente would slowly squeeze the life from Germany. He also complained that stress was turning his hair prematurely grey. As we shall see, however, Rupprecht's view of the chances of victory changed rapidly and frequently during the war and otherwise he remained upbeat. Indeed, when Rupprecht heard rumours that his father was considering asking the Kaiser to seek an early peace, he rejected this defeatism. His reply to Falkenhayn seems intended more to discomfit a superior he disliked and distrusted than to constitute a serious proposal for peace.[3]

The fall of Przemyśl soon rendered further discussion moot. The newly raised divisions had to go east to prop up Austria-Hungary with a fresh offensive at Gorlice-Tarnow. This was planned for 2 May. A major attack might be beyond reach in the west, but that did not preclude operations with more limited objectives, especially if they might divert attention from the main German effort against Russia. The most famous of these was the attack on French and British troops north-east of Ypres on 22 April 1915. This marked the first use of lethal gas on the Western Front. Weeks of violent fighting ran on almost to the end of May, in what became known as the Second Battle of Ypres. About another 100,000 men were killed, wounded, or captured.[4]

Rupprecht had no direct role in the planning or execution of the Second Battle of Ypres. He knew all about it, though. On 1 March Dr Fritz Haber, mastermind of the German chemical warfare programme, had visited Rupprecht's headquarters. According to Rupprecht's published diary, he warned Haber and Falkenhayn that they were gambling against the prevailing wind and, more importantly, with Germany's reputation. How could they be sure that the British or French chemical industries might not catch up with the Germans? Tellingly, this passage does not exist in Rupprecht's manuscript diary. It is a later insertion, designed to distance Rupprecht from the adoption of a controversial and unsuccessful weapon. The manuscript diary shows that he fully supported the use of gas, seeing it as a legitimate reprisal for British atrocities and expecting the German chemical industry to be able to outperform that of the Entente countries. He thought the attack itself was poorly executed: it took place on too narrow a front, too late in the day for proper exploitation, and there were too few reserves to hand. Still, German pressure forced the Entente back some 5 kilometres, to within 3,000 metres of the walls of Ypres.[5]

Rupprecht toured Flanders and the captured trenches in early May. He was unimpressed by the enemy's standards of engineering and hygiene. The trenches were too wide and looked unfinished. They were too shallow and there were not enough dugouts. Communications trenches were in a poor state and there was not enough wire. British trenches were a little better than French ones but still very dirty. Food leftovers, tins, and jars littered the dugouts. There were no latrines nearby. Corpses lay buried in the trenches and breastworks with their arms and legs sticking out. Dead bodies from the November battles still lay about in the open all over the place. The contrast with the German trenches Rupprecht toured the next day was dramatic: here 'everything was excellently maintained and lovingly tidied'. Telephone wires ran in neat channels in the trench walls; signposting was comprehensive and artfully painted; here and there little gardens were planted with snowdrops and other spring flowers. 'Everything was as homely as possible, and the men were in the best possible spirits.' The Germans had buried British dead from mid-April in a small cemetery on the side of the hill under simple wooden crosses. The village of Zonnebeke, by contrast, was 'a picture of devastation'. In places the foundations were all that was left. The bell tower of the church was split from top to bottom. The roofs of Ypres could not be seen through the mist, but Rupprecht was able to make out the succession of low ridges which made up the terrain of the salient. The subtle swells of the ground hardly showed on the map but offered good fields of fire to the defender, even if in 1915 enough trees still survived to restrict visibility in places.[6]

From the last days of April onward, German intelligence began picking up ominous signs of increased enemy activity opposite Sixth Army. By 2 May aerial reconnaissance had shown that the British were digging new assembly trenches opposite Aubers Ridge. Further south, French artillery fire was increasing almost day by day. The sector around Vimy Ridge held by I Bavarian Reserve Corps was especially heavily shelled. Sixth Army felt stretched thin. It had 90 kilometres of front to hold with thirteen divisions in the front line and just two in reserve. Artillery support was provided by 858 guns, of which 174 were heavy. When, therefore, on 21 April, Rupprecht was told to give up a regiment from the division responsible for defending Vimy Ridge, he protested. 'I told the Chief of the General Staff that I was not in a position to accept responsibility for the weakness of the front and that I took no responsibility for the consequences.' Falkenhayn replied: 'If your Royal Highness cannot bear the responsibility, I will just have to add it to my already heavy load. It cannot be changed.' On 8 May French engineers were spotted digging saps forward into No Man's Land and clearing lanes in their own wire. Clearly, an attack was now imminent.[7]

At quarter to five in the morning of Sunday 9 May, Rupprecht was woken by a bomb blast near his headquarters in Lille. A bomb had dropped near the garden wall of his old billet. Rupprecht had recently moved out after a newspaper published its location, but he did not think this was an assassination attempt. More probably the enemy was trying to destroy the nearby building which housed his telephone exchange to cut his communications. Other bombs later fell on nearby railway stations. At headquarters, the only real damage was to the composure of the cook. The blast had thrown him out of bed and he was so badly shaken that he made 'dreadful coffee' that morning. Rupprecht retained his poise better than his chef, rising and dressing as usual at seven o'clock. By then his army was already under attack.[8]

First into action were the British of Sir Douglas Haig's First Army. They launched two attacks some 5,500 metres apart, designed to converge on and capture Aubers Ridge. In the north, Rawlinson's IV Corps aimed to break through the 6th Bavarian Reserve Division near Fromelles, while further south the 1st and Meerut Divisions attacked the Westphalians of the 13th Division on a 2,200-metre front south of Neuve Chapelle. A short but sharp bombardment by 637 guns began at six o'clock. The artillery hoped to cut the wire and destroy both the front line and rear strongpoints. The forty minutes allotted was nowhere near enough. None of these objectives was achieved before the artillery fire, as planned, began to move off hundreds of metres into the German rear. The British were still forming up for their assault. When they did finally advance across No Man's Land, they found uncut wire and largely intact defences. The Germans were fully alert and poured rifle and machine-gun fire into the British ranks. Any small groups of attackers which managed to get into the German trenches were unable to hold out long before being overwhelmed. Most survivors found themselves pinned down in No Man's Land, unable to move either forward or back. Within twenty minutes the southern attack lost over 3,000 troops and had entirely broken down. The northern pincer had done little better. Again, some isolated companies had seized short stretches of the front line, but they were fighting for their lives. The Germans laid down murderous fire on No

Man's Land and the British trenches to prevent reinforcements coming up. The 2nd Battalion Devonshire Regiment, for instance, suffered 30 per cent casualties without ever going over the top.[9]

Repeated British attempts to get the attack moving again later that day were either stillborn or equally abortive. Such chaos reigned in the communications trenches that it was impossible to relieve the shattered units in the front line, even under cover of darkness. The few pockets hard won in the German lines were pinched out during the night. When the casualty returns came in, Haig had to accept defeat. Further attacks were suspended for now.[10]

The British were shocked by their defeat at Aubers Ridge. Confidence had been high. They thought they had learnt the lessons of Neuve Chapelle and had worked hard to improve planning and communications. Reserves were closer to hand, ready to deploy when needed. The reasons for failure, though, lay elsewhere. The British official history suggests that the initial forty-minute bombardment proved too short. Planners had failed to appreciate how much the Germans had built up their defences after Neuve Chapelle: they had doubled or tripled the thickness of breastworks and increased the depth of barbed wire, for instance. This explanation captures some, but not all, of the truth. A longer bombardment would probably not have solved the problem without measures to improve the accuracy and effectiveness of the British artillery. There was no allowance made for the reduced accuracy of worn gun barrels and insufficient time was allotted for target registration. More importantly, as Robin Prior and Trevor Wilson point out, the British failed to realize that, with fewer guns per metre of front and effort split between more than one German defence line, the intensity of their shelling was just 20 per cent that of 10 March. The tactical consequence was intact defences. Expecting the infantry to march forwards almost without having to fight in these circumstances was unrealistic. Aubers Ridge also displayed a weakness in British operational art, which had not yet internalized the need to match the scale of ends to the availability of means. This applied in particular to heavy artillery but had nothing to do with the shortage of shells Sir John French alleged in the political crisis over munitions he provoked back home, however. Plenty of ammunition remained available the next day. Although the 'shell crisis' hit on the deeper truth that war production and procurement needed reform, its origin was a sordid attempt by Sir John French to obscure his own command mistakes and counter likely criticism from Lord Kitchener, the Secretary of State for War.

Overall, Aubers Ridge, as Professor Gary Sheffield has written, 'most closely matches the stereotype of the First World War battle: soldiers advancing across No Man's Land only to be cut down by machine-gun fire; generals frustrated by the lack of progress ordering further fruitless attacks; minimal gains for huge losses'.[11]

The contrast between British failure and French success on 9 May was stark. Aubers Ridge was the British Expeditionary Force's (BEF's) contribution to a much larger French offensive, the so-called Second Battle of Artois. It is clear from Rupprecht's diary that the best efforts of the BEF caused him little or no concern on 9 May. Those of Victor d'Urbal's French Tenth Army, on the other hand, on the 20-kilometre front from the Lorette Spur down to east of Arras, worried him deeply. Word of trouble began to come in during the morning, with reports that Lorette was under such heavy bombardment that the entire hill was shrouded in clouds of dust. An enemy attack also seemed to be underway against I Bavarian Reserve Corps, whose 5th Bavarian Reserve Division held the front from Carency down to Neuville St-Vaast, about 4,000 metres west of the crest of Vimy Ridge. The 1st Bavarian Reserve Division extended the line south around Arras. The German front line constituted a network of trenches up to 150 metres deep. A second line, 2,000 metres or so back, had been begun but was not yet continuous. Many of the German defences had been badly knocked about by a methodical French artillery preparation from 3 May onwards. At seven a.m. on 9 May the French guns began firing once more with growing intensity. Four hours later, the infantry assault began. As the French infantry moved forwards, the guns either fired a rolling barrage in front of them or shifted their attention to the second line. Five French corps took part in the attack, supported by 782 field and 293 heavy guns. In all, the artillery dropped 265,430 shells on Sixth Army's positions between 3 and 9 May.[12]

By 12.30 on 9 May it was clear that the French had broken through the Bavarian line. Souchez and Vimy Ridge were under threat. If they lost Souchez, the Germans would have to evacuate the Lorette Spur. The loss of Vimy Ridge, the last high ground before the Douai Plain, would be even more worrying. Rupprecht asked Oberste Heeresleitung (OHL) for two divisions to prop up his reeling Bavarians. OHL agreed at once. Reserves would not be able to help before nightfall, however. In the meantime, Rupprecht would have to scrape together what units he could to contain what was increasingly looking like a major French breakthrough. No-one thought to send reinforcements to Aubers Ridge, which further confirms the insignificance of the BEF attack.

In fact, at around noon men of the French Moroccan Division were digging in on the crest of Vimy Ridge.[13] The Moroccan Division had advanced 5 kilometres in ninety minutes. This was so remarkable an achievement by 1915 standards that d'Urbal's staff officers could not believe it at first. On the Moroccans' left the 77th Division of General Ernest Barbot made similarly spectacular progress, occupying Souchez cemetery.[14]

Their success was based on three foundations. First, the attackers did several things right. Planning was painstaking and detailed. The artillery preparation had cut the wire so well and battered the trenches so thoroughly that in places the only way to move in daylight was on all fours. The French also used mines to blow large holes in the defences. The assaulting troops moved fast, leaving strongpoints to be mopped up by subsequent waves. Second, the men were well trained, experienced, and had high morale, partly due to good leadership. The commander of the Moroccan Division, General Ernest Blondlat, for instance, issued an order of the day which seems to have inspired his men: 'I am your father, you know that I love you like my own children, if you want to show me that you love me too, fight well and kill as many Boches as you can.' General Barbot seems equally to have personified French élan. When he was mortally wounded on 10 May, his dying words are said to have been 'Beautiful...Glorious day...Victory.' Third, the Germans they defeated had some very specific problems. While some defending units were on the alert, others chose to interpret French attack preparations as a diversion and were caught by surprise. In the crucial Vimy sector, the 5th Bavarian Reserve Division had been reorganized, with one of its original regiments replaced by a Landwehr regiment full of older men transferred from occupation duties in Belgium who resented their transfer. When the French attacked, this Landwehr regiment broke and ran.[15]

Things were going badly for Rupprecht in the centre but his men were doing better on the flanks, holding the French on the Lorette Spur and maintaining a firm grip on key villages such as Ablain-Saint-Nazaire, Carency, Souchez, and Neuville-Saint-Vaast. The Labyrinth redoubt also remained in German hands. Rupprecht's men were thus able to fire from both flanks and make it difficult for the French to reinforce success on Vimy Ridge. The defenders gathered together an ad hoc force to seal off the

French penetration by early afternoon. Under pressure from three sides the men of the Moroccan Division had been pushed back down the slope of Vimy Ridge by six o'clock that evening.[16]

The next day, 10 May, combat raged from house to house, sometimes from room to room, through the ruins of Neuville-Saint-Vaast, Ablain-Saint-Nazaire, and Carency. Equally vicious hand-to-hand struggles were fought out in the trenches of the Labyrinth, along the Souchez-Arras road and up at Notre Dame de Lorette. Both sides were too disorganized, however, to put together any coordinated attack. It was all many units could do to hold in place. Reliefs and resupply proved extremely difficult. In forty-eight hours of action, the Moroccan and 77th Divisions received almost no food, water, or ammunition. The French tried to improvise an attack in the afternoon of 11 May but it was unrealistic to expect their exhausted men to be able to restore momentum to an attack which had stalled, especially at short notice, with limited intelligence and poor communications. Most operations between 10 and 15 May remained small-scale and local.[17]

That did not mean they were not bloody. The Moroccan Division lost over 5,000 men in three days. One German regiment lost all three battalion commanders and nine of its twelve company commanders within thirty-six hours of coming into battle. Some of its companies were left just thirty men strong. Sixth Army counted 20,000 casualties up to 13 May.[18]

Partly to fill the gaps left by these casualties, but partly also with an eye to retaking the lost ground, between 9 and 14 May Sixth Army received reinforcements of four and a half infantry divisions, plus artillery. This was more than half the reserves OHL held on the Western Front. By 18 May another three and a half divisions had been sucked in, and OHL had just one division left in reserve for all of France and Flanders. This demonstrates how seriously the Germans took the threat in Artois. Tensions within the German high command further underscore the point. At noon on 11 May, Rupprecht received this telegram from OHL:

> At the very least, his Majesty expects the army to hold its present line under any circumstances. Whether this objective is accomplished defensively or with secondary attacks must be judged locally. In any case, with reasoned deployments and firmly coordinated leadership, the available infantry and heavy artillery ought to be strong enough to prevent a continued enemy advance. His Majesty acknowledges the outstanding bravery displayed in the recent battles with appreciation.

This was Falkenhayn writing, not the Kaiser. Rupprecht's reply was firm. He was keen to reject any implication that the effort so far had been less than wholehearted:

> His Majesty the Kaiser may rest assured that Sixth Army will do everything in its power to stop the enemy offensive. This commitment has been maintained from the beginning. We will not voluntarily relinquish any ground to the enemy. At this time a major counterattack does not hold any promise, but we continue to reserve this option.[19]

Falkenhayn, however, remained worried that Sixth Army's grip on the situation was not all it should be. In the evening of 11 May two OHL interventions in Sixth Army affairs underlined that fact, to Rupprecht's annoyance. First, a liaison officer arrived to provide a direct link between OHL and Rupprecht's two most menaced corps, bypassing Sixth Army headquarters, and to advise on the feasibility of a counter-attack. Rupprecht's complaints that this threatened the integrity of the chain of command were ignored. Second, a telegram arrived from Falkenhayn announcing that a fresh corps was coming to reinforce Rupprecht, which should be used 'under an energetic commander' to regain the lost ground. Rupprecht correctly read this as implied criticism of the general officer commanding I Bavarian Reserve Corps, Karl von Fasbender. To Rupprecht's mind, it was not Fasbender, but Falkenhayn, who was most responsible for the setback of 9 May. The latter had ignored warnings that the units in this sector were being stretched too thin. On 12 May, Falkenhayn was more explicit, wiring that any counter-attack needed a leader who 'is highly committed to the thing and is confident it will succeed'. He named a general (Claer) whom he knew full well Rupprecht thought unsuitable for special missions.

This was the last straw for the Crown Prince. He was no longer prepared to tolerate his authority being undermined. He would complain direct to the Kaiser. Before he could do so, however, he received further fuel for his resentment, both on his own account and on behalf of Bavaria. First, Falkenhayn appointed General Ewald von Lochow to command a semi-independent task force comprising three of Rupprecht's corps. Lochow was being squeezed into the chain of command rather as Fabeck had been at Ypres, nominally under Rupprecht but in reality reporting direct to OHL. Thus Rupprecht suddenly lost command of half his army. All his Bavarian staff thought he should resign in protest, seeing this as a 'war' with OHL. The next day, Falkenhayn twisted the knife further. When

Rupprecht requested reinforcements, OHL told him to consult Lochow—his subordinate—before deciding whether he really needed more men. Second, Rupprecht heard talk of a new military convention which would give the Kaiser power to appoint and promote Bavarian officers: an infringement of Bavarian royal privileges which Rupprecht neither saw the need for nor welcomed.[20]

Rupprecht wrote his letter to the Kaiser and sent it off on 17 May. He received two very different responses. The formal answer arrived on 23 May. It comprised two letters. One was from the Kaiser, agreeing with Rupprecht on all points. The other, from Falkenhayn, apologized for any misunderstandings. Rupprecht replied that he considered the matter now closed. There had already been a less formal, but more important, response, however. At one o'clock in the morning of 19 May, Rupprecht's chief of staff, Krafft, was shaken awake and handed an urgent message. He was ordered to depart the very same day for the Tirol, there to assume command of the Alpenkorps, a formation of mountain troops collected to fight Italy. 'That', thought Krafft, 'is Falkenhayn's answer to the Crown Prince!' Rupprecht felt that 'Krafft's transfer was a heavy blow for me: I'd known him well since the War Academy and I lost in him not only a trusted adviser but a loyal friend.' He also worried that it would create the impression that the command team of Sixth Army had failed and that Krafft's transfer marked another step in Prussian attempts to dominate the Bavarians. Krafft was replaced by a Prussian, Colonel Gustav von Lambsdorff. No effort was made to consult King Ludwig III about Krafft's transfer.[21]

While Rupprecht and Falkenhayn played out their political battle, a more deadly one continued to unfold in Artois. The British, under pressure from Joffre to add their weight to the offensive, began once more to batter away near Neuve Chapelle. This time, having seen a short bombardment fail, they experimented with a prolonged one. During three days of deliberate, observed fire, British guns fired over 100,000 shells, obliterating much of the German front-line breastwork on a 5,000-metre front north of Festubert. On the night of 15/16 May the BEF began its first night assault of the war. Two of the attacking brigades were detected by alert defenders; they were shot up and failed to get near the German lines, leading to the cancellation of planned follow-up attacks in this area. The third brigade was more successful, silently crossing No Man's Land and seizing part of the German front trenches. At daybreak, Major-General Hubert Gough's 7th Division joined the assault. It also took the German front and support lines, but by ten a.m. the attack had stalled. Resistance and rain prevented further progress that day but during the evening the Germans withdrew to a new line hastily built to the rear. Although fighting continued until 25 May, the British were unable seriously to threaten this defensive position. The BEF had advanced up to 1,500 metres on a front 5 kilometres wide but lost some 16,000 soldiers, while the Germans probably lost fewer than the 5,000 suggested by the British official history. German VII Corps drew down one brigade of reinforcements but was otherwise able to handle the situation with its own resources. Although Rupprecht did mention these operations in his diary, they clearly worried him little. He did not even bother to refer to another British attack on 16 June at Givenchy-lès-la-Bassée. This proved a 'rerun of Aubers Ridge', as Prior and Wilson put it: uncut wire and intact defences cost the BEF another 3,500 casualties for no gain.[22]

The situation further south, around Notre Dame de Lorette and Vimy Ridge remained Rupprecht's major concern. Neither army was seeing much return on the blood spilled in poorly coordinated attacks, hastily cobbled together by tired troops and staffs, so both sides rethought their approach. The German response, as we have seen, was to bring in Lochow to try to coordinate efforts in the central sector. The French took a different path. Foch told d'Urbal that improvised attacks must cease at once. Instead, a slow and methodical approach was called for, with assaults launched only after the 'fullest and most detailed preparation, along the lines of the 9 May attack. This preparation requires time.' In the short term, Tenth Army was to focus on local attacks to improve its positions and secure jumping-off positions for a full-scale attack to take place later. French pressure was sufficient to keep the initiative and prevent a coordinated counter-attack. Any fresh German troops found themselves being fed in to hold the line almost at once. By the end of May, despite heavy rain and much mud, the French had cleared the Lorette Spur and captured Ablain-Saint-Nazaire. German troops still held out, however, in Souchez, Neuville-Saint-Vaast, and the Labyrinth.[23]

By early June, OHL seemed to feel the pressure was easing somewhat. Falkenhayn sent two and a half divisions to the Eastern Front to reinforce the remarkable successes achieved in the Battle of Gorlice-Tarnow. He even travelled there himself for a few days to plan further exploitation. Rupprecht was not quite so sanguine. Between 9 May and 5 June, he noted, his troops manning the Souchez-Neuville sector had been subjected to fifty enemy attacks. On 7 June alone, no fewer than six French attacks were broken up by German artillery fire before they could gain any ground. Nonetheless, the strain on German units remained intense, and worn-out units needed to be rotated out of the line for rest. Rupprecht's dissatisfaction with Lochow grew: he found him lacking in dynamism and over-cautious in his preparations. On 15 June, in view of the apparent improvement in the situation, he suggested that Lochow's task force should be dissolved. Lochow, however, successfully argued for a fortnight's extension.[24]

In fact, at exactly this time, after five weeks of fighting and preparation, French Tenth Army was finally ready for a new attempt to capture Vimy Ridge and break through on to the Douai Plain. D'Urbal launched his assault on Wednesday 16 June. He tried to rectify what he saw as the three greatest shortcomings on 9 May. First, the Entente scaled up operations generally in an effort to tie down German reserves all along the line. The BEF launched operations at Givenchy on the La Bassée Canal and at Bellewaarde near Ypres. The former was a bloody failure, as discussed above. The latter seized a few hundred metres of front-line trench at a cost of nearly 4,000 men. More significantly, three French armies launched their own attacks to support the Tenth Army effort. Second, although Joffre could do little to reinforce d'Urbal's artillery, he could ensure better supplies of munitions. So, although the number of guns grew little, nearly twice as many shells fell on the German trenches in the week before 16 June than in the equivalent period in May. Third, this time the reserves would not be left too far back behind the line. Indeed, the attacking units were to commit every man they had to the first assault and keep no local reserve. Army reserves would follow up the advance and mop up as required.[25]

Significant obstacles to French success remained, though. The German defenders were fully alert. French troops were tired and intelligence was poor. At least one French division had been in the front line every single day since 9 May. Commanders did not always know the precise positions of their own men, much less where their opponents were. The flanks were still not properly secure. So any French advance would be exposed to German enfilade fire from Souchez and Neuville-Saint-Vaast, unless these villages could be rapidly neutralized when the assault went in. This proved impossible. As a result, although the Moroccan Division again did well, driving into the second line on Hill 119,[26] and a few other footholds were gained in the defences, yet again the attackers were exposed to cross-fire and the attack stalled. In many places, indeed, intact wire and heavy losses had stopped it almost before it had started.

The Germans were once more worried as 'the situation was becoming extremely precarious'. Rupprecht was gripped by insomnia. Lochow argued that Sixth Army should pull back behind Vimy Ridge, lure the French forwards, and then hit them from three sides as he had successfully at Soissons in January. Rupprecht, on the other hand, felt that his men were quite capable of holding in their current positions. In any case, he was not sure he had enough strength to execute a plan on Lochow's scale. Rupprecht's view prevailed. OHL did, however, think it worth sending significant reserves, totalling some five divisions and thirteen heavy batteries, over the next few days. In general, by the end of 18 June it was becoming clear to the Germans that the French drive was losing punch. Indeed, French losses between 16 and 18 June were 29,000, only slightly fewer than in the whole month of May. Foch and d'Urbal suspended major operations on 18 June, although heavy fighting went on locally until almost the end of the month. By 22 June German intelligence had convinced the high command that the Second Battle of Artois was over.[27]

Over 200,000 men became casualties during the Second Battle of Artois, half of them French. The Germans had reason to be pleased with their efforts. Although some ground had been lost, they had stymied Entente breakthrough attempts. Any lessons the British and French had learnt had been at a very high price, and both had shown themselves capable not only of inventing new mistakes but also of repeating old ones. They would need months to recover and get ready to try again.[28]

By the end of June the French had begun to move beyond the denial of early 1915 and grasp the scale of the challenge they faced. In February, Foch had still been maintaining that, if the defensive seemed superior to the offensive during the winter fighting in Artois and Champagne, it must be because the attackers had been doing something wrong. Similarly, Grand Quartier Général (GQG) still felt nothing had fundamentally changed:

> The present war has in no way undermined the principles which form the foundations of our offensive doctrine, but, because of the novel forms it has taken, operations are characterized by unfolding more slowly and methodically in both time and space. That is the result of firepower and the strength of defensive organization. The principles remain intact. Methods of attack must be adapted to this new situation.

Specifically, preparation should be thorough and methodical. With sufficient artillery support, getting infantry into the enemy defences was possible, so long as assaults were not made piecemeal but properly coordinated across a wide front. Success was to be followed up fast.[29]

Joffre developed the theme of speed further in his Note 5779 of 16 April, written to set the tone for the Second Battle of Artois: 'the aim of an offensive action is not merely to capture a line of enemy trenches but indeed to chase the enemy from the whole of his position and to defeat him without giving him the time to re-establish himself'. The initial assault must be 'sudden, violent and pursued ceaselessly and continually by the commitment of fresh units to the fighting front until the final result has been achieved'. In other words, Joffre was hoping to break through the German lines with one sharp blow.[30]

On 9 May, breaking in to the German positions indeed proved relatively straightforward but the results proved disappointing, as we saw above. The first lessons-learnt reports, produced within a couple of weeks, suggested moving reserves up nearer the front and some alterations to artillery-targeting priorities, but broadly upheld Joffre's operational approach. Even after another major failure on 16 June, GQG reckoned that

> the lessons of the most recent fighting prove that the first infantry attack, minutely prepared and vigorously executed, always succeeds. The enemy front is broken and his artillery unable to react. If our infantry stop, it is less because its offensive force is spent than the exploitation of initial success cannot be pushed far and fast enough.

As Joffre told Foch, more artillery was needed and any attack must take place on a broader front. More effort must be made, especially by the British, to tie down enemy reserves. Foch's reply was guarded about the possibility of a breakthrough. The German superiority in heavy artillery worried him and to rely on the British would be an error. Foch hinted that the poor results of 16 June, despite reinforced artillery and the improvements made after 9 May, in fact suggested that the problem might go deeper than poor execution or the application of insufficient resources. It was possible instead that the whole approach might be mistaken. The French might need to recalibrate their entire thinking. Not everyone yet agreed with Foch about the need for wholesale change. Nor had he worked out what reforms were necessary. But the fact that some, at least, within the French army were beginning to think in 'root and branch' terms represented significant progress.[31]

The British remained a long way behind. With a smaller army in 1914, they had been able to call on a narrower base of military expertise in the first place. The impact of the heavy casualties of the war's first months was therefore especially intense and it proved difficult to bring the rapidly expanding army up to par. Limited resources in manpower and artillery left BEF attacks necessarily only small-scale in 1915. While this reduced the absolute level of loss, if not the proportional rate, when they had the opportunity to experience large-scale operations, learning was sometimes erratic. The BEF misread the lessons of Neuve Chapelle at the tactical level, for example, and persisted in using short bombardments long after the French had given them up in favour of thorough preparation. When the guns failed either to break down the German defences or to achieve surprise, the consequence was the bloody failures of spring 1915. Operationally, British staffs and commanders had little chance to confront the issues of momentum and tempo in major battles which Foch was beginning to ponder. The political significance of the British army's effort in France as yet outweighed its military impact.[32]

To the German defenders, wholesale reform did not seem necessary. The heavy artillery had worked well. So had the newly rebuilt railways, allowing quick and efficient reinforcement of the defenders. Most of the lessons Sixth Army learnt were low-level tactical tweaks. For instance, units were reminded to counter-attack from the flank where possible, rather than frontally. What the Second Battle of Artois did close down, however, was any chance of continued debate about the utility of a second line of defence. A full second line was now clearly necessary. Falkenhayn ordered one to be built all along the front, about 1,500 metres back, to prevent the enemy overrunning both in a single rush. Both 'lines' in fact comprised linked systems of several trenches, a hundred metres or so apart, with sufficient dugouts to shelter the garrison. Specialist engineers and artillerymen were made responsible for inspecting the front and disseminating best practice in their spheres. The next time the British and French attacked, they would find themselves facing even stronger defences.[33]

8

Further Victories

The summer of 1915 passed relatively quietly for Rupprecht and his Sixth Army, although the steady drip of casualties continued relentlessly. Sharp fighting broke out from time to time, especially in dangerous flashpoints such as Souchez. Overall, however, the first anniversary of the outbreak of war allowed time for reflection. For Rupprecht, despite the defensive successes achieved, it had been a year of disappointment: 'How brilliantly the war began! What hopes we possessed a year ago! How differently everything has turned out.' To mark the anniversary of the Battle of Lorraine, the Kaiser honoured Rupprecht with the *Pour le Mérite*, the order founded by Frederick the Great informally known as the Blue Max.

On 29 June 1915 Rupprecht gave an interview to the *New York Times*, presumably to repair any damage done to his reputation by allegations publicized in May that his men had murdered prisoners of war.[1] If so, he did a good job. He described himself as 'the anvil in the west', whose job it was to hold the enemy back while the hammer struck in the east. He appeared 'simple, unpretentious and democratic'. He was 'not a voluble talker, particularly about himself, and [was] modest to a fault' but 'one quickly discovers that he has personality with a punch and an iron will. As a man and a fighter with something of the shrewd canniness of the Scotchman and all of the bulldog tenacity which is traditional of the British, relieved by native Bavarian good humour', he was 'soft of voice and slow of speech'. He took the opportunity to deny ordering the execution of captured British troops and to complain that American artillery shells, sold to the French army, were prolonging the war. Over a 'very small glass' of beer he showed his human side, chatting about hunting and expressing a wish to return to America after the war.[2]

The state of reserves would not allow the Germans to attack in force before November at the earliest. Oberste Heeresleitung (OHL) had just six

Figure 8.1. Kaiser Wilhelm II visiting Rupprecht's headquarters

divisions available. Intelligence suggested that the French, on the other hand, were actively preparing an offensive, perhaps in Alsace, with a possible diversion around Arras.[3] From late August into September, enemy activity certainly seemed to be on the rise opposite Sixth Army. French artillery fire was growing heavier and changing from routine harassment to something more deliberate. Enemy infantry were digging new assault trenches and pushing saps out into No Man's Land towards the German lines, in some places closing to within hand-grenade range. Prisoners of war began to report the arrival of extra heavy artillery. The British seemed active around Hulluch and the threat of a French offensive down in Champagne was also growing.[4]

What the Germans were observing were the preliminaries of a large-scale Anglo-French offensive which Joffre had been planning since July. The precise shape and timing changed over the summer as the French and British commands debated among themselves. The final idea, though, was for Castelnau's Groupe d'armées du Centre (GAC) to deliver the main blow in Champagne on Saturday 25 September with some thirty-five divisions, while French Tenth Army attacked on a 20-kilometre front in Artois with seventeen. On d'Urbal's left, Sir Douglas Haig's First Army would extend the offensive a further 10 kilometres north, driving on Loos and Hulluch with six divisions in the first line and a further three in reserve.

Haig possessed an average of eleven guns per kilometre, down from about thirty at Neuve Chapelle and compared with twenty-two for the French in Artois and thirty in Champagne. Haig hoped to offset his relative weakness in artillery with chlorine gas, which would panic the defenders and allow the British to carry both the first and second German positions in one bound.[5]

By 21 September, Sixth Army was braced for an imminent assault. Oberste Heeresleitung (OHL) sent Rupprecht additional artillery ammunition and guns. Enemy preparations were most obvious from Souchez down to the River Scarpe. Further north, in the sector of General Friedrich Sixt von Armin's IV Corps around Hulluch and Loos, the opposing lines remained far apart, there was little British sapping going on, and an attack seemed less likely. On Friday 24 September, however, the bombardment reached a new pitch of intensity along the whole front from the La Bassée canal south to Arras.[6]

The next day it took about three hours for the first news of major British attacks between Hulluch and Loos to reach Sixth Army headquarters. Rupprecht had not expected an assault in this sector, where mining villages provided good defensive positions and No Man's Land was open, overlooked by German-held slag heaps from the mining industry, and up to 800 metres wide. Thick clouds of gas covered the attack, however, cutting visibility to 3 metres in places. The British quickly overran IV Corps' front lines, destroying whole companies of the defenders and capturing their guns. No-one knew what forces, if any, were left to man the second line and fill the gap. The situation seemed critical. Rupprecht put all his reserves at Sixt's disposal and appealed for more from OHL. Falkenhayn agreed to help at once. By lunchtime it was clear that the British had captured Loos and were threatening the German second line along the Lens-La Bassée road, with fighting underway on Hill 70.[7]

With the situation around Loos obscure but troubling, further worrying reports soon began to reach Rupprecht's headquarters. This time, it was the French on the move. After a morning of carefully observed artillery fire their Tenth Army attacked at half past one in the afternoon. Seventeen divisions went over the top from Angres to Ficheux. South and east of Arras, Fasbender's Bavarians cut them down in No Man's Land and stopped the attack dead. From Roclincourt up to Souchez, however, the situation seemed more threatening. Again, as in May, groups of French troops broke through and even reached the crest of Vimy Ridge in places. They were isolated and wiped out in the course of the afternoon and evening, however.

To the north of Vimy Ridge, the French overran the German trenches, swept through Souchez, and drove up on to the lower slopes of the Gießler Heights. Here the advance was brought to a halt by the second-line defences and a round of local counter-attacks.

The situation around Loos was still Rupprecht's biggest worry. Falkenhayn, however, had larger concerns yet. Because of the pressure in Champagne, he sent reserves, originally intended for Rupprecht, down there. Sixth Army would have to hold out until the Guard Corps could arrive in forty-eight hours' time.

The question for all three armies was where to commit their reserves the next day. In Artois, Foch ordered his right wing to hold fast and reinforce the relatively successful left. Rupprecht overruled a complicated idea of Lambsdorff's and ordered the Guards to push straight into the most threatened sector, around Souchez. Meanwhile, the British thoroughly misjudged the situation. Sir Douglas Haig, convinced that he could have broken through the German second line around Hill 70 on 25 September if only reserves had been to hand, sent forward two inexperienced New Army divisions to attack that second line between Hulluch and Hill 70 in the late morning of 26 September.

The German position the Kitchener volunteers faced consisted of no more than a single trench, but it was intact and lay on a reverse slope, making it hard to spot or shell. They would have to cross more than 1,500 metres of open ground to reach it. Worse, both Hulluch and Hill 70 remained in German hands, exposing the British divisions to crossfire. Haig gambled on clearing both flanks as the main attack went in. After a very thin preliminary bombardment lasting just an hour, the British 21st and 24th divisions began their attack. Both had been in France less than a month. This was their first action. With staffs green and improvised, the troops underwent some chaotic night marches and were sent into battle worn out and hungry. The effort of the 21st Division in the south was also disrupted by a pre-emptive German attack. When the two British divisions advanced at noon, they were met by fierce and persistent machine-gun and artillery fire. They suffered heavy casualties and soon lost both direction and cohesion. A few groups of brave men reached the German wire but found it was uncut and could not get through. Within minutes the entire attack collapsed and the British broke. One German witness described the British advancing naively, as if on exercise, in dense columns twenty to thirty deep with officers leading the way. Field guns and cavalry trotted behind each column. Close formations made easy targets. Soon some 10,000 British lay dead and wounded in front of the German 117th Infantry Division. The rest ran away. Although an English prisoner of war (POW) said 'it was a very nice sport', Rupprecht noted that 'we Germans have a somewhat more austere impression of war'. That evening both British divisions were taken out of the line, each having lost some 4,000 men. The original assault waves of 25 September were also suffering badly by now. One Scots brigade, for instance, had suffered 65 per cent casualties. Any hopes Haig had cherished of breaking through now evaporated.[8] Further south, the French consolidated their hold on Souchez but were unable to make much progress against Vimy Ridge itself. Rupprecht was by now convinced that Sixth Army could contain the enemy. A day of small-scale attacks by all three armies on 27 September seemed to bear this out, with the Germans getting the better of the fighting, especially against the British.[9]

Events on 28 September shocked the German command in Artois out of its complacency. Joffre had ordered Foch that Tenth Army should, without letting the British Expeditionary Force (BEF) know what it was up to, scale down its offensive. This was designed to free up troops to transfer to Champagne, where the offensive was going relatively well. Nevertheless, local operations had been continuing around Angres, Souchez, and on the Gießler Heights. Slightly further south French troops continued probing up the western slopes of Vimy Ridge, around where the Canadian Visitor Centre now stands. Suddenly, during the early morning of 28 September, German resistance opposite them crumbled. Two French divisions made good progress towards the highest point of the ridge, the summit of Hill 140. General d'Urbal sensed an opportunity and ordered fresh attacks by three whole corps from Angres down along Vimy Ridge. Results, however, turned out to be limited. The French captured a few trenches on the Gießler Heights. Again, a few groups reached the crest of Vimy Ridge around Hill 140 and La Folie, but were cut off and crushed. Reinforcements could not have reached them even had any been available. Foch was normally an incorrigible optimist but even he did not think exploitation was a realistic prospect. The troops were too exhausted, the ground too chewed up, and German reinforcements would soon seal off the front once more.[10]

This attack caused deep and genuine concern in the German lines, however. When General von Pritzelwitz, in command of the Vimy Ridge sector, lost his nerve and demanded to be allowed to retreat, he was dismissed and replaced. Rupprecht's chief of staff, Lambsdorff, also dithered. His advice was, first, to abandon the ridge and pull back into a third line down on the plain; second, to attack; and third, to let the Guard Corps commander do whatever he thought best. 'The chief of staff is completely incompetent', noted one of his staff officers. Even Rupprecht, receiving reports of French troops in Givenchy, La Folie, and on Hill 140 and fearing a breakthrough, thought that 'this evening was the most frightening of the campaign so far'. The only reserves he had immediately to hand that day were two companies in training. He later considered that the French had indeed broken through, if only they had realized it.[11]

Rupprecht's response was, first, to send the Guard Corps in around Givenchy and Hill 140. Second, he inserted I Bavarian Corps into the line on the southern half of Vimy Ridge. Another corps was held in reserve in Douai. So, while French Tenth Army had initially been less successful than the British in pulling in German reserves, now they were beginning to have a significant impact. This was especially important since it was not only in Artois that the French were able to penetrate the German second position on 28 September: their offensive in Champagne similarly made good progress on that day.

By now, however, the French units around Arras were exhausted. They could make no headway in heavy fighting all along Vimy Ridge over the next week or so. Ammunition was scarce. Muddy ground, churned up by constant artillery bombardment, made movement difficult. There were no fresh French reinforcements to match those Rupprecht was able to throw in. Although the French occasionally made small-scale break-ins over the days that followed, by 29 September it was clear to Rupprecht that he had contained their primary drive. The next day he noted that 'the main crisis seemed over'.[12]

Plans for a renewed Anglo-French offensive on 2 October had to be postponed several times, partly due to weather, partly to allow time to secure vital tactical features before the main assault. A German counter-attack with five regiments at Loos on 8 October suffered heavy casualties and gained little ground. It did, however, disrupt British preparations and force a further postponement. Eventually, the French assault began in the afternoon of 11 October but progress was limited and by 14 October the Germans had regained any ground lost. Even to Rupprecht, it was clear that Anglo-French coordination had broken down: 'it was striking that while the French were making such efforts, the British were so passive'.[13] Delays and disappointments on both sides had eroded mutual trust between French and British commanders. Also, however, the inexperienced men and staffs of the BEF were having trouble keeping up with the intense tempo of local fighting.[14]

There was a third factor at work, too. British senior commanders were distracted by a row which flared up between Haig and French over the opening of the Battle of Loos. The Prime Minister, Herbert Asquith, wanted a scapegoat for the military failures of 1915 and Haig was determined it should not be him. He wrote to Kitchener claiming that his men had broken through on the first day, but that he had been unable to exploit their success because the commander-in-chief was holding reserves too far back and released them too late. Intrigues about the top job occupied the higher reaches of the BEF until they were finally resolved in Haig's favour in December.

When at last three British divisions attacked on 13 October, the result was another bloody disaster. In the unusually blunt words of the British official historian, it 'brought nothing but useless slaughter of infantry'. Although attempts had been made to learn from recent mistakes at the tactical level, operational planning remained muddled and over-ambitious, intelligence poor, and execution slipshod. Nick Lloyd suggests that 'in many ways the attack...typified much that was wrong with the BEF in this period'. The failure of this attack effectively closed down large-scale operations for the British at Loos, with Joffre officially suspending the French offensive on 15 October.[15]

The French deployed half as many divisions during the third battle of Artois as they did in Champagne. Artois was not solely a diversion from the main effort, but it was firmly a sideshow in comparison. The BEF committed twelve divisions to a sideshow of the sideshow. Casualties were, as always, heavy: about 150,000 men between the three armies. The Entente lost two men for every German but again had little to show for the price paid. The French and British lines had pushed a couple of kilometres east but had not won any truly significant ground. The German lines had buckled, but not broken. Nor did operations in the north significantly aid success in Champagne. Not even the Entente could afford a strategy of attrition with this loss ratio. Both British and French high commands were duly disappointed and the Battle of Loos offered the final pretext required to remove Sir John French. The German official history described the third battle of Artois as a 'clear—albeit costly—victory'.[16]

After the failures of autumn 1915, the French became more open to radical changes in approach. Foch was more convinced than ever that German defences were now too strong to break through with one 'coup de main'. Instead, a methodical approach, characterized by careful preparation, planning for multiple operational phases and close support from heavy artillery, was required. His opinion now won converts up to and including Grand Quartier Général (GQG). It was enshrined in a new series of doctrinal instructions issued in January 1916: 'In the current situation, specifically that of attacks on fortified fronts which present successive lines of defence, a breakthrough of the enemy front will not in general be possible in one operation alone.' These laid down the new offensive doctrine. New defensive instructions, released in December 1915, paid the Germans the compliment of imitation, by ordering units to establish a defence in depth.[17]

The Germans apparently had less to change. Autumn 1915 demonstrated how well they had learned the lessons of trench warfare over the last year. Their defensive tactics, it seemed, had been triumphantly vindicated. Nonetheless, Sixth Army carried out a thorough analysis of the fighting. It called in after-action reports and distributed a follow-up questionnaire. The final product was a printed twenty-four-page booklet, including maps. This distinguished between the enemy's initial tactical success and his eventual operational failure. The weakness of the defensive positions around Souchez was blamed for what progress the French made there, while the initial British break-in was put down to weight of numbers and surprise. It confirmed, however, that the basic principles of defensive tactics, such as the use of reverse slopes, had worked well. At the operational level, although in places enemy artillery had inflicted heavy losses on over-strong front-line garrisons, overall the battle seemed to validate defence in depth. Strongpoints scattered between the first and second positions had helped to break up enemy attacks, although poor enemy communications and control had also helped. Immediate counter-attacks on disordered and disorientated attackers by German reserve units had proved highly effective. Germany, it seemed, with a little help from its enemies, had learnt how to win defensive battles in trench warfare. The closest the report came to recommending a major change was to suggest that trenches should be dug more than 2 metres wide, to prevent attackers from jumping over them.[18]

At Rupprecht's headquarters, however, there was not much back-slapping going on. It was clear that a way must be found to turn tactical victory of this kind, a negative success which prevented the Entente from achieving its aspirations, into a more positive step which would bring German victory closer. Wars are not won by sitting forever on the defensive. To launch a decisive offensive in the west, Rupprecht thought, required reinforcement by twelve to fifteen army corps which simply were not available. To avoid a very long war, he told Falkenhayn on 13 October, the aim should become the best peace possible, rather than outright victory.[19]

The other factor contributing to an uncomfortable atmosphere in Sixth Army headquarters was growing discord within the staff. The focus of irritation was the new chief of staff, Lambsdorff. Anyone trying to fill Krafft's place was always going to find his relationship with Rupprecht difficult to manage, especially given the circumstances of Krafft's removal. Over the summer, however, Lambsdorff had become increasingly alienated not only from his army commander but also from the rest of the staff. When he dithered under strain in September, then failed to brief Rupprecht that the crucial Gießler Heights had been lost, and finally tried to cover his mistake up with a lie, it was time for him to go. His replacement was the highly experienced Prussian General, Hermann von Kuhl. Kuhl had served as chief of staff to Kluck's First Army in the early months of the war, and later with Fabeck's Twelfth Army in the east. Major Xylander of Rupprecht's staff was, as usual, dismissive: 'that's great! Things go from bad to worse! "Papa Kuhl" has become Chief of Staff, that common, lying, little tactical dead loss of a man. Nothing ever gets better.' In fact, however, when Xylander saw Kuhl at work, even he was impressed. Rupprecht and Kuhl would go on to form a highly effective partnership which lasted for the rest of the war.[20]

9

Verdun and the Road
to the Somme

Throughout 1915, Falkenhayn's main focus had been on the east, where the fighting had carried the Central Powers deep into the Tsarist Empire. Russia had lost two and a half million men but still her armies had not collapsed. Displaying extraordinary resilience, they were still in the field and fighting on. The German and Austro-Hungarian troops, on the other hand, were exhausted and had done all they could for now. There was little hope of them achieving in 1916 what they had not managed in 1915. If the war were to be won, it would have to be won in the west. And wars are not won by defensives. Somewhere, Germany would have to attack. The place she chose was Verdun.[1]

The Battle of Verdun is often held up as one of the archetypal attritional battles of the First World War. The briefest of glances into the ossuary at Douaumont tells you why. Although Falkenhayn pretended that his intention had always been to 'bleed the French army white', that was not his original plan, as his biographer Holger Afflerbach has shown. Kuhl and others criticized Falkenhayn for not knowing what he wanted and, Micawber-like, hoping something would turn up. In fact, though, Falkenhayn's plans were if anything too complex, rejecting the neat but artificial dichotomy between attrition and manoeuvre warfare and instead trying to synthesize the two.

In its final form, his plan consisted of two, or possibly three, phases. First, he would threaten or seize something the French could not afford to lose. The target he chose was Verdun, partly because it had a reputation as a strong fortress and partly because it sat in a salient. His artillery could fire into it from two sides. This would help during the second phase, when he expected the French army to counter-attack to try to regain ground they had lost. The German heavy guns would chew up these French attacks until morale collapsed. Falkenhayn hoped a third phase would ensue with a British attack around Arras to relieve pressure on their ally. He expected to have little trouble defeating this, but if necessary he would then launch a final attack near Arras to complete the overthrow of British and French armies. Within a few months, therefore, if all went according to plan, at a minimum Germany could hope to have broken the back of the Entente in the west, enabling Falkenhayn to send troops to finish off Russia. The key to the plan lay in the estimate of enemy morale. If Falkenhayn was right that the French army was close to collapse, Verdun might yield rapid strategic success. If he was wrong, however, Germany would be locked in to a slow grind with little hope of winning. Unfortunately for Falkenhayn and many of his men, his assumptions proved flawed.[2]

Rupprecht's part in the planning of Verdun was limited. By now, he and Falkenhayn had been sniping at each other for a year. Their relationship had deteriorated further in the wake of the third battle of Artois, when Rupprecht accused Oberste Heeresleitung (OHL) of losing the Lorette Spur, by stripping his army of reserves against his advice, in front of the Kaiser. It is hardly surprising, therefore, that Rupprecht only heard of Falkenhayn's plans for an attack on the French late, at Christmas 1915, or that he disagreed with them. As he had since the spring, Rupprecht argued against dissipating strength in local offensives against the enemy's strongest points. Instead, he advocated concentrating all possible resources for a knock-out blow, perhaps between Arras and the Somme, in the summer. It was equally predictable that Falkenhayn would ignore Rupprecht. Within days, Sixth Army was ordered to transfer all its supply lorries to Crown Prince Wilhelm and to prepare diversionary attacks for the end of January.[3]

Further meetings and memoranda in early 1916 served only to emphasize the gap in thinking between Rupprecht and Falkenhayn. The latter argued not only that large-scale reserves did not exist, but also that the previous year's fighting had demonstrated that it was impossible to maintain control of large forces on the modern battlefield. On 12 February, Kuhl came away from a meeting with Falkenhayn with the impression

> that Falkenhayn himself was not clear what he actually wanted and was waiting for something fortunate to turn up to produce a good outcome. He wanted a decision in the spring, but considered a breakthrough impossible and hoped that with the operation at Verdun he could shift over from position to mobile warfare. How else, I wonder, can that take place but with a breakthrough? Just because the French and English leadership of mass armies failed, must ours, too?

Falkenhayn was talking of fighting a decisive battle at Verdun, but for fear of a British counter-attack, which neither Rupprecht nor Kuhl thought likely, was not prepared to concentrate his forces to fight it. 'He who bets nothing, wins nothing', sniffed Rupprecht.[4]

On 26 February, Kuhl submitted a memorandum outlining his ambitious scheme for a decisive breakthrough. He and his staff had been working on this for weeks. It reiterated that ambitious objectives required sizeable commitment and underlined their opposition to smaller-scale operations. The memo remains interesting both as a summary of German thinking about the attack in early 1916 and because it displays considerable foresight about events later that year. Kuhl argued that the British at Loos and the French in Champagne had done their best. They had prepared carefully and brought maximum strength to bear. Both had come close to a breakthrough but ultimately failed. The German second-line defences had held them up. Entente attempts to break through that second line, whether improvised or set-piece with full artillery support, had failed because the defenders had been reinforced and surprise had been lost. Kuhl disagreed with the view that breakthroughs were therefore impossible and attackers should adopt a more methodical approach. He pointed out that proceeding step by step would only give the defender time to strengthen his defences and build whole new lines further back if necessary. Consequently, the Entente was right to seek a breakthrough. This meant punching through the enemy first and second lines and overrunning his gun positions, all in one bound, which would require several things. First, surprise was essential. Second, the attacker would need to work on a wide frontage: at least 20 kilometres. Third, he would require between twenty and twenty-four divisions and 320 heavy batteries plus field artillery. This represented roughly three times as many heavy guns as the Entente had just used in Artois and nearly a quarter of all the heavy artillery the German army possessed in 1916. Indeed, even the densest concentration achieved on 21 March 1918 was less intense. Kuhl was setting the bar too high and neither this memo nor its reasoning had much impact at OHL.[5]

On 23 January, Rupprecht's Bavarian troops along Vimy Ridge launched a series of local attacks, setting off mines, seizing the craters, and driving the French well back from the crest. Successful as they were, these actions indicate how dysfunctional German command had become. No-one had informed Rupprecht that the Verdun operation had been postponed so these diversions were wasted. Rupprecht was 'shocked at this irresponsible carelessness!' No less sloppy was the fact that, far from being a closely guarded secret, an attack on Verdun was the talk of Berlin. Right away, British intelligence had spotted that the German attacks north of Arras were 'diversions'. By the time the German attack at Verdun finally went in on 21 February, the French had done their best to reinforce the salient.[6]

Within a week at Verdun, it was clear to Rupprecht that forward progress was slowing. Although Falkenhayn remained convinced that a British attack was imminent, analysis of the British Expeditionary Force's (BEF's) reserve situation convinced Rupprecht otherwise. Intelligence suggested that Haig was not employing the divisions now arriving from Britain to build up reserves for an attack, but to take over more of the front line from the French. No British attack was likely before April or May, at the earliest.[7] By the end of March, with Verdun deadlocked and still no Entente relief offensive in prospect, Kuhl was ready to write off the possibility of a British attack: 'in that sense the plan certainly didn't work. Now the whole thing has become a test of strength at Verdun, a question of prestige.' Falkenhayn did not finally give up on the idea of launching his own attack at Arras until the end of April, when it became clear at last that the so-called 'mill on the Meuse' was grinding through reserves so fast that it would be impossible to spare any for Sixth Army. Losses were so heavy that some divisions were being kept in the fighting line even after they had lost half their men. Hope began to drain away. 'What distresses me most', noted Rupprecht, 'is that General von Falkenhayn apparently no longer thinks a decisive victory can possibly be won. In that event, how must the war end for us?'[8]

Prospects had not improved by early summer. 'Verdun is a real witches' cauldron which swallows our best troops one after the other', Rupprecht complained. Attrition at Verdun began to bite directly into Sixth Army, with Rupprecht forced to transfer out seven of his fresh divisions and receiving only five worn-out ones in return.[9] Even during quiet periods, the steady drip of casualties continued for Sixth Army. Artillery fire, sniping, patrolling, raiding, and accidents drained strength all the time. For instance, Sixth Army, now rather fewer than 200,000 men strong, lost 1,370 killed, wounded, and missing in the ten days between 11 and 21 January 1916. When combat grew more intense, inevitably wastage increased. The next ten-day period, which included the 'diversionary' attacks north of Arras, saw 4,700 lost. Small-scale operations to secure local tactical advantages were frequent. Thus, in the evening of 20 February Sixth Army recaptured the Gießler Heights. Accidents could be costly, however. On 29 April, for example, German gas drifted back into the assembly trenches of a Bavarian unit waiting to go over the top. The assault troops were wearing gas masks, but many were overcome nonetheless. The final death toll reached 307.[10]

Accidents or worse killed civilians, too. In the early morning of 11 January a dump of engineers' stores exploded in Lille, where Rupprecht's headquarters were based. Thirty German soldiers and seventy French civilians were killed. That was an accident, but the local population also fell victim to the stupidity or negligence of the occupiers. Also in Lille, an outbreak of typhoid was eventually traced to the latrines of a German artillery battery which had been built over the city's main water reservoir. Other diseases were also on the rise: no fewer than 400 Frenchwomen were detained in Douai on 8 March with venereal disease. Finally, in June 1916 a French teacher in Douai became the victim of a sex murder committed by a German soldier. This was the first case of its kind that Rupprecht had heard of, but no doubt not the last.[11]

The war remained the priority for both sides and the imperative was to absorb the lessons of Verdun. To the French, the fighting there seemed to reinforce the lessons of 1915 and validate the principles enshrined in their January 1916 doctrine, rather than throw up new ones. This applied equally to the attack and the defence. In particular, it showed that thorough preparation was more important than surprise. Otherwise, the only changes suggested were minor tactical ones. For Joffre, indeed, the main lesson was in fact an ancient one:

> The moral factor is more preponderant than ever. As the mechanical means of destruction grow in power, so the capacity for resistance grows in the soul of the warrior.... Troops who are well led, supported, informed, looked after, fed are capable of unlimited resistance.... The battle of Verdun has, in the view of the high command, taught us so far nothing we did not already know and teach; she must fix more deeply in the heart of everyone this truth: not a single inch of ground must be given up voluntarily under any circumstances. Troops, even when surrounded, must hold out to the last man, without retreating. The sacrifice of each is the very condition of victory.

Even on the industrial battlefield, Joffre was arguing, it was still human will which counted most.[12]

Joffre may have felt this a point worth making because throughout 1915 and 1916 the 'mechanical means of destruction' were growing in power. The war was becoming noticeably more scientific. For example, it was possible to locate enemy guns by taking bearings on the reports made as they fired and triangulating back. The Germans had experimented with this sound-ranging technique at La Bassée in late 1914. French scientists alerted the British to the method's potential the following March. The British were slower to pursue it than the French, but by the end of 1915 all three armies had established sections of both sound-rangers and flash-spotters. It would take time to prove their effectiveness, but the British alone had some 200 top-flight scientists working on the project. Likewise, now that artillery fire was taking place at longer range and without line of sight from gun to target, accuracy became both more important and harder to achieve. One of the improvements artillerymen tried was to take account of atmospheric conditions when calculating the trajectories of their shells. A more obvious example was the move over from cloth or leather caps to steel helmets. In autumn 1915, the iconic Adrian helmet replaced the képi in the French front line and by the middle of 1916 steel helmets were widespread on both sides of the wire. Most famously of all, the tank was coming. The British had developed a working prototype by Christmas 1915 and Joffre signed off on the first French designs around the same time. More broadly, generals on both sides were applying science to the problem of breaking in to the enemy front. Only after a careful calculation of what the available artillery could achieve would infantry objectives be set. Thus, for instance, Foch's instructions for the Battle of the Somme included the calculation that it would take 600 shells to clear 500 square metres of barbed wire. Similarly, Rupprecht noted that to prepare an attack on a front of 100 metres required 800 rounds from a field, or 400 from a heavy, artillery battery. A creeping barrage to cover an assault needed one field battery every 100 metres, or one heavy battery every 150. Once you knew how many guns and shells you had, you could work out how ambitious an attack you could plan. Wishful thinking could be challenged and ends could now be calibrated to fit the available means.[13]

One of the lessons Falkenhayn drew from the early fighting at Verdun and circulated to the army was that the front line must be thickly garrisoned and firmly held. Rupprecht disagreed. He thought May 1915 had shown that this approach left too many men exposed both to enemy artillery fire and to being overrun by the first assault. It was cheaper to hold the front line sparsely and counter-attack to win it back if necessary. Rupprecht decided to remind his corps commanders of this verbally, deliberately undercutting Falkenhayn's authority. It is rare to find a record of informal communication trumping formal doctrine in this way. This reminds us that, just because the written record survives when quick chats, raised eyebrows, and meaningful glances have been forgotten, not everyone always followed official doctrine. One wonders, in fact, how carefully the doctrinal literature was sometimes even read. Officers had many other calls on their time, after all, and often more pressing uses for paper.[14]

By the summer of 1916, all three armies were beginning to master at least some of the problems thrown up by the new warfare. They had surmounted the health and sanitary challenges of the first winter. Production was ramping up to offset shortages of equipment and weapons and they had learnt the logistics of sustaining millions of men in the field. They had dusted off old technologies, such as the mortar, and refined them for the new century, and were rapidly integrating brand new technologies, such as the aeroplane.

On the battlefield itself, the tactical and operational approach of the German army to defence had been thoroughly tested. Soldiers and commanders were confident in their methods and leaders. They had constructed defences in depth in case they needed them. The basic principle, however, at least officially, remained that every foot of ground would be fiercely contested. If the original garrison was forced to give way and the enemy broke in, reserves were to counter-attack and recapture the lost positions. French attack tactics had discarded surprise in favour of an artillery-heavy approach involving careful and lengthy preparation, with limited objectives set within range of the guns. They had yet to unlock the operational secret of maintaining offensive momentum, however. Debate continued over the best use of reserves and, although advocates of attrition such as Foch were in the ascendant for the moment, plenty of senior officers were unconvinced and still favoured going for a breakthrough. The British, as we saw in Chapter 6, remained behind the French and Germans both tactically and operationally.

The way of war of all three armies was on the brink of the severest test any of them had yet faced. Over the late spring and early summer of 1916, the first indications began to appear that the Entente was gearing up for an offensive in Picardy. Spies in London and The Hague reported that an attack was being prepared. Tactical intelligence was also generating worrying signs. General Fritz von Below's Second Army on the Somme first expressed concerns in mid-May. By early June Kuhl was persuaded. As tented camps sprang up around Albert and rail traffic increased, it became clearer that the British and French were making preparations. In mid-June the French 39th Division, part of the crack XX 'Iron' Corps, was identified in the line just north of the River Somme. When Joffre himself visited XX

Corps a few days later, he unwittingly but effectively confirmed that an offensive was imminent.[15]

Falkenhayn took time to convince. To begin with, he was distracted by the early success of the Brusilov offensive in Russia, which began on 4 June. He had to transfer troops from the west to counter it. When the situation in the east began to stabilize, for a while Falkenhayn remained concerned that Alsace-Lorraine was the likely target of any French offensive. On 20 June, however, he sent three divisions of reserves to reinforce General von Below if needed. The beginning of the Entente artillery bombardment on 24 June made it immediately clear that this was the real thing and that Second Army was the primary target. Falkenhayn sent further heavy guns and Kuhl concentrated Sixth Army's artillery reserves so that they were ready to move at short notice. He offered them to Second Army, but Tappen, still running the operations department at OHL, said no. Tappen and Falkenhayn remained concerned that the Somme operations were only a diversion, intended to distract from a full-scale attack at Arras. Not until 5 July did they acknowledge the severity of the threat facing Below and accord Second Army top priority. By then the British army had suffered 'the catastrophe of 1 July'.[16]

10

Early Days on the Somme

The first of July 1916 is, in the words of Gary Sheffield, 'the most notorious day in British military history'. Of the fourteen British divisions
which attacked that morning, nine either never made any progress or
lost any ground they had won within hours. A diversionary attack at
Gommecourt achieved nothing. Along much of the front when night fell,
the only British troops forward of the start line were the wounded or the
dead. Villages such as Thiepval, Beaumont Hamel, and Serre wrote their
fatal names into the history of the British army as the calvaries of the British
Expeditionary Force (BEF). By the end of that day at least 19,240 officers
and men lay dead. In all, 57,740 soldiers of Sir Henry Rawlinson's Fourth
Army had become casualties. Roughly every other man who went over the
top on 1 July was hit. Only on the British right was lasting progress made.
Mametz fell on 1 July, Fricourt the next day. Lieutenant-General Walter
Congreve's XIII Corps, next to the French, was the only British formation
to take all its objectives on the first day.[1]

It would be a mistake, though, to see the first day of the Somme through
British eyes alone. Three French corps (six divisions) extended the offensive
south of the river. They performed uniformly well and took many of their
objectives. They cleared the German first position and in places broke into
the second line. Fayolle, now promoted to command the French Sixth
Army, had the problem his British counterpart would have loved to face:
how to exploit success. Immediately south of the river, tough troops from
French North and West Africa, whom we last met rushing Vimy Ridge,
hesitated just long enough for the Germans to pull together local reserves
and stop up the gaps in their line. Further north, General Maurice Balfourier
was keen to push his XX Corps on but could not get the support he wanted
from the British. Congreve himself was keen, but Rawlinson had never
shared Haig's optimism and ambition and he was surprised by success where

none had been planned for. He would not permit the release of XIII Corps' reserves, which in any case were not ready to be committed so soon. This was an early but ominous portent that maintaining the coordination of the British and French armies on the Somme would not always run smoothly.[2]

One man's disaster is not necessarily his enemy's triumph. If Haig and Rawlinson did not realize quite how much they had lost, neither did German commanders yet feel that they had gained a lot. While they gathered that they had beaten off nine British divisions, the fact remained that on much of the Anglo-French front the defence had been overwhelmed.[3]

In the popular imagination, the first day of the Somme has become, in the words of the best recent historian of the battle, 'a metaphor for futility and slaughter; a national trope and tragedy that defies understanding'. In fact, however, there is nothing incomprehensible about the British tragedy that day. Multiple convincing explanations have been put forward. Almost at once, wounded British prisoners told their German interrogators that the defeat was the result of: 'the inexperience and uselessness of the young officers'; a failure to reinforce success; and inadequate artillery preparation which left German wire intact and machine-guns ready to cut down the attackers. To what extent the interrogators heard or reported what they wanted to hear, of course, is impossible now to reconstruct. The British official historian Sir James Edmonds offered a deeper analysis in the 1930s. For him, the problems began at the top, with the choice to attack where German defences were strong, rather than weak. This decision was forced on the British by the demands of coalition politics, as was the selection of day and even time for the assault. Disagreements within the chain of command over the objectives of the offensive, and so the correct operational method to pursue, introduced confusion. The French wanted to wear down the German army and relieve Verdun, proposing a series of limited-objective attacks to achieve this. Rawlinson also favoured a step-by-step approach, but Haig pushed for a deeper drive to try for a breakthrough. At the tactical level, the success of XIII Corps, where surprise was greatest and the artillery preparation most effective, partly thanks to French help, showed that progress was indeed possible. Problems with manufacturing quality, however, continued to reduce the effectiveness of British guns and shells. Lastly, Edmonds regarded British tactics as clumsy, inadequate, and an important cause of the high casualty rate. He saw this as the inevitable result of using ill-trained and inexperienced troops prematurely. Modern historians have tended roughly to work within the analytic template established by Edmonds.

Although they do not always agree on the exact weight to be attached to each factor, they tend to believe that fundamental conceptual differences, both between Haig and Rawlinson and between the British and French, underlay much of what went wrong. A litany of tactical and operational problems ensued, most of them at some point to do with the dominant weapon of the First World War: artillery.[4]

The German view at the time was much more straightforward: ground had been lost where Anglo-French artillery, guided by superior air power, had shattered the defenders' trenches and suppressed the German guns. Counter-battery fire became impossible and both protective barrages and harassing fire were weakened. Although Rupprecht criticized Falkenhayn for not sending enough reinforcements, the official historians, who were not normally sympathetic to Falkenhayn, judged that not even fresh troops would have saved the ground lost on 1 July.[5]

There was no time yet for proper post-mortems since Second Army remained under intense pressure. On 2 July German troops abandoned the second line and the Flaucourt Plateau, falling back in some confusion to a third position along the line of the river. The French had advanced nearly 8 kilometres and could see the rooftops of Péronne. By 5 July, however, the French advance on the left bank of the Somme had stalled. Further progress in the south would clearly require another major effort. Meanwhile the sector between the Albert–Bapaume road and the Somme saw a series of local British and French attacks to clean up the line and gain jumping-off positions for the next assault. It took the British six days and seven attacks to clear Trônes Wood. Contalmaison held out for four days, Mametz Wood for six. The three British divisions involved here lost over 12,000 men. British intelligence had under-estimated the speed of the German reaction and hence exaggerated the chances that 'just one more push' would bring success. These fights were poorly executed, small-scale, and uncoordinated, but eventually cleared the way for a British assault on the German second position along the Bazentin Ridge on 14 July. After an artillery bombardment of unprecedented concentration and a night approach march, Rawlinson achieved surprise and captured the German second position. As ever, however, exploitation remained problematic.[6] Between 2 and 13 July the British launched forty-six poorly planned and supported attacks. These cost 25,000 British casualties. Christopher Duffy has described this period as a 'prolonged chapter of wasted opportunities'. It did have the effect, however, together with the Bastille Day attack on Bazentin Ridge, of hammering home to the Germans that they had lost both their balance and the initiative.[7]

German unease manifested itself in four main ways. First, Falkenhayn and Below forbade any further voluntary withdrawals. Their men must hold their ground and fight to win back what they had lost. Second, reserves were pulled in with increasing urgency from other sectors of the Western Front. For instance, Oberste Heeresleitung (OHL) overruled Rupprecht's complaints that he could spare no troops and ordered him to transfer two divisions to the Somme. Third, reinforcements were thrown in as they arrived to prop up Second Army's line. This piecemeal approach created difficulties of command and control and inevitably undermined cohesion. As Rupprecht noted: 'When reinforcements eventually came up, it was too late. They arrived in dribs and drabs and had to be committed to action at once to block the gaps. Consequently, units are now so mixed together that no-one knows what's going on.' The headquarters of XVII Corps at one stage had units from no fewer than eleven different divisions under command. In all, slightly over forty-three divisions were sent to the Somme battlefront, between the end of June and the end of August 1916, with twenty-two being rotated out: a net reinforcement of twenty-one. Of those forty-three fresh divisions, twenty-one came from Rupprecht's Sixth Army, which received just fourteen worn-out formations in return. In just three months, therefore, the Somme consumed three times as many of Sixth Army's reserves as Verdun had in half a year: a useful index of stress.[8]

The fourth sign of nerves was turbulence in the command chain. Corps commanders and staff officers up to and including the Second Army chief of staff were purged. Second Army was split in two, with Below effectively demoted and left in charge only of the portion north of the Somme, now renamed First Army. The defensive expert Fritz von Loßberg was sent to keep an eye on him as chief of staff. South of the river, General Max von Gallwitz took over a new Second Army and was also given day-to-day command of the whole battle with Below a subordinate. Again the German army was improvising command arrangements, even after this had worked so poorly in 1914 and 1915.[9]

Rupprecht felt Falkenhayn was scapegoating Below to cover up his own failure to heed warnings of an attack. If anyone should be relieved or demoted, he thought, it was Falkenhayn himself. The cabal which had intrigued against Falkenhayn in January 1915 now saw another opportunity.

The Chief of the General Staff was vulnerable on many levels. He had failed to predict the attack on Second Army. More seriously, 1 July destroyed the last shreds of credibility of his entire strategy. The unexpected power of the Brusilov and Somme offensives had shown that he had under-estimated both the Russian and French threats. It also pointed up the bankruptcy of Verdun. Now that the British had failed to fall in with Falkenhayn's plans and rush an offensive at Arras, Verdun made sense only if it tied down and ate up the French army. Even this it was evidently unable to do. For the first time in the war, Germany felt menaced by enemies who seemed finally able to string together a series of coordinated offensives from the Somme to the steppes. The intrigue was not all about policy, of course. Power and personal concerns also played a part in uniting the cabal: Hindenburg and Ludendorff were agitating for greater independence of command in the east; Bethmann Hollweg was worried by repeated rumours that Falkenhayn had ambitions to take his job as Chancellor; and Rupprecht, quite simply, as Kuhl noted, 'hates Falkenhayn, anyway'.[10]

During the first few days of July Rupprecht heard from Bavarian diplomats in Berlin and at Imperial Headquarters that dissatisfaction with Falkenhayn was growing within the army, at court, and across the government more generally. On 5 July he wrote to the Bavarian representative in Berlin, Hugo von Lerchenfeld, arguing that Germany would lose the war unless Falkenhayn went. Lerchenfeld, as he was meant to, showed the letter to the Chancellor. Bethmann Hollweg's coded telegram in reply was supportive but cautious. Bethmann Hollweg said that, as a civilian, he could not be seen to interfere in military matters and that the message would be better coming from a soldier. Rupprecht was not discouraged. Instead he busied himself recruiting further members to the anti-Falkenhayn cabal. The Governor-General of occupied Belgium, General Moritz von Bissing, was a willing co-conspirator who also knew the Kaiser well. He proved a useful source of advice, as well as opening another channel of communication to the Chancellor. On 22 July, for instance, Bissing showed Rupprecht a letter from Bethmann Hollweg which made clear that the Chancellor was scared of moving directly against Falkenhayn himself. Bissing suggested Rupprecht approach the Kaiser directly. 'But how?' asked Rupprecht. Other help was offered from further afield. A Dr Gildemeister wrote from Bremen, offering to pay off Falkenhayn's allegedly huge gambling debts and suggesting Ludendorff as a replacement.[11]

Meanwhile, on 7 July Hindenburg demanded overall command of the whole Eastern Front. He and Ludendorff repeatedly pressed for more resources as a way of keeping up the pressure on Falkenhayn. Bethmann Hollweg overcame his former scruples about intervening in military affairs and sent a memorandum listing Falkenhayn's shortcomings to the head of the Kaiser's Civil Cabinet, Rudolf von Valentini. Gradually Falkenhayn's support began to ebb away. Influential courtiers such as Generals Hans von Plessen and Moriz von Lyncker, commandant of the Kaiser's headquarters and head of his Military Cabinet respectively, began to distance themselves. Even the Kaiser's backing was becoming more conditional and in late July, he reorganized command in the east to give Hindenburg and Ludendorff greater independence.

Falkenhayn's response was to work yet harder. He intervened in ever smaller details and tried to micro-manage the disposition of every battalion on both fronts. The result, predictably, was over-work, insomnia, and illness. By August, he was physically worn out and looked like an old man. The intrigue against him did not let up. On 9 August the Kaiserin wrote to Plessen asking him to set up a meeting for the Kaiser with Rupprecht and Duke Albrecht behind Falkenhayn's back. Four days later Falkenhayn told the War Minster, Wild von Hohenborn, that he would not be able to continue as Chief of the General Staff unless he possessed the full confidence of the Kaiser. The further Hindenburg's stock with Wilhelm II rose, the more insecure Falkenhayn felt. If this was an attempt to extract some sign of favour from the Kaiser, in the short term it worked. On both 13 and 24 August, the Kaiser assured him: 'we will stick together to the end of the war'.[12]

On 16 August Bethmann Hollweg sent an urgent telegram to the Kaiser, backing a request of Hindenburg's for reinforcements and sharply criticizing the way Falkenhayn was still concentrating on the Western Front. It was becoming ever clearer, Bethmann Hollweg argued, that the best hope was for a separate peace with Russia. The Kaiser, never the most tactful of men, promptly passed the telegram to Falkenhayn. The Chancellor kept up the pressure. Reinforced by a detailed brief from Lieutenant-Colonel Max Bauer on Falkenhayn's mistakes, he renewed his attack via the War Minister on 23 August. The response of both Lyncker and Wild showed how keen both were to follow, rather than lead, the Kaiser's opinion. Falkenhayn, they stated, was irreplaceable and enjoyed the full confidence of the army.[13]

Meanwhile, by coincidence or design, Rupprecht was also attacking Falkenhayn. Perhaps emboldened by his recent promotion to Field Marshal in both the Bavarian and German armies, on 21 August he sent off a formal letter to Lyncker for him to pass on to the Kaiser. He stated that Falkenhayn had lost the trust of the army and must go. He also requested a month's leave on medical grounds. His doctor was concerned about his heart and stomach, and Rupprecht was having trouble sleeping. So far in two years of war he had taken no leave whatsoever. The reply came in two parts. First, he was told that a reorganization of commands might be imminent and he might be needed. Rupprecht withdrew his leave request at once. Second, Lyncker wrote back, non-committally, that no decision had been made but that it was important to bear in mind Falkenhayn's good service in 1914.

Further developments on both scores followed rapidly. Late in the evening of 22 August a telegram arrived from OHL ordering Rupprecht to hand over command of Sixth Army to Colonel-General von Falkenhausen. He was being promoted to take over a group of four armies: Sixth in Artois; First and Second on the Somme; and Seventh from Noyon down nearly to Reims. Rupprecht was to be no longer a mere spectator of the struggle on the Somme, but in charge of the defence. 'Taking over command of this army group brings me the gravest concerns', he noted, 'since with it comes responsibility for the fighting on the Somme front: an extremely thankless task.'[14]

On 27 August neutral Romania, against Falkenhayn's predictions, finally joined the *danse macabre* by declaring war on Austria-Hungary. The news 'hit German headquarters like a bomb'. Here was something else Falkenhayn had got wrong. Did this mean defeat for the Central Powers and the end of the war? The Kaiser thought so, at first. Some of his advisers were less pessimistic. With the court divided, Admiral von Müller, head of the Imperial Naval Cabinet, suggested calling for Hindenburg and asking his opinion. If Hindenburg came, Falkenhayn would have to go. Everyone knew that. Valentini agreed with Müller. Eventually, even Lyncker and Plessen silently sided with the cabal.

If Falkenhayn ever had a chance to save his job by projecting optimism and showing his grip of the new Romanian development at his regular midday briefing to the Kaiser on 28 August, he was too tired and sick to take it. Indeed, his lacklustre performance increased Wilhelm's dissatisfaction with him. Plessen and Lyncker saw their chance. They suggested changing Falkenhayn for Hindenburg and Ludendorff. According to their accounts, the Kaiser took some persuading. Lyncker probably brought up Rupprecht's letter to prove that the army no longer trusted Falkenhayn. Finally they managed to win Wilhelm around. By lunchtime, the affair was settled: Hindenburg and Ludendorff were summoned to imperial headquarters. As anticipated, Falkenhayn submitted his resignation when he heard the news. Within twenty-four hours, Falkenhayn had handed over to Hindenburg and left.[15]

When Rupprecht heard the news, he was 'radiant'.[16] He wrote to his father that 'the change from Falkenhayn to Hindenburg is to be very much welcomed and it is only to be regretted that it did not happen before, since Falkenhayn messed everything up'.[17] The task he now faced was a big one, but at least he could have some confidence in his immediate superiors at last.

11

Rupprecht the General

Before we examine Rupprecht's part in the second half of the Battle of the Somme, it is worth pausing to address two important aspects of his military career. First, this chapter will explore his experience of daily life in wartime. Then, it will examine how he fitted into the command system of the German army. How did he relate to his chiefs of staff, his superiors, and his subordinates? It will thus begin to address the two stereotypes about the German army which were noted in the Introduction: that the General Staff ran matters and commanding generals were little more than decorative figureheads; and that Auftragstaktik, or 'mission command', was the defining principle of the whole system, lent the army a unique flexibility, and contributed to excellent battlefield performance.[1]

On an average day, Rupprecht rose and was dressing by seven o'clock in the morning. A naturally fastidious man, he knew the importance of dressing the part and setting a good example, so he always made sure he was immaculately turned out. Rather taller than average for the time at five foot ten inches, he was a naturally active man who ate simply and did physical exercises daily to keep his figure trim. His bearing was erect and martial. After breakfast, the first wave of reports and messages would arrive between eight and nine o'clock. If nothing urgent cropped up, he would then head out on horseback with one of his adjutants for his daily ride.

Unless a major battle was underway, the first important event of the day was the noon briefing. By that time Rupprecht's staff would have collated situation reports from the front and any incoming messages from Oberste Heeresleitung (OHL). The chief of staff and department heads would each make their report. Then action was discussed and any decisions necessary were made. Lunch followed at one o'clock. Rupprecht might spend the afternoon on paperwork, or drive to visit some of his units. There he met commanders, inspected troops, and awarded medals. It was widely accepted that it was important for generals to see and be seen by their men. Sir Douglas Haig, likewise, spent most afternoons on such visits. Rupprecht was not so assiduous as Haig, however. He was no natural orator and the common touch did not come easily to him. Consequently, early on Krafft had to push him to get out and about. Over time, however, Rupprecht grew accustomed to this aspect of his job. In November 1915, for instance, he spent several days reviewing various regiments, making a 'very good, brief address' to the assembled troops, and then making a point of speaking to many of the officers and men individually or in small groups. These visits also enabled him to cast an eye over his soldiers and their leaders.[2]

By seven o'clock, Rupprecht would be back at headquarters for the evening briefing, with dinner served at eight. He did not generally eat in the officers' mess but privately, with selected members of his staff and any guests. Food was generally plain, talk of the war discouraged, and after eating the time was spent chatting or playing cards. Occasionally they played Boccia, a form of indoor bowls. Entertaining distinguished visitors was an important part of Rupprecht's role. The famous Swedish explorer Sven Hedin has left a vivid, if rather gushing, portrait of Rupprecht and his hospitality in November 1914:

> He is one of those rare men whom all love and admire....In the German army he is looked upon as a very eminent general—a born strategist and a thoroughly schooled soldier. As regards appearance, manner and speech, he is fascinating and congenial in the highest degree, neither regal nor humble, but without artifice and modest like an ordinary mortal. When one *knows* that he has recently experienced the greatest private sorrow which could befall him, one fancies, perhaps, that one detects a trace thereof in his features—an air of sadness—but otherwise he does not betray, by a look or a sigh, how deeply he grieves over the death of the little prince of thirteen, the darling of all Bavaria. When the country and the empire are in danger, all private sorrows must be put aside! The Crown Prince has no time to grieve or to think of the void and bereavement which he will feel on his victorious return to Munich. He lives for and with his army, and is like a father to each and all of his soldiers. He devotes all his power of mind, all his physical strength, all his time, to the one great object which dominates all else in the minds of the whole German army.
>
> Crown Prince Rupprecht walks in with brisk and easy stride, stretches out his hands towards us and gives us a truly cordial welcome.

The twenty guests that night included Hedin, a duke of Mecklenburg who was also an explorer, Prince Löwenstein, and the Kaiser. They began eating at eight and left the table once the Kaiser had finished his cigar at half past ten. In May 1918 Rupprecht hosted four such banquets within a little over a week. Guests might include other royals, senior generals, politicians, bankers, and industrialists from Germany, her allies, or indeed neutral states. To entertain VIPs in the appropriate manner was an important part of his job.[3]

Circumstances could alter this routine, of course. Rupprecht might have to travel to OHL for meetings, or host conferences at his headquarters. Major battles obviously could become all-consuming as telephones jangled, reports arrived, and situation maps were updated. On 25 August 1914, Rupprecht did not leave the operations room for a minute all day. As both he and his staff grew more experienced, however, he learnt to stand back a bit. After all, there were limits to how much real-time control was possible with the communications available. After the war, Kuhl described Rupprecht's way of working. He had:

> a strikingly good grasp and deep understanding of operational situations. He was extremely hard-working, and had all the precise battle maps in his office and kept them up to date, he worked through all messages, letters, orders and reports in detail and was always perfectly informed. Consequently it was easy to brief him and to propose a decision. He would quickly grasp the situation and had himself already considered the conclusion. He was never nervy; even in the most difficult combat situations he allowed us in the staff the time to collate and inspect the messages and never pressed us or disrupted the process by interfering. He did not chase around after every message but waited until the situation had become clear enough that one could get a sufficient overview and a definite course of action could be decided on. He always made a bold decision. He was highly respected by his entire staff. Relationships within the staff and between him and his staff were the best imaginable.

It is impossible to be sure that Kuhl consistently felt so bullish about Rupprecht during the war itself, but nor is it clear what he had to gain from over-praising him in the 1920s.[4]

The size of Rupprecht's staff grew rapidly as the war went on. His immediate command group in August 1914 comprised fifteen officers. By September 1916 it was twenty-three strong and in late 1918 it had grown to forty-five officers within a broader headquarters over 1,000 strong. In 1914 it had been possible to squeeze headquarters into a school. By April 1917 it had expanded so much that half the old town of Mons was closed off to accommodate it, with departments filling offices throughout the southern and eastern parts of the town. The operations centre occupied 4, Avenue de Frère Orban. Officers were billeted around the Grand-Place while Rupprecht himself slept at the Chateau Hardenpont, 2 kilometres away on the outskirts of the town.[5]

Life for the members of Rupprecht's headquarters revolved around long hours of paperwork and meals in the mess. Officers paid 1.20 marks per day for breakfast, lunch, and dinner. These were served from seven a.m., one p.m., and eight p.m. respectively. Until August 1915 wine, schnapps, and cigars were free, but later they had to pay for their own. Hard as the work could be, there was always time to celebrate special occasions. Sometimes this might take place formally. In 1916, for instance, Rupprecht hosted a party for his officers on Christmas Eve before appearing as guest of honour in the Senior Officers' Mess on Christmas Day itself. The Junior Officers' Mess took their turn to lead the celebrations on New Year's Eve. At times the parties became more boisterous. On 26 January 1915 a 'lavish dinner' thrown by the Bavarian officers of Sixth Army headquarters for their Prussian colleagues to celebrate the Kaiser's birthday went on until half past one in the morning, despite a spirited argument over how to deal with Austria and the partition of Poland. Staff officers were afforded other comforts denied to their front-line compatriots. While Xylander was convalescing from an operation on his leg, his wife came to stay for several weeks to nurse him.[6] Some found other ways to enjoy female company. One evening in Douai the Turkish liaison officer attached to Rupprecht's headquarters, Zekki Pasha, entertained a young Frenchwoman for an hour or two. Losing track of time, she left after curfew. On her way home, three times she was stopped by patrols. Each time they refused to allow her to proceed and escorted her back to his quarters. Eventually, she decided that she might as well accept her manifest destiny and spend the night at his billet. Rupprecht had slightly more discreet arrangements. These included visiting a young Belgian who had previously been under the protection of a wealthy Douai businessman. Creeping out of his house at night to visit her was hardly dignified, however, and eventually the story reached the French newspapers.[7]

Rupprecht also kept up some of his other old hobbies, such as his interest in art and architecture. He carved out time where he could to visit collections and buildings of interest. One day in October 1916, for instance, on his way back from a visit to Seventh Army, he stopped off to tour the town of Laon, the Prince of Monaco's home at Marchais and the medieval castle at Coucy-le-Chateau: 'a unique sight, the proudest castle I've ever seen.... It would be a great shame, if the castle became a victim of this war.' Similarly,

Figure 11.1. Rupprecht and his son Albrecht

on 27 March 1917, Rupprecht visited Courtrai and Bruges, exploring Flemish decoration and architecture of the Middle Ages. Less cerebral pursuits, such as shooting hare or pheasant, were popular over the winter. When headquarters moved to Mons in spring 1917, a large area outside the town was set aside for hunting. Finally, Rupprecht's son Albrecht generally came to stay during his school holidays. Xylander described him as 'a really nice and well brought up young man, who speaks like a true Bavarian'. For Christmas 1915, Rupprecht gave Albrecht a bicycle. The fact that even when things were quiet, however, Rupprecht could spend no more than a couple of hours with him each day highlights the pressures upon the Crown Prince.[8]

The best way to escape the stresses of war was to go home. For the first two years of the war, Rupprecht did not take any leave at all. From late 1916 on, however, he made a total of five trips to Bavaria, each lasting on average between ten days and a fortnight. These trips were not all holiday. In Munich he often had to spend time meeting politicians, for example, and much of his February 1918 trip was filled by official duties connected to his parents' Golden Wedding anniversary. These trips gave him a break from the war, however, and allowed him to spend further time with his son. In season Rupprecht would go hunting in the Berchtesgaden Alps. Rupprecht was fortunate in this regard: ordinary soldiers might get no more than a week or ten days of leave once a year and Kuhl took none at all for four years, seeing his family only if he happened to be in transit through Berlin.

In summary, Rupprecht took the lead on ceremonial aspects of the job while his staff carried the main burden of administration and paperwork. Each army possessed a large and complex administrative apparatus. It needed to feed, clothe, train, and supply hundreds of thousands of men. Someone had to keep accounts and maintain military discipline, collate intelligence, prepare briefing notes, and draft orders. The lessons generated by operations must be collected, doctrine adjusted where necessary, and new techniques disseminated around the army. All these were jobs obviously best suited for trained staff officers to carry out. Equally, when it came to representing his command in negotiations with other formations or OHL, or to making the operational decisions which might make the difference between victory and defeat, and would certainly affect many lives, then charisma, and the habit of authority that the royal general possessed, might be more useful. When it came to decision-making, however, quite where the responsibilities of the army commander stopped and those of the chief of staff began is not easy to untangle. The two were expected to work together as a team but there was no set template of how they should do so. It was up to the individuals concerned to achieve their own equilibrium. Rupprecht had a different relationship with each of his three chiefs of staff. Indeed, each relationship itself evolved over time as the two partners developed and external stimuli changed.

The appointment of Konrad Krafft von Dellmensingen as his first chief of staff came as a pleasant surprise to Rupprecht. He was delighted to have a Bavarian officer to work with and knew Krafft of old. He respected his professional ability and the two men seem to have forged and maintained a close bond from the start. To begin with, Rupprecht seems to have deferred to Krafft. Krafft led most of the early strategy discussions with OHL, for instance. On occasion, he even appeared to boss Rupprecht about, asking him to go and hurry up a laggard corps on 27 September 1914, for example. Rupprecht had too much confidence in his own judgement to be a cipher, though. When he felt the need, he was happy to criticize the handling of his troops, as we saw with the Life Guards at Badonviller (14 August). Rupprecht was soon intervening in planning. On 18 November he argued that the strength available for a proposed offensive was inadequate. This happened 'without me suggesting it to him', Krafft noted. By January 1915, Krafft was beginning sometimes to defer to Rupprecht. He gave up the idea of taking Carency Wood after Rupprecht argued that the terrain was too difficult, for instance. Rupprecht had served his apprenticeship. His partnership with Krafft seems to have become one of military equals.[9]

Lambsdorff's appointment to succeed Krafft ironically helped Rupprecht grow as a general. Although first impressions were favourable, Rupprecht soon began to wonder whether he could trust him. During the dispute over Lochow's independent command in June 1915, the chief of staff seemed to be on Falkenhayn's side rather than Rupprecht's. When the French attacked in September, Lambsdorff seemed incapable of making a decision. By the middle of October, Rupprecht's patience was wearing thin:

> He wants to have control of everything, briefs me very poorly and was not always very well informed himself since he will not delegate to his colleagues. . . . His main activity was almost every day to visit one headquarters or another, inviting himself to breakfast [regardless of the needs of the situation]. . . . I did not trust Lambsdorff in a tight spot. A cold, smooth courtier, but not a real man.

Lambsdorff even began to try to cut Rupprecht out of decision-making. He showed him orders only at the last minute before they had to go out, or not at all. When Rupprecht found out that Lambsdorff had sought to conceal the loss of the important Gießler Heights, he was furious. Xylander reckoned that he had never seen him so angry. Rupprecht immediately wrote to the Chief of the Kaiser's Military Cabinet asking for Lambsdorff's relief and within the week he was moved sideways and out.[10]

Lack of trust in Lambsdorff forced Rupprecht to become more self-reliant. When Hermann von Kuhl became Rupprecht's third and last chief of staff, therefore, Kuhl found himself working with an experienced general. Kuhl was very thoroughly trained—he had been a protegé of Schlieffen's—and had spent the war so far serving as chief of staff to generals von Kluck and Fabeck. The former, especially, had a reputation for being tricky but Kuhl had managed him skilfully. Falkenhayn warned him that he would need to be diplomatic in his new post:

> Crown Prince of Bavaria [is] rather difficult, defensive about Bavarian rights, one minute exulting to the heavens, the next gloomy as death. Likewise he swings one minute from being unable to hold his position and having to give ground, to everything going brilliantly the next. His previous chief of staff, Graf Lambsdorff, and he could not get along.

Kuhl reached Sixth Army headquarters on 1 December 1915. He was welcomed with a gala dinner of Bavarian sausages and the two men rapidly grew to trust one another. They shared a view of offensive tactics and together disagreed with Falkenhayn's insistence that the British were planning to attack Sixth Army in early 1916. Rupprecht was fully capable of holding his own with his chief of staff as something close to military equals. As we shall see, during the second half of the war both Rupprecht and Kuhl were capable of taking the lead and proposing new ideas for how to proceed. Throughout the battles of 1916 and 1917 it is hard to see the join between the two men.[11]

Rupprecht's influence as a general was defined by his relationships, not only with his chief of staff, but also with his superiors and subordinates. Again, there was no agreed definition of the responsibilities and power of an army or Army Group commander. Rupprecht's role fluctuated in importance depending on how much latitude OHL was prepared to allow him and how far he in turn was willing to leave his subordinates to run their own shows. The traditional view of the German army has been that, by virtue of its tradition of Auftragstaktik, it has always been comfortable with a high level of decentralized command. However true this may be at the tactical level, the rest of this chapter will argue that operationally it is mistaken. Above divisional level, delegation was the exception, not the rule.

Rupprecht's boss was in effect the Chief of the General Staff, to whom the Kaiser tended to delegate day-to-day command of the German army. Traditionally, Moltke the Younger has been seen as a laissez-faire holder of this post. Through a combination of poor communications, illness, and incompetence, he passed decision-making power down to army commanders who, seeing themselves as some kind of semi-feudal paladins of the Kaiser, were more than happy to exercise their own authority. In reality, Moltke was consistent only in his inconsistency. Under him, OHL veered between trying to pull every string and abdicating all responsibility. As we saw in Chapter 2, the decision to let Rupprecht attack on 20 August 1914 was an example of the latter. Between 23 and 26 August OHL followed up with attempts at close central control, every day ordering him to attack in a different direction. Including Moltke, six different OHL officers worked liaison with Sixth Army at some point that month. Lack of consistency in personnel and intention generated destructive uncertainty which left decision-makers at all levels unsure of both their powers and responsibilities.[12]

This shambles could not, and did not, last. Neither did the promises of a free hand which Falkenhayn made to Rupprecht once he took over as Chief of the General Staff. His insistence that Sixth Army engage piecemeal as its units arrived on the Somme in September 1914 left Rupprecht no room for manoeuvre. In October, Falkenhayn would not allow Rupprecht to fight the Flanders battle as he saw fit. He insisted that Sixth Army wait for the new Fourth Army to arrive before advancing: 'even if the Crown Prince of Bavaria stands on his head, he may not attack!' Trust between Falkenhayn and Rupprecht rapidly evaporated and each began actively to undermine the other. In this environment, OHL was not keen to delegate. In any case, the changed realities of trench fighting, with nearly fixed battle-lines and telephones everywhere, permitted a degree of top-down control unimaginable during mobile warfare. When the French attacked in Artois in spring 1915, Falkenhayn tried to bypass Rupprecht by installing Lochow and telling him to report direct to OHL. Interestingly, Rupprecht does not seem to have complained about interference from OHL during the Third Battle of Artois in the same way, but that may be just because Artois was only a side-show and Falkenhayn's attention was elsewhere.[13]

When Rupprecht moved to command his Army Group in August 1916 and Hindenburg and Ludendorff took over at OHL, roles were recast. The Army Group was intended to be a high-level command which concentrated solely on tactics, operations, and related personnel matters. Administrative, financial, and legal matters remained the responsibility of each army. The Army Group was to take over the job of managing the process of roulement by which formations were rotated in and out of the line. From now on, Army Groups would be free to transfer formations from army to army without asking OHL's permission each time. They should be sufficiently large to generate reserves internally without having to request outside reinforcement. At their initial meeting at Cambrai on 8 September 1916, Ludendorff and Hindenburg reacted against Falkenhayn's record of interference and promised Rupprecht that they would leave him to run his Army Group. At least to begin with, they resisted the temptation to meddle as Falkenhayn had. After that first meeting, Rupprecht did not even see Hindenburg again for eight months. Once Ludendorff had checked and agreed Rupprecht's scheme of roulement, 'for the whole length of the immense and bloody Battle of the Somme', Rupprecht later reminisced, 'I was given a free hand'. This seems to have been part of a broader programme of allowing subordinate commanders greater latitude, as we shall see.[14]

Did Rupprecht make the same mistake of over-controlling those beneath him in the chain of command? Relations with his subordinates were not always easy, but on the whole he tried to leave them plenty of scope for exercising their own initiative. During the mobile warfare of 1914, Rupprecht had trouble with those under him. Some of this was the result of personality clashes. It was perhaps tactless to put Rupprecht in charge of General von Heeringen in the first few weeks of the war. Heeringen was a highly experienced general and former War Minister, nineteen years older than Rupprecht. More importantly, though, since neither had worked together before and all arrangements were being improvised, coordination remained poor. This ad hoc Army Group was soon broken up.

Communications proved another problem. As we saw above, the infrastructure did not exist for Sixth Army headquarters to keep in regular, much less continuous, touch with its units in mobile warfare. By the time of their attack on 20 August 1914, Rupprecht still had no established link to at least one of his corps. This gave ambitious generals such as Ludwig von Gebsattel scope to follow their own star, rather than the orders they had been given. The defeat of Gebsattel's attack on 25 August, undertaken despite instructions to remain on the defensive and guard the right flank, caused problems for Rupprecht's larger operations. Even where there was no active insubordination of this kind, it took time for all levels of command to adjust to the fact that battlefield communications were subject to even greater lags and friction than they had imagined. One way to get around this was to decentralize command, but this was a lesson not learnt until the fighting on the Somme in late September 1914.[15]

Once both sides settled into their trenches, the dynamic and rhythm of the war changed. Options closed down as the front froze, especially for the side on the strategic defensive. While Sixth Army did its best to ensure its troops kept up to date with the latest defence doctrine and organization, it needed to spend less time making operational decisions and more managing the flow of manpower and matériel which the new warfare devoured in ever greater quantities. Even if the enemy attacked, Sixth Army generally did little beyond allocating reserves where they were most required and reviewing performance to weed out tired and incompetent commanders and learn lessons for next time. Most of the time, the threat required little more.

On occasion, however, a major decision did become necessary. A good example is the counter-attack of VII Corps at Neuve Chapelle on 12 March 1915. Rupprecht set the objective and provided the resources required but left the detailed planning to the corps commander. As we saw, he regretted not having been firmer with Claer but did not alter his practice much thereafter. On the whole, although Rupprecht always offered advice and retained the right of veto, he tended to leave corps (and, later, armies) to fight their own battles. Rupprecht's headquarters was more often occupied with managing the overall effort than with minute-by-minute decision-making. Most of the time, the Entente attacks were not threatening enough to force more active intervention. One exception, the crisis of the Second Battle of Artois, proves the rule: such was the French pressure by 11 May that Rupprecht bypassed corps command and directly ordered one of the divisional commanders to clear the lines of communication to the village of Carency. This kind of intervention two rungs down the chain of command, while much simplified by the well-developed communications networks of trench warfare, remained rare. As we have seen, more often Rupprecht's interventions involved asking OHL for reinforcements, directing them where they were most needed, and approving or suggesting counter-attacks. The nature of defensive trench warfare left little scope for much else. The conduct of the Battle of the Somme generally unfolded along similar lines, as Chapter 12 shows.

PART III

Holding the Line
1916–17

12

Rupprecht Takes Command

Rupprecht wasted no time in getting briefed on his new command and the battle underway. Overall, although the Somme battle was putting the German army under considerable strain and losses were heavy, things appeared to be going tolerably well. German casualties so far totalled 195,172 men. The majority of the German divisions committed to action north of the river had lost at least half their infantry, and some had lost considerably more. These figures were too high for comfort but there was no cause for immediate panic. Germany still had some 1,400,000 men in reserve if required. Further, high as German casualties were, British losses were estimated to be five times as many. This was later revealed to be an exaggeration: the British had 'only' lost 190,000 men and the French 80,000. The balance of attrition was much less favourable than thought. Rupprecht, though, had no way of knowing this at the time.[1]

Manpower, however, was only one dimension of war, 1916 style. Machines were equally important. The bravest of soldiers could achieve nothing without the tools of battle. German industry was ramping up extremely rapidly. For example, monthly output of field artillery ammunition rose 60 per cent between the second half of 1915 and summer 1916. The trouble was that consumption had doubled and the German army had begun to eat into its stocks. Ludendorff vowed to increase supply again to 300 trainloads per month and re-establish equilibrium. Rupprecht, he promised, would receive 70 per cent of the output.[2]

At the operational level, in his four armies Rupprecht commanded forty-five divisions and some 700,000 men. Sixth Army, occupying the line from the Belgian border down to just south of Arras, of course, he knew well. It gave no cause for concern. The thirteen divisions which made it up were in good hands under Falkenhausen: 'despite his 73 years he is still very flexible and youthful, a handsome man with a sharply aquiline nose and

Figure 12.1. Rupprecht and his staff

bright eyes'. In any case, the British were unlikely to have the resources to attack here. Things were also likely to remain quiet on the front of Seventh Army between Noyon and Reims. The commander of Seventh Army, Heeringen, was quickly promoted away to avoid further clashes.

The main enemy pressure continued to be between the rivers Ancre and Somme against Below's First Army. Here, twenty-one German divisions, eleven in the front line and ten in reserve, were being attacked by thirty-two British and four French ones. In the six weeks since his success of 14 July, Haig had been trying to secure the observation posts and jumping-off positions he needed for his next major drive. A series of small-scale but intense battles for places such as Pozières, Mouquet Farm, and High and Delville Woods eventually added up to an advance of a thousand metres or so on an 8-kilometre front for Rawlinson's Fourth Army. The cost was 82,000 British soldiers.[3]

The enemy was most menacing in three sectors. First, his drive on Mouquet Farm threatened to cut off the salient at Thiepval. Second, British pressure around Delville Wood and Ginchy threatened the high ground there and at High Wood. Third, the French were driving eastward into the German second position on the right bank of the Somme. Below was confident that he could hold the first and last of these three sectors. In the centre, however, he was more concerned and was planning a large operation to recapture Longueval and Delville Wood on 31 August. The morale of his army, Below reported, was mixed. His men were unconcerned by the Entente advantage in manpower, but felt keenly that they were inferior in ammunition. Since enemy gunfire had destroyed fixed fortifications and barbed wire, leaving the defenders to fight from improvised positions in shell holes, they relied especially on protective barrages, which needed shells. Below seemed pleased with the new command arrangements. He and Rupprecht had always got on well but Below had found it difficult working for Gallwitz, whom he accused of funnelling resources First Army needed to his own Second Army. Gallwitz himself felt that he had been passed over for command of the Army Group and was prepared to be difficult with Rupprecht about it. As we shall see, he succeeded in causing considerable irritation as the battle went on.

The military situation of Second Army reassured Rupprecht, however. Intelligence counted twenty-two French divisions opposite Gallwitz's eleven. Although Second Army was low on reserves, it had plenty of guns and ammunition to hand. One difference between the two armies, though, was that under Below almost all the heavy artillery was parcelled out to the command of divisions. In Gallwitz's army, on the other hand, the majority remained under corps control. This more centralized approach ran the risk, in Rupprecht's opinion, of being slower to respond when needed in a hurry.[4]

The first test of the new Army Group and its commander was not long in coming. On 3 September eight British and four French divisions renewed the assault from Thiepval to the Somme. The defenders fought off rather clumsy British efforts at Thiepval, Mouquet Farm, and High Wood yet again. Further east, Rawlinson's men were a little more successful. After nearly a week of vicious fighting they finally cleared Ginchy, Delville Wood, and Guillemont, or what little was left of them. The French, however, gave the Germans a real scare. Fayolle's troops captured over 4,000 Germans and drove up to 3 kilometres into the German lines along the banks of the river. This Anglo-French attack on First Army was 'the strongest yet' and Rupprecht moved reserves up to support Below's left. Gallwitz protested noisily that he needed reinforcement, too.[5]

Gallwitz was proved right almost at once. At four p.m. on 4 September General Micheler's French Tenth Army attacked across the Santerre Plateau, aiming for the Somme crossings upstream of Péronne. By nine o'clock that evening, Second Army reported, the whole front line had been lost and there was a risk its guns might be overrun. Reserves would have to be sent to Gallwitz after all, however great Below's need. Rupprecht noted:

> Unfortunately our men on the Somme front are on the whole simply not the best and those who take their places certainly won't be any better. The veteran officers and other ranks become fewer every day and the replacements, however plentiful, have not had the benefit of the same military instruction and training. Physically also, they are mainly of low quality.... The situation is definitely extremely strained and dangerous for us.

The next day brought more heavy combat and further Entente gains, but also showed that the situation south of the Somme was not as poor as first feared. French progress in the south had been exaggerated. Much of the front line remained in German hands. Nonetheless, Oberste Heeresleitung (OHL) designated the situation 'very serious' and ordered six divisions, artillery, and air squadrons to be stripped from other sectors of the front and rushed to the Somme as quickly as the congested railways would allow.[6]

Rupprecht was impressed by the reaction of the new OHL to its first Western Front test: 'the change at OHL makes itself very pleasantly felt. What they arrange is effective and they take care to provide the best possible resources to their projects.' Ludendorff asked Rupprecht for the schedule of reliefs for the front-line troops and also how many replacements he needed. Falkenhayn had never been so professional. Managing a sustainable system of roulement to replace worn-out divisions with fresh ones now became thought so crucial that it sometimes took priority over other operational requirements. For example, Rupprecht refused to commit reserves to an attack on Delville Wood on 31 August because that would involve disrupting the relief schedule. He was worried about the resilience of his units: 'the ability of our men to resist is unfortunately not what it once was, and I can see with concern the time coming when divisions which have already been committed once at Verdun and on the Somme must be put back in to where the heat of battle is highest'.[7]

The question of roulement came up at a conference of Western Front commanders held at Cambrai on 8 September. Present were Hindenburg, Ludendorff, Rupprecht, Crown Prince Wilhelm, Duke Albrecht of Württemberg, Fritz von Below, Gallwitz, and their chiefs of staff. In general, Rupprecht found himself impressed with the two men now running the army.

In his diary he recorded his impressions with a typically nineteenth-century emphasis on physiognomy:

> Hindenburg creates a good impression. His forehead is strikingly broad, his eyes are blue and create an open and kind effect. His bearing is composed and determined. He loves hunting and is a joker but very approachable . . . Ludendorff has a well-defined, smart head. His face is very pale and I had the impression that he ought to take better care of himself. What he said was all spot on.

At the conference it was announced that eight new divisions were to be raised, five for the east and three for the west, of which two were intended to reinforce Army Group Crown Prince Rupprecht. More detailed discussion followed. The Second Army chief of staff, Colonel Bernhard Bronsart von Schellendorff, proposed speeding up reliefs by rotating divisions in and out of the line, rather than corps. He argued that imitating the British Expeditionary Force (BEF) and leaving corps headquarters in place at the front would generate greater continuity in command. There were obvious drawbacks, however. First, command cohesion would suffer: divisions would take time to get used to their new corps and vice versa. Second, corps played a vital role in coordinating artillery which it would be a mistake to dilute. Third, corps commanders were less likely to push strangers as hard as they could those they knew well. Lastly, rotating divisions rather than corps would make the army commander's job harder. Below's chief of staff proposed instead that part of the staff of the corps being relieved should stay *in situ* for a few days to ease the transition. Rupprecht preferred this solution.[8]

As Alexander Watson has pointed out, the Germans suffered more casualties at the start of September than in any other ten-day period on the Somme in absolute terms, with the exception only of the first ten days in July. As a proportion of overall strength, early September was probably the bloodiest period of the whole campaign. First and Second armies lost 13 per cent of their strength, compared to 10 per cent casualties between 1 and 10 July and considerably higher than the average 'normal' rate on the Somme of between 6 and 8 per cent every ten days. Concerns were now beginning to grow about both the quality and quantity of manpower. OHL began to toy with the idea of withdrawing to the line Arras–Laon–Verdun to shorten the line and free up reserves. At the Cambrai conference of 8 September, when he warned that if losses carried on at the present rate they would be forced to make peace before being bled dry, he found German Crown Prince Wilhelm agreeing with him.[9]

In the middle of September, the pressure ratcheted up another notch. By now, Foch had given up trying to arrange a tactically synchronized British and French attack. The two armies seemed never to be ready to attack simultaneously. The British official historian blamed the French for not trying hard enough to support their ally and repeatedly requesting postponements to operations. He did not mention that British requests for delay had become fairly frequent, too. The two allies were, however, capable of offering each other a measure of support at the operational level. They could stage assaults close enough together to generate some overall momentum. Some historians see this as a deliberate policy by Foch. Given the emphasis usually placed on simultaneous attacks, however, one suspects this was a militarily second-best method which had the political advantage of tactfully minimizing inter-allied recrimination.[10]

Either way, on 12 September the French struck again. Fayolle's Sixth Army tried to overrun the German third position and outflank Péronne from the north. Five divisions drove eastwards towards Bouchavesnes and the Bapaume–Péronne road. The attack was extremely successful. According to the official history, German protective artillery fire came down too late and missed the attackers. Consequently, the French were able to overrun the Saxon defenders in their dugouts. In Rupprecht's version, the Saxons simply ran away. Within half an hour Bouchavesnes had fallen to the French, who went on to seize nearly 7 kilometres of the German third position and open a gap 1,500 metres wide. To many on both sides, it seemed that the elusive breakthrough might at last have been made. Fayolle, much to his surprise, found himself enthusiastically embraced by the normally stolid Joffre.

The next German defensive line remained only sketchy and could not be relied upon to offer much obstacle. First Army began preparations to recapture Bouchavesnes, although it would take time to bring up reserves and they could not launch a counter-attack for several days. When the counter-attack finally took place, on 20 September, it failed. By then, however, French efforts to exploit the breakthrough had also ground to a halt. The gap had simply been too narrow and any attempt to push on had been chopped up by fire from the flanks. Moreover, the problems of moving up timely supplies and reinforcements, especially in heavy rain and mud, remained as yet insurmountable.[11]

In the meantime, after a three-day bombardment, on 15 September the British and French launched the Battle of Flers-Courcelette. This, in Haig's mind, would be the climax of the campaign, an assault designed to capitalize on all the hard-won progress of July and August. He hoped finally to break through the last German defences and into open country. To shatter the deadlock and return to mobile warfare would redeem all the frustrations and casualties of the last two months. One tool to help smash a hole was, for the first time in history, the tank. The story of the Battle of Flers-Courcelette is often told primarily through the prism of tanks. In particular, the narrative has tended to be dominated by debates about whether, in the first place, their use was a premature mistake; and secondarily about whether doling them out in twos and threes all along the line was the correct tactic, or they might have been more effectively employed en masse. As we shall see, there was more to the battle than tanks.[12]

At about eight a.m. on 15 September 1916 the front from Thiepval to Combles burst into life as the British Reserve and Fourth Armies lurched into action once more. Of the fifty tanks planned to participate, thirty-six reached their starting positions, twenty-five got to the German front line, and just six achieved their final objective. Inevitably, the British made mistakes with their handling of this new weapon. Fear of friendly fire, for instance, led them to leave lanes in the barrage for the tanks to advance down. Since many of the tanks failed to arrive, however, wide stretches of the defences were left intact and able to inflict heavy loss on the assaulting infantry. Harder to comprehend was the failure to find time for joint infantry–tank training. Likewise, it is unclear why one general elected to ignore his tank experts' advice and sent four tanks into the unsuitable terrain of High Wood. Nonetheless, where artillery preparation had been effective, the creeping barrage worked well, and infantry followed up closely, sometimes aided by tanks, good progress resulted. Within four hours, tank D-17, 'Dinnaken', led cheering British soldiers up the main street of Flers. 'In some places the appearance and fire of the tanks caused panic and terror', noted the German official historian, who also observed that the defenders' resistance at Flers and Gueudecourt was as good as broken. Here, where the British penetration was deepest, they had advanced some 2,000 metres. High Wood, Martinpuich, and Courcelette also fell, and some 4,000 metres of the German third position had been cleared.[13]

Rupprecht watched the fighting that afternoon from the upper window of a building in the village of Bihucourt. At four p.m., he noted 'the battle was in full swing. The drumfire roared constantly like a powerful waterfall, sometimes dying away a little but then growing once more in strength.... Judging by the smoke clouds, a counter attack to recapture the lost village

of Martinpuich was underway.' At about the same time on the other side of
the line, it was becoming clear to Rawlinson that no decisive victory was to
be won that day. It would be pointless to commit further reserves without
moving guns up. He would have to prepare a fresh set-piece attack once
more from scratch. Again, over-ambitious objectives, beyond the range of
the guns, had been set. Just because Rawlinson was not ready to force
matters did not mean the battle was over, of course. Strong German counter-
attacks to regain lost ground were made throughout the afternoon and
evening. They failed. 'Even by the standards of the Somme, 15 September
was an unusually intense day of combat', according to the German official
historian. The majority of British battalions had lost 300–400 men each.[14]

In Rupprecht's view, the fact that the defence around Flers had given way
in the first place, and the failure of the counter-attacks, could both largely
be blamed on exhaustion. The Bavarian troops holding the crucial sector
had been in the line for twenty-one days straight. They were slow to react
to defend Flers and some soldiers were so tired that they were falling asleep
even as they advanced across No Man's Land under heavy fire. Basic errors
were repeated as a result. For example, Ginchy, which lay on the boundary
between two divisions, had fallen on 9 September because neither thought
to garrison the village properly. Less than a week later, Courcelette fell for
the same reason. 'The whole staff of First Army, except for the Chief of Staff
Colonel [von] Loßberg, struck me as overworked and exhausted', thought
Rupprecht. 'The tension of recent weeks has brought some of the staff,
especially some of the over-strained Corps chiefs, close to breakdown.'[15]

Rupprecht also felt that the enemy had exploited a greater weight of
artillery fire. The Entente, he reckoned, fired four times as many shells as the
Germans. One thing he remained unimpressed by was British tactical skill:

> The enemy brought up armoured vehicles for his successful attack against 3rd
> Bavarian Division in the area of Martinpuich yesterday which drove straight
> across country at our trenches and fired on them with machine guns and
> small-calibre cannon. Under the protection of these armoured cars the British
> infantry pushed forward in thick bunches. The attackers seemed drunk; they
> staggered slowly forwards, rifles under their arms, regardless of the gaps our
> infantry and machine-gun-fire tore in their ranks, which were always filled up
> with men from the rear.

Although the French made little progress on the east side of the bulge on
15 September, and reserves soon came up to contain the British, nonetheless
the situation of First Army was far from ideal. First, its front line had been

stretched by another 8 kilometres. Second, it seemed that the Entente were trying to drive a wedge between First and Second armies. The counter-attack at Bouchavesnes designed to forestall this would not be ready for days and indeed some of the reserves intended for it were needed instead to plug gaps between Flers and Courcelette. Third, the loss of Flers left German positions in Combles extremely vulnerable and if Combles fell, the Bouchavesnes attack would be impossible. Lastly, the Canadian capture of Courcelette left just one communications trench running up to Mouquet Farm. German positions in the Thiepval salient were becoming dangerously exposed.[16]

If the situation north of the Somme was critical, on the other side of the river Gallwitz, too, was feeling the pressure. The French Tenth Army ground forwards on the Santerre Plateau between 15 and 18 September, forcing the Germans to pull their heavy guns back to the right bank of the Somme. Gallwitz directed a stream of warnings of impending disaster to Rupprecht and Kuhl at Army Group headquarters. When his demands for reinforcements were ignored, he wrote a formal letter complaining that First Army was receiving preferential treatment. Relations with the Army Group went from chilly to frosty. When Rupprecht and Kuhl visited Second Army headquarters in Saint Quentin, no-one was waiting to meet them, to hang up their hats and cloaks, or to direct them to Gallwitz's office. The subsequent interview between Gallwitz and the Crown Prince was animated. More damaging was the fact that both Kuhl and Rupprecht suspected that Second Army was, at best, not keeping them properly informed and, indeed, possibly downright lying. When Rupprecht asked why he never saw copies of Second Army orders, chief of staff Bronsart claimed that everything was done by telephone so there were no written orders to see. Rupprecht was not convinced. Kuhl went further: 'Reports are biased... Gallwitz is embittered and makes continual difficulties. Given his intelligence, I wouldn't have considered him such a small man. Bronsart is dishonest and Faupel [the operations officer] is also a weasel. A completely crooked crew.' Eventually, in late October, Bronsart was transferred elsewhere.[17]

While Haig and Foch prepared a new push, the Germans finally launched their counter-attack at Bouchavesnes on 20 September. Two important points came out of this particular phase of the battle. First, the balance of air power was shifting from the Entente to Germany. Throughout July and August, British and French airmen had possessed general air superiority. They were able to operate almost at will even over German lines. The Germans responded by reinforcing their air force on the Somme. New squadrons arrived, armed with the latest and best designs. Consequently, the intensity of air combat increased as the Germans began to contest control of the sky more fiercely. On 20 September, when elements of six German divisions attacked either side of Bouchavesnes, air support was ample and the German fliers were largely able to go about their work undisturbed. Second, Bouchavesnes reminds us graphically how difficult it was, even with air reconnaissance, for those up the chain of command fully to understand what was happening on the First World War battlefield. The first reports Rupprecht received were of enemy artillery silenced by gas; a defence caught off balance; and an attack carrying all before it. In short, he thought he had scored a stunning success and he regretted not having set deeper objectives. He encouraged Below to push on. Only later in the day did he find out that progress had not been quite so dramatic and that the advance had in fact been stopped on the western edge of Bouchavesnes. Stubborn resistance and a strong French counter-attack were apparently to blame. The next day, the picture of the situation was revised once more. The attack, it was now clear, had been a failure. Bouchavesnes had never been in German hands at all. The attackers had finished back where they started, in their own trenches. The preliminary bombardment had been insufficient. The attacking corps commanders had rushed the execution of the operation because they had not built enough cover for the assault troops and they did not want to leave them exposed out in the open for too long. 'Or maybe', Rupprecht wondered, 'our infantry simply possesses no offensive power any more.'[18]

The attack unleashed by the British and French on 25 September showed what could be achieved if the two allies could ever coordinate their attacks properly. The British Fourth and French Sixth armies conducted a major set-piece assault simultaneously and side by side for the first time since 1 July, and seized the largest slice of German-held territory taken so far. Seven British divisions attacked Morval and other German strongpoints, aiming eastwards for Le Transloy and the new German fourth line. A further corps drove north to protect the left flank. Fayolle, with seven French divisions, attacked north-east into the German defences in villages such as Sailly-Saillisel and Rancourt and the huge Bois de St Pierre Vaast. With luck, he might thus turn the flank of the formidably strong Mont St Quentin and threaten Péronne town from the north. Reserves of both infantry and cavalry stood by in case resistance suddenly collapsed and deeper exploitation became possible. A further linked operation the next day, by the British Reserve Army, would try once more to seize the bluff at Thiepval.

On 25 September the British did well. They captured Morval and Lesboeufs. The next day they occupied Gueudecourt and Combles. The French had a tougher time. Rancourt fell quickly but, caught between machine-gun fire from Bois de St Pierre Vaast and artillery dug in on Mont St Quentin, it proved hard to make progress over the open ground and losses were heavy. Local actions continued over the next couple of days, and nowhere along the Somme in the autumn of 1916 was ever completely quiet; but the Battle of Morval had died away by the morning of 29 September. Any idea that the Germans might counter-attack faded away when OHL told Rupprecht that reserves were running short and in future his Army Group would have to rely more on its own resources. Units in line would just have to accept longer intervals before relief if necessary. Rupprecht thought this unhelpful advice. It would work only if the intensity of enemy attacks slackened, but that seemed unlikely. In the event, OHL was forced to send five divisions from its reserves to help him withstand the impact of the battle, not only of Morval, but also of Thiepval Ridge.[19]

General Sir Hubert Gough attacked on 26 September with four divisions from Courcelette to Thiepval. His objective was to clear the crest of the ridge, prevent German observation of Albert, and enable the British to see down into the Ancre valley. Fighting was heavy but by early the next day both Mouquet Farm and Thiepval at long last lay in British hands. Poor weather and the usual problems of coordination rendered further progress slow, however, and heavy trench fighting continued in and around the Schwaben Redoubt well into October.

The battles of Morval and Thiepval Ridge, taken together, won the British and French the whole German line from Thiepval to Bouchavesnes, a front 25 kilometres long, to a depth of about 1,500 metres. Christopher Duffy has described the battles as 'the supreme effort of the British on the Somme, and the one that brought the Germans closest to collapse'. Certainly, they showed a British army which had learnt much over the previous three months. The attack of Major-General Ivor Maxse's 18th Division on Thiepval, for instance, is evidence of two major tactical improvements. First, the assaulting troops had learnt the importance of crossing No Man's Land fast to avoid the German protective barrage. Second, everyone now knew that the Germans were likely to counter-attack. Lieutenant-Colonel Frank Maxwell VC distinguished himself by rapidly organizing the mixed-up units which had stormed Thiepval village into an effective defence. As William Philpott has argued, 'by the end of September 1916 British junior officers and other ranks were no longer naive or casual in the military arts'. Indeed, in the words of Robin Prior and Trevor Wilson, 'in this grim, intense, close-quarter fighting, the troops from the British New Army and the Dominions were quite capable of outfighting the German defenders'. If it had ever been true that the German soldier was man-for-man superior to his British counterpart, this edge was now eroding.[20]

Rupprecht noted and lamented this, too: 'while in the past, although our infantry were fewer than the enemy, they were qualitatively superior, as a consequence of the heavy casualties, especially in officers and NCOs, this qualitative edge has declined'. Manpower problems seemed to be getting worse. The British were rotating divisions through the front line every six days but it was becoming harder to organize timely reliefs for German front-line troops. Eight days under enemy artillery was enough to wear out most units, even if there was no infantry fighting. Rupprecht, however, was having trouble getting Ludendorff to agree even to a fourteen-day relief cycle. Further, morale was suffering as a result of fighting bloody battles for land which in itself had no obvious value and which was ultimately lost. The same was becoming clear the other side of the wire, too: British intelligence officers 'have never seen the moral[e] of the Germans so low as at present'. First and Second Armies between them had lost 135,000 men. September was by far the Germans' bloodiest month on the Somme.[21]

Where the strain was even more marked, however, was in matériel. German infantry as yet had no answer to the tank, although they soon began experimenting with trench mortars and 37 mm naval guns in an anti-tank role. In the air, the German air force, as we have seen, was back on level terms by the end of the month. While the British and French lost 123 aeroplanes in September, the Germans lost just twenty-seven. Nevertheless, Germany remained outnumbered by at least three to two in aircraft and could not ease up. German gunners, noted Rupprecht, 'were on a par in quality with the British, but not with the French, and in terms of numbers they have not been able to keep up with the ever rising number of enemy batteries'. The crews were becoming overstretched and exhausted, in action night and day. The field artillery fired over four million rounds in September, up from one and a half million the previous month. Heavy howitzers expended 907,000 shells, compared with 643,000 in August. Inevitably, tired crews sometimes performed poorly. Infantry–artillery cooperation remained less than ideal, with protective barrages coming down too late and targets of opportunity being missed. The guns themselves were wearing out and breaking down, too. Half of the field guns and a third of the light howitzers had to be replaced during the month.[22]

So far, Rupprecht and his men had clung on, but the strain was telling. Would October be the month that saw the German army break?[23]

13

Autumn on the Somme

The Somme was simultaneously slaughterhouse and war school, where three armies struggled to adapt to the protean challenges they faced. This can be seen most clearly in the to-and-fro between offensive and defensive tactics. We have already seen, for instance, how by late September the British Expeditionary Force (BEF) had lost its July naivety and began to learn how to exploit the predictabilities of the German defence. Once the attackers knew that the Germans would advance to recapture any ground lost, they could plan to consolidate their gains and dig in, catch the counter-attack in the open, and inflict further losses. For their part, the Germans realized they must eliminate this predictability. September saw the incoming senior commanders propose a new means of fighting the defensive battle, spread their ideas, and begin to build consensus for change. By the beginning of October, their new methods were starting to bite and have effects across the battlefield.[1]

The key issue was how rigid the defence should be. Falkenhayn, as we have seen, had always been firm that his men should not give up an inch of French soil voluntarily, contesting the front line ferociously and counter-attacking to regain any ground lost. His aim was to make every Entente advance as expensive as possible, both politically and strategically. If France and Belgium discovered that they could only liberate their homelands by destroying them, so much the better. Operationally, he considered this the neatest way to maintain the integrity of the defensive line and prevent a chain reaction of units being outflanked and withdrawing in turn. Retreats, he also feared, might damage morale.

Ludendorff had different ideas, however. He outlined them at the Cambrai conference of 8 September. His suggested approach was much more elastic. He wanted the front trenches manned only thinly, mainly with machine-guns. They would function as an outpost line to identify and disrupt enemy

Figure 13.1. Hindenburg with Ludendorff

thrusts. The weakened attack would then break on the stronger defences of the second and third German lines. Light machine-guns and trench mortars would substitute firepower for manpower. Artillery should not act purely defensively but should aggressively target enemy concentrations of guns and infantry. Now that the enemy possessed artillery superiority and had evolved effective drills for mopping up any trenches he overran, fixed positions and underground shelters had become liabilities rather than assets. It was too easy for troops to be overrun in their dugouts: better for them to stay mobile. Further, the defenders were no longer automatically to counter-attack. Only significant terrain was worth losing more men for.[2]

Soon it became clear that Ludendorff was not thinking about applying this new flexibility merely at the tactical level. He was considering using it operationally, too. On 12 September Oberste Heeresleitung (OHL) mentioned the idea of building a new defensive line from Arras to Laon via Saint Quentin to enable Rupprecht's Army Group to shorten its front by 50 kilometres and free up reserves. This position eventually became known to the Germans as the *Siegfried Stellung*. The British and French called it the Hindenburg Line. We will discuss it further in Chapter 14.[3]

Debate on the new elastic defence went on throughout the month. Second Army orders issued on 17 September still stuck to the old principles but a consensus was already emerging in favour of Ludendorff's ideas. The ground was fertile since, as we saw in Chapter 10, front-line troops had already begun to ignore Falkenhayn's official doctrine when it conflicted with practicalities on the ground. Several details of the new approach needed filling out, however. Who was to control any local counter-attacks, for instance? Could it be left to the initiative of company, platoon, and even section commanders?

On 27 September Kuhl summed up what had been learnt over the previous few months. The situation was now so different from what had gone before, he wrote, that 'only experience on the Somme is important. The lessons of earlier battles must be corrected from now on.' Operationally, everything was about holding on: 'on the Somme, victory will go to whoever lasts longest in matériel, munitions and manpower. There is nothing else for it. We will prevent an enemy breakthrough, if we provide for timely reliefs.' Tactically, he identified five areas for improvement. First, units should be deployed in greater depth, so divisional frontages should be reduced from 4 kilometres to under 3. Second, better cooperation between artillery and infantry was desirable. Once an enemy assault was underway, the guns should concentrate solely on the attacking infantry. Third, more fighter aircraft were required, more contact patrols should be flown, and spotter crews needed better training. Fourth, staffs were being stretched too thin. Divisions, in particular, needed to have a second properly trained staff officer. Corps commanders who knew their sectors well might be left in place even when their men had been relieved to avoid losing the benefit of their experience. Fifth, defences should be positioned on reverse slopes and eschew deep dugouts, and the front line should be only thinly garrisoned and not automatically held to the last man. The front line could best be held by counter-attacks coming from deep. Counter-attacks were more effective when they were quickly improvised locally (Gegenstoße) rather than deliberate set-piece operations (Gegenangriffe).[4]

Tactics of this kind had already contributed to the breakdown of French attacks on 25 September along the Bapaume–Péronne road.[5] They were far from the only factor sapping momentum from the Entente advance throughout October and into November, however. With the passing of the autumn equinox, the weather changed for the worse. Mist and rain grounded spotter planes and so weakened artillery preparation. They also made objectives harder to spot, especially in the featureless wasteland that was being fought over. Consequently, barrages tended to fall either short and hurt the attackers, or too far ahead and miss the defenders. The ground, stripped bare of vegetation and pock-marked with shell holes, was soon churned to a liquid yellow-grey mud. This stuck to everything and made walking a slow-motion torment. Guns which could normally be pulled by six horses now required teams of twelve, if they could be moved at all. Stable firing positions were increasingly hard to find. Moving food and ammunition across country had rarely been easy. Now in places it became all but impossible. Where there were roads, they were worn out after months of heavy traffic and began to break up. A lorry passed every four seconds along the main French supply road east from Amiens: the traffic was twice as heavy as along the famous voie sacrée at Verdun. Where Foch's staff had originally estimated they would need three steamrollers to keep his roads open, by November forty-nine were at work. The British supply network, hastily cobbled together and patched up over the previous two years, reached breaking point. Attempts to imitate the French and build a light railway network looked promising, but this solution came too late to solve the supply problems in heavy artillery munitions, roadstone, and timber.[6]

In the face of these major challenges, at times the tempo of French and British operations slackened, granting the Germans crucial breathing space. Still, it would be a mistake to see the October battles as mere postscripts to the 'real' fighting of July–September. The Entente retained considerable punch yet. Indeed, Rupprecht considered that two days in October (9 and 12) saw the hardest fighting the Germans had yet faced. Even as late as 5 November, he ranked the battle among the most savage they had experienced.[7]

The pressure of the September fighting had taken its toll on Rupprecht and when October opened with fresh British and French attacks, he became rather depressed. Kuhl was forced to intervene. On 2 October, for instance, Rupprecht told his chief of staff that they could not hold out like this for much longer and it would be better to pull back into a new line of defence to the rear. Kuhl responded that there was no proper fortified position ready to allow such a move; that trying to break contact with the enemy in the middle of heavy fighting was an invitation to disaster; and that, in any case, even if they did withdraw, they would only find themselves in the same predicament again within a few days. The prince was still quite down two days later. It was clear to him that Foch and Haig were now taking an attritional approach, launching small-scale attacks to keep up the pressure in between large set-piece operations. He worried that 'the large number of prisoners we have recently lost is an evil sign'. 'But he can straighten himself up again', added Kuhl.[8]

The British and French continued to nibble away at the German defences. They were trying to establish good jumping-off positions for another major assault. Rawlinson's Fourth Army's objective remained Bapaume, while Gough's Reserve Army was still working to capture the crest of the Thiepval ridge. With Mont St Quentin firmly in German hands, French Sixth Army could drive only north-eastwards, on Sailly-Saillisel and Bois St Pierre Vaast. South of the Somme, meanwhile, high ground around Lihons and Chaulnes continued to block the French advance eastwards.

Entente plans for a joint attack had to be postponed when heavy rain set in, and fighting degenerated into small-scale pushing and shoving very reminiscent of the August struggles. An attempt to coordinate a large Anglo-French operation on 7 October delivered only disappointing results for the Entente and attempts to get the offensive moving again the next day yielded little. In a vivid illustration of the difficulty of communication on the 1916 battlefield, Major Prager of Rupprecht's staff happened to be watching the action from an artillery observation post. The forward observer told him that it would take at least an hour and a half to pass any message to the guns defending Le Sars. Rupprecht and his men could feel some satisfaction, nonetheless, that they had beaten off the 'strongest attacks to date' on the Somme front. The weeks of fighting which now began in the twin villages of Sailly-Saillisel, house by house and cellar by cellar, were characterized by a ferocity fit for Stalingrad. It was, according to William Philpott, 'the worst fighting that [the French army] was to see in the whole Somme battle'.[9]

The Germans were suffering, too. 12 October in fact marked another very heavy day of fighting. Five British divisions of Fourth Army went over the top but, encountering an alert and ready defence with machine-guns deployed and concealed in considerable depth, often out of range of the British creeping barrage, they achieved little of value. Nor did further set-piece offensives on 18 and 23 October. Fourth Army held a conference on 13 October to discuss improvements in tactics, but the weather and terrain prevented implementation of any recommendations it made. The same day, men of the German 15th Infantry Division mutinied and refused to enter the line. Their corps commander claimed never to have seen such poor troops. The problem was not limited to the full-scale attacks which make the history books; nor yet the innumerable little patrols and raids which do not. Rather, reported First Army, they faced a more relentless opponent: 'our worst enemy unfortunately remains the enemy superiority in ammunition, especially in heavy calibres. These knock down our defences, cause most of the casualties, disrupt traffic in the rear areas and deprive troops who are supposed to be resting of true quiet.'[10]

On the other side, the Germans had rotated their forces, shifting out exhausted divisions and artillery batteries and bringing in fresh ones. The extensively fortified Butte de Warlencourt, a prehistoric burial mound 20 metres high, dominated the centre of the front. The British attacked it again and again throughout October and November, each time without success. As Gary Sheffield has argued, 'like Monte Cassino in a later war, the Butte exercised a powerful and malevolent grip on the minds of the British soldiers crouched in its shadow'. Unlike Cassino, it never did fall. Despite the impossible mud and painful evidence that the offensive had stalled, Haig insisted on a final British attack on 5 November. The XIV Corps commander, Lord Cavan, lodged a rare formal protest, but the operation went ahead nonetheless. It captured but a little ground of limited significance.[11]

In the centre, therefore, the British and French were stuck firm. On the Santerre Plateau on the left bank of the River Somme, however, the attackers had greater freedom of movement and resupply and reinforcement were slightly easier than in the devastated centre but even here, after some progress in heavy fighting on 6 and 10 October, by the second half of the month French momentum was fading. Indeed, by the end of October the situation of the German army on the Somme felt much more comfortable than it had only a month earlier. German casualties in October dropped to 85,000 from 135,000 in September. Fresh divisions had been committed to relieve those worn out by the fighting and a proper system of *roulement* was in place. As the tempo of operations dribbled away, divisions were beginning to endure in line for longer than the fourteen-day target. One Bavarian division managed to last three weeks before it was relieved. A French offensive at Verdun on 24 October, although successful in recapturing Forts Douaumont and Vaux, could not be sustained for long enough to disrupt the German reliefs rota. In any case, the Somme was supposed to be relieving pressure at Verdun, rather than vice versa.

Stronger artillery increased German confidence. On the main battlefront there were now four times as many heavy artillery batteries as there had been on 1 July. A new Army Artillery Reserve had been established to replace worn-out guns more promptly. Infantry and artillery were liaising more effectively and increased ammunition supply enabled deeper defensive barrages to be fired. More ammunition was being manufactured and supplied and it was being distributed more efficiently. OHL delegated to Rupprecht the power to decide where to send ammunition, so he could direct shells where they were needed in a more responsive and timely fashion. In the air, the Germans were still outnumbered, although not by so much. They had, however, mastered new machines and famous units such as Oswald Boelcke's Jagdstaffel (Jasta) 2 led the way in developing new tactics to fly and fight in large formations, rather than as individual machines. The Entente had lost air superiority. Although Boelcke himself was killed on 28 October, by then his most famous pupil, Manfred von Richtofen, had already begun his lethal career.[12]

On the British left flank, Gough's Reserve Army was rechristened Fifth Army at the end of October. The name changed but the mission stayed the same. This remained the elimination of the Thiepval Salient. In what was later called the Battle of the Ancre Heights, Gough's men spent October and early November launching a series of limited-objective assaults designed to nibble away at the German hold on Thiepval ridge. At last by 21 October they had cleared the Stuff and Schwaben Redoubts and reached the crest of the ridge. It had taken a month to advance 750 metres. German intelligence had been monitoring the build-up of British strength here closely for some time, fearing a more ambitious scheme was being prepared. Both Rupprecht and Ludendorff suggested evacuating the salient, but Below was reluctant to give up the good observation posts he held there. He felt that his defences were strong and he should hold there as long as possible.[13]

Finally, on 13 November, after a week-long bombardment, the British attacked with five divisions. The focus was on the far side of the River Ancre, around the villages of Serre and Beaumont Hamel, where the BEF had suffered so badly on the morning of 1 July. This time the German wire and fixed defences were systematically destroyed. A creeping barrage, incorporating machine-gun fire, covered the infantry advance closely. At least, that was the case where the attack went well. Inevitably, that did not happen everywhere. Tanks were unable to have much impact: the ground was too boggy. Beaumont Hamel and St Pierre Divion fell to the British, but other objectives of the original attack, such as Serre, remained firmly in German hands. Even another follow-up attack on 18 November could not prise them free. Casualties were heavy: battalions of the 51st (Highland) Division lost up to half their strength. Nevertheless, the Battle of the Ancre (13–19 November)

was considered successful enough that Haig could, at last, declare victory
and formally suspend the offensive.[14]

On the other flank, by 12 November the whole of Saillisel was finally in
French hands. It was, however, evident that operations were winding down
at last. The first snowfall on 18 November gave a final sign that winter was
at hand and that the time for major operations was past for another year.
By that time, Rupprecht had already decided he could finally get away on
leave for the first time in over two years. He left for Munich on the evening
of 16 November.

On the face of it, the German army had done a good job of frustrating
the Entente armies in the Battle of the Somme. After 141 days of fierce
fighting, it had allowed the French and British to advance about 10 kilometres
at most. Two of the attackers' main geographic objectives, the towns of
Bapaume and Péronne, both remained firmly in German hands. Casualty
statistics are not straightforward for the Somme. British casualties probably
totalled 419,654, with the French losing half as many: 204,253 men. Most
estimates for the Germans range from a conservative 429,209 to a frankly
implausible 680,000. About 500,000 seems roughly right.[15]

With casualties so high, and results apparently so meagre, was the Entente
right to fight and then persevere with the battle? Debate continues about
this, so, before we leave the Somme, we might briefly review some of the
arguments and explore what light Rupprecht's evidence sheds on them.
Sir Douglas Haig was quick to justify the Battle of the Somme in his official
despatch of December 1916. No-one was more aware than he that his early
hopes for a breakthrough and a return to mobile warfare had been dashed.
So Haig offered not just one, but three objectives which he argued the
campaign had achieved. These were: first, to relieve Verdun; second, to tie
down the German army in the west and prevent it being transferred to fight
in the east; and, third, to wear down the enemy. 'Any one of these three is
in itself sufficient to justify the outcome of the Somme battle', he said.
'[Together] they have brought us a long step forward towards the final
victory of the Allied cause.' How do these three justifications stack up?[16]

The weakest of the three is Verdun. While it is true that the Germans
suspended active offensive operations at Verdun on 12 July, it had been obvious to everyone for months that they were going nowhere and would have
to give up anyway. Rupprecht had privately written it off in his diary as
early as 20 March. Long before 1 July it was clear that the British were not
going to do what Falkenhayn had so painstakingly planned for them. When

the attack on the Somme came, and proved much heavier than Falkenhayn had anticipated, this served as final proof not only that there was still life in the French army but also that Haig was not going to play neatly into Falkenhayn's hands. The Verdun business had long been bankrupt: the decision of 12 July merely shut down the shop. In any case, if the Somme were seriously intended as an offensive to relieve Verdun, it was hardly a very timely one. Over four months had passed since the fighting at Verdun began.[17]

Did the Somme prevent the Germans from transferring troops from the Western Front to other theatres? No: possibly as many as fifteen divisions were transferred from west to east during the campaign, although nine of them were exhausted and in any case some six fresh divisions went back the other way in exchange. If we step back from the statistics, however, the larger picture is equivocal. On one hand, the Central Powers remained capable throughout 1916 of fighting off multiple opponents on widely separated fronts. Indeed, from August onwards, Germany could take on the new commitment of Romania and crush her army in just four months. On the other hand, though, the Entente strategy of concentric offensives was actually beginning to operate rather well. OHL sent divisions east because it had to. Germany was having to juggle multiple threats and beginning to find doing so a considerable strain. We will never know how much strength Germany could have moved east if the Somme, or some other very similar campaign, had not been fought, but politically Haig and Foch had little choice if they were not to let down their allies.[18]

If the verdict on the second justification seems evenly balanced, the third appears more clear-cut. Whether attrition was always in Haig's mind as a back-up plan or put forward as a rationalization after the fact, the Somme certainly wore down the German army. Every time a German division spent a tour in line on the Somme it lost, on average, about 3,000 men or about a third of its infantry. Losses on this scale inevitably depressed morale and the quality of the troops suffered. In October Rupprecht wrote to his father, King Ludwig III, that 'sadly it's becoming ever clearer that our troops lack attacking power since almost all our attacks, even the limited ones, fail. The troops are not what they were in the spring.' Alexander Watson has demonstrated the psychological damage suffered by the German army. This comes through strongly in Rupprecht's papers. The Somme did not break the back of the German army, but it weakened it considerably. To expect any battle at this stage of the war to do much more is probably unrealistic.[19]

Some have argued that the Somme was a necessary learning step for the Entente forces. The tactical lessons the BEF learnt there, or the refinements Foch made to his operational method, contributed to final victory in 1918. We shall explore the changes made over the winter of 1916/17 in more detail in Chapter 14, but this is true, in a sense. The only way to learn how to fight is to do it. They were horribly expensive lessons, however. Worse, Rupprecht's view of how British combat effectiveness developed is mixed. Throughout the campaign he saw them as dangerously brave. They were less proficient and menacing opponents than the French, however. They often relied on sheer weight of numbers, of artillery and men, to blunder forwards. As the campaign developed, he accepted that the qualitative gap between German and British infantry was closing, although he attributed that more to his men getting worse than to the British getting better. By November 1916, he actually noted signs of British tactics becoming clumsier once more, with a return to the old-fashioned close formations which had proved so vulnerable earlier in the war.[20]

Finally, some historians have argued that the Germans became so keen to avoid a repeat of the Somme that they decided to pull back into the Hindenburg Line in spring 1917 and wait for the U-boats to win the war instead. In fact, there was no strategic master plan. The Hindenburg Line was originally constructed as a contingency measure, and the decision to retreat into it was taken only shortly before implementation. The German army was under no illusions that the retreat would prevent another Somme-style offensive from the enemy: it would just delay one for a few weeks and give the defenders a better chance of withstanding it, when it came. We shall discuss this decision further in Chapter 14.[21]

14

Scorched Earth

By the end of 1916 it was at last clear to all that this war could end only when one side or the other toppled into the abyss. As Hindenburg wrote to the Chancellor that autumn, the outcome 'would decide the survival or destruction of the German people'. Only if Germany mobilized all her resources, he argued, could she prevail. Victory required a radical and ruthless remobilization of society and industry to feed the military's needs. Such was Germany's relative weakness in manpower, raw materials, industry, and transport that a land offensive was unthinkable. Some, Rupprecht and Kuhl among them, went further: they were beginning to doubt whether a military way out of the nation's difficulties existed. They kept their doubts to themselves, however, for now.[1]

Hindenburg and Ludendorff remained optimistic. The military establishment was not prepared to accept that victory was beyond reach. Oberste Heeresleitung (OHL) was agitating for a renewal of unrestricted submarine warfare. Earlier in the war Rupprecht had opposed this, not on legal or moral grounds but because he was concerned that the risk of provoking the United States outweighed the benefits the relatively small U-boat fleet might achieve. Now that more U-boats were available, however, and with American entry seeming more likely in any event, his attitude changed. OHL also recast the army to increase effectiveness. Over the winter of 1916/17 Hindenburg and Ludendorff built thirty-three new divisions, from a mix of fresh recruits and existing units, bringing the total to 232. The cavalry was reformed and infantry establishments were standardized. In theory, each division now had three infantry regiments, each of three battalions; fifty-four heavy and 108 light machine-guns; and thirty-six field artillery pieces. The distinction between active, reserve, Landwehr, and Ersatz formations was abolished. In practice, these ideals were not always achieved. Nonetheless, in total, the army deployed about 9,300 field, and nearly 5,000 heavy, artillery guns, together with 2,271 aeroplanes and 150 balloons.[2]

The German army also had to reconsider its battlefield approach. As we saw, it had started the Battle of the Somme somewhat complacent. 1915 had shown that it was perfectly capable of containing Entente attacks. Along much of the British Expeditionary Force's (BEF's) front on 1 July, this complacency proved justified. Defensive firepower had shredded the British ranks. Any break-ins the British managed were cut off by artillery and soon pinched out. Where the British and French had scored successes, the weight of their artillery seemed to have made the difference. The French, in particular, had concentrated their guns and systematically destroyed German strongpoints one by one. Next, a thick and effective barrage kept the defenders in their dugouts while the assault troops overran the shattered trenches and seized their objectives. As fighting on the Somme continued it became ever clearer that this was not a battle of genius and manoeuvre, but of matériel and attrition. The Germans called it Materialschlacht.

This called for new tactics. Evidently, troops in the front line often achieved least and suffered most. In response, several corps and divisional commanders began to downgrade the forward crust defence and hold more of their strength rearward, whatever Falkenhayn's orders said, as we saw in Chapter 10. Other changes followed, too. To improve air support, for instance, each corps was given a specialist air commander in the middle of August. Further, First Army experimented with delegating control of all bar the very heaviest artillery batteries right down to divisional level. Response times improved as a result.[3]

These lessons were among those digested by the new team: Rupprecht, Kuhl, Ludendorff, and Hindenburg. Their first priority was to increase the flow of food, ammunition, and matériel to the troops. Once they had taken steps to improve that, they began to re-examine everything else with fresh eyes. In this case, it is possible to follow the learning process closely. They discussed new tactics at Cambrai on 8 September and began to codify their ideas in a circular of 25 September. Kuhl developed them further in his memo of 27 September, which we discussed in detail in Chapter 13. OHL then called in after-action reports from headquarters at every level from regiment to Army Group that had fought on the Somme. The archives in Munich preserve at least sixty-eight of these reports which, together with lessons gathered from the defeats suffered at French hands at Verdun in the autumn, provided the raw material from which OHL pulled together a major revision of defensive doctrine over the winter of 1916/17. A team within the Operations department worked on a slew of memoranda covering topics such as the construction of trench systems, the use of mortars, and effective liaison between spotter 'planes and their artillery.[4]

These documents were together known as 'Collected Instructions for Trench Warfare'. The keystone Part 8, 'Principles for Command of the Defensive Battle in Trench Warfare', was released on 1 December 1916. With attrition now beginning to bite, the objective ceased being to hold every inch of ground regardless of its value. Instead it became to cause the enemy maximum losses while minimizing one's own. Four core ideas were to work together to achieve this. First, the defender must remain active and not allow the enemy the initiative. Instead, he must keep the other side off balance by aggressive patrols, raids, and local attacks. Second, the defence must be built around machines rather than manpower. Third, ground must not be held unthinkingly, regardless of its tactical value. It was acceptable to pull back a little if necessary in the face of a major enemy attack. Any ground yielded should be immediately counter-attacked and regained. If that proved impossible, however, and only a full-scale set-piece operation seemed likely to regain it, the importance of the terrain should be weighed up before any decision to proceed. Counter-attacks were resource-intensive and should no longer constitute an automatic response. Lastly, the defence should be deployed in depth to drain the attacker's momentum and leave him vulnerable to counter-attack. Under the new regulations the distance between trench lines in each defensive position was to extend from 50–100 metres to 150–300. Similarly, the depth between first and second positions was increased from a kilometre or 2 up to somewhere between 4 and 10. Some debate ensued about who should control any counter-attacking reserves. Should they stay under the control of their own division or be commanded by the man leading the front-line garrison? The latter, it was eventually decided. The same commander also won control of all the heavy guns in his sector. To increase the elasticity of the defence, the commander on the spot was to be given greater scope to use his initiative. He would only be permitted to do so in two very specific circumstances, however: he might choose whether to pull back temporarily if under heavy attack and whether to recapture lost ground. Otherwise, OHL reserved decision-making power to itself. This was, therefore, far from a general delegation of authority.[5]

The aim of codifying doctrine in this manner, in one set of documents, was to increase uniformity of practice. Previously, each individual army had kept separate files on the methods they expected their formations to follow. Now the 'Collected Instructions for Trench Warfare' offered a single ready reference in case of need, a foundation for all subsequent debate and adaptation, and a benchmark against which practice could be checked. Thus, the 'Principles for Command of the Defensive Battle in Trench Warfare' document, for instance, was revised five times to incorporate new lessons before the war was over. When First Army issued a report nearly seventy pages long on the lessons of the Somme, Rupprecht told his officers to read it in conjunction with the 'Defensive Battle' document. Comparing the two would throw into relief differences in approach between the two, particularly as regards elastic defence. Kuhl took care to highlight and explain the changes made in a subsequent edition. More practically still, in January 1917 OHL ordered subordinate headquarters to present detailed schemes of defence, following the new regulations. Staff officers scrutinized the maps and went through the calculations to check compliance.[6]

In November 1916 Hindenburg issued another significant memorandum, 'Command in War and the General Staff'. In it, he warned that Germany's enemies were starting to surpass her in some respects as her pre-war edge in training, discipline, and drill was eroded. It was noticeable, he complained, 'that we have in some respects learned more slowly than our enemy'. The solution lay in improved training. Rupprecht picked up on this, establishing a school at Solesmes to train divisional commanders and staff officers. The first course began in February 1917. The new 'Collected Instructions for Trench Warfare' were at the centre of the curriculum. Demand was so strong that Rupprecht soon set up a second school and in March Crown Prince Wilhelm established one at Sedan for his Army Group. This provision of new training for senior officers built on attempts to improve that of officers and non-commissioned officers (NCOs) at company and platoon level. These had been underway since October 1916 with the establishment of 'Field War Schools' in each Army Group. These lasted five to six weeks and trained 100 officers and 100 NCOs each time. Specialist schools, for instance for stormtroop tactics and artillery techniques, were also expanded and improved. In addition, each division was to spend three weeks of uninterrupted training over the winter of 1916/17. All in all, the Somme proved 'the high school of the German army for the defensive battle in position warfare'.[7]

All these changes would, it was hoped, improve the quality of the army; but quantity remained a problem. At best, Ludendorff and Hindenburg

Figure 14.1. Rupprecht inspecting his troops

would be able to count on a reserve of twenty divisions in the west in spring 1917. The BEF alone would have as many and the French another seventy-two. A meeting of army chiefs of staff on 2 January 1917 was almost unanimous that a major breakthrough operation was out of the question. Offensively, the best that could be achieved was a series of limited-objective local assaults. These might hurt the enemy but could not defeat him. There was no alternative to assuming the strategic defensive and ceding the initiative to the Entente. Kuhl put together a detailed memorandum along these lines. The question now, therefore, became how best to meet the enemy onslaught intelligence was predicting for the beginning of March.[8]

Two possibilities presented themselves. Either the army could stand and fight where it was, much as it had throughout the previous two years. Or it could trade space for time and pull back some 30 kilometres into the position known to the Germans as the Siegfried Stellung and to the British as the Hindenburg Line. This was not a new idea. OHL had already been thinking about it since early September 1916. They calculated that a retreat to the Arras–Laon line would shorten the front by some 50 kilometres and free up about ten divisions. Construction began in autumn 1916.

Ideas about how best to use the Hindenburg Line evolved over time. To begin with, and indeed well into 1917, it was seen as no more than a safety net which might come in handy if enemy pressure, especially in the Somme sector, became intolerable. When morale at OHL, which had been high after the capture of Bucharest and defensive successes on the Somme, was knocked by General Charles Mangin's victory at Verdun on 15 December, orders went out to accelerate construction. Still, however, the Hindenburg Line seems to have been viewed primarily as a contingency measure.[9]

In the course of January, views changed. To see the decision to retreat as purely driven by a negative desire to avoid a renewal of the Battle of the Somme is to over-simplify a more complex process. In fact, it was the result of a combination of positive and negative considerations. First, the Kaiser's decision in favour of a resumption of unrestricted submarine warfare on 8 January 1917 seemed to open another possible path to victory. If U-boats could throttle Britain and force her out of the war, all that was necessary on land was to avoid defeat. Moving back into a strong defensive position could obviously help. Ludendorff told Kuhl that once they had defeated the enemy's next attack, the war would end in the summer. Neither Kuhl nor Rupprecht was quite so optimistic, but they disagreed more with the timing than the logic.[10]

The second factor was more negative. First Army had originally argued against withdrawal. Below believed it would damage the morale of the men who had fought so hard to hold the line on the Somme. More junior commanders, however, began to press for a retreat. Their troops, they suggested, could not withstand another battle like the Somme. One First Army corps commander, General Georg Fuchs, made a particular impression. He warned Kuhl that the morale of his men was vulnerable and the condition of their defences lamentable. The front line near the Ancre, for instance, consisted of little more than shell holes. The dugouts were flooded and communications trenches unusable. Better, he argued, to pull back. Convinced, Kuhl suggested withdrawing into the Hindenburg Line as soon as possible. Discussions went back and forth between Army Group Crown Prince Rupprecht and OHL. Finally, on 4 February 1917, the Kaiser signed off on Operation ALBERICH, the code-name for the retreat into the Hindenburg Line and the devastation of the evacuated zone. The commanders of the armies in line thus found themselves overruled by a coalition of their subordinates and seniors.

OHL hoped that pulling back into the Hindenburg Line would advance four objectives. It would free up reserves by shortening the line. The strength of the position itself would save further manpower by enabling each division to hold a broader sector. The Hindenburg Line was based on multiple defensive positions, echeloned in depth and wherever possible sited on reverse slopes to prevent enemy observation. Thick belts of barbed wire offered further protection. Large numbers of machine-gun strongpoints dotted the defensive zone. Next, withdrawing would buy time. Before the enemy was able to attack, he would have to establish new lines of communication forward to the new front line. Then he would have to make all the time-consuming preparations for a new offensive again, this time from scratch and on new ground. The evacuated area would be harrowed, with villages burnt, bridges blown, and rails and roads torn up, to make the enemy's job harder. German and Russian retreats in Poland earlier in the war had demonstrated how effective a scorched-earth policy could be. Third, every day bought on the Western Front might give the U-boats another twenty-four hours to throttle Great Britain. Lastly, if the enemy did eventually attack, the German army would be more likely to beat him off.[11]

Rupprecht's attempts to exercise direct influence over decisions made regarding the Hindenburg Line enjoyed little success. First, when the whole idea had originally come up, Rupprecht had proposed a different course for it, retreating further and incorporating cities, such as Lille and Cambrai, which the Entente would be unwilling to attack and destroy, into the defences. OHL rejected his suggestion on the grounds that it would require too much manpower. Second, Rupprecht objected to orders to deport local inhabitants, raze their homes, destroy their livelihoods, and demolish the road and rail networks. Military necessity required only that fields of fire in front of the new defences be cleared and he was concerned about both the humanitarian issues involved and possible damage to Germany's reputation. He was also concerned that discipline would suffer. At first, his protests seem to have remained fairly quiet, largely because he considered the scheme impractical. He could not believe that either the labour or explosives would be available to carry out these orders. In the event, when Operation ALBERICH was put into motion on 9 February 1917, within three weeks 126,000 civilians deemed capable of working in the Reich were shipped away without trouble. Some 12,000 children, mothers, and old people, 'useless mouths', were left in towns such as Noyon to be liberated— and fed—by the enemy. Trainloads of useful machinery were also removed. Only when the final demolitions were scheduled to start on 16 March and it was becoming clearer that Ludendorff was in earnest about scorching the French earth did Rupprecht contemplate resigning in protest. Fearful, however, that such a move would suggest disunity between Bavaria and Prussia, he signed the order. He sadly noted in his diary that he had watched the villages burning as he drove back to his headquarters.[12]

Retreating in the face of an alert enemy is always a risky operation and Rupprecht had to coordinate the movements of three different armies. Security was extremely tight. The OHL Intelligence Staff made up elaborate deception plans in the press and leaked dummy operations orders. German aeroplanes repeatedly bombed the railway stations of Amiens and other communications nodes in an effort to slow any enemy response. Although preliminary limited withdrawals on the Somme front had gone well, nerves grew tense as 16 March approached. In fact, good staffwork contributed to a well-organized move. The British official historian Cyril Falls gave Rupprecht and Kuhl generous credit for that. Patrols stayed behind to create the illusion of normality while the main forces slipped away during the night. The Germans leapfrogged back through a series of successive rearguard positions until they were safely in the Hindenburg Line on 19 March.[13]

Enemy interference was minimal. Both the British and the French seemed slow to detect German movement, slower to grasp what was underway, and slower still to follow up. 'It's really amazing, how inactive the enemy is being', noted Rupprecht. 'He still seems to have noticed only small parts of our withdrawal and has not yet grasped the big picture. The French are even more in the dark than the English.' Entente troops and staffs had become attuned to the rhythms of trench warfare and were perhaps not as alert as they might have been. Also, British intelligence had been caught off balance. Jim Beach has demonstrated that this marked a failure of both collection and analysis. Spy networks in the German rear areas were unable to provide sufficient information for a reliable picture to emerge and, deep down, the British simply could not believe that the Germans would willingly yield something they had fought so stubbornly to keep for two years. A third factor was that Sir Douglas Haig was wary of over-extending his forces and, while ordering his men to take any opportunities which presented themselves to inflict loss, warned against large-scale attacks in force unless fully supported by artillery. Such support was hard to provide in mobile warfare over broken ground. Fourth, conducting a pursuit over what Falls described as 'a zone of morasses, the joint product of shell-fire and rain' was undeniably difficult. Finally, both Haig and the French commander-in-chief, General Robert Nivelle, were focusing on their own impending attacks, at Arras and along the Aisne respectively, rather than on the space between the two.[14]

According to the German official historian, ALBERICH boosted, rather than depressed, morale: it proved to the rank and file that their leaders knew their business. There were two further positive outcomes from the retreat, he argued. First, Entente offensive planning was gravely disrupted: the whole area between Arras and Soissons became a no-go area for months. The British official history corroborates this view. Second, the German army now found itself in powerful defensive positions in which it would be easier to withstand Entente attacks. He suggested that the German defensive victories which followed, at Arras, on the Aisne, and in Champagne, owed much to the withdrawal to the Hindenburg Line. We shall examine the first of these battles in Chapter 15. It is worth noting first, however, that little time was in fact bought. Within three weeks of the German withdrawal, Rupprecht's Army Group found itself entangled once more in a full-scale attritional battle which in many ways resembled the Somme.[15]

Once the retreat to the Hindenburg Line was successfully completed, OHL revised its estimate of enemy intentions. In the west 146 German divisions now faced 183 enemy ones. The deployment of Entente reserves seemed to suggest two, possibly connected, operations: a British effort around Vimy and Arras and a major French push near Reims. From late February, traffic analysis by signals intelligence suggested enemy reinforcements were arriving at Arras, opposite Falkenhausen's Sixth Army. German intelligence soon picked up on work to improve road and rail links in the area, as well as more air activity. Rupprecht secured reinforcements of artillery, aircraft, and infantry for Sixth Army. By 22 March Falkenhausen appeared to have all he needed to withstand a surprise attack. As the weight of enemy artillery fire grew from 26 March, any remaining doubts evaporated and within days Rupprecht was formally warning OHL to expect a major offensive between Lens and Arras. In early April OHL gave him authority over four divisions held in reserve behind Sixth Army.

On 4 April, a major bombardment began east and south of Arras. Overall, 320,000 rounds fell on Sixth Army between 29 March and 5 April, more than double the amount fired the previous week. It was evident that an attack could be expected in days, rather than weeks, but, even though Sixth Army was outnumbered twelve divisions to nineteen, there seemed little cause for real concern. An OHL liaison officer sent to inspect the defensive preparations went away satisfied that Sixth Army was ready to repel anything the British might manage to launch. The German forces defending the Souchez and Vimy sectors, he noted, were especially well prepared. Falkenhausen was keeping five reserve divisions well in the rear, out of British artillery range, where they could rest and train undisturbed. On 6 April both Ludendorff and Rupprecht ordered Sixth Army to move these reserves up closer to the front line at once. The threat was now imminent and grave.[16]

Before we explore the Entente offensives, we should briefly outline how the British and French armies reacted to the lessons of the Somme and hoped to change the way they fought in the new year. It was easy enough to accept the need for change after a year which left neither army happy with results. It was harder, however, to choose which lessons to learn.[17]

The French army found sifting the lessons of 1916 particularly difficult. It was true that the methodical, artillery-dominated, 'scientific battle' employed on the Somme had enjoyed considerable tactical success and reduced French casualties. An average infantry company which might have lost seven men killed for every day of combat in 1914, and five in 1915, in 1916 lost just one. However, the need always to follow the plan had prevented exploitation of success. Worse, as an operational approach it clearly was not getting the job done. It was hard to see how a method which had failed to liberate Péronne, just 10 kilometres away, in four months could free France. Meanwhile, down at Verdun General Robert Nivelle had secured impressive results on 24 October and 15 December with a very different approach. In some ways returning to the tactics of 1915, French troops swept forwards in a single, brusque onslaught, well supported by artillery and aiming for deep objectives including the enemy's gun lines. In December 1916 Joffre signed off on a 160-page memorandum on offensive methods for the following year. This followed Nivelle's method more closely than Foch's. When Nivelle took over as commander-in-chief on 17 December, 'scientific battle' became discredited and its practitioners, such as Foch and Fayolle, were sidelined. As we shall see in Chapter 15, the new methods yielded only renewed disappointment. Major reform of training and doctrine formulation would have to await the arrival of Pétain as French commander-in-chief in the summer of 1917.[18]

The British on the Somme were starting from a much lower base than the French. According to a German after-action report, in July 1916 British infantry remained less dangerous than the French, even though they had improved since Loos. The troops were not as well trained and they were unsure of themselves tactically. British artillery fire was better directed than before, but it still lacked the effectiveness of the French. We have already seen that the BEF improvised and experimented frantically throughout the battle and that GHQ collated the most important lessons and distributed them, especially via the doctrine manuals printed by the Army Printing and Stationery Service (SS). Over the winter of 1916/17, however, GHQ undertook a major revision of the BEF's manuals.[19]

In February 1917 the new Director of Training, Arthur Solly-Flood, wrote and published two new tactical manuals: SS 143, 'Instructions for the Training of Platoons for Offensive Action' and SS 144, 'The Normal Formation for the Attack'. These introduced two main principles. First, the infantry platoon now replaced the company as the basic tactical unit. Second, Solly-Flood tried to integrate new technology better. The platoon was reorganized. Rather than the old four rifle sections, each platoon now deployed specialist bombing, rifle, Lewis gun, and rifle grenade sections, along similar lines to the French model. The platoon should form an 'army in miniature' with its own integrated firepower and be able to fire and move independently. Moreover, these pamphlets re-emphasized the need for platoon and section commanders to act on their own initiative without waiting for orders from above. This was a principle enshrined in pre-war practice, but wartime experience had shown how vital it was on a battlefield where communication was slow and difficult, at best. SS 144 also grappled with the perennial tension between regimented step-by-step plans and a more laissez-faire approach which might make it easier to exploit success. The compromise it proposed was that commanders should act in a manner appropriate to the situations they found themselves in. This advice was sensible and sought to prevent the micro-management that had been prevalent in many formations. It did not, however, offer much guidance and so was not terribly helpful, but then no attempt to reconcile two fundamentally opposed operational ideas at the tactical level was likely to be.[20]

The most important new contribution to the BEF's operational thought was SS 135, 'Instructions for the Training of Divisions for Offensive Action', issued in December 1916. This came down firmly in favour of the methodical, 'step-by-step', approach. It stressed the importance of painstaking preparation and of setting limited objectives within range of effective artillery support. In essence, therefore, the British were now subscribing to what the French called the 'scientific' method and moving away from deep-objective breakthrough attempts. They were, in other words, signing up for the approach the French were in the middle of jettisoning.

In some ways, then, the thinking of the BEF had made a major advance. It had absorbed the tactical lessons of the Somme and was moving towards finding repeatable solutions to the 'break-in' problem, largely by adopting tactics reminiscent of those the French had developed in 1915 and 1916. At the operational level, however, they remained behind. They had not yet identified, much less solved, the problem with 'scientific battle': the slow tempo which allowed the defender to maintain his equilibrium, reinforce his defence, and dig in again.[21]

The British were not only learning new things, however. They were also changing the way they learned. In February 1917 GHQ set up a new Directorate of Training, under Solly-Flood, to coordinate and improve uniformity in training across the BEF. In addition to the new doctrine he produced himself, it was his job to reform and integrate the network of schools, which had sprung up informally around the BEF from 1915 onwards, into some kind of system. Eventually, in June 1917, SS 152 'Instructions for the Training of the British Armies in France' was distributed, laying out establishments and model curricula for all the schools. Learning, it was clear, was now a serious business.[22]

15

The Battle of Arras

At half past five in the morning of Easter Monday, amid driving rain and flurries of sleet and snow, the British attack at Arras began. The intention was to break into the German defences, roll up the Hindenburg Line from the north, and then push on Cambrai. Fourteen British divisions took part in the first assault, a similar number to the first day of the Somme, but the artillery on hand was much stronger. Where in 1916 Rawlinson had one field gun every 20 metres and one heavy gun every 52, Generals Sir Henry Horne (First Army) and Edmund Allenby (Third Army) now deployed one field gun every 13 metres and a heavy piece every 25. Better ammunition, and more of it, multiplied the effect. The shallowness of the German defences up on Vimy Ridge allowed the attacking Canadian Corps to concentrate its fire yet further. Proportionally, the Canadians unleashed twice the weight of heavy artillery shell fired on the Somme, and thirty times that fired by the French in May 1915.[1]

The main force of the attack fell on six front-line German divisions arrayed in three 'Gruppen' ('groups'): from north to south, Gruppe Souchez, Gruppe Vimy, and Gruppe Arras. Each 'group' equated to, and was built around, a traditional corps. The Germans were outnumbered by some three to one in artillery and their guns were closely targeted, and much neutralized, by British counter-battery fire both during the preparatory bombardment and on 9 April.[2]

The German defenders were caught off balance by the timing of the attack and were soon overwhelmed along much of the front. The wire had been well cut and their trenches were badly damaged. Following closely behind a creeping barrage, the attackers washed over the front line with relative ease. Often, the garrisons never made it out of their dugouts. Up on Vimy Ridge, the Germans lost the crest and were pushed back into their third line on the eastern downslope. By eleven o'clock, a few companies of defenders still held out in a strongpoint on Hill 145, but most of the ridge otherwise was firmly in Canadian hands. (Hill 145, where the Canadian National Memorial now stands, was marked as Hill 140 on French and German maps and referred to as such in Chapter 8.) Further south, between Bailleul and the River Scarpe, 14th Bavarian Infantry Division collapsed altogether. Troops from British 4th Division advanced 6 kilometres, further than anyone had managed since trench warfare began. For a giddy moment, they thought they had broken through and called for cavalry to exploit, but their success was so unexpected that none were on hand in time. South of the river, also, the Germans lost villages such as Neuville-Vitasse, together with many of their guns, and were driven back almost to the hilltop village of Monchy-le-Preux.

Any confidence, or even complacency, that Sixth Army was ready for anything had been shattered. As ever, early reports were sketchy. Communications had largely been cut by enemy shell-fire. One runner took three and a half hours to cover the 2 kilometres from the strongpoint on Hill 145 down to regimental headquarters. When news did get through, it was universally bad. At half past four Gruppe Arras reported despairingly: 'Situation poor, casualties very heavy, much artillery lost.... Ammunition and reinforcements crucial. Number and weight of shell-fire much stronger than Battle of the Somme. We have destroyed fifteen tanks but there are many more still there.'

The worst news was that all attempts to counter-attack had collapsed. The reserve divisions, whose job it was to seal off any enemy penetrations and drive the attackers back, were nowhere to be seen. Falkenhausen and his staff had ignored repeated instructions to close them up to the front and all bar one of the five reserve divisions remained east of Douai, a full day's march from the battlefield. Although Rupprecht tried to hurry them along, little could be done now. Even the ready reserves of the garrison divisions arrived too late and were too weak to do anything more than plug gaps. The tired and disordered remnants of troops who escaped being overrun that morning had no chance of recapturing the ground they had lost. By nightfall, reinforcements were on their way. Rupprecht sent Sixth Army two divisions at lunchtime. That evening, he added another five. These new formations, he made clear, were to be moved up tight behind the front at once, without worrying about possible billeting problems. These reserves, at least, would be available if required.[3]

The question, of course, was whether they would arrive in time to hold the British, or whether Haig's men would be able to exploit their stunning successes first. Rupprecht remained sure that this time his line would hold. He was less convinced, however, how much that would achieve. He noted that 'the situation is undoubtedly serious, certainly as serious as that in First Army at the beginning of the Battle of the Somme'. Although the Germans had more reserves available this time, the terrain was more difficult and it was very doubtful whether his men would be able to recapture Vimy Ridge. He eyed the future with foreboding: 'for the moment we can certainly contain this push; but it's questionable whether we'll be able to withstand further attacks supported by this weight of artillery. This poses a further question: is it worthwhile for us to carry on fighting this war under these circumstances?'[4]

Whatever the long-term outlook, in the short run the bad news kept coming. Up on Vimy Ridge, the last defenders of Hill 145 were finally overcome that evening. Over the next couple of days the British tried to exploit their victory by pushing forward all along the line. They seized the high ground of Monchy-le-Preux on 11 April, and the next day finally cleared the defenders from their last footholds on the ridges of both Vimy and Lorette. The British were not having it all their own way, however. An Australian attack at Bullecourt turned to bloody disaster when they encountered the fresh and highly trained Württembergers of 27th Division. The Australians broke in to the German trenches but communications collapsed and confusion followed when the Germans counter-attacked. About 1,200 Australians were taken prisoner. Other British attacks were also repelled. Indeed, British momentum was draining away. The attackers were tiring; there were no fresh reserves or, at least, those which did exist were not released by GHQ; coordination between units and arms was deteriorating; and all the time the German defenders were improving their positions and getting stronger.

By the evening of 11 April Rupprecht was optimistic that the worst of the crisis was now past. The idea of Sixth Army launching an attack to recapture lost ground, which Rupprecht and Kuhl had resisted, was now abandoned. The decision was taken once more to trade space for time. During the night of 12/13 April, the Germans abandoned their exposed positions at the foot of Vimy Ridge and pulled back 4–5 kilometres into more sustainable defences in their third line, running from Méricourt to Oppy and Gavrelle. The British followed up slowly. To crack the new line would require a full set-piece assault, which would take the British Expeditionary Force (BEF) time to prepare. Fighting over the next few days became increasingly scrappy and small scale as the intensity of operations died away.[5]

Figure 15.1. The front-line trenches of the Hindenburg Line (Siegfried Stellung) near Bullecourt

The British lost 13,000 killed, wounded, and missing in the first phase of the Battle of Arras, a quarter of the losses of 1 July 1916. The normally understated British official historian described 9 April as 'one of the great days of the war. It witnessed the most formidable and at the same time most successful British offensive hitherto launched.' The advance averaged 6 kilometres on an 18-kilometre front. The Germans lost 233 guns and 23,000 men, of whom 16,000 were captured or just went missing. Seven German divisions were so badly chewed up that they had to be relieved without delay.[6]

Inquests into the disaster began at once. Why had the German army been unable to contain an attack it had seen coming? With another huge French offensive known to be imminent, there was an urgent need to check whether the new defensive doctrine was flawed. Oberste Heeresleitung (OHL) began a thorough debrief, interviewing officers who had taken part. Every level of command involved, from regiment up to Army Group, wrote a report on their experiences and what had gone wrong. The independence and objectivity of this process, however, was immediately prejudiced by a wave of sackings, instituted by OHL over Rupprecht's objections. Sixth Army's chief of staff, Major-General Karl von Nagel, was fired on 11 April. Loßberg replaced him. Nagel's assistant, Rudolf von Xylander, was also let go. Both men were blamed for the failure to move reserves up in time. Falkenhausen, the army commander, was badly shaken and offered his resignation to the Kaiser. This was rejected, but a few days later an opportunity arose to promote him out of the way when the Governor-General of Belgium died in office. Falkenhausen replaced him in Brussels and Otto von Below took over Sixth Army.[7]

These dismissals set the tone. It was now clear that OHL would be comfortable with reports which blamed the defeat of 9 April on the mistakes of individuals, not on the new defensive system itself. Not surprisingly, most of the after-action reports which came in took their cue from this. A preliminary memorandum from Rupprecht on 12 April, for instance, suggested a couple of reasons for failure. First, reinforcements of guns had not been properly dug in and registered and so were of little use. Second, infantry reserves were in the wrong place. A fuller report on 21 April discussed a broader range of factors but re-emphasized these two as the most important. Some points that subordinate formations made, which OHL might not like, were not repeated on up the chain of command. For instance, suggestions that the British might actually have planned and executed a sophisticated combined arms attack rather well were suppressed. On the other hand, the principles of defence in depth were, it was argued, shown to have worked, even if in places on 9 April the terrain or state of the defensive works made them impossible to apply.[8]

That the boss sometimes gets told what his subordinates think he wants to hear is hardly news in any context, much less in the history of the German army between 1914 and 1918. This instance, however, represents the first time that we can see this process so clearly in action under Ludendorff and Hindenburg. In the autumn of 1916 the thought processes of the chain of command had briefly been characterized by a level of rigour and intellectual honesty which permitted the German army to tear up established methods and bring in a largely new defensive doctrine. This was possible partly because Ludendorff and Hindenburg possessed a measure of self-confidence which Falkenhayn had long ago lost and partly precisely because their new approach overturned his ideas. The result was a level of objectivity much greater than the chain of command had achieved previously. The British success on 9 April, however, applied a new level of pressure to the system, which reverted to its default setting: too much truth hurts.

This becomes only clearer when we examine why the British thought they had done as well as they had. The official historian identified three main factors at work. Two of these, British artillery superiority and the slow arrival of the defender's reserves, corresponded closely with those identified by the Germans. He also suggested a third factor, however. The German defensive scheme, he argued, being new, was not only grafted onto fortifications not suited to it, but indeed was imperfectly understood by the defenders and not properly implemented. He argued that the British artillery plan, despite intelligence that German defensive methods had been reformed, was designed to overwhelm an old-style defence. It only worked because 'the new German system had not made very much progress'. Instead, 'contrary to Ludendorff's original design, the infantry had received orders to hold the forward system at all costs, instead of regarding it as a true outpost system. Not only so, but it was held in such strength that when it was overrun each division lost about one-third of its infantry.'[9]

After the war, the German official historians accepted that the new principles were not properly applied. Partly this was because they were hard to implement. The terrain, most obviously up on Vimy Ridge, offered little depth: the eastern face was so steep that losing the crest meant losing the whole thing. Partly it was the result of a failure of higher command, from army level up to and including OHL, to understand how imminent an enemy offensive was. Preparations had not been made with sufficient thoroughness or urgency. Too few shelters had been built behind the front lines, so the garrison was left forward, where it proved highly vulnerable to British combined arms tactics. Building the Hindenburg Line had diverted resources which might have helped construct Sixth Army's defence in depth. The success of ALBERICH promoted a sense of security which proved all too false. But partly, also, it was based in a failure to understand and apply the new doctrine. Although, as we have seen, the after-action analyses did not emphasize this, there is nonetheless evidence to that effect. Even where the ridge was not a problem, units had been ordered to defend well forward and to hold their positions to the last, rather than to roll with the punches. A good example is the 8th Bavarian Infantry Regiment, holding a sector of flat ground just north of the River Scarpe. One battalion was being held right back in the outskirts of Douai, some 22 kilometres and at least six hours away. Of the remaining eight companies, six and a half were in the front line.

Nine hundred metres of the second line ended up being held by one non-commissioned officer (NCO) and twelve soldiers. This sector was one of those which collapsed most disastrously on 9 April.[10]

The significance of the British assault on 9 April must not be exaggerated. Tactically, it showed that the BEF, given sufficient preparation and resources, could break in to a strong defensive position on a broad front, as it had failed to do on 1 July 1916. The cost was also lower. This represented a measure of progress. Vimy Ridge, with its views across the Douai Plain, the key to Artois, constituted a prize in its own right. It was a prize, moreover, which had eluded the French army twice in 1915. Impressive as the Canadian capture of Vimy was, however, it is important to remember that it was a sideshow, designed to secure the flank of the broader British attack, which was, itself, a sideshow designed to draw attention away from Nivelle's offensive further south.[11]

Moreover, in one important respect the British seemed to have made little headway. They remained as incapable as ever of turning tactical advantage into operational success, much less strategic victory. Even on 9 April, this had been a factor. We have already seen that the cavalry were not in position to exploit success on the north bank of the Scarpe. More generally, decisions made in planning reduced the chances of successful exploitation on the first or second day. For instance, each corps was set up with three divisions in the first wave of the assault and just one ready to leapfrog through them and continue the advance to the final objective. Since the final objectives were not reached, either the objective was too deep; or a single division on a three-division frontage was not enough; or both. Another example arises with the handling of XVIII Corps, the three divisions of which constituted the Third Army reserve. The choice of when and where they were to be used belonged not to the army commander on the spot, General Sir Edmund Allenby, as one might expect, but to Haig. No units were to move without GHQ's permission. Perhaps Haig did not fully trust Allenby, who certainly lacked experience of command at this level. Still, this was a strange arrangement, not least after Haig had criticized something similar at Loos eighteen months before.[12]

The British made other old mistakes all over again. During the days immediately after 9 April, in an attempt to maintain momentum and exploit gains against an enemy whose weakness Allenby misjudged, they rushed through the planning and execution of a cluster of narrow-front attacks. All too often these achieved little, foundering on tired troops, poor intelligence, and insufficient coordination. The attack of the 9th Division on the Roeux chemical works on 12 April was a good example. No-one thought to synchronize this operation with the attack of the neighbouring division. There was no time to arrange a smoke screen to cover the approach march and German guns disrupted the assembly of the assault units. The troops were cold, wet, and tired. They had received no hot food for days and were unable to keep up with a creeping barrage which advanced unrealistically fast. The British heavy artillery bombardment was inaccurate and ineffective. Ground gained was minimal and soon abandoned. As the official history noted, 'it is one thing to plan and organize when there is plenty of time, but ... in modern war it is often quite another matter when there is time only for hurried improvisation, carried out by largely amateur staffs'. Bashing away in this fashion had not achieved much on the Somme and it yielded little in 1917, too. Haig recognized this on 15 April when, after representations from some of Allenby's division commanders, he ordered a halt to such attacks and an operational pause.[13]

Abandoning the Arras offensive was not yet an option. The main purpose, after all, had been and still was to prepare the way for the French offensive which General Robert Nivelle had promised would win the war. This main push began along the Chemin des Dames on 16 April. Ground was made both here and in a subsidiary effort in Champagne. Some twenty-nine French divisions took part, twice as many as the British used at Arras. OHL was never really concerned, however, and the Germans were inflicting very heavy losses on the French. By 20 April it was clear to Paris that the offensive had stalled and breakthrough remained a dream. The French attacked again on 4 May, this time with more limited objectives. They found resistance no less ferocious. Over the next week the main operation was wound down. Nivelle, after much politicking, was finally removed on 15 May. Haig had been astute enough to suspect that the French were struggling and that Nivelle's position was under threat almost from the first. Nevertheless, politically he could hardly suspend British operations until he was officially told that French plans had changed.[14]

Rupprecht, of course, was unaware of any of the intrigues behind enemy lines, although on 15 April he correctly judged that the crisis for Sixth Army was past. On 21 April the Germans began to pick up signs of a renewed British attack at Arras. When this assault duly unfolded on 23 April, it was carried out in a very similar fashion to that of a fortnight earlier, under a thick smoke screen and heavy bombardment. Nine British divisions took part. Although Loßberg described this as the heaviest attack he could remember, British gains amounted to no more than a few hundred metres for the loss of 8,000 men. The German corps commanders were able to cope using only their own resources and required no extra help from army or Army Group reserves. Three major factors contributed to the disappointing outcome. First, the British never achieved the same artillery dominance that they had on 9 April. German artillery had been reinforced while the British had not. Counter-battery intelligence had been unable to plot the positions of German batteries so thoroughly. On 9 April many of the German observation posts on Vimy Ridge had been overrun, leaving the guns blind. The same did not recur on 23 April. Second, the British troops were tired, in some cases having been in action repeatedly for a fortnight. Third, this time the German reserves were quickly on hand. Already by midday they were working to seal off and eliminate enemy break-ins. Another British attack on 28 April with six divisions suffered from all the same drawbacks and managed only to capture the village of Arleux.[15]

On 3 May Sixth Army found itself under full-scale attack once more, as fourteen British divisions from three different armies attacked over 22 kilometres from Bullecourt to Fresnoy. Once again, the Germans felt under little threat. British command mistakes helped. A late change of time for Zero Hour left plans in confusion and formations in disarray. The assault waves found themselves silhouetted against a setting moon, offering easy targets. When German infantry judged the assault imminent, they moved forward into the shell-holes of No Man's Land to escape the bombardment and fight a mobile battle, disrupting the enemy until he was thrown back by a counter-attack coming from deep. British units seemed unable to cope with these counter-attacks, in some cases breaking and running. Overall, progress was minimal. The only gain, the village of Fresnoy, was recaptured by Bavarian troops a few days later. 'We have every reason to be happy about yesterday's events', wrote Rupprecht in his diary. Although Bullecourt remained the focus of bloody combat for another fortnight and there were occasional flare-ups of violence elsewhere along the Sixth Army front until 24 May, the Battle of Arras had lost any purpose it might ever have had by nightfall on 3 May. Rupprecht noted that British attacks later that month were merely repeating the pattern observed in the later Somme battles: uncoordinated, poorly synchronized, small-scale, local operations. German attention began switching to Flanders and on 30 May Sixth Army formally reported that it expected no further major offensives in its sector.[16]

Nearly another quarter of a million men were killed, wounded, or captured in the Battle of Arras. Again, for every soldier the Germans lost, the British lost two. The original idea for the battle had been 'to pin the enemy... draw in his reserves, and thereby facilitate the task of the main French attack'. None of these objectives was achieved. Even the normally sympathetic British official historian could not resist a jibe: 'as usual, performance had lagged behind promise'. The British never looked like breaking through to Cambrai. Even before it became clear that Nivelle had failed, any idea of joining hands with the French seemed far-fetched. Arras neither distracted the Germans away from the impending French attack nor sucked in their reserves before the main blow fell in the south. The Germans knew Nivelle was coming and bolstered their defences accordingly. Indeed, if anything Arras served to make the Germans even more alert. There were plenty of fresh formations available to meet the double threat. Between 1 March and 20 April, the Germans sent more divisions to reinforce the Chemin des Dames (eighteen) than to Arras (fourteen) and still held at least another dozen in reserve. Short-lived and unsuccessful as the Nivelle offensive was, it accounted for nearly twice as many German soldiers as Arras did.[17]

Even seen purely as an exercise in attrition, while the Entente of course could absorb more casualties than the Central Powers, especially now that the United States had joined the war, to be losing men so much faster than Germany was hardly a palatable long-term approach. There was a danger that, as the French General Fayolle had noted of his men on the Somme the previous year, men of the Entente might become 'fed up with getting themselves killed, with no important success, no decision'. This was all the more true when it seemed that at least some of the losses were rooted in a failure to learn from previous mistakes. The British official historian, with uncharacteristic bluntness, asked why the Battle of Arras became 'profoundly disappointing' after the triumph of Easter Monday. He identified three problems which impacted the British ability to fight effectively after the first day. The first was an external factor, to some extent beyond British control. The difficult terrain, and especially the problems faced building roads across the shattered battlefield, constrained supply and slowed the tempo of operations, allowing the Germans time to prepare their defences. Second, commanders erred in repeatedly sending tired troops into improvised local attacks when the situation called for a pause to prepare a new large-scale full-dress offensive. The third factor was more fundamental, however. The underlying problem was that, as Cyril Falls put it, 'the atmosphere of siege warfare hung about the British army when it passed to open or semi-open warfare, and it was by no means only the rank and file or junior officers who were still affected by it'. This came through in many ways. Staffs would plan thoroughly for the first day, but fail to consider what might happen thereafter, becoming intellectually paralysed by the inevitable uncertainties involved. Too often, instead of the chain of command remaining flexible, it became rigid. With communications inevitably poor, the centre tried to exert greater control itself rather than to delegate authority to the man on the spot. Artillery might be devastating to begin with but, once deprived of thorough intelligence and struggling with the problems of redeployment forwards, the guns rapidly lost effectiveness. Infantry performed well when working to the script, but improvised less impressively, at least until it had the opportunity to learn on the job. In summary, the army could be quite effective on the first day of an offensive but became hesitant and unsure when asked to go off-script. That, Falls implied, was largely a failure of training.[18]

To Falls' three we can add three more. First, as Jim Beach has shown, Haig and his intelligence staff made the mistake, for neither the first nor the last time in the war, of under-estimating available enemy reserves and reading too much into strategic reports of uncertain value. They assumed that anecdotal reports of German home-front discontent would translate into exploitable battlefield weakness. Second, the new German elastic defence, when properly used, was sufficient to contain and ultimately defeat British attacks. The contrast between outcomes on 9 April, when the defence was shallow, and 23 April, 28 April, and 3–4 May, when it was arrayed in depth with reserves ready to counter-attack promptly, demonstrates the truth of this at the tactical level. But it was true operationally, too. While the British were able to overrun the first and second German positions, the next line of defence stood firm and prevented a breakthrough. Third, the Germans proved quicker to learn and adapt than the British. The tactical tweaks the BEF had introduced over the winter of 1916/17 could overwhelm an old-style German defence, as 9 April showed. When the Germans began to defend more skilfully in depth, however, the British were lost once more. As Rupprecht reported to OHL on 13 May, elastic defence had now worked well in three major battles. It was not leading to increased casualties, as had been feared. According to Loßberg, the troops liked the new approach.[19]

The Germans worked hard at learning and disseminating lessons as they went along. For instance, in early May Rupprecht held a conference where the General Officer Commanding (GOC) of the 3rd Bavarian Infantry Division ran through recent lessons of the fighting in which he had taken part. A practical demonstration of how to operate a mobile elastic defence followed on the training ground, with every formation in the Army Group represented.[20] OHL was continually collating data on enemy attack methods and comparing them with German tactics.[21]

That is not to say, however, that everything was for the best in the best of all possible German worlds. In particular, there were signs of growing rigidity within the German command set-up. On 1 May, for instance, Sixth Army sought to increase its tactical control at the expense of its subordinates' initiative. Below ordered generals commanding divisions and corps to check with Army headquarters before undertaking any retreat.[22] Less than two weeks later, Ludendorff started micro-managing the deployment of a division in Second Army and even ordered that henceforth no division was to be moved without his agreement. 'Such a reduction of my powers is definitely too much', complained Rupprecht in his diary. 'What's the point of having army groups, if every decision must be approved by OHL? Ludendorff cannot oversee every detail on every front. If he wanted to do so he inevitably would neglect some other and more important missions. The paperwork generated by [his] inquiries and answers to them has in any case already grown a lot.'[23] By the spring of 1917, the relaxation in command Ludendorff and Hindenburg sponsored the previous autumn was fading away. Central control was being reasserted and the flow of information upwards, as we have seen, was losing its purity. The German army was reverting to type and the weaknesses which would lose it the war were coming once more to the fore.

16

The Battle for Flanders

Summer 1917

The double failure of the spring smashed British and French hopes. With Nivelle's methods discredited and the morale of the French army vulnerable, they would obviously have to change approach. On 4–5 May statesmen and soldiers meeting in Paris resolved to carry out a series of low-risk, limited-objective attacks. With luck, these might achieve local successes and over time build up to exhaust Germany's power of resistance. The Germans needed little more than common sense to guess this would be the case. Nonetheless, it was confirmed by one of their highly placed agents in Paris.[1]

Where would the next offensive strike? Back in April Oberste Heeresleitung (OHL) had already begun to worry about the threat to Flanders. If the British Expeditionary Force (BEF) drove east and swept the Germans from the higher ground overlooking the Ypres Salient, it might be able to threaten vital railway nodes at Roulers and Courtrai, undermining the whole German position in Belgium and threatening the U-boat bases along the coast. Worryingly, rail activity in the British rear seemed to be picking up so Kuhl visited the German Fourth Army, commanded by General Friedrich Sixt von Armin, which was responsible for the defence of Belgium. After his tour, Kuhl highlighted the weakness of the defences in the mini-salient south of Ypres around the villages of Wytschaete and Messines. The Germans had held the high ground here since autumn 1914, not least because the ridge commanded excellent fields of fire towards the British lines. To cover No Man's Land, however, the defenders had to occupy trenches on the westward, forward slope. Such positions, once relatively sensible, were now highly vulnerable to the artillery-intensive methods of the BEF, as the battle for Vimy Ridge had shown. Further, the terrain of the

ridge itself militated against a defence in depth, as it had at Vimy. If the
Germans lost the crest, the next suitable position to defend was the Flanders
Line, some 10 kilometres back. To avoid this danger, Kuhl suggested withdrawal to an intermediate Third, or Warneton, Line, but Sixt and his commanders all argued for holding in place. Rupprecht and Kuhl were not
prepared to overrule the men on the spot. Instead, they sent a division of
infantry and some gun batteries as reinforcements.

Throughout the second half of May it became more obvious almost
every day that an attack on Messines was approaching. British artillery more
than doubled in strength between March and June. The Royal Flying Corps
was getting more active in the air and almost every night the British sent
groups of infantry off across No Man's Land to raid the German trenches.
Equally, British forces further south seemed to be thinning out, making
operations there less likely. Radio intercepts showed that Canadian troops
around Loos were being sent on leave. Relative quiet in the rest of the Ypres
Salient suggested that any attack on Messines would be a local attack, rather
than part of a larger operation, at least for now. By early June it seemed
imminent.[2]

The Germans were as prepared as they could be. The garrison had been
reinforced and no fewer than four defensive positions had been built, one
behind the other. Concrete pillboxes and blockhouses protected command
posts and machine-gun nests. Reserves stood nearby. The British artillery
bombardment, three and a half million shells between 26 May and 6 June,
flattened the villages of Messines and Wytschaete, cut barbed wire, and neutralized German batteries. About a quarter of German field guns, and nearly
half of the heavy artillery, was put out of action by counter-battery fire. The
front line was reduced to a wasteland of craters a kilometre deep. Only one
artillery observation post survived. Two of four German divisions garrison-
ing the front under this bombardment had to be relieved even before the
enemy infantry assault began.[3]

For all the warnings the defenders had received, when the attack came it
still took them by almost complete surprise, because the British used a
weapon the Germans had overlooked: the mine. Under-estimating the British
ability to tunnel deep, the defenders discounted the possibility of large-
scale mining against the Messines Ridge. At ten minutes past four on the
morning of 7 June 1917 they were proved catastrophically wrong. Half a
million kilograms of explosive, in nineteen different mines, went off together
underneath the middle of the German front lines. The German official

history quotes an observer: 'we saw nineteen giant roses with bright red petals, or immense mushrooms, rise slowly and majestically out of the ground. They then broke apart with a dull roar. Immediately afterwards bright multi-coloured pillars of fire and smoke shot skyward, carrying earth and debris up with them.' The earthquake was felt 30 kilometres away; the roar could be heard in London. The 3rd Bavarian Infantry Division, defending Messines itself, effectively lost all its three forward battalions in the mine explosions. Only three officers and thirty men survived.[4]

Even before the roar of the explosions had faded away, the guns of British Second Army opened up again. The artillery plan was the most sophisticated yet. It incorporated three main belts of fire, 650 metres deep. Two-thirds of the field artillery delivered a creeping barrage which rolled forwards ahead of the assaulting infantry at a rate of 100 metres every two minutes. Machine-guns also took part. Further ahead, targets of importance such as command posts and machine-gun nests were singled out and bombarded until overrun. All the while, counter-battery missions neutralized enemy artillery. The infantry of nine British divisions advanced to the attack, supported by seventy-two of the new Mark IV tanks.

The resistance they faced was, on the whole, feeble. Those defenders who had not been killed or wounded by the bombardment or mine blasts were badly shaken. In many cases they either gave themselves up or headed for the rear. Clouds of smoke and dust blocked both defensive fire and effective command and control. The latter had been further complicated by a decision to split responsibility for the defence between two ad hoc battlegroups. The British rolled easily over the front line and, by four hours after Zero Hour, had seized control of almost the entire German second line along the crest of the ridge, including the ruins of Wytschaete and Messines. Here they planned to dig in, consolidate, and, with the benefit of uninterrupted observation over the German rear, meet and defeat any counter-attacks. At around three p.m. a second phase would follow, with fresh troops passing through to continue the attack. Their objective lay down the east side of the ridge at the Oostaverne Line (known to the Germans as the Sehnenstellung) which ran across the base of the salient.

As the British troops dug in along the crest they found themselves silhouetted against the skyline and uncomfortably tightly packed into a small area. Losses to machine-gun and artillery fire were heavy. Nonetheless, the British plan seemed to be working well. German reserves turned out once more to be too far back to counter-attack effectively. Some had to march 16 kilometres before they reached the battlefield. Worse, they were unfamiliar with the ground and exposed to British shelling as they approached. Conflicting orders from the two battlegroup commanders injected further confusion. The reserve divisions ended up being committed piecemeal and late. Counter-attacks which were planned for the morning did not take place until mid-afternoon. By then, the British were easily strong enough to beat them back into the Oostaverne Line, although the BEF's second-wave attack then met little success in turn.[5]

Rupprecht could not achieve much on 7 June. This was a short, sharp corps-level defensive battle which even the men on the spot had difficulty keeping control of. In his diary, he queried some aspects of the handling of the battle. Why did the reserves arrive late? Why had Fourth Army not rotated divisions out of the line sooner, if they were worn out? He doubted his men were strong enough to recapture the Messines Ridge. Could they hold on to the Oostaverne Line, though? Rupprecht felt that, as soon as the British moved guns up on the high ground, this position, too, would become untenable.

What to do next? The corps commander at Messines, General Maximilian von Laffert, had also been shaken by the events of 7 June. His first reaction was to retreat over the River Lys. This risked losing much of the artillery, though, and Fourth Army forbade it. Sixt proposed staying put and seeing what turned up. Rupprecht favoured a retreat of some 10 kilometres into the Flandern-Stellung (Flanders Line), while Kuhl was more conservative. He expected a major follow-up offensive at Ypres and was keen to protect the southern flank of their positions there, so did not want to pull back too far. He again suggested a compromise, pulling back into a new position built around the old Third (Warneton) Line and along the banks of the Ypres–Comines Canal. Eventually, after repeated pressure for a decision from Ludendorff, on 10 June Kuhl told Sixt to withdraw to this intermediate position that evening. The British took over the evacuated Oostaverne Line but were in no position further to exploit their success. By 14 June, major operations in the Battle of Messines ceased.[6]

Messines was, without doubt, a BEF victory. The British achieved their objective of seizing the ridge. They could now push ahead with their plans for a further drive out of the Ypres Salient in July. They took over 7,000 prisoners and inflicted some 25,000 casualties on the Germans. They owed their success, the German official history later concluded, to five main factors. First, the British were superior in both manpower and matériel, especially in artillery where they outnumbered the Germans by more than three to one. Second, the mines had a tremendous impact, destroying defences and demoralizing defenders. Third, the German forward slope positions were flawed and vulnerable. Fourth, the British had been able to enfilade the defenders from both flanks. Lastly, the counter-attack divisions arrived too late.

The German command, however, need not get too depressed by the Battle of Messines. At least one of these five factors was unrepeatable. Mining on such a scale would not be feasible again. Further, as Rupprecht noted, 'the British are great at painstaking planning of attacks, but never manage to exploit their initial success'. The British remained unable to earn maximum return on the huge investment of resources involved in battles such as Messines. British casualties were also around 25,000 men. How long would they be able to carry on with such a costly way of war, when the returns were so slight? The main lesson Rupprecht drew from Messines was that his defence must be more elastic and mobile, not only to pull back from positions that were vulnerable to superior enemy artillery, but also to exploit the German army's perceived comparative advantage in open warfare.[7]

That the Battle of Messines would be followed by a further British attack in Flanders was partly a matter of common sense. Unrest in France, both at home and in the army, made a major French effort unlikely. The British could not logistically support an attack across the old Somme battlefield and the area devastated by ALBERICH. They had been fought to a standstill in Artois. Only Flanders remained. German intelligence estimated the most likely effort would combine a drive up onto the ridges surrounding Ypres with a push along the coast, perhaps supported by amphibious landings. It was clearly desirable that Germany have the ablest possible command team in Flanders to meet this onslaught. Messines had shown that Sixt and his chief of staff, Stapff, were not the best. Loßberg, the acknowledged defence expert in the German army, was currently chief of staff to Sixth Army around Arras, under the tough and experienced Otto von Below. Kuhl and Ludendorff discussed the problem on 12 June. They felt that, since Loßberg and Sixt would not collaborate well, just swapping over the chiefs of staff would not work. Instead, Kuhl proposed exchanging the entire staffs of Fourth and Sixth Armies. Ludendorff agreed. So did Loßberg. Rupprecht approved the idea and forwarded it to Hindenburg. When the Field Marshal took the proposal to the Kaiser, however, Ludendorff told Kuhl, something seemed to go wrong. Stapff and Loßberg were ordered to change places without anything further being mentioned about the army commanders, much less the rest of the staffs. Two days later, Kuhl and Loßberg tried again to get Sixt moved. This time, Ludendorff told the full story. There had been no mistake on the first occasion. Instead, the Kaiser had vetoed any change of army commander. This was his form of revenge. Six months previously, Rupprecht had got two corps commanders sacked for poor performance after the Somme, despite both men having served at the Kaiser's court as imperial adjutants. Wilhelm II remained piqued. Kuhl's diary entry finishes on an incredulous note at this pettiness: 'Does he not realize the seriousness of the situation?'[8]

Hard evidence that the British were planning an offensive in Flanders multiplied as the summer continued. The Germans watched as enemy engineers built roads, railways, and camps for the new troops arriving. Diversionary operations around Arras fooled no-one. British artillery began to build up in the salient and BEF units replaced Belgian troops in the bridgehead over the Yser at Nieuport, which Sixt attacked on 10 July in a successful attempt to disrupt plans for an attack along the coast.

On 11 July the Royal Flying Corps launched an offensive to win control of the air over Flanders. The result was some of the largest aerial battles of history so far. On 26 July, for example, a battle developed over Polygon Wood in which no fewer than ninety-four fighters eventually became embroiled. By then, the pace of the British concentration was picking up. German intelligence identified nearly twice as many batteries opposite Fourth Army as a fortnight previously. In response, Rupprecht built up Fourth Army's reserves of both manpower and matériel. Net, Sixt received eight divisions in May, five in June, and a further four in July. Fourth Army expanded to seventeen divisions in the front line and thirteen and a half in reserve, representing nearly half the strength of Rupprecht's Army Group. Loßberg began to build new defensive positions on the Passchendaele Ridge and Gheluvelt Plateau, so that the British would now have to fight through between five and seven lines of defence in a zone more than 12 kilometres deep.[9]

On 15 July the British guns began to register their targets with ranging shots. Within ten days it was clear to Rupprecht that a full-scale artillery battle was underway. Despite poor weather, German guns could not always keep up with the pace of action. Thirty per cent of the heavy guns in Gruppe Wytschaete had broken down or were put out of action by enemy fire. Rupprecht noted that the bombardment was heavier than during the

worst days on the Somme. Indeed, where in July 1916 the British had fired
1.7 million rounds from about 1,400 guns, a year later at Ypres a little over
3,000 barrels let loose nearly 4.3 million shells. Three times as many shells
hit each kilometre of front as on the Somme. One single German battery
reported being targeted by no fewer than a thousand rounds. Although the
bombardment did a good job of destroying the German front line on the
left and centre of the planned attack, little damage was done on the right,
on the Gheluvelt Plateau, where the terrain was more difficult, or to the
German rearward defences. The British commander at Ypres, Sir Hubert
Gough, was once again setting objectives too deep for the weight of fire he
had available.[10]

On 31 July nine British and two French divisions launched the main
attack, jumping off at ten minutes to five in the morning. On the left, the
French made their objectives and more. Their mission, however, was only to
guard the flank of Gough's Fifth Army. The main British attack had mixed
results. On the left and in the centre, Gough's men advanced about
2,700 metres and captured their second objectives. Stiffening resistance prevented them reaching the third, as did a breakdown in coordination with
the artillery. On the right, up on the Gheluvelt Plateau, the British were
much less successful. The German artillery here had escaped the worst of
the counter-battery fire and was able to target the British infantrymen, who
were advancing too slowly to keep up with the creeping barrage. Soft ground
and the need to clear the many copses and woods in their way caused delay.
The defenders had plenty of time to block this increasingly uncoordinated
assault. They restricted the British to a gain of about 900 metres.[11]

Fifth Army remained less than halfway to its day one objectives, had suffered heavily, and had badly under-estimated German powers of resistance
and counter-attack. Nevertheless, relative to some of the operations which
had gone before and, indeed, some of those which came later, it is possible
to see 31 July as a success of a kind. Robin Prior and Trevor Wilson have
pointed out that overrunning a couple of defence lines, capturing 45 square
kilometres of enemy territory, and clearing away German observation posts
overlooking the town of Ypres were all solid achievements, especially compared to the 6 square kilometres taken on the first day of the Somme.
British casualties, at 31,850 men, were heavy in absolute terms but unsur-
prising for an attack of this scale and nature, and again looked light relative
to 1 July 1916. In any case, the Germans had suffered heavily too. Fourth
Army lost about 30,000 men in the last ten days of July. The failure to clear

the Gheluvelt Plateau, however, left the Germans able to enfilade the flank of any attack further north and would haunt subsequent British operations for weeks.[12]

The action of 31 July, now known as the Battle of Pilckem Ridge, caused little concern within the German command. Fourth Army had everywhere been able to contain the attack with its own resources. On the first day of every previous battle examined so far, the defenders' almost immediate reaction was to call for reinforcements. This time, Fourth Army felt no need. Rupprecht looked on with great calm:

> I was looking forward to the attack with the greatest equanimity, since we had never been so strong on a front under attack and our reserves had never been so rehearsed in their roles as we were that day.... Considering the strength of the enemy attack and the fact that experience tells us that the first blow is the most dangerous, we have plenty to be happy about with the events of today's fighting.

Ludendorff alone seems to have fretted. He telephoned Kuhl many times for updates during the day. This may tell us more about the stress he was feeling than about the battle. By 2 August, however, he was more confident and asking Fourth Army to give up divisions for the sake of operations in Russia.[13]

There was no room for complacency, however. The usual process of after-action review went ahead. Some intriguing points emerged. Rupprecht blamed the French success on the collapse of a Saxon division and poor leadership by the corps commander, General Martin Chales de Beaulieu. The most noteworthy feature was the poor quality of the British infantry. They were over-reliant on artillery support and went to ground as soon as they came under even the slightest machine-gun or rifle fire. Another old issue came up again: who was to control counter-attacks by the rapid response (Eingreif) divisions? Was it to be the commander of the division itself, or the man in charge of the defence forward? It is striking that this obvious and important question, which we saw come up before at Arras, had not been resolved even after some six months of practical experience of the new defensive methods.[14]

Rain started to fall late on 31 July and did not stop for three days and nights. August continued wetter than average, with only three dry days, and the salient rapidly became a series of huge swamps. The poor conditions inevitably made operations more difficult for the attacker. It became especially hard to move guns and shells. Even for the defenders, though, the weather caused major problems. Shell holes and trenches filled with water.

Troops were left out in the open, huddling under scraps of corrugated iron and wood in a desperate attempt to stay dry. Rupprecht worried that, in these conditions, with sleep difficult, units would wear out and need relief more rapidly. This concern proved exaggerated, but it was not groundless: on the Somme, the average division had sustained 4,000 casualties during a fortnight's stint in the front line, whereas in early August 1917 German formations were having to be replaced after losing only half as many. The mud made reliefs themselves tricky. Heavy British use of gas made moving food and supplies up to the front even more difficult. Bearers slipped and slid through the slime as they carried supplies forward in the dark and found it hard to fit their respirators in time. One Bavarian division alone had 1,200 men gassed. On balance, though, Kuhl felt the rain was more help than hindrance: 'We're lucky, the weather is very bad, constant rain, in Flanders the soil is without foundations, so one can only proceed on the roads. Thus we have time to regroup, carry out reliefs, etc.'[15]

Regardless of the poor weather, General Gough was eager to push his men on. In addition to a number of smaller actions, he launched a series of major attacks over the next few weeks, all of them disastrous, all of them suggesting that he had learnt none of the lessons of previous battles. Ill-prepared and poorly coordinated attacks threw tired units against unsuppressed defences. The results were depressingly predictable. On 10 August, two British divisions again made no significant progress on the Gheluvelt Plateau but lost 2,200 men. The Battle of Langemarck on 16 August saw a broad-front assault by nine British divisions, plus the French again. Again, the Germans lost ground in the north but their defences in the centre and south held firm. On the difficult terrain of the Gheluvelt Plateau, the British made their third assault on alert defenders and chalked up their third failure. Altogether, the British suffered 15,000 casualties. The Germans lost St Julien to a special operation involving tanks on 19 August but larger operations, such as those on 22 and 27 August, made little progress. From now on, Gough's troops were capable only of sporadic and disjointed narrow-front assaults, five of which were launched in the early days of the next month. By then Haig had finally stepped in and forbidden exactly that kind of penny-packet attack. He had also transferred responsibility for capturing the Gheluvelt Plateau from Gough to Plumer, so it is hard to understand what Gough was trying to prove.

The results of the August fighting were, for the British, extremely disappointing. There had been no breakthrough, much less any chance of linking up with an amphibious force. Indeed, the final objectives set for 31 July mostly still remained in German hands. By 28 August, Gough had lost 68,000 men with little to show in return. Within the British ranks, the official history noted, 'discontent was general' at the poor decisions taken and worse conditions endured. To Rupprecht, British troops were definitely inferior to their German opponents: they would not advance under fire and were offering almost no resistance to counter-attacks. Even officers were surrendering freely. British bravery seemed to have declined since Arras. A Fourth Army conference reviewed German defensive tactics since 31 July. Unsurprisingly given his success, Sixt decided that there was no need to change anything. Even through the prism of attrition, the Germans had little as yet to worry about. Although the rate of ammunition consumption was worrying, Fourth Army losses between 21 July and 31 August were 58,794, almost 10,000 fewer than the British had suffered. Early worries that the pace of rotation of divisions in the front line would need to increase, putting unsustainable pressure on reserves, were proving unfounded. The average German division was managing to stay in line for twenty-two days or even longer. However grim the conditions the front-line soldiers were having to endure, British pressure was plainly insufficient. Indeed, Rupprecht was amazed by the slow pace of British operations and keen that his Army Group should hold out without begging for aid from OHL. Kuhl estimated that they could do so until the beginning of October. A heavy attack from the supposedly exhausted French at Verdun on 20 August only made this more important. In the course of August, eighteen divisions were rotated in and out of Fourth Army but there was no need yet to reinforce the defenders at Ypres in net terms.[16]

Indeed, as the British push petered out in early September, Ludendorff felt able to transfer three divisions and twenty-five artillery batteries away from Fourth Army to support operations elsewhere. By the middle of September morale among the defenders was extremely high. Rupprecht and the German high command were convinced that the enemy offensive at Ypres had fizzled out. They were almost ready to declare victory. When heavy artillery fire opened up on the southern half of the salient on 15 September, it was at first written off as being just for show. When the bombardment intensified two days later, however, it became clear that there was no room yet to relax. To the front-line commanders on the spot, another major British assault seemed imminent.[17]

17

The Battle for Flanders
To Passchendaele

On the morning of 20 September, Kuhl arrived back at headquarters from an overnight visit to Oberste Heeresleitung (OHL). He was astonished to find a full-scale battle underway. The campaign had kicked back into life. What became known as the Battle of the Menin Road Ridge began at twenty to six that morning when nine British divisions attacked on a front 9 kilometres wide, supported by some three times the weight of fire laid down on 31 July. German after-action reports later stressed the sophistication of the attackers' fire-plan but expressed pride that machine-guns, deployed in depth, had halted the British assault short of the artillery positions. The Germans, however, were merely stopping the British from something they had no intention of doing in the first place. General Sir Herbert Plumer had taken over the main British effort and made two changes to British Expeditionary Force (BEF) assault methods. First, he adopted looser infantry formations to avoid the thick concentrations of troops which had been so vulnerable to enemy fire, for instance at Messines. Second, he chose not to set objectives deep in the rear. Experience had shown that doing so risked the attackers losing momentum and outrunning their artillery support, leaving tired troops vulnerable to counter-attacks. Instead, he opted for shallow objectives, less than 1,500 metres deep and well within his own artillery range. He aimed to overrun the thin enemy front-line garrison, seize a manageable bite of the enemy defences and rapidly consolidate what he had grabbed, then defeat the inevitable counter-attacks. This is in fact what happened on 20 September. The whole process would then be repeated a few days later, with another operation following soon after, and so on. The British intention, therefore, was to grind, rather than burst, through the German defences, chewing up defenders as they went.[1]

Plumer's next operation, the Battle of Polygon Wood on 26 September, reinforced the effectiveness of the new British methods. Plumer had trouble moving artillery up to new positions so he reduced the scale and ambition of his operation, narrowing the frontage to 8,000 metres and setting even shallower objectives, not much more than 1,000 metres deep. The British broadly achieved these, clearing most of Zonnebeke and Polygon Wood. Again, German counter-attacks developed too late in the day and broke on the new positions the attackers had speedily dug themselves into.[2]

The Germans seemed powerless to prevent the relentless British march forward and they were getting rattled. In late September, for the first time in the campaign, OHL decided to reinforce Fourth Army with three fresh divisions. Less could be done about ammunition consumption, which remained worryingly high. Even on relatively quiet days, Fourth Army was firing off more train-loads of shells than the whole Army Group was receiving daily. During days of battle such as 20 September, they might use more than twice as many.[3]

With hindsight, we can see that the Germans had less to worry about than they thought. It is hard to interpret the Battles of Menin Road Ridge and Polygon Wood as significant British successes except relative to the disasters which had gone before. The casualty figures, as always, are heartbreaking. The two armies together lost 75,000 men in the September fighting, about half each. Since 31 July the British had lost 86,000 men and had advanced 6 kilometres towards the German rail junctions still over 30 kilometres distant. How many more men must fall to get that far?[4]

At the time, however, German commanders were deeply worried that there was something wrong with their tactics. In a flurry of meetings and memoranda, they frantically tried to diagnose what was going wrong. There are two different narratives of how the Germans responded to the threat of Plumer's 'bite-and-hold' approach. The traditional version was set out in the official history and has been repeated frequently since. It is flawed but worth outlining before we look at this in a more fruitful way.

According to the German official history, the Battles of the Menin Road Ridge and Polygon Wood underlined once more the fundamental flaw of elastic defence. Relying on counter-attacks could work, if they were mounted at the right time. To do so, however, was nearly impossible on the often devastated, and always lethal, First World War battlefield, where communication and movement were so difficult. As Rupprecht pointed out, if reserves were stationed close behind the front line, they were not only vulnerable to artillery fire, but would also often find themselves in action before the enemy's main axis of thrust had become clear. If they were kept too far back, on the other hand, they arrived too late, when the enemy had already had a chance to dig in.[5] Loßberg proposed reverting to the old style of holding the front line much more firmly to make an enemy break-in harder. If ground was lost nonetheless, Eingreif divisions should be held back to take part in a well-organized set-piece offensive at a later date, rather than frittered away in improvised attacks at short notice. These ideas were formalized in orders issued by OHL on 28 September and by Fourth Army two days later.[6]

Loßberg's new tactics failed completely, however, at the Battle of Broodseinde on 4 October. After no special artillery preparation, twelve British divisions attacked. One of Rupprecht's staff officers, Major Prager, described this as 'surely the toughest battle so far', with the British heavy artillery fire being particularly 'smothering'. The German front-line garrison was suppressed and swamped. For example, the 4th Guards Division had increased the proportion of their strength in the front line as instructed. When the attack began, the forward garrison was taken by surprise, blinded by thick clouds of smoke and dust, and overrun. Thickening up the forward defence in this way, the Guards reported, only increased casualties. The Germans lost another kilometre of ground and the village of Broodseinde. For a while, indeed, Rupprecht thought his line was broken. The Eingreif divisions had to be thrown in to prop up the buckling line and were no more available for set-piece counter-attacks than they had been under the previous scheme. The Germans had at last been pushed off most of the Gheluvelt Plateau, exposing the southern flank of the Passchendaele Ridge. The British lost 20,000 men.

The next day Rupprecht advised Fourth Army to end the experiment with holding the front line rigidly and move back to an elastic defence in depth. On 7 October this policy, the third in two weeks, was written into orders from both OHL and Fourth Army. From now on, the front line was to constitute little more than a screen. A small force, based in shell holes rather than trench lines, would cover a Forward Zone ('Vorfeld'), between 500 and 1,000 metres deep. This stretched back to the Main Line of Resistance (MLR; in German, 'Hauptwiderstandslinie'). In the event of a major enemy offensive, the forward garrison was to pull back across the Forward Zone and into the MLR, where the battle proper would be fought, supported by reserves moving up from deep.[7]

According to the German official history, therefore, the move away from a 'modern' elastic defence in depth was largely the idea of one man: Fritz von Loßberg. When Broodseinde showed that his rigid forward defence did nothing to help stop the British either, the German army quickly wrote it off as an aberration and reverted to an elastic defence. This traditional narrative very neatly suited the German military writers who constructed it. First, it blamed a single individual, Loßberg, and deflected criticism from OHL and the rest of the General Staff. Second, it painted a rational and systematic picture of the German way of working. Most of the historians concerned, of course, had been members of the General Staff, and many of OHL, during the war and liked to think of themselves as the brains of the army. Third, it reinforced the case for elastic defence, which was an important tenet of German military thought between the wars.[8]

This traditional narrative considerably over-simplified what had happened, however. More importantly, it deflected attention away from the real problems the Germans were facing in the autumn of 1917. First, although it is impossible to untangle exactly who first advocated the switch back to a more forward approach, it was not all Loßberg's fault. OHL was heavily involved. Indeed, OHL issued orders calling for a forward defence on 28 September, two days before Loßberg spoke at Courtrai and issued similar orders to Fourth Army. Second, whatever the orders, it is far from clear that every front-line unit was able to adjust their tactics in time for that to be a major factor in defeat at Broodseinde. For every formation which followed the new instructions, like the Guards, there were others which complained that it was impossible to follow all the twists and turns of new doctrine. The 119th Division, for instance, was at the front for sixty-seven straight days from 11 August to 18 October. It pointed out that new orders incorporating the latest lessons learnt were of only limited use with no opportunity to train. Third, there were simpler explanations for the problems the Germans were facing. These spoke far more to the operational level of war than the tactical. The cumulative effect of attrition was beginning to make itself felt. Although a net six divisions reinforced Fourth Army in the first ten days of October, quality was slipping. Rupprecht noted on 5 October that the only replacement divisions available were either inexperienced and in need of further training, or those whose confidence had been shaken by repeated defeats. Even formerly good divisions had been weakened by absorbing large numbers of recruits. Poor leadership was a problem, too. Rupprecht felt that even Loßberg temporarily lost his nerve at one point during the

Battle of Broodseinde. The commander of Gruppe Ypern, General Alfred Graf zu Dohna-Schlobitten, had more experience at the imperial court than he had of the Western Front, let alone commanding at this level. Rupprecht regarded him as 'a military non-entity' and he was sacked from the hottest seat on the Western Front the day after Broodseinde, after three defeats in less than a month. The most decisive factor on 4 October, however, was, as so often during the war, the guns. As Rupprecht noted in his diary the next day, even though Fourth Army fired off a record thirty train-loads of ammunition, British firepower was overwhelming. The Germans had no answer.[9]

The response to Plumer's 'bite-and-hold' operations of September and early October teaches us two interesting broader lessons about the German army. First, the German General Staff sought tactical solutions to what was in fact an operational challenge. This was not because they were stupid, but because they knew they had no operational solution to offer. Ludendorff, for instance, as he warned of the dangers of high enemy tempo and the problems this was causing on the railways, explicitly spoke of the need to use tactics to reduce attrition. The tendency of the German military to seek military solutions to political problems and to attempt to offset operational weakness with tactical brilliance is a recurring theme in its history from Schlieffen to Stalingrad. Second, it highlights the intellectual arrogance of its commanders. Men such as Ludendorff were convinced not only that a single solution to their difficulties existed but also that they could find it.

This had two important consequences. First, it blinded them to the possibility that in fact there might be no panacea, and that different situations might require different responses. Second, it meant that doctrine formulation became increasingly centralized and dogmatic. While this did not altogether preclude bottom-up innovation, it did restrict the initiative of subordinate commanders and render the Germans predictable to their enemies. Although neither Rupprecht nor Kuhl was comfortable with this tendency, it proved difficult to overcome. On 2 October Rupprecht visited Fourth Army and told Sixt to avoid over schematic approaches and over-centralization. He was to allow his subordinates more latitude for initiative so they could operate less predictably. When Rupprecht got back to his headquarters at Mons, he was infuriated to find there a copy of a highly detailed and schematic order just issued by Loßberg, setting out an artillery defence plan which even laid down the deployment of individual batteries. Two days later, Rupprecht again told Fourth Army to allow the corps commanders more scope to use their own initiative and to avoid employing the Eingreif divisions in too formulaic and predictable a manner. Kuhl, too, was worried: 'the new tactics which Loßberg invented were much too schematic. That is in general Loßberg's big mistake. We must leave more freedom.' 'Loßberg', Kuhl noted, 'is a great organizer, but not much of a tactician or strategist.' Rupprecht agreed, noting in his diary that the new tactics introduced on 7 October, which relied on close coordination between infantry and artillery as the forward garrison deliberately gave ground in the face of an enemy attack, displayed Ludendorff's lack of understanding of the difficulty of communications on the modern battlefield: 'it would be better if he did not bother himself with intervening too much in the details of tactical methods', he remarked. Further, the continuous stream of tactical instructions was proving bewildering: 'There is no cure-all. A pattern is harmful. The situation must be dealt with sometimes one way, sometimes another.' This tension between central and local solutions and control was not new in 1917, although we see it particularly clearly around the Battle of Broodseinde. We saw it at work on the Somme and before, and we shall see it again in 1918, for it was never resolved.[10]

Four days of heavy and persistent rain followed the Battle of Broodseinde. Both Gough and Plumer proposed closing down the Flanders campaign but Haig was determined to capture the Passchendaele Ridge. The next attack was set for 9 October and would involve eleven French and British divisions. In normal conditions, to launch another major attack after just five days would be ambitious. In the mud and wet it proved calamitous. Even to move troops and guns up proved extremely challenging. The night before Zero, some of the assault battalions took nearly ten hours to march 4 kilometres. Divisions which had enjoyed support from ninety guns on 20 September could now call on just twenty-five. The barrage was weak or invisible and 'no previous attack organized by the Second Army in the war had such an unfavourable start', wrote the official historian. In many places, the main attack did not even reach the German first line, much less penetrate it. Most of the defending divisions did not even have to call on their reserves. Total British casualties are unknown but heavy: just three of the assault divisions alone lost nearly 7,000 men between them.

Although the Battle of Poelcappelle was a clear German tactical victory, the operational strain on the defenders was worsening. Rupprecht was growing increasingly worried. The first ten days of October were the bloodiest single period of the whole Flanders campaign for Fourth Army.

It lost 29,000 men, or 17 per cent of its combat strength. Only September 1916 on the Somme had seen a higher casualty rate for any of Rupprecht's armies. The average battalion in late July had been 713 men strong. By 11 October, it was down to 621. Rupprecht noted that enemy artillery superiority was so stifling that nothing the Germans did seemed to help. 'Our most effective ally', he suggested, 'would be rain.' It was still just possible to find enough replacements but if the French renewed offensive operations further south, OHL would be unable to help further and Rupprecht's Army Group would have to stand alone. It might be necessary to pull the line back to dodge enemy attacks. Morale was also suffering, both in the trenches and at headquarters. To Kuhl, both Loßberg and Sixt seemed depressed and borderline unfit.[11]

Plumer remained committed to a high tempo of operations. The British decision to attack again on 12 October, however, was founded not in any understanding of the level of worry Rupprecht and his men were suffering, but in much vaguer intelligence about German home-front morale and a misunderstanding of the situation on the ground. By the time Plumer and Gough realized that the Battle of Poelcappelle had not been the success they had first imagined and that Passchendaele remained both further away and more heavily defended than they thought, it was too late. The British enjoyed even less success on 12 October, in the First Battle of Passchendaele, than they had three days previously. Poor weather, deep mud, and insufficient artillery support all contributed to disaster. In the rare places progress was made, it was measured in metres. Although Rupprecht believed that the new Forward Zone tactics had worked well, it is clear that he was misinformed about the extent of their use and over-estimated their impact. German tactics were not the decisive factor. Not only did different German corps try to employ different methods; even divisions within the corps went about things in a variety of ways. In the centre of the British attack, Gruppe Ypres in theory evacuated their deep Forward Zone when the enemy attacked, while on either wing Gruppe Dixmuide and Gruppe Wytschaete relied on a more traditional rigid forward defence. Even within Gruppe Ypres, divisions such as the 195th Infantry Division were unable to use the new tactics properly. Nonetheless, 13,000 British troops became casualties for no significant gain. Between 11 and 20 October, on the other hand, Fourth Army lost fewer than 10,000 men, a third of the casualties in the previous ten days.[12]

Such was the nature of 1917 communications, though, that the initial reports reaching Rupprecht on 12 October were worrying. The Passchendaele

Ridge, it seemed, was under serious threat. The Crown Prince moved two divisions up from reserve to restore the situation. By the next day it was clear that the situation was under control and Rupprecht felt free to go off hunting. Congestion on the railways was now his most immediate concern. The army was running some 900 trains daily and the network was so overloaded that no fresh reinforcements could reach him before 18 October. Still, the front-line troops were adequately rested, reserves were relatively plentiful, and there was no need for worry, in the short term at least. Observers such as the chief of staff of Gruppe Wytschaete, Lieutenant-Colonel Albrecht von Thaer, who had been very downbeat in later September, were pleased that things now seemed to be going well. Ludendorff was actually upbeat, telling Rupprecht that within two weeks they would have won the war. Rupprecht could not understand or share his optimism. The British, he felt, were quite capable of hammering away for another four to six weeks. After all, they had only suspended the Somme campaign when the weather made it impossible to carry on.[13]

A few days of relative quiet followed. Kuhl and the staff took advantage of the lull to begin planning for 1918, as we shall see in Chapter 19. The British restricted themselves to small-scale operations designed to keep the defenders busy and prepare for the next big push. The first stage of this unfolded on 26 October, with a main attack launched by two Canadian divisions aiming at the village of Passchendaele on its ridge. On the first day they made only 450 metres, about half of what they had hoped. Rupprecht noted another defensive victory. Although, as he also observed, 'the state of the ground defies all description', on 30 October another Canadian push saw them drive another 800 metres and reach the outskirts of Passchendaele itself. Five of the six Canadian battalions which spearheaded the assault suffered 50 per cent casualties.

Reinforcements and artillery ammunition were becoming causes for concern in the German ranks again. By 29 October Rupprecht's Army Group had no reserves left and even OHL could not be relied on to provide more than another two divisions, at best. Consumption of ammunition was running so high that Rupprecht worried he would run out within eight days. Finally, on 6 November the Canadians cleared the village of Passchendaele. The German defenders were blasted out of their positions by British guns. Yet again, communications broke down. It took three hours for counter-attack orders to reach the reserves, by which time it was too late to have any hope of success. Although, as Rupprecht said, 'the loss of Passchendaele is painful for us', lack of reserves due to transport delays meant the idea of a full-scale attack to recapture the ridge had to be abandoned. On 10 November the Canadians launched a further operation to consolidate their hold. This proved the last day of major fighting in the Second Battle of Passchendaele. The Canadian Corps lost nearly 13,000 men between 26 October and 11 November.[14]

On 12 November Fourth Army reported that there were no signs of preparations for a further attack. Rupprecht could begin to hope that the Battle for Flanders was over. This was confirmed three days later when intelligence noticed French troops being replaced in line by British and Belgians. OHL had already begun to redeploy forces away from Flanders and in all thirteen divisions were pulled out of the line for rest and retraining during November.[15]

The fighting in Flanders of the summer and autumn of 1917 devoured manpower and matériel at a ferocious rate. Hundreds of thousands of men fought on both sides and battle casualties probably totalled nearly half a million. Almost every division in the BEF fought at Ypres in 1917, as did nearly half the German divisions in the west. German casualties, at the worst estimate, were 217,000, British losses either 238,000 or 244,000, while the French lost about 8,500 men. The German Fourth Army fired 18 million shells or nearly 2,000 train-loads of ammunition; the British used perhaps six times as much. The emotional impact of the horrendous conditions cannot be over-estimated. Even Ludendorff realized that, for the soldiers fighting on the Passchendaele Ridge in the last stages of the campaign, 'it was no longer life at all. It was mere unspeakable suffering.' More soberly, the Bavarian history suggested that 'in probably none of the big defensive battles did the soldier suffer as much as in Flanders. Nowhere offered so little protection from enemy fire and the weather.'[16]

The British official history argued that 'no great victory had been won; it was . . . an ordinary, not an annihilating victory'. Clearly, the most ambitious hopes of Haig and those around him were unfulfilled. No breakthrough took place. The German army did not collapse. The rail junctions at Roulers and Thourout remained firmly in German hands. So did the Belgian coast. The British official historian claimed, however, that Rupprecht's diary proved that the German army in Flanders was broken and contemplating a major retreat. At a time when it was politically vital to show shaky allies that Great Britain remained committed to the war, the BEF had kept the initiative, working and bleeding hard. More directly, the British had, he argued, distracted the Germans and so ensured the security of the wobbly French army. The British had advanced as much as 8 kilometres and captured the crest of the high ground encircling Ypres. This reduced German ability to shell into the salient. And the damage done to the German army both compelled Ludendorff to gamble on the success of offensives early in 1918 and weakened the forces he had at his disposal for those attacks, thus ensuring they failed.[17]

From the German perspective, things look rather different. Army Group Crown Prince Rupprecht's War Diary records the battle as 'a big defeat for the enemy, a major victory for us'. The official history agrees, describing Flanders as a 'major German victory' born of outstanding defensive organization by Fourth Army. The British offensive had been halted on the third of Loßberg's five lines. True, the German army had been worn down, but in some ways the impact had actually been rather less than that of previous battles. The absolute number of German divisions sucked into the fighting was down by a quarter from the Somme, for instance (71 versus 95.5) and the proportion of the army in the west involved fell to under half from 70 per cent. The impact on other fronts was minimal: seven German divisions left the Western Front in July 1917 and were not replaced until the end of November, after the Third Battle of Ypres had been closed down. German casualties in Flanders in the six months from June to November were roughly the same as had been suffered in the Anglo-French attacks of April–May, less than half those on the Somme and less than in the first six months at Verdun. As Alexander Watson has demonstrated, 'although by the end of the Ypres offensive the German army's confidence had been shaken, the bulk of the force was not yet ready to collapse', not least because it appeared to German intelligence that the British were experiencing similar problems. Incidents of indiscipline were on the rise, but more often involved men being transferred from Russia than soldiers who had been through the Flanders campaign. Soldiers' complaints were about lack of leave and poor conditions on badly organized troop transports, rather than a rejection of the war or their duty. While it is true that Rupprecht discussed withdrawal in his diary, he did so only in the context of a temporary pull back to unbalance the British before counter-attacking them. The collapse of Russia and imminent arrival of a large American contingent were at least as important as drivers of Ludendorff's decision to attack the next spring as his wish to move from defence to offence.[18]

It seems perverse to argue that a campaign which achieved none of its strategic objectives was any kind of British victory and few modern historians have dared to do so. Although, as Gary Sheffield argues, the offensive did allow the Entente to retain the initiative on the Western Front, the impact on German operations elsewhere was extremely limited. Further, J. P. Harris has pointed out that the worst of the French army's problems had in fact been resolved well before 31 July. A wave of mutinies had briefly gripped the French army in May but was largely resolved by the end of June. French troops proved effective in the attack at Ypres itself, at Verdun in August and at La Malmaison in October 1917. The lag between the Battle of Messines and the beginning of the main attack, however unavoidable, significantly undercut at least one of the strategic rationales proposed for launching the Ypres offensive. The decision to continue attacking, given the scale of the problems involved, the high cost, and scanty returns on the blood and treasure invested, is harder to defend. As Jim Beach has argued, weak understanding of the state of the German army played a part but was not the determining factor: GHQ Intelligence tended to follow Haig's optimism, rather than lead it. Poor intelligence, primarily strategic, merely lent weight to a campaign which already had its own political and tactical momentum.[19]

Did that momentum need to extend as far as the capture of Passchendaele village, with all the horror that entailed? The British salient thus created was highly vulnerable and had to be rapidly evacuated when the Germans went on the offensive in spring 1918. Robin Prior and Trevor Wilson have argued that it was quite possible to suspend the campaign at any point. One option might have been to pull back to the Pilckem Ridge, won in the early days of the attack, although the morale and political costs of doing so would have been high. Nonetheless, the military logic, once the British had started to clear the high ground overlooking Ypres, of pushing on to finish the job is clear. Indeed, Rupprecht saw it, too: 'it can be said of Passchendaele that it forms the keystone of the entire high ground east of Ypres and that is why the enemy fought so hard to possess it', he noted on 16 November. If you look back at Ypres from Passchendaele, then walk around to the back of the church and look out over the plain stretching away to the east below you, it is easy to see what Rupprecht meant.[20]

Even if it made sense at some level to push on to Passchendaele, however, that does not mean that the tactics used to do so were sensible. Prior and Wilson argue that the British had failed to understand and employ the 'bite-and-hold' tactics which offered a tactical solution. They have a point. Certainly in October Plumer was rushing his attacks, not allowing enough time for adequate artillery preparation. He was out of touch with conditions on the ground. J. P. Harris, on the other hand, has suggested that in fact, for a frontal attack into the teeth of alert defenders, British losses were relatively low and bespoke increased efficiency of tactical method, at least compared to, say, the Somme. The casualty returns were probably, however, reduced as much by the low numbers of attackers getting into action as by skill in avoiding enemy bullets and shell fire.[21]

The central point about the Entente in late 1917, though, is a chilling and dispiriting one, which David Stevenson has identified. The Allies confronted a terrible dilemma. Fighting on as they had at Third Ypres 'promised to cripple the British army as surely as it had crippled the French and Italian ones'. On the other hand, the methods which had proven successful at Messines and La Malmaison would be prohibitively expensive in lives, matériel, and destruction of the land they were supposed to be liberating. Doing nothing was hardly an option, but doing anything seemed to invite disaster, even if successful. Neither the Entente in general, nor the BEF in particular, seemed any closer to finding a way to win the war on the battle-field than they had been in the three previous years of fighting. Both sides continued to experiment with new tactics to break the Western Front impasse, though, as we shall see when we explore the Battle of Cambrai in Chapter 18.[22]

18

Cambrai

Although winter was near and further sustained operations were unlikely, Rupprecht never expected the end of the Flanders campaign to mark the end of the fighting season. Local enemy attacks remained likely and indeed on 19 November Second Army reported that they were picking up indications of an assault involving tanks at Havrincourt, a previously quiet sector of the Hindenburg Line 15 kilometres south-west of Cambrai. Rupprecht and Kuhl reinforced the division holding the line there and moved reserve battalions closer up to the line.[1]

At quarter past seven the next morning, 20 November 1917, six divisions of the British Third Army under Lieutenant-General Sir Julian Byng attacked on a 9-kilometre front stretching from the Canal du Nord, just west of Havrincourt, down to Banteux. There had been no preliminary bombardment. Instead, 378 tanks cut gaps in the wire for the infantry to rush through. Over a thousand British guns laid down an effective lifting barrage and intense counter-battery fire. The Germans had three divisions holding the front, with a fourth in reserve at Cambrai.[2]

The first reports to reach Rupprecht caused little real concern. He heard that the defenders had been caught by surprise and the front line overrun in places. The tanks had proved surprisingly effective, moving quickly across the dry and firm ground, and ploughing up the hundred-metre-deep belts of wire in front of the German lines. They had demoralized some of the defending infantry, too. 'I never expected tanks would be able to break through so fast', wrote Rupprecht. Nonetheless, in many places the enemy had been repelled or had gained only toeholds in the German lines. Only in one spot had he driven beyond the front line. Soon, however, the news grew more serious. Both the front and support lines had been lost. Brave German resistance at Flesquières, coupled with timely counter-attacks by the reserve division, had absorbed much of the sting of the British attack, but the unfinished reserve line remained under threat and 126 guns had been overrun. The Germans would have to evacuate Flesquières that night before it got completely cut off. The British had crossed the St Quentin Canal at Masnières and Indian cavalry had been spotted approaching the outskirts of Cambrai. Ludendorff accused Rupprecht of getting distracted by the situation in Flanders, a charge Rupprecht refuted in his published diary, although the manuscript version admitted Ludendorff was right. Clearly, a powerful counter-attack would be required to restore the situation and Rupprecht rushed reinforcements to Second Army. Six divisions began arriving the next day and in the course of 21 November a new defensive line was stitched together to contain further British thrusts.[3]

The dramatic British success of 20 November was seized on as great news in Britain. At last, it seemed, a clear-cut victory had been won. The bells of churches across the country, including St Paul's Cathedral, rang out, the first time they had done so in this manner since the Boer War. King George V congratulated Sir Douglas Haig and promoted Byng in the field. First reports emphasized the role played by massed armour in securing this victory. This theme was picked up by cheerleaders for tanks between the wars, by men as influential as Winston Churchill and Basil Liddell Hart. More recently, modern historians have questioned their importance. For instance, Bryn Hammond's excellent book on the battle argues convincingly that it was no complete victory, much less the 'first great tank battle' and a victory for the tank. In his view, what success the British enjoyed on 20 November was based not on any single weapon, but on the convergence at last of a whole range of strategic, political, scientific, technological, and tactical factors, allowing an integrated combined-arms approach.[4]

German views of why the British succeeded on 20 November, however, put more stress on armour once more. The key issue, according to after-action reports and the diaries of Rupprecht and Kuhl, was that tanks had enabled the attackers to achieve surprise. German reports on tanks should be treated with a little suspicion, however. The tank was, after all, a convenient scapegoat to explain away failure, distracting attention from defensive short-comings such as insufficient artillery support. Neither Kuhl nor Rupprecht had shown much concern about armour before. Indeed, even this time they seemed comfortable that they had discovered an effective counter-measure, using lorry-mounted anti-aircraft guns in a mobile anti-tank role.[5]

Haig had originally intended to suspend operations quickly if progress stalled. His troops found themselves in a valley, however, overlooked by the high ground of Bourlon Wood. Staying where they were would be difficult and painful. Either they must go on and take Bourlon, or they would have to pull back to the next defensible position along the Flesquières Ridge. As in the final stages of the Third Battle of Ypres, tactical considerations were permitted to warp the operational design. Bourlon Ridge proved as magnetic as Passchendaele. Several days of bitter fighting rolled to and fro in the wood and outskirts of the village. The longer the fighting went on, the less palatable a retreat became. British momentum slowed as logistics came close to breakdown, and attacks became increasingly spasmodic and uncoordinated. The German line held. Remarkably, as late as 25 November the British were still hoping for a breakthrough and sent cavalry up to exploit. Left standing on an exposed hillside while they awaited their chance, the cavalrymen achieved little except to offer German gunners target practice.[6]

German commanders had already begun planning a full-scale counter-attack. As early as 21 November Rupprecht ordered Second Army to prepare to pinch out the new British salient from north and east. Kuhl suggested that the main attack take place on the left-hand, southern pincer. Presumably his idea was to avoid the difficult ground of Bourlon Wood and a frontal attack on the alert British troops already fighting there. Instead, he would drive from east to west into the flank of the bulge, across open downland. When Rupprecht and Kuhl visited Second Army the following morning, Marwitz outlined a plan along exactly these lines. Kuhl was impressed by the calm atmosphere in Second Army headquarters.[7]

Ludendorff, in contrast, remained flustered. Once more he could not refrain from interfering. To Rupprecht he seemed 'very nervous. On the telephone he enquired into a thousand details which had a very disruptive effect.' For instance, even as fighting raged, Oberste Heeresleitung (OHL) was demanding to know at once how many batteries of which calibre guns were firing on this target or that. Ludendorff was so worried by the British success that he insisted Flanders be stripped of reserves to meet the new threat, a step Rupprecht did not think necessary. Ludendorff also involved himself closely in planning the counter-attack. On 27 November he, Rupprecht, and Kuhl attended a meeting at Second Army headquarters in Le Cateau to discuss the coming operation. Rupprecht, in particular, was excited by the prospect of breaking in and rolling up the British front from south to north. It offered 'the best opportunity we've had for years' to give the British a real knock. A total of fourteen German divisions were involved.

On 30 November, after just one hour of artillery bombardment, two corps were to launch a surprise attack into the vulnerable eastern flank of the British salient. As the infantry advanced, it would use infiltration or 'stormtroop' tactics, bypassing enemy strongpoints and leaving them for subsequent waves to mop up. The attackers would infiltrate deep into enemy lines and seize the village of Metz-en-Couture. Further north, a third corps would drive south either side of Bourlon Wood. The task here was harder. There was no chance of surprise because the enemy would be on the *qui vive* after recent fighting. Consequently, the northern attack would be delayed until two hours after the southern force had jumped off, in the hope that resistance would be beginning to weaken by then. Once Metz-en-Couture had fallen, the British in Flesquières and Havrincourt would be isolated and they would have to evacuate the salient they had won on 20 November. At a minimum, Rupprecht's aim was to recapture the sections of Hindenburg Line lost the previous week.[8]

In the event, the attack in the south overran the thinly stretched British front line. Desperate defence and a timely British counter-attack, carried out with style by the Guards Division, eventually brought the Germans to a halt, but not before some units had driven up to 6,000 metres into the British positions. Metz remained out of reach, however, as did the Flesquières Ridge. The standard of cooperation between German infantry and their trench mortars was high. 'Stormtroop' tactics clearly had merit, although Kuhl identified plenty of areas for improvement before next time. The failure of the northern attack, which substituted mass for tactical finesse, reinforced the point that surprise was a more effective weapon than weight of numbers. Here, British artillery had shot the assault columns to pieces as they crossed open ground and progress was slight. Vicious fighting on both flanks over the next couple of days produced further heavy casualties but little change to the overall situation. Ludendorff suspended offensive operations during the evening of 1 December. Forty-eight hours later, Byng gained Haig's approval to withdraw from Bourlon Wood and Marcoing back to a more defensible winter line along the forward slope of the Flesquières Ridge. This manoeuvre was carried out over the next few days and the fighting died away.[9]

By every measure, honours at Cambrai were even. Once the front had re-stabilized by mid-December, the British had gained 20 square kilometres of ground on the left, but lost 16 on the right. British casualties between 20 November and 8 December totalled 44,207, while the Germans lost

41,000 men, 14,000 of them in their counter-attack. Both sides could and did claim a sort of victory. As Rupprecht noted, his men had scored the biggest offensive success over the British since the Second Battle of Ypres two and a half years earlier.[10]

Neither side, however, had accomplished what they had hoped with their attacks and the British had come close to defensive disaster on 30 November. As a result, commanders on both sides had some explaining to do. Sir Douglas Haig took full responsibility for the decision to carry on bashing away against Bourlon. General Byng was rather less gallant, blaming the collapse of his eastern flank on poor training, weak leadership, and low morale among his junior officers and men. Although his version of events was upheld by a Court of Enquiry early in the new year, historians subsequently have tended to place more blame on the senior commanders, including Byng, who had under-estimated the German capacity to counter-attack, had drawn up no proper defensive plan, and had allowed themselves to be taken by surprise. Haig's chief of intelligence, Charteris, was replaced within a couple of weeks, although, as Jim Beach has demonstrated, Cambrai was more pretext than cause for the removal of an unpopular officer who had already lost the confidence of many in both France and Whitehall. Further, the 30 November attack, Beach points out, was inherently 'difficult to anticipate because of the relative haste with which it was improvised and because it was hard to distinguish between defensive reinforcement and offensive preparation'.[11]

The reasons for the failure of the German northern attack on 30 November were clear: lack of surprise, an alert enemy, and poor tactics. Events on the southern wing were more interesting. According to Ludendorff's memoirs, the counter-attack there was less successful than it might have been because an otherwise good division, rather than pushing on to its objectives, stopped to ransack an enemy supply depot. Rupprecht blamed Ludendorff instead. At the 27 November conference, Ludendorff had emphasized the importance of the Flesquières Ridge position, marking up a map with charcoal crayon to show how it might be captured from the south-east. According to Rupprecht, Marwitz replied 'I will take special notice of this sketch' and subsequently, rather than driving deep for Metz-en-Couture and bypassing enemy strength as Rupprecht's plan envisaged, directed a shallower advance towards Trescault which ran directly onto the British defences. Ludendorff's explanation, which foreshadows disciplinary problems encountered among hungry troops in the spring 1918 offensive, seems convenient. When he wrote his memoirs he was an ex-general trying to shift the blame for defeat from his own decisions to a lack of home-front support and supplies. That said, there is evidence that at least some troops were off scavenging for food in British dugouts when the enemy hit back. Similarly, if Rupprecht knew that Marwitz had shifted the axis of attack to Trescault from Metz, why did he not tell him to revert to the original plan? As at Neuve Chapelle in 1915, he seems to have felt constrained not to interfere with his subordinate's decisions. In any case, the Germans never got close even to the tricky Flesquières Ridge position, much less Trescault or Metz.

There are simpler explanations for the incomplete success of the German southern wing, as the after-action reports themselves demonstrate. First, as we have seen, resistance never completely collapsed; a defensive line was eventually improvised; and some local British counter-attacks worked well. Second, the German thrust was short of resources, and especially manpower. Lack of reserves meant too much was asked of the assault divisions, which inevitably soon became burnt out. There was no second wave ready to leap-frog through and continue the assault, which prevented exploitation of early success. Third, what reserves were to hand were often held back by corps headquarters located too far to the rear to keep up with events, rather than under the direct command of the men leading the attack. Fourth, staff work on logistics was sometimes poor and caused confusion and delay. For instance, five divisions were all trying to draw ammunition from the same supply depot and three different divisions were routed through a single crossroads, causing traffic jams so snarled that ammunition columns were lucky to move 1 kilometre in an hour.[12]

The Battle of Cambrai, in the words of the British official historian, 'had little effect upon the general situation'. It made no difference to the stale-mate on the Western Front and neither helped nor hindered the situation across the Alps after the Italian defeat at Caporetto in October. The material impact on both sides was approximately equal. If 20 November provided any boost to British morale, the German counter-attack ten days later undid it. Similarly, any damage to the defenders' confidence caused by the British assault was offset by the demonstration that the German army remained a potent attacking force which could accomplish much, even without the mechanical panoply deployed by the British. Politically, both sides could claim at least some sort of a victory to end the year.[13]

The importance of Cambrai lies not in what it achieved, but in what it promised for the future. On 20 November the British had, for the first time on a large scale, successfully pulled together a range of technological, organizational, and tactical advances, integrating artillery, armour, and airpower with infantry to fight in a new and recognizably modern fashion. Equally the Germans had, in places, showcased a style of warfare, first advocated as early as 1915 but now being employed more widely, which became known as 'stormtroop' tactics. Assaults were to use speed, infiltration, and close cooperation between guns, infantry, and aircraft to overrun defences and unlock the stalemate of the Western Front. The urgent need now, for both sides, was to learn the lessons they would need to refine their methods ready for the fighting of the year ahead. On 4 December, Rupprecht stressed the importance of learning from the recent offensive. It was, after all, his Army Group's first large-scale attack. 'The lessons learnt... are extremely valuable. They must be integrated at once into the winter training of staffs and troops and be incorporated into the design of further offensive operations. An accelerated working out of lessons learnt is thus pressing.' Commands at all levels were to write up after-action reports. Rupprecht and Kuhl set out a list of topics they wanted information about within days. Divisions were to report on each arm, both independently and in combination, the preparation and organization of the attack, staff work, communications, and mobility. Gruppe and army headquarters were told to focus on preparations, organization and leadership, transport, secrecy, cooperation with neighbouring formations, the dissemination of orders, intelligence and communications, and supplies and munitions. They were to concentrate on hitting the most significant points, rather than capturing every little detail, and not to worry about style or presentation. Speed was essential because the German high command had already decided that they would strike in the west in the spring. Cambrai had shown that, if the German army was to be ready to fight a mobile war, a winter of intensive analysis and training lay ahead.[14]

Kuhl summarized the reports he received in three memos he issued during December, making a series of recommendations. He highlighted the importance of achieving surprise and the need for a follow-up wave to maintain momentum and exploit success. Units must advance at all costs and pay no heed to the situation on their flanks. Reserves should be at the disposal of the commanders leading the assault, not held back under the grip of senior commands. Decisions would need to be made quickly, so the power to make them must be delegated to the man on the spot, not jealously held onto higher up. 'In many cases we must return to the principles which worked well at the beginning of the war', wrote Kuhl, appealing to the past to show the way to the future. The memos also addressed a number of detailed tactical issues which needed to be dealt with during winter training. For instance, units should attack in small mobile assault squads, not in the long skirmish lines laid down in the pre-1914 manuals.[15]

The lessons from these and other reports, for example from the Battle of Caporetto and Haig's despatch on his 1917 operations, were incorporated into the new doctrine publication *The Attack in Position Warfare*, written by Captain Hermann Geyer and published on 26 January 1918. This was intended primarily to provide the operational framework within which the stormtroop tactics laid out in a new edition of the *Training Manual of Infantry* could work. Geyer put special stress on the need to maintain the attack's momentum with quick decision-making. Spearheads were to advance at speed, leaving centres of resistance and threats to their flanks to be neutralized by the troops coming up in support. Ludendorff shared Geyer's view and emphasized momentum in the series of planning conferences held throughout the early months of 1918. These will be discussed further in Chapter 19. According to Rupprecht, however, Ludendorff was underestimating the difficulties of maintaining momentum. Ludendorff seemed to think that all that was required was good infantry–artillery cooperation and smart traffic management behind the lines to keep reserves moving. He thought divisions could continue in combat for several days at a time. Rupprecht, on the other hand, believed that twenty-four hours was the most they could manage. Rupprecht also had broader worries. 'It is regrettable that OHL is once more interfering in tactical details which should better be left to individual commands to determine according to their experience and requirements', he complained. 'I think that armies should not tie themselves to the standardization laid out in the memorandum but rather should conduct themselves as circumstances dictate.'[16] 1918 would fully bear out Rupprecht's concerns.

PART IV

Year of Defeats 1918

19

Planning the Spring Offensives

In October 1917, even before the fighting in Flanders had finished, the German high command began turning its attention to the year ahead. On paper, Germany had three options. She could settle for a negotiated peace. She could stay on the defensive in France and Belgium, while eliminating other enemies such as Russia and Italy. Or, she could attack in the west to drive Britain, France—or both—out of the war. In reality, her choice was considerably more limited. First, as David Stevenson has shown, there was no possible peace deal on the table. Public opinion in all the combatant nations had hardened over time as the treasure and blood flowed. The prospect of compromise was more distant than ever. No-one was more intransigent than Ludendorff. In his mind, anything less than victory meant defeat, and defeat probably meant revolution back home. His ambitions were almost limitless, but discounting these, he was even at a minimum not prepared to concede military control over Belgium. Neither Chancellor Georg Michaelis, nor his successor, the Bavarian Georg von Hertling, was able or willing to pursue a line independent of Ludendorff and Hindenburg. On the other hand, for London, Paris, and probably Washington a full restoration of Belgian sovereignty was the *sine qua non* for any agreement. There was no common ground on this issue and consequently no basis for a settlement. The German government rejected out of hand even President Wilson's 'ostentatiously moderate' peace proposals, the Fourteen Points of January 1918. Second, Britain, France, and the United States were apparently determined to continue the war to the end, Russia or no Russia on their side. Ludendorff had to find a way to defeat them. All his senior generals agreed that the only way to do so was by attacking. To sit on the defensive would achieve nothing except give the Americans time to build up their strength in Europe and shift the odds further against Germany.[1]

The question, then, was: how, where, and when to attack? On 23 October, his chief of operations, Major Wetzell, recommended a knock-out blow against the British before the Americans could arrive in force, using thirty divisions. Two days later Rupprecht and Kuhl submitted a memorandum so much less ambitious that Kuhl was 'curious what OHL [Oberste Heeresleitung] will say about it. Probably that we're washed out. One must tell the truth, though.' They argued for only limited offensives in the short term. Working on the assumption that they could count on no reinforcements from the Russian front and that the British would continue their offensive in Flanders, they argued that the best way to avoid the pain of another attritional battle in the new year was to pull back deeper into Belgium before launching an upper cut from Armentières into the flank and rear of the advancing British Expeditionary Force (BEF) around Ypres. Ludendorff asked for a detailed study of the forces that would be required for such an attack, noting that events in other theatres would determine its practicability. Rupprecht was worried that Ludendorff was concentrating on the tactical issues involved and losing sight of the need to inflict a decisive operational, or even strategic, defeat on the enemy. He also noted that much would depend on the spring weather. If the River Lys stayed high and the valley was marshy, the attack could not work.[2]

On 11 November, Ludendorff visited Rupprecht's headquarters at Mons to discuss offensive plans for 1918. Also present were Kuhl and a clutch of staff officers from OHL and elsewhere, including Colonel Friedrich von Schulenberg, chief of staff to the Prussian Crown Prince. The Bolshevik revolution in Russia, underway now for a few days, had not yet delivered a ceasefire on the Eastern Front but held out the prospect of freeing up troops and artillery for the west, so Kuhl proposed a variant of his 25 October idea. Some thirty-five divisions would strike north-west between the Lys and the La Bassée Canal, cutting up through Bailleul and Hazebrouck and driving for the Channel at Calais. To ease the task of slicing the BEF in two, it might be necessary to pull back in front of Ypres and draw the British eastwards. The British breastworks would be easy to break down and the Portuguese contingent holding the line was especially vulnerable. The only drawback with this plan was that the state of the ground would make it impossible before the beginning of April at the earliest. Ludendorff insisted that any attack must begin by the end of February or beginning of March at the latest.

Schulenberg then suggested attacks either side of Verdun, arguing that a French defeat there would shatter her resistance for good. To Ludendorff, however, not only was the ground at Verdun difficult and enemy defences strong, but an attack there would leave the British still free to fight in Flanders. Thus the Germans might end up fighting two major battles when they had only enough ammunition for one. In Ludendorff's view, it was the British who were the engine of the Entente war effort and so the main effort must be directed against them. The British also had the advantage of being less formidable opponents than the French. If the Lys were ruled out, the only viable sectors left were Arras and the area around the Somme near St Quentin. Formidable enemy defences at Arras, not least on the blood-soaked ridges of Vimy and Lorette, made an attack there unappealing. Further south, the ground was more favourable and rail junctions such as Amiens offered attractive targets. Crossing the wastelands created in 1916 and 1917, however, would be tricky. Ludendorff ordered further studies, with five operations to be developed in greater detail: Kuhl's proposal for a drive on Hazebrouck (Operation St GEORG, later plain GEORG); an attack on Arras (MARS); St MICHAEL (MICHAEL), centred on Saint-Quentin; and twin attacks north and east of Verdun (CASTOR and POLLUX).[3]

The Mons conference of 11 November shows the best and worst of German military planning during the First World War. The German army has often been accused of focusing so keenly on the tactical that it lost sight of the political dimension of war. In fact, however, Ludendorff and his advisers seem to have displayed a shrewd insight into Entente dynamics, fully appreciating the depth of French resilience and the extent to which Britain was the driving force of the alliance. The decision to target the British shows, indeed, that OHL was building its military plans around this political understanding. What Ludendorff proved unable to do, however, was to translate and sustain that insight throughout the planning process. He failed to appreciate, for instance, that attacking astride the join between the British and French armies was more likely to push them together than to pull them apart.

Rupprecht put his name to the study which Kuhl sent to OHL on 20 November. This reiterated that, along the whole front of Army Group Crown Prince Rupprecht, the sector west of Armentières remained the most promising. A decisive attack should employ forty divisions and 400–500 batteries of heavy artillery and drive into the British rear to cut off and crush the main body of the BEF. If available strength permitted only a smaller effort, this would still be the best ground for a shallower diversion involving twelve to fifteen divisions. Kuhl also briefly discussed other options. With MARS, he worried about taking the high ground around

Arras and calculated fifty divisions would be needed. MICHAEL, he argued, brought several problems. First, the Germans would have to sustain the attack south-westward across the devastated zone left by ALBERICH. Second, they would then have to wheel ninety degrees right and head north-west to roll up the British line, while holding off French counter-attacks from the south along an ever-expanding front. At least fifty-five divisions would be required to achieve an operational objective which remained vague, at best.[4]

The 20 November memorandum made no allowance for Russia dropping out of the war. When she signed a cease-fire, Kuhl judged that the British were unlikely now to attack in Flanders but would expect a German offensive. He revised his plan. The best chance to achieve surprise and reduce the chances of another Materialschlacht remained where British defences were weakest, between Armentières and the La Bassée Canal, with an attack in April. It would be important, however, to tie down enemy reserves with a series of diversions up and down the Western Front first. These should begin in early March and also aim to exacerbate frictions within the Entente command. Local attacks around the Ypres Salient, north of Lens, and at St Quentin would precede a large push at Cambrai aiming to suck in British reserves. An offensive at Verdun would do the same for the French. Kuhl was now proposing, in fact, not just a plan for a single hammer blow, but a design for a whole campaign. By pulling together a series of operations, he expected to deliver a cumulative effect much greater than the sum of its parts. He was also keen to keep options open. If the Germans failed to achieve surprise in one place, rather than hammer away fruitlessly like the British, he wrote, they should reorganize and attack elsewhere. Speed was essential.

In some respects Kuhl's approach resembled that of Wetzell's latest staff study, dated 12 December, which also called for a series of operations. According to this, Second and the newly formed Eighteenth Armies would begin with an attack by twenty-two divisions at St Quentin. A couple of weeks later, Fourth and Sixth Armies would drive on Hazebrouck. The difference between the two plans lay partly in the different sectors they chose for the main preliminary attack. More importantly, however, while Kuhl and Rupprecht seemed still to believe that a single knock-out blow was possible, Wetzell did not. He expected no single operation to be decisive on its own. In this, he was also out of step with Ludendorff, who remained, as David Zabecki says, 'fixed in his mind to a single great attack— a Schlieffenesque Battle of Annihilation'. Ludendorff also remained committed to attacking the British, while Wetzell believed that the French constituted a more enticing target. Wetzell reiterated these points in a memo written on Christmas Day.[5]

In theory, no final decision had yet been reached. At another planning meeting on 27 December, all the Army Groups were told to continue planning for a range of options from the Swiss border to Flanders. Kuhl was asked to pull together plans for six different attacks. Fourth Army was to work on GEORG II, an attack on Mount Kemmel and Bailleul, while Sixth Army studied GEORG I, a drive on Hazebrouck, and MARS, aimed at Arras. Meanwhile, Second and Eighteenth Armies drew up MICHAEL with objectives Bapaume, Péronne, and the Somme. In reality, however, Ludendorff had already made up his mind. Much of the paper trail comprises contingency plans or efforts to confuse and deceive. Ludendorff's intent was clear, however, in the orders he sent out. For instance, on 19 December OHL ordered Eighteenth Army to take over the front from St Quentin down to the River Oise. General Oskar von Hutier was in command, with his artillery under Colonel Georg Bruchmüller. This was the team responsible for stunning victories at Riga in the autumn and their deployment here was taken by British intelligence to indicate a possible attack. Similarly, on 29 December OHL told Rupprecht that he was to have a new Seventeenth Army under him. The commander, Otto von Below, the victor of Caporetto, brought a reputation as a good attacking general. His chief of staff was Rupprecht's old comrade, Krafft von Dellmensingen. Rupprecht and Kuhl realized that enemy intelligence would be alerted by Below's presence and considered sending him temporarily to Sixth Army before switching him back at the last minute. This deception plan faded away, however, when Below objected to any changes in the composition of his staff.[6]

Rupprecht finished his 1917 diary optimistically. It was true that the German army had been unable to break through in 1914, and that the Entente had failed to do so every year since. In spring 1918, however, the Germans would be able not only to maintain their battlefield superiority over the enemy but deploy reserves and artillery on a scale never before seen. The chances of ending the war with a major blow were reasonable. Although Germany would be in trouble if the offensive failed, Rupprecht was almost more nervous that the British might imitate ALBERICH and pull back. While 1918 thus certainly held dangers, the situation for Germany was overall better than it had been a year previously and he could hope that the new year might bring victory and peace.[7]

Planning continued in January under conditions of the utmost secrecy. At Rupprecht's headquarters, even members of the operations staff such as Captain Wilhelm von Leeb, a future field marshal, were deliberately shut out. Rupprecht was not happy with the plans the armies submitted. Sixth Army's ideas for GEORG I were too academic, especially because they under-estimated the difficulties of re-taking the Messines Ridge. Without clearing enemy observation posts from there, it would be impossible to move supplies and reinforcements up to maintain momentum and seize Mount Kemmel. The terrain for MARS, also, especially the high ground at Vimy and Monchy-le-Preux, was very favourable to the defender. MICHAEL presented fewer tactical problems but led in a less decisive direction. The scale of forces necessary to turn any tactical success to strategic effect was beyond what was ever likely to be available.[8]

On 18 January, after a couple of weeks of political distraction over Russia, Ludendorff began a three-day tour of the front to discuss the offensive. He followed this with a conference at Avesnes on 21 January. Again, he stressed the importance of close artillery–infantry cooperation, as well as the need to keep moving forward. Operationally, first-wave divisions must fight on without relief for at least the whole of the first day of the assault. Ludendorff also explained that OHL currently had sixty-three divisions on hand in the west. By the end of March a further twenty-four would probably arrive from Russia and Italy. This would create a reserve of eighty-five to ninety divisions. Where to use them? He summarized his view of the options. GEORG I was too dependent on the weather. If spring came late, it might be May before it became feasible. MARS was tactically too hard. Therefore, they would adopt a version of MICHAEL. To the objection that MICHAEL lacked any defined objective, Ludendorff replied that 'in Russia also we always just pushed on to a nearby objective and then saw how we could carry on'. Seventeenth Army would be slotted into the line between the Sixth and Second Armies, occupying the sector between the River Scarpe and Flesquières, whence it would launch MICHAEL I south-westwards towards Bapaume. Second Army would drive due westwards on Péronne (MICHAEL II), while the task of Eighteenth Army with MICHAEL III was to cover the left flank. This last army, Ludendorff announced, was to be transferred from Rupprecht's Army Group to that of Crown Prince Wilhelm. He made a point of asking for Rupprecht's agreement to the change. Rupprecht could not publicly object but told Kuhl that 'now the war is lost'. The decision, he thought, made no military sense. It would obviously be better for the whole attack to be controlled by a single commander. He saw it as nothing more than a political gesture designed to rehabilitate Wilhelm's military reputation after the failures at Verdun. In his memoirs Ludendorff claimed that his motives were exclusively military: 'though profoundly loyal to my King, I am an independent man and no courtier'. In fact, this decision would allow Ludendorff to maintain overall control as he could not if the operation was delegated to a single Army Group. Finally, Rupprecht was to continue preparing for GEORG, which might be executed if MICHAEL failed.[9]

Over the next few days OHL sent out formal orders codifying what had been discussed at Avesnes. Rupprecht told his armies to be ready for MICHAEL by 20 March and GEORG I and II by early April. After the plans were wargamed in early February, Rupprecht proposed cancelling the difficult MARS operation south of Arras. Instead, he proposed diversions to draw British reserves to Flanders, but Ludendorff rejected this suggestion. Further meetings took place across February and March but the overall shape of the offensive from now on changed little.

Much of the discussion at these meetings centred on tactics. Ludendorff, and indeed the whole German army, has been criticized for being obsessed with the tactical level of war and paying too much attention to the trees at the expense of the forest. Ludendorff had logical reasons for his approach, however, as the words with which he had opened the Avesnes conference on 21 January show:

> We talk a lot about Operations and not much about Tactics. I have taken part in many operations. But I have never known in advance how an operation would unfold. Decisions must be made day by day, often hour by hour. Whether one will be in a position to strike in the direction originally intended, or whether one will be forced to veer off elsewhere, it's not possible to say in advance. Not even three or four days ahead. The picture can change so much in the meantime, that the original design can't be carried through. So I warn you against committing to any particular course of action, even if it's the best one. Instead, one must think, using all possible means, 'How do I defeat the enemy? How can I break through his front line?' What happens thereafter in many cases depends on making a split-second choice. The choice you make then must be correct. I advise you therefore to pay greater attention to tactical matters.

During the same meeting, Ludendorff pointed out that 'tactics must be given precedence over abstract strategy. Without tactical success there could be no strategy. Strategy which gives no thought to tactics is doomed to failure.' He had a point, although uncertainty about the future hardly absolves one from contingency planning. In any case, Rupprecht resented Ludendorff's tactical interventions as interfering in the proper business of subordinate commands and risking excessive standardization.[10]

Rupprecht was growing increasingly concerned that they were taking a path which could lead only to disaster. 'Do we have enough resources for a major offensive?' he asked his diary on 30 January. 'I doubt it myself and am deeply worried.' When Ludendorff argued that 'thorough preparation is more important than surprise of execution', Rupprecht disagreed: 'I think the opposite. If we can't surprise the enemy with our attack, it will definitely become a fruitless Materialschlacht.' On 4 February he wrote to his father: 'Sadly I cannot see the military situation in a rosy light: reserves of manpower are running short and we're losing many horses to malnutrition. Raw materials of all kinds are in short supply.... It is now impossible for us to end the war victoriously.' Extreme war aims in the east were a mistake which would make a negotiated settlement harder. Kuhl shared Rupprecht's concerns: 'we will do our best but I now have not much confidence in the attack, unless we're especially lucky'. The MICHAEL attack risked driving into a devastated wasteland and creating nothing more than a bulge in the line. On 7 February, Kuhl spoke out 'unsolicited' to Rupprecht after dinner, arguing that they were not strong enough to succeed until peace with Russia was final and the army there could be sent west.[11]

When Rupprecht visited Munich for his parents' Golden Wedding celebrations on 20 February, he tried to persuade his father how poor the outlook was. Ludwig III would not be convinced. More importantly, Rupprecht also buttonholed the Kaiser, warning him of the difficulties facing the offensive, including shortages of manpower and horses, the fact that they were playing their last card, and the danger that they might gain nothing more than a partial victory and a useless and vulnerable salient. Wilhelm II was unconcerned. He replied that they were not seeking a major breakthrough but would damage the enemy with successive operations in different places. He was parroting Ludendorff's line. It remained doubtful, however, whether Germany possessed the strength for multiple operations on the scale required. Rupprecht made sure also to talk to the Kaiser's military advisers, Generals Plessen and Lyncker, along similar lines. 'Who knows', he asked his diary, 'whether we'll ever again get so good an opportunity as we currently have to begin peace talks with the Western powers and America?' By early March, however, as preparations began to come together, Rupprecht's spirits had risen once more: 'when you spend three and a half years purely on the defensive, you easily become a pessimist', he noted ruefully.[12]

On 6 March Rupprecht issued orders for the offensive to his armies. The first objective was to cut off the Cambrai salient 'and thus win a major tactical victory'. While it was not possible to be dogmatic about what should follow, since circumstances might change, the general intention was for Seventeenth Army to pivot north-west, rolling up the British line, while Second Army headed west, driving deep into the enemy rear. Eighteenth Army was to guard the southern flank. Hutier's Eighteenth Army had been pushing for a more ambitious role than flank guard for some days, so on 7 March Ludendorff called a meeting to ensure proper coordination between Eighteenth and Second Armies. Ludendorff agreed that it made sense for Eighteenth Army to seize bridgeheads on the far side of the Crozat Canal if possible, but refused to unleash Hutier fully until they had all seen how the battle was playing out. Another decision made at Mons that day set Thursday 21 March as the start date.[13] OHL issued its formal written orders for Operation MICHAEL on 10 March, with final orders from Army Group Crown Prince Rupprecht going out six days later. By now there were indications that the British were strengthening their defences all along the front, but there was no evidence that they knew where the attack would fall. Nothing, however, could halt MICHAEL's momentum now.[14]

The sky was clear the night before the attack, the weather better than expected. Rupprecht was relieved that the British had done nothing to disrupt his build-up. He was disturbed that evening, however, when Ludendorff told Kuhl that, if the Allies were defeated, his ultimate intention was for Army Group Rupprecht to establish itself along a line St Pol–Doullens–Amiens while Eighteenth Army held Roye–Noyon. Eighteenth Army was clearly no longer meant purely to guard Rupprecht's flank, but was expected itself to form a major part of the offensive. What had always been a highly complex manoeuvre was now developing into a widely divergent attack. This risked dissipating, rather than concentrating, German strength. When Rupprecht protested, Ludendorff replied: 'In Russia we always set ourselves only a close objective. We just cut a hole in the enemy's lines. The rest takes care of itself!'[15]

20

Operation MICHAEL

Rupprecht woke up on 21 March to find the countryside blanketed in a dense fog. Visibility in places was just a few metres. At twenty to five in the morning the German guns opened up. The preparatory bombardment went on for five hours. Altogether, over 6,600 guns and 3,500 trench mortars fired 3,200,000 rounds that day, including gas shells, along a 100-kilometre front from Croisilles down to La Fère. The climax was five minutes all-out shelling of the enemy front line, after which, at a quarter to ten, the barrage began to creep forward. A first wave of twenty-one specially trained and equipped assault divisions followed close behind. They were supported by twelve regular divisions of the line. A further twenty-nine assault and six line divisions formed two further waves behind. The defenders were eighteen divisions from the British Third and Fifth Armies, with a further eight infantry and three cavalry divisions in reserve. In the air, for once the Germans outnumbered the British by almost two to one.[1]

At Rupprecht's headquarters, it took until midday for any news of the attack to come in. The first reports were highly encouraging. The enemy front line had fallen almost without resistance and second-wave divisions were moving up as scheduled. British units were transmitting by wireless en clair: 'We are in extreme distress!' The prospects for cutting off the British salient at Flesquières looked encouraging. Once that had fallen it would be possible to shift heavy guns to get ready for MARS-SOUTH. The only oddity Rupprecht spotted was that his men did not seem to be capturing as many enemy guns as expected. The British batteries seemed to have pulled back out of harm's way. There was no need to worry too much yet, however: they would soon fall into German hands.[2]

Rupprecht's instinct proved correct. Returns the next day showed that Second Army had captured just fifty British guns. The first day of the offensive, however, undoubtedly constituted a German tactical victory. The artillery preparation had been effective, surprise was achieved and infiltration tactics worked well, especially in the fog. Particularly on the British Fifth Army front in the south, the defenders were stretched too thinly. Even where resistance was stout, it was disjointed. British communications collapsed, so combined arms cooperation broke down, too. Guns were left blind while all around them the battle swirled. Yet German progress fell short of expectations. Eighteenth Army penetrated deepest, in places up to 13 kilometres, closing up towards the Crozat Canal. Hutier had deployed only two of his second-echelon divisions and still held twelve in reserve. Seventeenth Army's attack on the right flank, on the other hand, faced much tougher resistance and at best made only some 5 kilometres, finishing the day still nearly 8 kilometres short of its objectives at Bapaume and Ytres. It had been forced to commit all the divisions of its second wave to get even that far. Ludendorff chose to reinforce success rather than relative failure, sending six fresh reserve divisions to Eighteenth Army. On the other side, Haig transferred five divisions down from the north to prop up his Third Army south of Arras.[3]

The next day brought Rupprecht more encouraging reports. Seventeenth Army forced Byng to withdraw and abandon the vital high ground at Monchy-le-Preux. A counter-attack by British tanks was driven off with heavy losses. Below's flank was now more secure and the way seemed clear for Ludendorff to extend his attack northwards. He ordered Kuhl to prepare for Operation MARS both sides of the River Scarpe. At the same time Sixth Army was instructed to get ready for an attack on the Lorette Spur under the code name RIDE OF THE VALKYRIES. Second Army drove on despite tough resistance, and captured, among other places, Gouzeaucourt, forcing the British to evacuate the Flesquières Salient that night. Further south still, disarray within the command of Gough's Fifth Army led to a premature retreat, leaving a gap in the British line north of Ham which the Germans were quick to fill.[4]

German hopes were high. Reserves remained plentiful. Some twenty fresh divisions were standing by and morale was good. Rupprecht found a train of wounded soldiers, on their way home for treatment, waiting outside his headquarters. He stopped to chat to them, finding them full of high spirits and convinced of victory. Events had moved faster than he had anticipated:

> I always hoped indeed that, if the attack restored mobility—which in any case is not such an easy thing to do—the British higher command would fail. They're only used to set-piece attacks with very detailed painstaking planning

while our leaders are better trained and more skilled at manoeuvre warfare. But I am surprised that the endurance of the British soldier—which I know well—did not last longer and that things have moved so quickly. The British are now in a very tricky spot.

Now that the British would be forced to fall back over the Somme, 'their biggest defeat of the war definitely awaits'. When news arrived that the left of Second Army had broken clean through the British defensive system and was out into open country, Rupprecht exulted: 'Victory is ours! Who could have hoped for such a success 24 hours ago!'[5]

The next day brought further good news, south of the Somme at least. Indeed, 23 March saw the deepest single advance of any day of MICHAEL: 16 kilometres. Along most of the front attacked, the Germans had now bundled the British out of all three lines of their defensive system. Eighteenth Army seized crossings over the Somme and broke out from its bridge-heads along the Crozat Canal. The British Fifth Army was beginning to disintegrate, with most of the divisions hit by the first assault reduced to mere remnants. Worse, a gap was growing between British Fifth and Third Armies which even the arrival of some French reinforcements was not yet able to fill. British artillery fire was weakening noticeably. Reports of chaos in the British rear were multiplying. Although north of the Somme progress was slower, the Germans did manage to capture Mont St Quentin, just above Péronne. They had taken 40,000 prisoners and seized some 400 guns.

Ludendorff estimated that the British were down to about fifty divisions and that the French would stand on the defensive to cover Paris. He issued orders to exploit the success won so far. Seventeenth Army would head north-west, resting its left flank on the Somme all the way to Abbeville. Second Army would drive due west towards Amiens while Eighteenth Army headed south-west. This was no new brainstorm on Ludendorff's part. As we saw above, he had outlined something very similar to Kuhl on the eve of the offensive. His estimate of the British and French was roughly right for now: not until 26 March, when the Doullens Conference gave Foch authority to coordinate the Allied response, did more aggressive French support for the British become possible. Nevertheless, however good the intelligence seemed, Ludendorff was increasing the ambition of his offensive considerably. Where the original plan had envisaged merely holding off the French while the British were crushed, now Ludendorff expected his men to be able to take on and defeat both at the same time.

Figure 20.1. German troops in the streets of Bapaume, March 1918

He was over-estimating the resilience of his increasingly tired troops and the ability of his logistic system to maintain momentum along ever-lengthening supply lines across devastated terrain. Moreover, an eccentric attack of this kind would dissipate strength, rather than concentrate it. An attack like that might come off against an already defeated enemy, but the British army was not yet weak enough for it to work.[6] MARS-SOUTH was now pencilled in for 27 March, MARS-NORTH for the next day, and RIDE OF THE VALKYRIES for 29 March. Eight days or so later, Sixth Army would attack on the River Lys. The deep objective for this last attack, code-named KLEIN-GEORG, was ambitiously set as Boulogne.

Second Army occupied Bapaume again and started to fight its way across the old Somme battlefield on 24 March. By the end of the day, fighting had broken out in High Wood once more. The British could no longer organize a continuous line. Instead the defence comprised a series of islands around which the rising German tide lapped. Soon the Germans were back on the River Ancre. Eighteenth Army, however, was starting to feel the effects of fatigue and stretched supply lines, managing to advance only 4 kilometres rather than the planned 12. Still, Hutier managed to drive a wedge between the French and British lines around Roye.[7]

We now know that this period marked the nadir of Anglo-French cooperation. Neither commander-in-chief trusted the other. By 24 March Pétain felt that the British were not trying hard enough and that Haig was already falling back on the Channel ports. Paris remained his own priority. Exactly what happened at a meeting between Pétain and Haig late that evening is disputed. So are Haig's actions that night in response. But the next day he warned Byng that he could no longer rely on either Gough's army or the French and must assume responsibility for the British Expeditionary Force's (BEF's) southern flank. At GHQ, Haig's staff officers began working up logistics plans in case the line of communications southwards was cut. Foch was concerned that the French and British were fighting different battles and, by drifting ever further apart, were playing into German hands. At Doullens on 26 March senior political and military leaders from both Britain and France decided to forestall this danger by agreeing to unify command under Foch. His first order was that Pétain and Fayolle should defend Amiens and maintain contact with the British. David Stevenson has described the Doullens Conference as 'one of the great symbolic moments of the war, although', he warns, 'its practical import was greater for the future of the 1918 campaign than for the battle in progress'.[8]

Foch possessed the attribute Napoleon most looked for in his generals: he was lucky. He took over at just the right time. Although Hutier took Roye and Noyon on 26 March and Marwitz's men occupied Albert, the power of the German offensive was fading. Seventeenth Army was still struggling to make headway near Arras. Resistance had been determined and German casualties were heavy. They had lost 90,000 men in five days. The troops were getting tired. Of the thirty-seven divisions in action, eight were already doing their second stint in the line. Supplies of ammunition, food, and even water were problematic. The railheads had been left far behind and transport was in short supply. The first thing the troops who captured Albert did was loot the town for food and drink.

Ludendorff was frustrated at the lack of progress. He telephoned Rupprecht in a rage. Units were being left too much to their own devices, he argued. They must be pushed harder to attack. Worse, they were using the wrong tactics. Rather than infiltrating in the proper stormtroop style, they were attacking head on in close-order formations. Rupprecht told Kuhl to find a way for Second Army to ease the pressure on Seventeenth Army and help it forward. Oberste Heeresleitung's (OHL's) solution was to order the launch of MARS either side of the Scarpe for 28 March.[9]

Rupprecht described 27 March as 'a disastrous day'. His staff officer, Major Prager, considered it the turning point of the whole campaign. Neither Seventeenth nor Second Armies managed to get much further forwards that day. Although Eighteenth Army seized Montdidier, it was clear that even here resistance was intensifying as French reinforcements arrived. That was bad enough. Worse still, however, was a dispute between Rupprecht and OHL over three divisions held in reserve. Rupprecht wanted to commit them to support the bogged-down right wing of Seventeenth Army. OHL refused. It diverted all three south of the Somme. When Rupprecht heard this, in the early afternoon of 27 March, he exclaimed 'now we have lost the war'. Why he felt three divisions were likely suddenly to make a difference on a flank where the Germans looked increasingly stuck, and why OHL was wrong to refuse to reinforce failure, he did not make clear. In any case, it is possible that Rupprecht was getting his dates confused. According to Kuhl, the three divisions were sent to Second Army only in the afternoon of 28 March, after it became clear that MARS was misfiring. Prager could not recall which day the transfer took place and Rupprecht admitted that his notes for both days were sketchy. The true significance, perhaps, of this story is that it shows how tightly nerves within the German high command were stretched and how swiftly the mood could and did swing. In only four days, triumph had collapsed into despair.

This was not only the case at Rupprecht's headquarters. On the night of 27/8 March Ludendorff sensed that the road from Montdidier to Amiens lay open. He told Crown Prince Wilhelm to send forces up the valley of the Avre and seize this vital city and rail junction, but Eighteenth Army refused to advance. At the time, Wetzell thought this showed that MICHAEL had run its course and should now be suspended. He argued that resources should be shifted north for GEORG. Later, he felt the failure to push for Amiens a decisive error, although it is not clear that Eighteenth Army could realistically have done so. Amiens lay over 30 kilometres from Montdidier, deep in the enemy rear. To ask tired troops, who had taken a week to advance 50 kilometres and whose supply lines were already stretched, to wheel right and strike for it was surely to ask a lot. French reinforcements were arriving all the time and making the task ever harder. Eighteenth Army eventually did send a corps up the road towards Amiens but found the way blocked. On 28 March Rupprecht's troops overran British supply columns at Le Hamel. For a few hours he thought that perhaps at last they were about to break through, but such hopes soon evaporated. General Debeney of French First Army was beginning to close up the gaps, not only between British and French, but also within the French line. He no longer had to throw all available troops straight into the line as soon as they arrived. Instead he was at last able to build up reserves near Amiens.[10]

If 28 March was a day of missed opportunities south of the Somme, north of the river it was one of dashed German hopes. Operation MARS was designed to break the British defences around Arras and get the right wing of MICHAEL moving once more. Nine German divisions launched the attack, supported by 1,250 guns. The bombardment was less thorough than it had been one week before, counter-battery fire less effective, and the barrage crept forwards too quickly for the infantry, who took time to fight their way through largely intact defences. Partly because not all the troops had been properly trained in stormtroop tactics, and partly because the enemy positions here were well established and complex, the tactics used were relatively traditional. Close-order replaced small-group infiltration. With little fog to mask the attackers, the British shot them down with ease. By early afternoon MARS had clearly failed and OHL suspended the operation. Kuhl later judged that Ludendorff was excessively concerned about casualties on 28 March, that he lost his nerve that day, and that one more push might have broken the BEF's backbone. But now that MARS had failed, any attempt to capture the Vimy and Lorette Ridges was obviously out of the question. Second Army was stuck in the Ancre valley. Rupprecht felt the need to remind his men that, with resistance now stiffening, frontal attacks without proper artillery preparation invited only casualties and must be avoided. Instead, they should probe to identify weak points and work around the flanks of enemy defences.[11]

Good Friday, 29 March, was the quietest day on the Western Front in over a week, with the only change being a small German advance north of Montdidier. More interesting were the deteriorating relations within the high command. In the morning Ludendorff telephoned Kuhl and told him to put Seventeenth Army on the defensive while Second and Eighteenth Armies continued the attack in the Amiens–Noyon–Montdidier sector. Kuhl and Rupprecht objected that this deviated from the original plan to crush the BEF first and only then turn on the French. It would give the British breathing space at precisely the time when one more good strike might finish them off. Further, they were worried that the scaled-down

GEORGETTE, now intended for launch in a little over a week, was being rushed.

Ludendorff was proving increasingly awkward to work with. He had always been impatient and highly strung but was now becoming especially aggressive and hostile. Further, he was increasingly bypassing the proper chain of command, intervening directly in the operations of Rupprecht's armies. Often Kuhl and Rupprecht learnt of orders issued not from OHL but from their subordinates. Rupprecht thought Ludendorff had lost his nerve. A couple of days previously the second of his stepsons to die in the war had been lost in action and the news had hit him hard. Captain von Leeb of Rupprecht's staff reckoned 'Ludendorff's nerves have completely gone. It is a crime to leave him in charge of commanding the armies. All our divisions will be placed in an operationally impossible position, facing stronger resistance in tactically disadvantageous conditions. So our last divisions will be rendered useless. We could have forced a decision, if we'd been handled properly! Now it will be too late, we've used up our strength to no purpose.'[12]

Ludendorff continued to push his men hard, but even he was beginning to realize there were limits. When the attacks of Eighteenth and Second Armies ground to a halt on 30 March, he ordered them to regroup and try again. Marwitz protested that his troops were worn out. They could do no more. Ludendorff gave way, suspending the MICHAEL operation until 4 April. The Germans spent the first three days of April resting their men and bringing up supplies. This was no easy task: reinforcements heading south had to march across the lines of communication of two attacking armies and kilometres of devastated ground. Rupprecht's diary entry for Easter Sunday, 31 March, gives a vivid impression of the chaos and devastation he observed as he motored through endless columns of marching men to visit Second Army. Leaving Mons at eight a.m., he first came across evidence of fighting at Cambrai, where almost no window was left intact. He crossed the St Quentin Canal at the ruined village of Masnières. From a distance, Gouzeaucourt looked intact, but in reality it lay amidst 'a labyrinth' of trenches, wire, and shell holes. Destroyed tanks and abandoned artillery guns lay round about. From there he drove up Mont St Quentin to look down at Péronne. The town appeared welcoming and picturesque in the rays of the spring sun. Again, though, the reality was different. The houses were mere shells, glowing only because their shattered walls let the sunlight through. The nave of the gothic church lay in ruins, its towers missing.

Second Army headquarters had been set up in an old British field hospital in the little village of Tincourt, which had been otherwise wiped from the map. In a valley north of Cléry he found the remains of a British artillery regiment which had been shelled as it tried to get away. Field guns stood abandoned, together with a piece of heavy artillery and a tank. Most of the crews had already been buried, but horses still lay dead all around. He drove on to Bapaume over the old Somme battlefield. Grass had already grown over the trenches and shell craters. No villages were to be seen: they existed only as place names on sign posts. All that remained of the mighty forest of St Pierre-Vaast was two clumps of low tree stumps. All over the steppe-like rolling downs were planted countless wooden crosses with red, white, and blue cockades, marking graves. 'A bleak landscape!' he called it. 'A sad picture of unbounded devastation which I'll never be able to forget.' The Bapaume–Cambrai road was in a very poor state, but Bourlon Wood, for all the fierce fighting of the autumn, was relatively intact. He got home at nine p.m. having travelled about 250 kilometres in thirteen hours.[13]

The German breathing space proved even more useful to the defenders. The British and French were able to bring up fresh reinforcements and reorganize themselves, consolidating their hold on Amiens and improving positions all along the line. When Ludendorff renewed the offensive on 4 April, his objective was to take Amiens, or at least to get close enough for his heavy guns to interdict the important railway lines running through the city. Fourteen divisions attacked in the early morning of 4 April but only four of these were fresh formations and progress was limited. Second Army reached the outskirts of Villers-Bretonneux, 16 kilometres east of Amiens, but stalled there. Attempts to get the attack moving again the next morning collapsed. At Army and Army Group level, the feeling was unanimous: MICHAEL must be suspended. During the evening of 5 April, OHL agreed. All efforts now would be directed to the attack code-named GEORGETTE, up in Flanders.[14]

In some ways, Operation MICHAEL had been a stunning success. The concentration and delivery, in secrecy, of such an immense offensive constituted, as even the British official historian noted, 'one of the most remarkable pieces of staff work that has ever been accomplished'. On 21 March, David Zabecki has calculated, the Germans captured more ground than the Entente did in 140 days on the Somme. Overall, they penetrated up to 60 kilometres into the Allied lines and captured 1,200 square kilometres of France. As we have seen, Ludendorff's objectives kept changing but the important fact remains that he achieved none of them. Initially, he sought to hold the French at bay while he destroyed the BEF. Apparent success emboldened him to order his armies to fan out across northern France and defeat both British and French simultaneously. When this more ambitious plan soon became obviously impractical, he scaled his objectives right down, now seeking merely to capture Amiens and the vital supply lines running through the city. This failed, too.

If he did not break the British or French armies, however, he did hurt them. Eighteen British divisions were worn out by the fighting and could not be reconstituted, at least in the short term. A further sixteen were being rebuilt. Haig's GHQ reserve consisted of just one fresh division. Altogether, the British lost nearly 178,000 men, 75,000 of them as prisoners of war. More British troops went into captivity during the two weeks of MICHAEL than in the whole of the war on the Western Front so far. French casualties totalled 77,000, of which 15,000 were prisoners. The Entente, therefore, lost a little over a quarter of a million men. The Germans also captured 1,300 guns, almost half the number the British had started with on 21 March. German losses, however, were also very heavy: maybe up to 239,000, almost equally split between the three attacking armies. Ludendorff had thrown in about ninety divisions, including nearly all those trained and outfitted to lead the assault. Each division had lost 2,000 men or more. Neither side could easily afford losses on such a scale, but Germany could spare fewer than Britain and France. Time, also, was working against the German army. Both factors made it all the more vital that such a high price be made to count for something. Perhaps another attack, this time in Flanders, would knock over the tottering BEF. Once more, Rupprecht's Army Group had a lead role in executing it.[15]

21

Operation GEORGETTE
and Summer 1918

At quarter past four in the morning of 9 April 1918, guns of the German Sixth Army began shelling the British and Portuguese troops defending a 27-kilometre stretch of front between Givenchy-lès-la-Bassée and Bois Grenier. After four and a half hours of bombardment, ten German divisions advanced to launch Operation GEORGETTE. Further divisions of Sixth Army were in support, and the next morning Fourth Army would extend the front another 16 kilometres northward, driving into the British line between Frelinghien and the Ypres–Comines canal. Altogether, twenty-nine divisions were on hand. Overhead, nearly 500 aeroplanes set off on missions in support. Thus the second of the German spring offensives began.[1]

Rupprecht and Kuhl were far from happy with the concept of GEORGETTE. It fell a long way short of their idea for a decisive haymaker aimed at the Channel ports to split the British Expeditionary Force (BEF) in two, trap a large part of it in Ypres, and cut it off from its supplies. At one stage, planning envisaged 30–40 divisions taking part in the main attack, with another twelve to fifteen in support. As we saw in Chapter 19, however, Ludendorff preferred MICHAEL. This reduced the resources likely to be available for operations in Flanders. GEORG became KLEIN-GEORG and eventually the even smaller GEORGETTE. What was originally intended as a knock-out blow became first a diversion and then a contingency plan in case MICHAEL alone failed to win the war. At one stage in late March it fleetingly almost seemed that no operation in Flanders might be necessary, but on about 26 March the decision was taken to launch GEORGETTE.

It was not just wounded pride making Rupprecht and Kuhl unhappy. They had other reasons for unease. First, they were unclear how much good a half-strength attack could do, but it was obvious that Calais and Dunkirk were now out of the question as objectives. The strategic effect, even if they could crush the British Second Army and clear the Ypres salient, was likely to be limited. The MICHAEL experience, indeed, set Rupprecht wondering whether Ludendorff had any plan at all: 'it is striking that in all OHL's [Oberste Heeresleitung's] instructions no single intention can ever be distinguished. Instead the talk is always only of territorial objectives to be reached. It gives me the impression that OHL is living from hand to mouth without professing any definite operational aims.' In a footnote to his diary he remarked: 'before starting the second operation of the spring... I asked OHL what the operational objective was. Ludendorff's reply on the telephone was "I forbid the word 'operation'. We bash a hole. The rest takes care of itself. That's how we did it in Russia!"' Kuhl complained that 'OHL's orders for GEORGETTE are again not clear, no clear objectives and missions, always just points on the map and tactical measures.' Second, Rupprecht and Kuhl were concerned that GEORGETTE was being rushed. Most of the artillery and aircraft needed for the attack, and even some of the infantry, had to be redeployed northwards from MICHAEL. This could not even begin until they were no longer needed there, and then the transfer would take time. Lack of rail capacity meant some of the infantry divisions would have to march the whole way. The decision to continue with MICHAEL, even after 30 March when it was clearly losing momentum, ate into that preparation time. Leeb was furious, accusing Kuhl of refusing to stand up to OHL:

> The Army Group plays a miserable role. If I were in Kuhl's shoes I'd ask them to back me or sack me. I'm just sorry for the Crown Prince. Kuhl is a very clever man but he has no character. He's not nicknamed 'Mr Look-out-for-number-one' for nothing. He definitely knew, quite clearly, that OHL was not running operations on the right lines.

With Kuhl's position and seniority, Leeb thought, it was his responsibility to say something. 'He owed the Crown Prince that much, at least.' In fact, after the war Kuhl at first tried to defend Ludendorff's decision to persevere with MICHAEL into April. In his evidence to the government commission investigating the causes of Germany's collapse in 1918, he gave two reasons. First, he argued that any pause would have given the enemy time to regroup, too. There is something in this: Sixth Army had already warned that they would not be ready until about 8 April and there was an argument for keeping up pressure on the British somewhere, especially since driving towards Amiens might interdict rail movement there and ease GEORGETTE's progress. Second, Kuhl suggested that it is always difficult to know when to suspend an attack. One suspects that Kuhl was endeavouring to present a united military front to the politicians looking to criticize the army in the immediate aftermath of the war. A few years later, in his 1929 history of the war, when the political storm had passed, Kuhl accepted that it would have been better to suspend MICHAEL sooner. Either way, where MICHAEL had taken seven weeks to organize, now GEORGETTE was being thrown together in twelve days.[2]

Whatever his reservations beforehand, Rupprecht was pleased by Sixth Army's results on 9 April. The barrage crept forwards more slowly than on 21 March so the German assault troops were better able to keep up with it. Infiltration tactics again proved effective in thick fog. The Germans easily rolled over the defending divisions, many of which had been battered in the recent fighting on the Somme and were still in the process of being rebuilt. A Portuguese division evaporated almost at once. Rupprecht's men had overrun the front three trenches by noon and by nightfall had seized some of the crucial crossings over the River Lys. Soft ground was making it difficult to move artillery forwards and caused some of the immense German tanks to ditch, but only on the left, where the British were defending Festubert and Givenchy stubbornly, was there cause for concern. Fourth Army joined in the next morning and enjoyed similar success, storming Messines village and forcing the British to evacuate Armentières.

On 11 April progress was slower, but the lead German units finished the day well established across the Lys. They were ready to drive through the Nieppe Forest for Hazebrouck, having advanced 14 kilometres in three days. Haig was worried enough to issue his famous 'Backs to the Wall' order, calling for every position to be held 'to the last man' and for each soldier to 'fight on to the end'. On 12 April Plumer, worried for his southern flank, pulled his troops back at Ypres, giving up, among other hard-won ground, the ruins of Passchendaele. Elsewhere, though, the pace of the German advance slowed further and Ludendorff, impatient at Sixth Army's progress, switched the main effort from Hazebrouck to the capture of Bailleul. He was doing exactly what Kuhl had warned against: swinging north too soon, in close behind the Ypres salient, rather than driving deep into the British rear. Perhaps Ludendorff realized that he had not the strength to cut off and destroy the BEF north of his break-in and would have to settle for the more limited achievement of clearing the Ypres salient. There is evidence in Rupprecht's diary that Ludendorff was giving up on the idea of large knock-out blows and expecting instead to launch a series of smaller-scale offensives. His attention was beginning to drift to planning a renewed attack towards Amiens by Second Army. Rupprecht thought this a mistake which demonstrated that 'Ludendorff is a superb organizer, but no great strategist.' Whatever the reasoning, the change of German direction gave the British time to reinforce this sector: any chance to seize Hazebrouck and pull off a deep envelopment of the Allied north flank had gone.[3]

Over the next few days the pressure from OHL to keep up the pace of advance remained intense but, as Rupprecht noted, 'what good are orders to attack, if the troops are no longer capable of it?' The situation reminded him of the First Battle of Ypres, when attack orders kept coming which the men were in no position to carry out. One of the symptoms of exhaustion was a slip in discipline, with looting and drunkenness a common feature in captured towns: 'what a difference from our magnificent army of 1914!' Rupprecht complained. 'We are all stressed and over-tired', he admitted in his published diary. In the unpublished version, he was more direct, noting that 'Kuhl seemed entirely exhausted' and saying of himself: 'I am still very depressed and my nerves let me down badly.' Friction within the German command was reaching new heights, and Ludendorff seems to have been at the root of the problem. On 2 April Kuhl had noted that

> Ludendorff is very agitated, intense and nervous, he wanted to some extent to excuse himself for the multiple changes of decision and orders and blames the army commands for not orienting him sufficiently and not giving him important information. For example, a few days ago Second Army all of a sudden reported that they didn't have enough ammunition and that consequently they would be unable to execute the attack he wanted, and so on. But that kind of friction cannot be eliminated in warfare: one just has to deal with it. If you always want to have perfect information for your decisions, you'll never reach any decision at all. What he said about his intentions was not at all clear, he gave no end-objectives or clear missions for the armies, just lots of tactical odds and ends.

In the middle of April the Sixth Army chief of staff complained to Kuhl about Ludendorff's interfering. Not only was he uptight and micro-managing the smallest details, he also had a habit of demanding changes to orders issued by the army after they had been sent out, which caused severe friction and disorder. Kuhl was in little position to help:

> I myself am continually being called up by Ludendorff about tiny details, such as that one division doesn't have the correct maps, and so on. Unfortunately

his liaison officers go around looking for negative things to tell him which will make them look good. Recent days were frankly dreadful because of all this flapping around, you can't even think for the endless telephone calls. The army group was cut out of the chain of command with Ludendorff dealing directly himself with the army commanders and giving them their orders. We had to ask the armies first of all what Ludendorff had ordered them to do, so as not to contradict him. I had to keep these interventions secret from the Crown Prince [Rupprecht]: he is already very worked up by them and it could easily turn into a proper fight, since the Crown Prince is furious about it. He is becoming in fact entirely excluded.

Later, during the fighting on the Aisne, OHL cut Crown Prince Wilhelm out of the command loop in much the same way. This sometimes extended even to important personnel decisions. When Kaiser Wilhelm II returned from a visit to General von Stetten's II Bavarian Army Corps, he complained that Stetten seemed out of touch and had made a poor impression on him. However little trust anyone had in the Kaiser's judgement, his will must be obeyed. Stetten, even though he was a personal friend of Rupprecht's, was unceremoniously sacked.[4]

On 15 and 16 April the Germans managed to establish toe-holds on the lower slopes of the Flanders Ridge but within a couple of days the advance had come to a complete standstill. Ludendorff ordered a pause to prepare a set-piece resumption of operations on 25 April. This new assault seized the vital high ground of Mount Kemmel from its French defenders but the Germans proved unable to exploit their success. Operation GEORGETTE had run out of steam. Indeed, when Second Army's drive south of the Somme on 24 April did not manage even to take and hold Villers Bretonneux, it reinforced the feeling that Rupprecht's whole Army Group was worn out and needed a rest. Ludendorff would have to look elsewhere for his victories. GEORGETTE was officially suspended on 29 April. A few days later, Ludendorff suggested using a couple of divisions to renew the attack on Festubert and Givenchy. Rupprecht refused.[5]

Once again, as on 21 March, the Germans had managed an impressive tactical break-in and caused considerable concern within the Allied high command. At the operational and strategic levels, however, even though the British lost more ground around Ypres in three weeks than they had gained in four months of bloody fighting the previous year, GEORGETTE was a failure. Again, the fundamental problem was the difficulty of maintaining the momentum of an attack. The scaled-down operation launched on 9 April was, perhaps, never strong enough to have much chance of achieving its most ambitious aims. With the forces available, to take Hazebrouck, drive for the Channel ports, and cut off the British and Belgian coast was not considered a very realistic objective even by the most optimistic voices at OHL. Only if the BEF instantly crumbled might that be on the cards. When it became clear that the British would not collapse, the Germans began to work towards the more limited objective of levering them out of the Ypres salient. This also failed. The cost to the German army was 86,000 men, a little over one-third as many as MICHAEL. British casualties were roughly the same: 82,040. Overall, in a little over a month, more than 650,000 men had become casualties, half of them German.[6]

Today, we know that the spring offensives so far had proved a double defeat for Germany. For Entente commanders at the time, blessed with none of our perfect hindsight, however, the situation still appeared extremely dangerous. At the end of April, German armies remained poised 16 kilometres from Amiens and only 60 from both Abbeville and Calais: one good victory away. The British army had taken a beating. Of its sixty divisions, all bar five had been heavily engaged, with twenty-nine used twice and six in action three times. The French situation was better: of their 103 divisions, forty-one had fought in March and April, three of them twice. Nevertheless, the French had been compelled to extend their front by some 100 kilometres, eating into their reserves. On the other hand, French intelligence estimated that, thanks largely to transfers from Italy and Russia, Germany's available reserves, which had been seventy-four divisions on 20 March, had been reduced to only sixty-four by 1 May. Worse still, the whereabouts of forty-nine of them were unknown. The threat remained very real and very large.[7]

Ludendorff felt that the Allies were now too strong north of the Somme. While defeating the British remained the main priority, he would have to draw French reserves away down south before attacking Haig again. His plan was for Crown Prince Wilhelm's Army Group to hit the French line along the Chemin des Dames, north-west of Reims, with Operation BLÜCHER. Eventually some forty-two divisions took part. Execution was planned for 27 May. Rupprecht's Army Group was to follow this up as soon as possible with a resumption of its offensive against the BEF. Early thinking favoured NEU-MICHAEL, a renewed push between the Somme and Arras, targeting Doullens, but Kuhl eventually managed to convince OHL that a NEU-GEORG in Flanders would be more practical and offered greater rewards. NEU-GEORG would attack between Ypres and the Forest of Nieppe, aiming for Poperinghe and Cassel. It was later re-designated HAGEN.

Since it would take time to re-deploy guns and equipment for this up from operations further south, the launch was originally planned for late June, although by 31 May that had been pushed back to mid-July.[8]

While planning continued, the German army tried to pick out the lessons of the offensives so far. The way it did so reveals a further deterioration in its capacity to think. All the attacks of March and April 1918 bogged down in the face of logistic difficulties and the exhaustion of the attackers. As the Germans began to analyse these offensives, however, they concentrated not on operations, but tactics. The lessons-learnt system had started to creak at Arras and in Flanders the previous year. It now seemed to be losing the ability to identify even the most important questions to ask. Worse, it was even less able to put forward honest answers to the questions it did ask. After-action reports parroted the dogma that recent fighting had demonstrated the efficacy of tactical doctrine, even as commanders complained that their troops were unable to shake the habits of trench warfare and keep up with the increased tempo of mobile operations. Many units did not even employ the new tactics. Corps and army headquarters, far from leaving subordinates free to use their initiative, had been trying to exercise too much control, intervening even in the movements of individual regiments. The General Staff seemed to Rupprecht to be part of the problem:

> Higher commands are paid ever less attention to. Their reports go immediately to OHL to mostly young General Staff officers, who have little of the important understanding of personalities. These judge them and the judgements they make often have huge impact. The quest to present one's own performance in the best possible light tempts them to over-sharp and not always accurate criticism.

Albrecht von Thaer, an experienced staff officer, shared a similarly low opinion of what he called the 'demi-gods' who surrounded Ludendorff at OHL, none of whom was prepared to pass on unwelcome news. The learning process was beginning to prove itself incapable of keeping up with the pace of change. Indeed, more generally, paralysis was gripping the German army. Control was becoming increasingly centralized but those at the top who insisted on making more and more of the decisions were receiving ever less reliable information on which to base them. The consequence, inevitably, was poor choices.[9]

Rupprecht was growing intensely concerned: 'if our next big blow fails, our situation will certainly be poor and there will be little hope that we can bring the war to a tolerably satisfactory conclusion', he noted on 29 April.

About a week later he reported to his father that although 'the overall situation is at the moment not unhealthy', Germany needed to win by midsummer if she were to avoid the war dragging on into the unforeseeable future, but Kuhl and Rupprecht agreed that she would not be able to do so. Since U-boats were unlikely to force a submission from Britain, the only way to end the war was to drive the British into the Channel but, with recent victories 'largely Pyrrhic ones' which ate into German strength, and hunger a growing issue in the Central Powers, this would only become more difficult over time. The replacement situation was deteriorating. Divisions arriving from Russia consisted exclusively of men who were either over forty or very young. One whole company of this kind had raised the white flag the first time they came under enemy shell-fire. The only solution, Rupprecht felt, was to restore independence to Belgium and trade Alsace-Lorraine for colonies to achieve a compromise peace. OHL seemed at one level to see the situation clearly: they grasped the need to avoid heavy casualties. They were unwilling, however, to follow their own logic through, accept that military victory was beyond Germany's strength, and start to negotiate. 'It's the policy of the ostrich', Rupprecht noted.[10]

One man who agreed with Rupprecht was the aspiring politician, Prince Max von Baden. One of the candidates to replace Bethmann Hollweg the previous summer, he offered a relatively moderate voice in German affairs. Since February, he had been pushing for peace talks, quoting the view of the well-respected Germanophile Swiss war correspondent, Hermann Stegemann, that Germany's position was 'splendid, but hopeless'. Continuing the war, in Max's view, increased both Germany's war guilt and the risks of Bolshevik revolution across Europe. Military action would only drive her enemies together, while diplomacy might prise them apart. Max was gathering like-minded people to build a power base. On 19 May he began a three-day visit to Rupprecht's headquarters, in the course of which personal empathy developed into political collaboration. Rupprecht agreed with Stegemann's analysis. Max and Rupprecht worked together to influence other German royals, Ludendorff, the chancellor, and even the Kaiser. For instance, Rupprecht suggested Max to Ludendorff as a foreign minister to replace Kühlmann. Results, however, as we shall see, were slow to come. This should not be mistaken for an exclusively progressive alliance to build a better future. Their aims remained poorly defined but centred on making the Kaiser see the true seriousness of the situation in which Germany found herself. Their main motivation was a shared dread that defeat would bring down the monarchy. Only by contrast with a world as stubborn as the Kaiser's court might theirs seem truly liberal voices.[11]

Rupprecht's pessimism was growing again. He told Kuhl that, if the war could not be concluded by winter, there would be a revolution. Kuhl thought he had picked up this idea from Max, but other factors also were conspiring to lower Rupprecht's morale. On 12 May, Rupprecht made a dispiriting visit to the Bavarian Lifeguard Regiment, with which he had begun his military career. They had been one of the first units to the summit of Mount Kemmel. It proved 'a painful reunion! Many dear old comrades were missing. The regiment's casualties in the recent fighting were quite severe, in officers alone they lost 40.' He was having trouble with insomnia, barely managing four hours of unbroken sleep per night. This left him feeling exhausted.[12]

BLÜCHER began on 27 May with another stunning success. For the first time, the German artillery all fired by the map as the British had at Cambrai six months earlier. This helped achieve surprise. The bombardment was heavy but very sharp, lasting less than three hours. The German infantry attacked just before first light and quickly overran a garrison which, rather than defending in depth, was packing the front line. They seized the Chemin des Dames, overran much of the enemy's artillery, and swept on across the River Aisne. By nightfall Seventh Army had advanced over 20 kilometres, the largest one-day advance of any Western Front attack. Rupprecht was especially pleased that the Germans were finding and defeating British divisions in the line: five of them had been sent there to recover from the battering they had received in March and April. BLÜCHER seemed to be doing its job of softening up the BEF. German forces captured Soissons and were threatening both Reims and the River Marne. By 1 June their forces were only 60 kilometres from Paris. French reserves were being rapidly chewed up and Foch had ordered troops down from Amiens to prop up defences in the Marne sector. Ludendorff was so keen to exploit the success of Crown Prince Wilhelm's Army Group, however, that he also began stripping divisions from Rupprecht. A diversion was becoming a distraction. Even worse, BLÜCHER was now losing steam. Progress slowed and stopped. On 4 June Seventh Army had to pause to regroup. An attack between Montdidier and Compiègne on 9 June (Operation GNEISENAU), designed to ease pressure on one shoulder of the huge salient created by BLÜCHER and suck further Allied reserves down from Flanders, accomplished little.[13]

Neither Rupprecht nor Kuhl agreed with Ludendorff that HAGEN would decide the war. With the thirty-nine divisions likely to be available, the most they could hope for would be to take Hazebrouck and Cassel and clear the Ypres salient. In any case, Ludendorff decided on 6 June that the next attack after GNEISENAU should not be HAGEN, but an operation to push across the Marne and capture Reims. This was eventually scheduled for 15 July and given the codename MARNESCHUTZ-REIMS. HAGEN would not be feasible before 1 August at the earliest.[14]

While Rupprecht planned his next move, the British demonstrated that they would not sit on the defensive for ever. June saw the beginning of a series of local, limited-objective attacks. Most famously, on 4 July ten battalions of Australian infantry, accompanied by four companies of Americans and supported by sixty tanks, attacked north of Villers Bretonneux and, in a model combined-arms action lasting ninety-three minutes, captured the village of Hamel. On 19 July, the Australians were in action again, this time with South African and Scottish troops, to capture Meteren village.[15]

As usual, the first place OHL sought explanations for the success of these British attacks was in tactics. The high number of German prisoners taken suggested to the General Staff that the defenders were packing too much of their strength forward. Maintaining a Forward Zone only 100 or 200 metres deep was insufficient: 500 or 1,000 metres would be more appropriate. OHL re-emphasized that the primary defensive effort should concentrate on the fight, not for the front line, but for the Main Line of Resistance. What OHL did not comment on was that much of the German army was by now in a bad way. Rupprecht noted that some of his infantry companies, which should have had 124 men in the field, in fact numbered only fifty. This undercut the troops' ability to mount a proper defence in depth. Food was in short supply. There were no potatoes for front-line troops and they were only receiving fresh meat nine days per month. With widespread exhaustion and hunger lowering resistance, disease spread quickly. A first wave of the notorious Spanish 'flu which ravaged Europe and America in 1918 and 1919 swept the army from late June for a month. A second wave followed in September. In Sixth Army alone, some 15,000 men were hospitalized.[16]

Meanwhile, Rupprecht was finding out for himself that there was plenty of aggression left in his enemy. Soon after midnight on 2 July enemy aeroplanes raided his headquarters. The account Rupprecht left is vivid:

> When the alarm sounded, I went down into the cellar, as I previously never had. No sooner had I entered than I heard the buzz of the enemy aeroplanes

and the whistle of dropping bombs. A dull thud, a violent crack! Suddenly the doors from the shelter out into the garden blew open and down the stairs stumbled the sentry who had been standing outside, a member of the Landsturm, blown in by a bomb which exploded in the garden. I caught him: he was bewildered, but unwounded.

The walls were shaking and the doors were banging backwards and forwards. We closed them. There was no doubt about it: the conservatory adjoining my bedroom was hit. You could clearly hear the sound of the glass roof falling in. Captain Gerke, who was struggling to count the bombs, had just said 'five' when a bomb fell immediately on the shelter itself, which was installed in the cellar under the stone staircase leading into the garden. The blast was extremely strong. I saw the roof of the shelter buckle, then the light went out and a thick cloud of dust and smoke blew through the doors which had once again sprung open.

I grabbed my electric torch and checked that everything was all right. But where was my adjutant, Captain von Hirschberg? We searched the cellar, then heard his voice. He tottered into the shelter covered in blood. He had been slow to get out of bed and was caught by the blast of an exploding bomb as he neared the steps down into the cellar. He had bomb splinters in his legs and was blown into the cellar, where he sustained other further injuries from splinters of glass. We examined his wounds at once: luckily, they were light.

Already we wanted to leave the dark cellar, but then heard other bombs land further away. In the morning it became clear that it was not only the house I lived in and its outbuildings that were badly damaged. A bank was also hit and reduced to rubble. The only person inside, a Belgian, was miraculously spared. A building diagonally across from mine, which was occupied by Belgian nuns, was likewise completely destroyed without its inhabitants coming to any harm. An ill Franciscan sister was eventually dug out of the ruins of the upstairs, after much hard work.

The story of the raid seems to be as follows. The enemy aircraft had followed one of our bomber squadrons returning from a night flight to hide the sound of their motors. Then they split up. Some bombed the nearest air defence batteries while the others attacked my house. It's not clear how many enemy squadrons were flying over Tournai that night, but in any case there were several. Bombs were also dropped near army headquarters. In the morning, two squadrons appeared again, the first consisting of only three machines, to inspect and photograph the damage.

I took my usual morning ride to the park at Froyennes for my exercise, accompanied by Major von Behr. I always got back from there in time for the mid-day briefing at the HQ building. This time, I luckily stayed a bit longer than normal in the park. While I was still there, I heard firing from a nearby anti-aircraft battery and immediately thereafter the whistle of a bomb, probably dropped on the flak battery. After the first impact came several others, bit by bit moving away towards the city. As it turned out, the fliers flew along the road to the town and damaged some houses by the entrance to the city. It was as if someone knew at what time I took this route every day. This suspicion was close to the mark, as also in Douai, at the hour at which the general commanding Seventeenth Army usually journeyed from his residence to his HQ, his route was bombed from the air.

When searches were carried out they turned up hidden wireless transmitters in various places, used by spies to communicate with the enemy.

In all, four bombs fell on Rupprecht's house or in his garden. Hirschberg was hospitalized but there is no record of other casualties. Contrary to Rupprecht's suspicions, it is unlikely the RAF were targeting him directly that night. Especially by night, they had no way of achieving that level of accuracy at this time. It is more probable that he was caught up in a raid on Tournai station, one of a series of experiments targeting the German railway network.[17]

HAGEN never happened. When MARNESCHUTZ-REIMS began on 15 July, it did not go at all to plan. A total of nearly fifty German divisions took part, supported by 6,400 guns, over 2,000 mortars, and 900 aircraft. Although the artillery support thus came close to the level available on 21 March in absolute terms, the ratio of German to Allied guns was the lowest of any of the 1918 offensives, at 2:1. Worse, the French defenders were well dug-in and alert. Foch was actively preparing a counter-attack on the west face of the Marne salient, designed to retake Soissons. This was planned for 18 July so the French were watching the sector very closely and picked up indications of the impending German attack. For once, the Germans failed to achieve surprise. In the face of intense enemy artillery fire, many of the assault troops lost the cover of the creeping barrage. A few divisions managed to gain toe-holds on the far side of the River Marne but found themselves very exposed there. Their artillery support was still struggling to get forward. It soon became clear that Reims would not fall anytime soon. Within less than thirty-six hours the German advance stuttered to a stop. By the end of 17 July OHL was ordering the evacuation of the furthest bridgeheads over the Marne and everywhere attackers became defenders. Within hours, during the early morning of 18 July, the German troops manning the western face of the Chateau-Thierry salient were attacked by General Charles Mangin's Tenth Army, supported by 346 tanks, swinging out of the Forest of Villers-Cotterêts and striking towards Soissons.

OHL suspended all transfers of men and resources for HAGEN. It despatched two of Rupprecht's divisions, which he was keeping back for that operation, down to prop up the defence in what is now known as the

Second Battle of the Marne. Although over the next fortnight of heavy fighting the French failed to cut off and destroy the German salient, they did push its defenders back across the Aisne and Vesle rivers. In all, seven divisions earmarked for HAGEN had been diverted to the Marne. More importantly, the French had made it clear that the initiative now lay, not with the Germans, but with the Allies. Loßberg proposed an immediate withdrawal into the Hindenburg Line. Ludendorff was not prepared to go so far. Maybe he did not think it militarily necessary yet. Maybe he was unwilling to acknowledge in public that his offensives had failed. He was prepared, however, to cancel HAGEN, at least for now, despite objections from Kuhl. This took place on 20 July. Kuhl noted tersely that 'this is the turning point of the war!' The next task for Rupprecht and his Army Group would be not to attack, but to defend.[18]

22

The Hundred Days

It is easy to forget now that, even after the Second Battle of the Marne (15 July–6 August 1918), most people still had little clue how and when the war would finish. This war had been unlike any other and had touched so many so deeply. How could it possibly end? What might victory or defeat even look like, when the cost in blood and treasure had been so high? Could old-world diplomacy possibly silence the still-loud beat of the drums of war? In the summer of 1918 to suggest that it might all be over by Christmas would have seemed a joke in the worst of taste. Part of the story of what we now know to have been the last few months of the First World War is how and when the German military at last began to understand the true nature and meaning of defeat.

In July and early August 1918 Rupprecht and Kuhl began doing what they could to improve their defences against an Allied attack. In places, they straightened the line, pulling out from some of the most vulnerable positions. They were handicapped by a shortage of labour and transport, and by poor morale. The 111th Division, for example, was exhausted. It had been in the front line for 138 straight days, with just one twelve-day break. It had lost nearly 6,000 men. Letters home were arguing for strikes and revolution. One man in the sick bay wrote that he was being treated worse than a convict or an animal. The replacement situation was so dire that only Saxony still had men to spare: the King of Saxony decided to allow his soldiers to be drafted into Prussian regiments, to Rupprecht's predictable disapproval. Oberste Heeresleitung (OHL) reorganized command arrangements. Rupprecht's Army Group had become unwieldy: controlling five separate armies was too burdensome. A new Army Group was to be created on 12 August under General Max von Boehn to take over the three armies between the rivers Somme and Oise, including Rupprecht's Second Army.[1]

Before that reorganization could take place, though, in the early morning of 8 August, a ferocious Anglo–French assault began on Marwitz's Second Army east of Amiens. Spearheads from the Australian and Canadian corps, supported by 430 tanks and over 2,000 guns, attacked along a 17-kilometre front. Debeney's French First Army soon joined in. Nearly 2,000 British and French aeroplanes took to the air. German resistance crumbled fast. By nightfall the British and French forces had driven up to 12 kilometres and captured almost all their objectives. The Germans lost 27,000 men that day, 12,000 of them as prisoners. Kuhl's diary describes how they were taken completely by surprise and how the attack had simply overrun the burnt-out defenders. It was, he concluded laconically, 'a hard day'. Rupprecht put part of the blame on a morning fog which blinded his anti-tank guns and allowed enemy armour and infantry to work closely together. Surprise was another important factor. As at Cambrai, British guns had fired no preliminary bombardment and Rawlinson's Fourth Army did a good job of concealing its other preparations.[2]

The next day, the pace of the British advance slowed, gaining only another 5 kilometres. Although some German reinforcements had come up, the resistance Marwitz could offer was still very limited. Again, however, the British had not planned adequately for the second day of operations. They were unable to coordinate their actions effectively and launched a weak series of piecemeal attacks. Nevertheless, a worried Marwitz proposed falling back behind the Somme. Ludendorff responded by firing Marwitz's chief of staff and ordering him to hold firm. On 10 August the British proved Ludendorff right. They struggled to make another 1,500 metres and, after another day of disappointing results on 11 August, Haig and Rawlinson suspended the Amiens operation. The British had suffered casualties of about 20,000 men; the French a similar number; and the Germans 48,000. Of those, no fewer than 30,000 had been taken prisoner.[3]

The Battle of Amiens has tended to occupy a more prominent place in histories of 1918 than, say, the Second Battle of the Marne, especially in the Anglo-Saxon world. This is partly because the British Expeditionary Force (BEF), rather than the French, took the leading role. Partly also, however, it is because the Battle of Amiens is often seen as the beginning of the German army's final decline. The German official monograph argued that 'as the evening of 8 August settled over the battlefield of the Second Army, the heaviest defeat of the German army since the beginning of the war was an established fact.... The first steps along the dark road through the forest of Compiègne to the Hall of Mirrors at Versailles were taken with the catastrophe of 8 August 1918.' In his memoirs Ludendorff famously called 8 August 'the black day of the German Army in the history of this war', primarily because it showed how far the combat effectiveness of the army had fallen. 'The war', he decided, 'must be ended.' His most recent biographer, however, argues that although he offered to resign, he was far less convinced that Germany had lost the war than he later pretended. Defeats, for Ludendorff, remained the result of poor individual decisions rather than systemic failings. He blamed Wetzell for the Marne and Marwitz's chief of staff for Amiens. He was constantly on the look-out for scapegoats and redoubled his efforts to win the war single-handed. Rupprecht was

> amazed at the patience of my chief of staff, who doesn't let himself lose his cool at the endless telephone calls from Ludendorff, even when he's trying to lay down what even individual battalions...should do. To keep Ludendorff calm he always agrees with him or at most says 'that depends on how things play out, we can't predict that yet', or so on. The telephone has some draw-backs: it gets used too often, and in direct communications between OHL and the chiefs of staff of armies and corps, the commanders get totally shut out. Just recently one army commander said to me in this regard: 'I no longer really know what I'm there for, since everything has always been decided before I am consulted.' Ludendorff's impatience is to blame for much of this, however understandable it may be in the current circumstances. If only Ludendorff would not ring up every single corps direct, as well as the army group and army chiefs of staff! ·

Ludendorff's nerve was clearly cracking, his screaming at his staff officers audible throughout his headquarters. He was changing chiefs of staff 'like underwear' and developing the shakes.[4]

It was not just Ludendorff feeling the strain. Rupprecht was finding it hard to recover from a bout of influenza and his spirits, too, were low. He could not see how Second Army would be able to hold out. On 13 August he went back to Bavaria for a couple of weeks to recuperate, but his mood did not improve much. He wrote to Prince Max that 'I no longer believe that we can hold out over the winter.' Rupprecht spent his leave fishing with his son and stalking stag in the Alps. He also acquired a wife thirty years younger than himself: Princess Antonie of Luxembourg. Since July 1917 he had been spending time with the young Grand Duchess of

Luxembourg and her five sisters, aware that his son needed a mother and the Wittelsbach dynasty needed a spare heir. The fourth sister, Antonie, seemed keenest and got on well with her future stepson, Albrecht. The engagement was announced on 25 August.[5]

By the time Rupprecht got back to his headquarters on 2 September, the situation had deteriorated badly. While he was away, Foch had orchestrated a sequence of attacks up and down the Western Front. The French struck one day, the British somewhere else the next, and the Americans on a third in a different sector again. As part of this, Rupprecht's Army Group came under British attack between Arras and Albert on 21 August. Employing similar tactics to those used at Amiens, the BEF drove forwards 5 kilometres. To the south Rawlinson's Fourth Army soon resumed their push along the Somme. The whole right flank of the British army began chewing through the German defences across the old Somme battlefield towards Bapaume and Péronne. In all, seven British and French armies were locked in battle with five German ones over 200 kilometres of the Western Front, from Lens almost all the way to Reims. Not since the autumn of 1914 had the fighting been on such a scale.

The strain on the Germans was intense. In Kuhl's view:

> We stand now at the crisis. Questions of prestige have no role to play. Cold, sober calculation is all. We can't pull the wool over our people's eyes. We can't force a decision. We are worn out. The divisions are in disorder. We can only fight a delaying action, with skilful retreats, losing ground in some places and holding it elsewhere. I wish I was wrong.

The war could no longer be won, but might it still be possible to force a draw? Kuhl envisaged fighting a long delaying action, slowly pulling back from defensive line to defensive line. In this way the Allies could be prevented from reaching the Rhine until sometime in 1919. This would require coherent operational planning if it was to work, but Kuhl saw two obstacles to this taking place. Loßberg, now Boehn's chief of staff, was one: he would have to be involved, especially given the influence he had with Ludendorff, but he was a tactician, incapable of thinking operationally on the scale required. Rupprecht's absence in Germany would also make decision-making harder.[6]

Through the last days of August, German resistance was fierce. Nonetheless, the Allied armies ground inexorably forward. Progress was slow: it took the New Zealand Division eight days to drive 12 kilometres and liberate the ruins of Bapaume, for example. This was lightning fast compared with earlier years, but at this rate it might indeed take nine months to reach the Rhine, assuming they did not run out of manpower first. Boehn's attempts to hold the old German reserve position from 1916 along the Bapaume–Péronne road failed. He was outflanked by Australian troops to the south at Mont St Quentin and Canadians driving down the Arras–Cambrai road to the north. OHL accepted the inevitable and ordered Boehn's and Rupprecht's Army Groups to fall back into the Hindenburg Line. Finally Ludendorff told Hindenburg that 'we no longer have any prospect of winning the war'.[7]

By 7 September the Germans were back where they had begun the year. The Allies began closing up to the Hindenburg Line and positioning all the men, machines, and munitions they would need to assault it. While preparations went on, relative calm descended on the front. The Germans had recoiled up to 50 kilometres from their summer high-water mark. Losses on both sides had been heavy. British Third Army had lost 23 per cent of its infantrymen, while 29 per cent of German Seventeenth Army's combat troops had become casualties. Over half of the German soldiers went missing in action, most of them ending up fit and healthy but in British hands. This was partly because open fighting made it easier to cut off and capture individuals and whole units. Partly, however, it was also a symptom of declining morale. Other signs of defeatism came across in the mail censorship summaries, in increased desertion and 'shirking' behind the lines, and even in reports of whole units running away at the first rumour of an enemy. The story of the morale of the German army during late 1918 is complex and historians are still debating it, but all can agree that it was significantly worse than it had been earlier in the war.[8]

On 6 September Hindenburg, Ludendorff, and some of the chiefs of staff met to discuss what had gone wrong and what to do next. Ludendorff looked 'completely ill and exhausted'. He argued that MARNESCHUTZ-REIMS had been defeated because security had failed and the French had been expecting it, while conversely the Germans had let themselves be taken by surprise by the French counter-attack. More recent setbacks in Picardy were the result of poor leadership. 'So it is everyone's fault—except OHL's', Kuhl noted sourly: 'in reality, it's the other way around'. OHL's view was superficial but some units carried out sophisticated analysis which gives a better explanation of the recent setbacks. For example, the 3rd Marine Division drew four conclusions from the fighting for Bapaume (21–31 August). First, German infantry was weaker than before, particularly in morale. Second, defensive doctrine was too complicated and cumbrous. Using multiple different names for each defensive line was causing confusion. Third, divisions were being committed piecemeal, mixing up units and reducing cohesion. Lastly, 'tank shock' was a problem. Units were dissolving at the sight of enemy armour. Poor leadership, of the kind Hindenburg and Ludendorff were fixated on, was only one factor among many.[9]

The German supreme command was not entirely blind to the tactical problems front-line troops were facing. Between July and September OHL issued eleven different memoranda tweaking defensive tactics to counter new Allied methods. There were multiple problems with how it went about this, however. First, it once more assumed that its doctrine was perfect and defeats must be the result of failure to follow instructions properly. There was little evidence for this. Second, defence in depth required manpower that was no longer to hand. The average infantry battalion had begun 1918 with 850 men. By the end of September this was down to 540. Even achieving this strength had required breaking up no fewer than 22 whole divisions. Third, as we have seen before, the standard of instant communications assumed in OHL's instructions was impossible given the technology available and conditions on the battlefield. Fourth, setting up field guns near the front line to kill tanks proved highly effective when visibility was good. In fog, however, they were useless and quickly overrun. More importantly, detaching guns in this way distorted and unbalanced the overall defence. Lastly, and most significantly, there was a hidden assumption underpinning OHL's analysis that German troops were better than the enemy. So, if they were beaten, they must have done something wrong. The possibility that the enemy might be doing something right was never admitted. Now, of course it made sense to concentrate effort on improving things the Germans could control, rather than those they could not. Moreover, to accept that the British or French had got better and developed tactics to which the Germans had no answer might damage morale. Nonetheless, failure to face the tactical facts infected and prejudiced operational and strategic decision-making. Wishful thinking was no basis for sensible planning. Tactically, the Germans were being outfought every time and they had run out of useful responses. On 21 September OHL revised its tactical doctrine again. Units were no longer to defend elastically but were to fight in, and at all costs hold, the main line. The wheel had turned full circle, back to the tactical rigidity Falkenhayn had espoused in 1915 and 1916. Operationally, too, the Allies were posing problems all up and down the front too quickly for the Germans to respond, even had the resources to do so been available. The only concrete decision reached on 6 September was to try more of the same of an operational recipe that patently was not working: they would hold in the Hindenburg Line as long as possible to buy time to build the 'Hermann Line' 15–20 kilometres further back.[10]

The time had come to address the increasingly obvious problem of Erich Ludendorff himself. Doctors prescribed more sleep and relaxation to counter his nervous strain. Boehn went to see him on 5 September, on behalf of all the commanders of armies and Army Groups. He asked Ludendorff to stop short-circuiting the chain of command and interfering so aggressively in day-to-day operational details. Ludendorff promised to behave better. He also agreed to a reorganization of his staff. Wetzell, after two years as chief of operations, was out. Colonel Wilhelm Heye became Ludendorff's deputy. Speculation that Ludendorff himself might be replaced was widespread. For a while, Ludendorff was calmer. Before September was out, however, he was back to his old tricks, sacking army commanders he felt had let him down, including Marwitz from Second Army, and fiddling with the deployment of the anti-tank defences of one of Rupprecht's corps.[11]

The middle of September was taken up with battles for the outposts of the Hindenburg Line at Havrincourt (12 September) and Épehy (18 September) as well as the American clearance of the St Mihiel salient (12–16 September). The Germans remained uncertain about where the Allies would strike next. Rupprecht was still most concerned about his left flank, south of Cambrai. He could not understand why the British were not being more aggressive here. He also wondered, however, whether Haig might assault Sixth Army north of the River Scarpe. Later in the month he began looking for reinforcements to send to Fourth Army, having received intelligence of an imminent enemy attack on the Flanders coast. A simultaneous attack on all three armies seemed possible and Kuhl was well aware that they did not have the strength to withstand that. Ludendorff was also worried about threats at Verdun, in Alsace, and in Lorraine. No part of the front seemed safe.[12]

One huge, coordinated offensive was precisely what Allied supreme commander Ferdinand Foch had in mind. On 26 September the largest battle of the Great War opened with a Franco-American drive between the Meuse and Reims towards the rail junction at Mézières. The next day, the British attacked west of Cambrai, crossed the Canal du Nord, and established bridgeheads across the St Quentin Canal. Belgian, British, and French troops launched an offensive around Ypres on 28 September. Finally, on 29 September a Franco-British force attacked the Hindenburg Line around

St Quentin. Bitter fighting flared from Flanders to the Meuse. Not one of these attacks created a clean break in the German lines. Indeed, early results were disappointing. After three days of savage combat in the Argonne Forest, American forces had only advanced 12 kilometres at best. General Pershing suspended his attack on 29 September after losing 45,000 men. The drive on Cambrai, similarly, ran out of steam by the end of the month. The Australian, American, and British troops of Rawlinson's British Fourth Army managed to break in to the Hindenburg Line on 29 September, but it took them several bitter days of combat to clear the Germans out. Only at Ypres did the Allies win quick success. Within forty-eight hours they had cleared the ridges up which the British had toiled so painfully in 1917 and were heading down the far slope towards the rail lines at Roulers. The Flanders operation only ground to a halt when the difficulty of transport over the shattered battlefields of the salient choked off supplies and prevented further progress. Foch's plan, however, did not depend on a breakthrough at Ypres or indeed anywhere. He was betting that the cumulative effect of these attacks would exceed the sum of the parts.[13]

Foch was proved spectacularly correct. At 6 p.m. on 28 September Ludendorff and Hindenburg agreed that it was time to ask for an armistice: now, without delay. The next day they informed the Kaiser and decided to form a new government to approach President Woodrow Wilson and request a ceasefire. In his memoirs, Ludendorff tried to maintain that it was not the military situation on the Western Front, but the imminent collapse of Bulgaria, which provoked his decision. This was a transparent attempt to deflect blame. Both Kuhl and Rupprecht thought little of this spin at the time and the briefing Ludendorff gave to his staff makes clear that he was desperate rather to forestall the collapse of an already unreliable army. He wanted the army to remain, at a minimum, strong enough to crush any Bolshevik revolution back home. If the army were defeated in battle, not only might it not be strong enough to do so but it might even precipitate the very revolution it was supposed to be guarding against.

Also on 28 September a telegram had arrived at Rupprecht's headquarters from Hindenburg warning all Army Groups that OHL was no longer in a position to send them any more reserves. Manpower was not available and, even if it had been, the transport situation prevented movement. Even before he heard of the decision to put out peace feelers, Rupprecht had been deeply worried: 'our situation has further deteriorated and is now critical as never before', he wrote. The only way to save Fourth Army in

Flanders, he thought, would be to retreat to Ghent, even at the cost of giving up the U-boat bases along the Belgian coast. Even Loßberg, 'the man with nerves of iron', had lost hope and was reporting that Army Group Boehn was at the end of its strength. Rupprecht told his father that 'the military situation has got worse once again'. OHL was still playing the ostrich game. Rupprecht re-emphasized the point in another letter: 'What I have been afraid of already for a long time, has now come to pass as I expected: the decisive defeat. . . . We must definitely achieve peace at once and at any price, since we are as good as defenceless. . . . It is the decisive moment in Bavarian history since 1866. If only I could be at home!' The same day, Leeb wrote in his diary that 'the campaign is lost'. Not everyone agreed yet, however. When Ludendorff rang Kuhl to admit defeat and tell him about the request for an armistice, Kuhl's first reaction was that this was premature and that they should at least try to make one more stand before giving up.[14]

The new Chancellor, Rupprecht's friend Prince Max von Baden, despatched a Peace Note to the United States overnight on 4/5 October. Even now, Ludendorff harboured unrealistic expectations of the Allies' likely demands, under-estimating their determination to ensure that Germany was in no position to resume hostilities. He thought he had more room for negotiation over the territory Germany still occupied than was ever likely to be the case. He told Kuhl that it would take nine months for German troops to evacuate Belgium and France. As Kuhl sardonically noted in his diary, 'I was afraid that the enemy might not give us so much time.'[15]

By 4 October the Germans had been pushed back into the reserve positions of the Hindenburg Line. To overwhelm this last belt of defences the Allies prepared another set-piece attack. While they did so, there was another brief lull in operations, during which Rupprecht slipped away to Luxembourg to visit his fiancée. On 8 October came news that the British were attacking once more. After heavy fighting and the last German counter-attack of the war, eventually the British smashed through into open country. Canadian forces finally liberated Cambrai in the morning of 9 October. By then, Rupprecht's armies were in full retreat back to the so-called Hermann Line, a sketchy set of defences on the east bank of the River Selle. Again, the Allies rolled forward and began to prepare a full-scale assault. By 11 October, Rupprecht's Army Group reserves had run out. He could offer his armies no further reinforcement.[16]

Pessimism spread through the German command. On 8 October Boehn and Loßberg reported that their troops were no longer capable of putting up a defence. This gave Ludendorff an excuse to sack both men and break up their Army Group. Three days later, the commander of Seventeenth Army, Otto von Below, also buckled. He telephoned Kuhl, insisting that his troops must retreat at once. To avoid leaving a gap in the line, and since anyway it was too late at night for such a manoeuvre, Kuhl said no. In that case, Below threatened, he would march anyway, orders or no. Insubordination of this kind could not be tolerated. Both Below and his chief of staff were rapidly sacked.[17]

The state of morale lower down the army is harder to untangle. There is evidence that, already depressed by the failure of the spring offensives and the defeats of July and August, it entered a final crisis, especially among rear area troops, after news of the Peace Note to President Wilson. Desertion and shirking were problems, albeit probably not on the scale some historians have suggested. Equally, however, there are indications that, particularly in some front-line units, spirit remained remarkably firm even in October. Better food, now that supply lines were shorter, played a major role in improving mood and the number of men taken prisoner declined in both absolute terms and as a proportion of total casualties. The slower tempo of operations in October made the situation appear less critical. Wilson's second note, which arrived in Berlin on 16 October, provoked resentment and stiffened resolve in some quarters. The idea that the German army was a morally beaten force, even after the Peace Note, is an over-simplification and it is the resilience, not the vulnerability, of the German army, even into the dying months of the war, that is one of its most striking characteristics.[18]

On 17 October the Allies went on the offensive once more, clearing the Belgian coast and liberating towns such as Bruges and Courtrai. Further south the British marched into Douai and Lille, although an attempt to bounce across the River Selle at first bogged down. Still, by 23 October the British were advancing on Valenciennes and the Forest of Mormal, while the French and Americans continued to grind forward in the south.

After weeks of increasingly erratic judgement and behaviour, Ludendorff was finally removed from his post on 26 October. Within a fortnight of demanding an immediate armistice he had begun to argue that the situation had improved, that Germany could afford to take a hard line, and that it might make sense to fight on into the new year. The final crisis came when he issued an order of the day to the army which rejected peace negotiations and so directly contradicted the civilian government. Max von Baden refused any longer to serve alongside Ludendorff. The Kaiser could hardly lose two Chancellors in less than a month, especially with his own position and prestige with the population at large falling fast. He accepted Ludendorff's resignation. Even Hindenburg made no more than a token effort to save the man who had been his partner for more than four years. The two men never spoke again. Ludendorff suggested Kuhl as his successor but the job went instead to Wilhelm Groener, a railway expert, chosen because the government's priority was now demobilization, not fighting on.[19]

On 30 October Kuhl and some of his other staff officers managed to escape their new headquarters in Brussels for a few hours' sightseeing on the battlefield of Waterloo, but from 1 November renewed Allied attacks shattered any relative quiet. Ghent and Valenciennes fell in the north while American and French forces resumed their drive towards the Meuse at Sedan and Mézières. On 4 November three British armies attacked on a 65-kilometre front and crossed the River Sambre. Rupprecht's report to OHL was bleak:

> The heavy fighting of 4 November on the fronts of Second and Seventeenth armies caused heavy wastage in personnel. Units on the front line, whose combat power had already been seriously reduced before the battle, have mostly been weakened to the limit by the losses they suffered in this heavy fighting. It is no longer possible to supply combat-capable reserves to the front.... The commanders of Seventeenth and Second armies dutifully report that, because of exhaustion, low unit strengths, and particularly the limited steadiness of their men, they are not capable of withstanding a new major offensive. There is a danger that a new large-scale attack would break through, or at least cause us heavy losses, and that we would have to start the move to the Antwerp-Meuse line in considerable disorder.

Soon after midnight, he ordered a general retreat. The rearguards detached to slow the British advance did a good job of holding up the enemy. Poor roads, worse weather, and an over-stretched supply network delayed the British even more and by 8 November they were losing all touch with the retreating Germans.[20]

Rupprecht's units were not the only ones on the brink of collapse. The navy mutinied in Kiel on 3 November and within days soviets of sailors, soldiers, and workers formed all over Germany as revolution spread. The German government hurried to send a delegation to discuss armistice terms with Foch. On 7 November the negotiators arrived at the French lines near Guise and were led to Foch's train, parked near the village of Rethondes in the forest of Compiègne. Several days of long and blunt talks ensued. While they went on, Germany descended into chaos. As soon as it became clear that the army would not fight for his throne, the Kaiser abdicated and fled into exile in Holland. On 9 November, Germany was proclaimed a republic, with the Socialist Friedrich Ebert taking over in Berlin as Chancellor. By now, the Allies were standing on the banks of the Rivers Scheldt and Meuse. On 11 November British troops reached the grimy Belgian town of Mons, where their war had begun. Early that morning, the German delegation finally signed the armistice and by noon the war, at long, long last, was over.

By then, Rupprecht's war had already finished, cut short by revolution in Munich. On the afternoon of 7 November, as many as 60,000 people packed onto the Theresienwiese fields in the south-west of the city, where the Oktoberfest is now held. Overlooked by a huge bronze statue of Bavaria, speaker after speaker demanded the immediate abdication of Kaiser Wilhelm II and his son, plus a package of political and social reforms. No mention was made of the Wittelsbachs. The demonstrators decided to process through the government quarter to the Angel of Peace monument, high on the bank of the River Isar and, as they marched, red flags appeared in the crowd. From the steps of the Feldherrnhalle, the monument built outside the royal palace to commemorate Bavaria's military past, agitators harangued the marchers, demanding an end to the monarchy. The leader of the Independent Social Democrats, Kurt Eisner, began to seize control of armouries and barracks throughout the city, persuading the soldiers to join the revolution. Resistance was slight. The War Minister had no troops on whom he could rely and soon even the royal guards at the palace began to slip away. By eight o'clock, Eisner's small but growing band controlled the barracks, the main railway station, the post office, and government buildings. A Soldiers' and Workers' Soviet set itself up in the Mathäser Beer Hall. It was the very model of a modern coup d'état: fast, effective, and mostly peaceful.

The masses on the streets of Munich made no attempt to storm the palace or detain the royal family. The writer Thomas Mann found the atmosphere peaceful and celebratory, rather than menacing. If there was any political sentiment, he thought, it was pro-Bavarian and anti-Hohenzollern. The government, however, was worried that revolutionaries might rush in during the night and round up the royal family. They advised the King to leave town until the situation became clearer. Later that night, three cars slipped out of the royal mews carrying the King and Queen, four princesses, Rupprecht's son Albrecht, and various members of staff. After a dramatic

Figure 22.1. The demonstration of 7 November 1918 on the Theresienwiese, Munich

night drive through thick fog, in the early morning of 8 November they took temporary refuge at one of their countryside castles on the road to the Austrian border. Within hours, Eisner proclaimed that the Wittelsbachs had been deposed and a republic set up: 'the Free State of Bavaria'. When Ludwig heard that revolutionaries were on their way to force him to abdicate, he fled, first to a hunting lodge in Berchtesgaden and then across the Austrian border to Salzburg. On 12 November 1918, Ludwig III signed a declaration releasing all officers of the Bavarian army from their oath of loyalty. Although he never formally abdicated, thus ended over seven centuries of Wittelsbach rule.[21]

About nine o'clock in the morning of 8 November, Rupprecht received his first news of the revolution from Munich. The telephone call was interrupted and information remained fragmentary for some time, but it was clear that no troops could be relied on to restore order and there was little Rupprecht could do from so far away. He issued a proclamation to all his Bavarian troops, claiming that the King was acting under duress and the government did not represent the majority. He called for a national convention to draw up a new constitution and a free vote to redefine the relationship between people and the royal family. Rupprecht evidently still saw a future for himself and his family in the government of a new Bavaria.

In the short run, however, it was possible that he was in personal danger. Soldiers' soviets were being set up throughout the army, including in Brussels, the site of Rupprecht's headquarters, just as they had been in Russia in 1917. The Bolsheviks' murder of the Tsar and his family was fresh in Rupprecht's memory. He may not yet have known that his father was fleeing into Austria, but he did hear of the Kaiser's flight on 10 November. The city of Brussels was sliding into anarchy as armed mobs of soldiers roamed the streets seeking loot, and it was becoming dangerous for Rupprecht to stay. He was, in any case, according to one of his staff officers, a 'broken' man. When Hindenburg ordered him to cooperate with the soviets, he could not bring himself to comply. Instead, he burned his personal papers, turned over command of the Army Group to Sixt von Armin, bade an emotional farewell to his staff, and took refuge in the Spanish Embassy late on 10 November.[22]

In some ways one almost feels that Rupprecht's war had already been over for a while. His behaviour during the Hundred Days was rather detached at times. He was absent on crucial occasions and was less determined to organize the defence and influence the campaign than he had been. His influenza did not help. Even after Rupprecht recovered from that illness, he continued to be troubled with insomnia and migraines. It is not hard to diagnose exhaustion and stress. Family was a further distraction. He was surely too experienced to be carried away by his new fiancée, but relations with his father remained an irritant. More importantly, one suspects he was demotivated by Ludendorff's habit of marginalizing Army Group and commanders and working through staff officers instead. The last occasion Rupprecht and Ludendorff met in wartime was on 18 July. More than anything else, however, one suspects that Rupprecht had simply realized that the situation had reached the point where there was no longer anything he could do.

23

Rupprecht on the Run

The Spanish ambassador provided Rupprecht with a car and a passport into the Netherlands under a false name. Travelling as Mr Landsberg, presumably to avoid getting interned or embarrassing the Dutch government, Rupprecht crossed the border on 12 November. In Amsterdam he stayed with an art connoisseur friend and studied pictures in the Rijksmuseum while he waited for news of the political situation back home. Eventually the government guaranteed his safety and, still incognito, he travelled back to Bavaria. A rising wave of political violence soon forced the Wittelsbachs abroad once more, however, and it was not until the autumn of 1919 that he was able to settle permanently back home. He finally married Princess Antonie of Luxembourg in April 1921.

Although she bore him a son and five daughters, the marriage seems not to have been a happy one. The couple spent increasing amounts of time apart as the years rolled by. Perhaps old habits died hard. Perhaps the Crown Prince was unable to meet the expectations of a much younger bride. Neither case would be the first or last of its kind in history. When his father died in October 1921 Rupprecht was able finally to agree a settlement with the government over the status and finances of the royal family. The Wittelsbachs received a lump sum and possession or residence rights in a number of palaces, castles, and estates. The state took over the rest.[1]

One threat hanging over Rupprecht was that of prosecution for war crimes. He featured at number 33 on a list of 895 alleged war criminals published in December 1919, facing accusations of ordering the murder of British prisoners of war, of the destruction of villages and execution of innocent civilians in Lorraine in 1914, and of the burning of Cambrai during the German retreat. The whole war crimes process provoked testy disagreements between France, Britain, and Germany, and collapsed soon after it began in Leipzig in May 1921. Ironically, the case which led the French to withdraw was that of Major-General Stenger, accused of issuing a 'take no prisoners' order in August 1914 while under Rupprecht's command. With the French gone, the prosecutions lost any teeth they might ever have had. In January 1922 the Inter-Allied Commission declared the Leipzig process 'highly unsatisfactory' and, although war crimes trials of a kind continued until 1933, it became increasingly clear that none of the accused would be found guilty by a German court. The charges against Rupprecht were formally dropped in June 1923 and he was free to travel all over Europe, including to England and even France, as he had before the war.[2]

The death of his parents left Rupprecht the pretender to the thrones of both Great Britain and Bavaria. The British claim could be dismissed: he had already made clear that he had no intention or chance of becoming King Robert I and IV. The Bavarian issue, however, had to be treated with care. For the rest of his life, Rupprecht styled himself in public as 'Crown Prince' rather than 'King'. There were plenty of monarchists keen to restore a Wittelsbach to the throne. Inevitably, they were concentrated on the political right. The number of true conservatives looking only to wind the clock back was relatively small. Most people, including Rupprecht, realized that the obstacles to returning the sweeping powers that his predecessors had enjoyed were immense. More often, the monarchy was seen as more of a symbol and embodiment of Bavaria. Rupprecht seems to have shared that view: while keen to take up the crown, it remained important to him that he do so only by legal means and to popular acclaim. In theory seeing the monarchy as rising above faction and politics, he was not prepared to let himself be identified with any particular party.[3]

His attitudes, sympathies, and interests, however, left him much more in tune with the right than the left. During the economic and political crisis of 1923, amid rising political violence, dissatisfaction with the weakness of the Weimar government set off rumours of putsches against the government. Rupprecht backed the declaration of martial law and the installation of the nationalist Gustav von Kahr as a kind of dictator in September 1923. Kahr was to form a united front of relatively moderate Bavarian 'patriotic' groups to forestall the extremism of radicals such as Adolf Hitler's Nazi Party. One of Kahr's policies envisaged expelling the so-called 'Ostjuden', recent Jewish refugees, largely from Poland. This was both a convenient stick with which to beat Berlin and reflected genuine anti-semitism. On both grounds, Rupprecht supported the deportation policy.

Figure 23.1. Crown Prince Rupprecht and Princess Antonie with their family between the wars

It is hardly surprising that anti-semitism constituted part of the mental furniture of a Bavarian aristocrat born in 1869. It was equally predictable that he should find the vulgarity of the Nazi Party unappealing. Rupprecht and Adolf Hitler certainly met, in the summer of 1922, but the ex-corporal made little impression on the former field marshal. Rupprecht might have seen the Nazis as possible anti-socialist allies but their pan-German nationalism did not attract him. He was too committed to preserving the rights of individual states within the federation. On the other side, Hitler's interest in the monarchy was tactical and pragmatic. If he could exploit it to help achieve his own objectives, he was prepared to do so, but he had no real commitment to either the Hohenzollerns or the Wittelsbachs. Indeed, he viewed both dynasties as degenerate. Men in his entourage, however, such as the head of the Brownshirts, Ernst Röhm, remained keen to bring the Führer and the Crown Prince closer together. As the strength of the far right, led by Hitler and Ludendorff, grew during 1923, Rupprecht did hold meetings with the latter. Their relationship was no easier than it had been during the last year of the war. Rupprecht attacked him in public, pointedly remarking that 'not every general can be a statesman like Frederick the Great'. Although the Crown Prince declared himself willing to receive Hitler once more, that meeting never took place.[4]

On the evening of 8 November 1923 Hitler stormed into a meeting attended by Munich's politicians in the Bürgerbräukeller. In what became known as the Beer Hall Putsch, Hitler, claiming to be righting the wrong done to the monarchy in 1918, held Kahr and other members of the government at gunpoint and forced them to endorse the Nazis' plan to seize power in Munich, march on Berlin, and overthrow the government there. The whole scheme was poorly planned and incompetently executed and it quickly began to lose momentum. As soon as Kahr regained his freedom, he repudiated the putsch. Hitler and Ludendorff tried to fan it back into life next morning with a march on the War Ministry but their followers found their way blocked by loyalist policemen on the Odeonsplatz. There, in front of the Feldherrnhalle, shots rang out. When the smoke cleared, four policemen and sixteen Nazis lay dead. Hitler escaped but was arrested a couple of days later.

Rupprecht was out of town at his castle in Berchtesgaden, near the Austrian border, probably seeking to put distance between himself and a coup of which he had some foreknowledge, although we will probably never know for certain the depth of his involvement. Even if Rupprecht had a broad idea of the plotters' general intentions, he probably had little warning of the attempt itself, not least because it was put together only at the last minute. The next day, when he was told what had happened, his primary concern seems to have been to avoid bloodshed, rather than to intervene on his own account. Later, Hitler bitterly blamed Rupprecht for the failure of the putsch, but that hardly proves that the Crown Prince had let the conspirators down. Hitler under stress was quite capable of lashing out at even the most innocent, as his subsequent career amply demonstrated. Ludendorff accused the Catholic church and royal family of cooking up an unholy alliance to smash the putsch and claimed Rupprecht himself had broken his word. Rupprecht's attitude to the conspirators, during the trial which followed, was ambiguous. On the one hand, he was in favour of trying them thoroughly, which suggests he had little to hide. On the other, though, he also argued that they should be treated clemently. He felt Ludendorff was the prime mover and main danger: Hitler was no more than Ludendorff's stooge.[5]

Rupprecht was far from the first person to under-estimate Adolf Hitler. Tragically, he was also not the last. In 1923 Rupprecht had little reason to fear the enmity of a failed rabble-rouser now locked up in prison. By the time the gaol-bird had moved into the Chancellery in January 1933, however, there was plenty of reason to be scared. Politicians in Bavaria, across the political spectrum, identified the threat the Nazis posed and scurried to find some way to protect the rights of Bavaria and themselves against a Hitler dictatorship. One option might involve Rupprecht in some capacity. The Crown Prince's prestige was high. He had spent more than a decade establishing himself as a king without a crown, working with Bavarian veterans' organizations and touring the country. His popularity underpinned renewed ideas of restoring the monarchy in some form. When he visited the Opera soon after Hitler came to power, he was greeted with applause and the audience roared out the old royal anthem. In a measure of the growing desperation of those opposed to the Nazis, even some Socialists were coming around to the idea of installing Rupprecht as State President or in the emergency post of State Commissioner. Prime Minister Heinrich Held, however, was unwilling to concede the all-party government of national unity which Rupprecht demanded.

While the politicians talked and talked, the Nazis acted. Having secured the loyalty of the army and emboldened by success in the plebiscite of 5 March, the Nazis seized control of the Bavarian government and simply tore up the old constitution. Rupprecht's protests to the German President, Hindenburg, received no more than a polite acknowledgement. Within a fortnight, the concentration camp at Dachau, a short tram ride from downtown Munich, opened its gates. If Rupprecht's restoration had ever been a serious option, it never was again.[6]

That Hitler feared Rupprecht's prestige, and had neither forgotten nor forgiven him for the collapse of the Beer Hall Putsch, was soon made devastatingly clear. On 13 March four men from Rupprecht's inner circle were arrested. One remained incarcerated for over a year. In autumn 1933, his son Albrecht was denounced as an enemy of the Nazis and was only saved from Dachau by the intervention of Ernst Röhm. The murderous 'Night of the Long Knives' in 1934 was further proof, if any were needed, of the Nazis' violent lack of scruple: among the many victims was Gustav von Kahr, killed for his 'betrayal' of Hitler in 1923. Nonetheless, Rupprecht would not allow the Nazi swastika to be flown outside his Munich palace and continued to appear in public into 1935, mainly at church or veterans' events. Hitler and Rupprecht took care to avoid each other when their paths might otherwise have crossed. When the Nazis established their summer playground in the Alps above Berchtesgaden, Rupprecht stopped using his castle there, and during the second half of the 1930s he retreated into 'internal exile'. He did his best to protect his children from Nazi indoctrination, sending his son Heinrich to be educated by independent-minded monks at Ettal Abbey while his daughters attended the Convent of the Sacred Heart in Roehampton.[7] Approaches from monarchist resistance groups were treated with extreme and warranted caution: the Gestapo was watching and in August 1939 most of the members of these were rounded up and thrown into gaol.

These arrests were a clear sign that conditions were becoming more dangerous in Germany, and on 13 August 1939 Rupprecht left Germany to visit his brother in Hungary. When he returned to Munich briefly in October 1939, he faced police questioning about possible links to monarchist sympathizers in the anti-Hitler resistance group known as the 'Harnier Circle'. Thereafter he spent the rest of the war in exile in Italy. Here, with support from the Italian king and Pope Pius XII, he divided his time between Florence and the beach at Forte dei Marmi, while his wife preferred the mountain air of the Tirol or Dolomites. In September 1943 Italy surrendered to the allies and the Germans seized effective control of the north of the country while the British and Americans advanced slowly from the south.

With the Gestapo active in Florence and military pressure on Germany growing, life was becoming dangerous for anyone with a record of anything other than wholehearted support for the Nazis. In early June 1944 Rome fell to the Americans and on 6 June the Allies landed in France. Rupprecht thought it best to disappear. On 19 June he went to Florence railway station and bought a ticket to travel and rejoin his wife in the Dolomites. Instead of boarding the train, however, he disappeared into the crowd on the platform, left the station by a side entrance, and doubled back to the apartment of an Italian friend. Here he went into hiding.

The wisdom of doing so soon became apparent. On 20 July 1944 Hitler narrowly escaped with his life when a bomb went off at his headquarters in Prussia, the 'Wolf's Lair'. The Nazi regime lashed out at anyone with even the vaguest record of opposition to Hitler or the most tenuous link to the conspirators responsible for the attempted assassination. Rupprecht was vulnerable. He knew the uncle of the would-be assassin, Claus Schenk von Stauffenberg. Indeed, much of the conspiracy centred on the traditional officers of the old general staff, and their families, some of them Bavarian, whom Rupprecht had known for many years. The Gestapo searched Rupprecht's old apartment in Florence, but they had missed him and now time was running out. As the boom of British guns crept ever closer, the

Gestapo scoured the city but eventually even they gave up and pulled out. After a lawless few days of street fighting between Italian Fascists and partisans, by 14 August it was finally safe for Rupprecht to emerge into daylight once more. He had been indoors for nearly two months and was pleased to be reunited with his son, Heinrich.

Rupprecht did not yet know what had happened to the rest of his family. On Hitler's personal order, the whole Wittelsbach family had been arrested in the summer of 1944. They spent the winter that followed imprisoned in a series of concentration camps, including Dachau. American soldiers finally liberated them on 30 April 1945. By that stage Princess Antonie weighed less than 40 kilograms. She refused ever to return to Germany. The family met up but she never lived with Rupprecht again. Antonie died in Switzerland on 31 July 1954, aged just fifty-four. At her request, she was buried not in Bavaria, the country of her birth, but in Rome.

Rupprecht returned to Munich in November 1945. He had spent much of the previous year writing memoranda for Eisenhower and the Allies with suggestions for a federal constitution of the new Germany, but his time was past. The Americans had hardly fought a world war to restore crowned heads to the thrones of Europe. Supporters of the Wittelsbachs set up a 'King's Party' to argue for a constitutional, parliamentary monarchy but the party was banned from taking part in municipal elections in May 1946 and soon collapsed. Any hopes Rupprecht might have harboured for a restoration died away and his life became less and less political. He continued his travels, especially to Italy, and resumed his ceremonial 'duties' around Bavaria. His eightieth birthday in 1949 was celebrated with a week of festivities at his country estate at Leutstetten and with march-pasts and receptions at Schloss Nymphenburg.

Age was now catching up with Rupprecht. In October 1954 he contracted pneumonia. July the next year saw him return from Italy with a bit of a chill and soon his heart was weakening fast. On 2 August 1955, at five minutes to three in the afternoon, he died in his bed at Schloss Leutstetten. Rupprecht was eighty-six years old. The government ordered Bavarian flags to be flown at half-mast. Over two days some 50,000 people filed past his open coffin, lying in state in Schloss Nymphenburg, to see his body, dressed as a Bavarian field marshal. On 7 August, some of his veterans, dressed in the uniforms of a bygone age, led the procession which carried his body to its final resting place in the Theatinerkirche St Kajetan, opposite the royal palace. He was buried, with ceremony and pomp fit for a king, next to his first wife Marie-Gabriele and their son, Luitpold.

PART V

Conclusions

24

Rupprecht the Field Marshal

This chapter continues the assessment of Rupprecht's command which we began in Chapter 10, picking out broader lessons about Germany, her army, and the role of the Kaiser. Chapter 25 then builds on this by looking at Rupprecht's attempts to have his voice heard in wartime politics. Finally, Chapter 26 sets Rupprecht in the context of broader history and explores some of the lessons his career teaches us about the First World War and modernity itself.

Rupprecht's promotion to field marshal and command of an Army Group in August 1916 changed his daily routine and relationship with his chief of staff very little. His duties remained the same mix of administration, operational decision-making, and ceremonial as before. The only difference was that it took longer to drive to visit units spread out over a broader front. His partnership with Kuhl remained solid. Inevitably, relations cooled from time to time. Between December 1916 and February 1917, for instance, an exhausted Kuhl sulked after he was shut out from personnel decisions about his staff. On the whole, though, they made a formidable team, complementing each other well. On occasion, Rupprecht was the dominant partner. He seems to have been first to see the counter-attack opportunity presented by the Battle of Cambrai in November 1917, for instance. At other times, Kuhl was the prime mover. It was Kuhl who went to Ludendorff on 6 April 1918 and demanded the suspension of Operation MICHAEL.

The cooperation between Rupprecht and Kuhl was eventually destabilized, not by any disagreement between the two, or even by enemy action, but by Ludendorff. We saw in Chapter 11 how Ludendorff and Hindenburg took over at Oberste Heeresleitung (OHL) and began by delegating authority to subordinates such as Rupprecht to fight their own battles without interference. Quickly, however, OHL started to demand information on an ever-widening list of questions, some of them minute details. Already by

8 October Kuhl was noting that the burden of reporting was obstructing the conduct of operations. Worse, Ludendorff's demands for immediate responses to his many enquiries grew increasingly shrill: a hint perhaps that his nerves were already becoming strained. When some people realize they have taken on too much, they cut back to their core roles and delegate secondary tasks to others. Ludendorff's response was the opposite. As the pressure mounted he tried to exert greater control, centralizing power and authority in OHL and intervening even in low-level tactical decisions and doctrine.[1]

From the Battle of Arras on, as noted in Chapter 15, instances of Ludendorff increasingly being told what he wanted to hear multiplied, so he was making decisions on the basis of incorrect reports and warped analysis. With information not always flowing freely around the institution, the army's intellectual honesty and ability to innovate were threatened. General von Gebsattel summed it up well:

> Very often there have indeed been false reports made by many units, on all sorts of topics, even very important ones. I am firmly convinced that several severe defeats we had to suffer during this war were caused by such false reports.... From the very beginning of the war it was clear that army commands and higher reacted very negatively to reports that relayed inconvenient facts and did not suit the plans of the commanders in question. Whoever made such reports was accused of being a merchant of doom, a pessimist, to be lacking in energy or even worse. He would be heavily criticized and in some cases even bluntly told that he could not be employed in such a position when acting like that.[2]

Ludendorff also began to intervene directly well down the chain of command. On 12 May 1917 he issued orders that henceforth OHL must approve all divisional transfers, bypassing three steps in the hierarchy: corps, army, and Army Group headquarters would all be sidelined. 'Such a reduction of my powers is definitely too much', complained Rupprecht. 'What's the point of having army groups, if every decision must be approved by OHL? It is impossible to attend to every detail on the whole front from one place.' Such an approach risked both poor decisions and the destruction of any sense of initiative further down the chain of command.[3]

A good example of this came during the Flanders campaign, with the to-and-fro over defensive tactics around the Battle of Broodseinde (4 October 1917) discussed in Chapter 17. Ludendorff's intervention created three problems. First, his suggestions were not always practical. For instance,

the new revised defence in depth introduced in October relied on a standard of real-time infantry–artillery liaison which was impossible with 1917
communications. Second, it dented the self-confidence of his subordinates,
who became scared of being second-guessed by the chief. Third, he set a
poor example which some of his subordinates began to imitate. Loßberg,
for example, tried to dictate every detail of his army's operations. The
arrogance of Ludendorff's clique of 'demi-god' staff officers increasingly
alienated them from the line commanders, further reducing the flow of
information. The result, Rupprecht thought, was over-schematic approaches
which tied the hands of subordinate leaders and made their moves predictable to the enemy. 'There is no cure-all. A pattern is harmful', Rupprecht
wrote on 9 October. 'The situation must be dealt with sometimes one way,
sometimes another. It would be better if he [Ludendorff] did not bother
himself with intervening too much in the details of tactical methods.'[4]

As the stress mounted in 1918 and Ludendorff tried to control ever tinier
details on the basis of distorted reports, he grew increasingly out of touch
with everyday reality. He lost sight of the broader picture and his capacity
to make decisions deteriorated. We saw a clear example of this process at
work during spring 1918 in Chapter 20. On 9 June, Kuhl complained that:

> Since the Army Group was set up we have hardly had a single quiet day. The
> period of the big offensive, which should have been fine, was made dreadful
> by Ludendorff's nervous excitement. The continual rush, blame and threats of
> dismissal were appalling. One got stuck on the telephone so much that one
> could hardly issue any orders or even think properly.

By August, Ludendorff was telephoning Kuhl at least five or six times a day:

> There's no dealing with Ludendorff... Ludendorff has endlessly something to
> say about every detail, speaks directly to every army and their chiefs of staff,
> and gives them detailed instructions often completely opposite to what he
> ordered me. When we talk to the chiefs of staff, we find out that they're doing
> something completely different from what we told them to. That makes every-
> thing much harder. He is extremely nervy and won't take no for an answer.[5]

Ludendorff increasingly worked through junior members of the General
Staff, bypassing his Army Group and army commanders because he could
bully them if necessary. Accordingly, generals such as Rupprecht became
increasingly marginal and demoralized. The clearest sign of this lies in
Rupprecht's attitude to home leave. As we saw in Chapter 10, he took none at
all in the first two years of the war. From November 1916, he began to do so,

both because he realized his health required it but also because he found out that counterparts, such as the Prussian crown prince, were enjoying lots. At first, he was extremely diligent about returning to his post if bad news arrived. Reports from Flanders in September 1917, for instance, made him cut short a trip home. By August 1918, however, when the situation was arguably more serious, with his Army Group under British pressure and Bapaume just lost, Rupprecht made sure to finish his leave before he returned to duty. He only got back a fortnight after fighting had resumed. Here was a man who no longer felt indispensable.[6]

Rupprecht's career demonstrates that the German army's approach to command was not, as the myth would have it, universally pragmatic and decentralized, with authority consistently delegated to the man in the best position to give the orders required. Instead, decision-making power shifted up and down the command hierarchy in a highly contingent manner, driven primarily by the pressure of events and force of personalities. Other factors, such as internal politics within the clique-ridden German officer corps, were also at work.[7] We saw how Rupprecht had trouble getting rid of Lochow in May–June 1915, largely because he was a client of Falkenhayn's whom Lambsdorff was not prepared to alienate. Men such as Dohna-Schlobitten were selected for important posts on the strength of imperial connections rather than experience or qualifications, with sometimes disastrous results. Not all the Kaiser's appointments were useless, though: indeed, some proved extremely successful. The selection of Rupprecht's chiefs of staff, Krafft and Kuhl, for example, depended on politics as much as merit but in the event succeeded well. Even Lambsdorff's selection was justified by his record, although in fact he did not work out.

The case of Major Max Stapff offers another example of this. Stapff began 1917 as chief of staff to Fourth Army. As we saw in Chapter 16, after the Battle of Messines Stapff was transferred to the less threatened Sixth Army around Arras. Here, he soon began to worry that his sector might be the next British target and wanted reinforcements. To get them, he bypassed Rupprecht and the chain of command, going straight to his friend Wetzell, the chief of operations at OHL. Stapff did not get the men he wanted but he did convince Wetzell that Artois posed a major threat. This proved a distraction from the real danger in Flanders. Even when Stapff had lost the confidence of his corps commanders, Wetzell's influence kept him in post. Wetzell resented the role Kuhl had played in sidelining Stapff back in June, which contributed to friction between the OHL operations department and Rupprecht's Army Group. Wetzell was 'a dangerous enemy, since he can't be controlled and can do much damage behind my back', Kuhl thought. In late October 1917, Wetzell sent reinforcements Rupprecht badly needed to the Aisne instead, where they achieved nothing. The Stapff–Wetzell friendship undermined Kuhl's ability to extract the resources he needed from OHL.[8]

In the German army, therefore, rational modern efficiency coexisted with patronage structures which Frederick the Great would have recognized. It was simultaneously capable of disinterested meritocracy and personal intrigue. Human tensions within the officer corps introduced an element of uncertainty and instability to its processes. There were at least two other factors getting in the way of the German army fighting its war, however: distrust and antagonism between the different regional contingents, and the Kaiser himself.

The German army was the midwife of national unity, its guardian and guarantor. The Reich, founded on Prussian battlefield victories between 1864 and 1871, brought together communities long divided by religion, money, culture, diet, dialect, and geography. The extent to which these and other fault-lines divided—and still divide—German society never fails to surprise non-Germans. The army was far from immune. Much of the time, the fault-lines ran beneath the surface, but under wartime pressure several broke into the open. The relationship between Bavaria and Prussia is a good example. Between 1914 and 1918 the two largest German states were frequently wrangling. There were two underlying sources of friction. First, Bavaria was sensitive to any infringement of her rights under the 1871 constitution. Second, a deeper thread of low-level prejudice also infected relations. There was, for instance, a long tradition in Prussia that Bavarians made poor soldiers. They had been ineffectual opponents in 1866 and performed scarcely better when they were allies in 1870. This was in turn a symptom of a deeper cultural divide between the educated, Protestant north of large-scale farms and industry and the bucolic peasantry of the Catholic south.

As the second largest block in the German federation, Bavaria sometimes played a special role as representative of the non-Prussian states. She held the permanent chair of the foreign affairs committee of the federal upper house, the Bundesrat, for instance. She also had other, less formal, paths to influence. Her ambassador in Berlin, Lerchenfeld, had been in post since 1880 and was both highly experienced and well respected at the Kaiser's court, for example. Nevertheless, as Stefan März has argued, 'the tension between unitary and

federal characteristics constituted an essential element of the Kaiserreich'
and the Prusso-Bavarian relationship was rarely straightforward.[9]

Relations between the two royal families were cordial without being
close. Religious differences prevented intermarriage and Ludwig III had
been wounded fighting against the Prussians in 1866. He limped for the rest
of his life as a result. His relations with Wilhelm II were not always smooth.
Both men were volatile and prickly. At the coronation of Tsar Nicholas II
in 1896, for instance, Ludwig had complained loudly at being treated like
the Kaiser's vassal, rather than his ally. Wilhelm II summoned Ludwig to his
yacht and dressed him down 'like a schoolboy'. Nonetheless, Ludwig
retained the right of access to the Kaiser and the senior members of both
families crossed paths frequently, not least at official events such as the
funeral of the Habsburg Emperor Franz Josef in 1916. Wilhelm attended the
golden wedding celebrations for the Bavarian king and queen in February
1918. Rupprecht had known Wilhelm II, who was ten years older than him,
since at least his student days in Berlin in 1890.[10]

Rupprecht supported a united but federal Germany led by Prussia, seeing
that as the best defence against the clericalism and Vatican interference a
closer union with Austria might entail. For him, though, Germany had to
be more than just a Greater Prussia. The constitutional rights and prerogatives of the other states must be safeguarded. Even before the war began, he
had been nervous of Prussia's centralizing ambitions. In January 1914 his
suspicions were reinforced when Moltke told him that Rupprecht was to
have a Prussian chief of staff in the event of war. The clear implication was
that only thus could Moltke be sure to avoid mistakes which might otherwise endanger Prussia. The outcome of war, Moltke tactlessly reminded
Rupprecht, would be crucial for Prussia. 'No less so for Bavaria', Rupprecht
drily replied. Krafft, the Bavarian who eventually got the job, possessed a
level of anti-Prussian paranoia which reinforced Rupprecht's suspicions.[11]

Once war broke out the pious hope was that 'as in 1870 will Bavarians,
Prussians and Badeners fight together and win as German brothers'.
National sensitivities soon surfaced, however. Perceived threats to Bavarian
reserve rights under the constitution generated resentment. Rupprecht was
especially sensitive to encroachments on the military convention, such as
any suggestion that the Kaiser might appoint or promote Bavarian officers
or install Prussian officers in command of Bavarian units. Likewise, he
opposed the extension of censorship from Berlin to include the traditionally lightly regulated Munich newspapers.[12]

At times, Prusso-Bavarian tensions had a direct and evident impact on operations. An early example occurred in late August 1914 when OHL decided to send two army corps over to East Prussia to oppose a Russian invasion. When a railway expert suggested that I Bavarian Corps was one of the easiest formations to send, Moltke's deputy exclaimed: 'that's impossible. We Prussians can't let it be said that East Prussia was liberated by Bavarians.' Prussian units were transferred instead. Second, as the war continued, it proved neither militarily efficient nor politically desirable to maintain Sixth Army as a predominantly Bavarian formation. After the Lorraine campaign, contrary to Rupprecht's wishes, Bavarians were dispersed up and down the front and formed only a minority of Rupprecht's command. Third, in 1916 Ludendorff originally wanted to give Rupprecht overall command of the whole Western Front. To promote the Bavarian crown prince over his Prussian counterpart, however, might prove diplomatically tricky and Ludendorff had to drop the idea. A fourth example took place in October 1916: at a parade in front of the Kaiser, General von Boehn made a speech boasting that no enemy would break through his corps while a single Prussian heart was still beating. Unfortunately, two of his three divisions, and many of the men on parade, were in fact Bavarian. After complaints reached King Ludwig III, Boehn was transferred away at the first opportunity. Lastly, in March 1917 Rupprecht wanted to resign in protest when ordered to scorch the earth as he fell back to the Hindenburg Line. He did not do so for fear that this would be interpreted at home and abroad as betraying a split between Bavaria and Germany.[13]

Where Prussian arrogance met Bavarian inferiority complex, further friction arose. The Bavarian general Fasbender stormed out of a meeting to plan an attack at Arras in October 1914 after being provoked with 'typical Prussian condescension' by Claer. Casual contempt was widespread: during the Somme fighting, when told that the unit which had lost a given position was Bavarian, Loßberg had muttered 'of course'. During a tricky period for his relations with Kuhl, Rupprecht wrote:

> I regret ever more that I haven't had a Bavarian chief of staff since the beginning of the campaign. It would have made things much smoother. The Prussian chiefs of staff tend to be overbearing and behave as if they are only subordinate and responsible to OHL. In the future we must try to ensure that Bavarian troops fight together under their own staff and are not treated as mere contingents of the Imperial army.

Low-level discourtesy did little to promote smooth working and at times could cause discomfort. General Wenninger at imperial headquarters noted on 6 September 1914 that 'my first week in our new headquarters as the only Bavarian was as miserable as that in Koblenz was enjoyable. The thermometer rises and falls with the performance of our troops on the battlefield.'[14]

Wartime not only exacerbated existing tensions: it also created new ones. Any suspicion that Bavarians were being exploited and making a dispropor-tionate sacrifice provoked fury both within the army and at home. Nowhere were emotions rawer than when it came to food. In October 1916, for example, the Munich meat ration was cut to 187 grams per head, while it remained 250 grams in Berlin. Outrage was the predictable result, made worse by the fact that Bavaria supplied much of the food to Berlin.[15]

Not only should Bavaria pay a fair share of the costs of the war and no more; she should also receive her deserts when it came to sharing out the spoils of winning. From Bethmann Hollweg's 'September Programme' of 1914 onwards, the German leadership debated the annexations which would follow victory and how to split them up between the different federal states. Rupprecht was as keen as the government in Munich that Bavaria should gain her rightful share of anything on offer and his contacts kept him well informed about the various schemes which came up. Tracking the evolution of all the competing proposals would fill much space to little purpose, since none of them became a reality. One point is crucial, however: annexations represented an impossible problem for Germany because there was no way to reconcile everyone's interests. The tone was set as early as November 1914 when the question of the post-war future of Alsace and Lorraine came up. The 1871 solution of making them directly administered imperial prov-inces had created an awkward administrative anomaly and failed to make good Germans of the inhabitants as hoped. Instead, it seemed that Alsace and Lorraine should be transferred to one or more of the German states. How to do this was not straightforward, however. Bavaria was not prepared to let Prussia take both: this would make her too powerful and undermine federalism. Some conservatives in Prussia did not even want Alsace-Lorraine, since they worried that the Catholic population there would disturb the confessional equilibrium in their largely Protestant kingdom. The possibil-ity of Bavaria taking either or both, however, provoked opposition from Württemberg and Saxony, who worried about the spread of Catholic influ-ence. Baden, meanwhile, wanted Upper Alsace and was not prepared to let herself be encircled by Bavarian territory. No consensus was possible.[16]

After Russia's collapse, Hindenburg and Ludendorff designed a new Prussian order for Europe which ignored, or was ignorant of, complexities of this kind. In December 1917 Ludendorff wanted Prussia to annex Lithuania, Courland and Riga in the East, and both Alsace and Lorraine in the west. The furthest he was prepared to go to buy off the lesser German states was to offer the rulers of Bavaria and Saxony the thrones of Belgium and Lithuania respectively, via a personal union. In other words, a Wittelsbach would rule Belgium, although it would not become part of Bavaria. Rupprecht was scornful:

> The Prussian motto 'Suum cuique' ('each to his own') should be translated into German as 'everything for me'. Since the start of the war, from my knowledge of the Prussian character and the weakness of our leading men in Bavaria, I foresaw that, whatever her commitment to the war, Bavaria would suffer only harm and lose respect.

The idea of a personal union was an echo of a bygone age which could not work in modern conditions.[17]

What this brief discussion of the annexations problem has demonstrated is that Germany did not know what world she wanted to create even if she somehow managed to win. She had gone into the war with no clear political vision and proved unable to develop one. Even in the best case, there was no territorial settlement which could possibly satisfy all those who were bleeding to achieve it. Just as annexing Serbia would destabilize the fragile balance between Austria and Hungary, any move to incorporate Alsace-Lorraine threatened the 1871 Reich settlement. Adding Belgium, Poland, and the Baltic states into the mix only made affairs more intractable. Probably only Ludendorff's brutal approach of ignoring the sensitivities of the lesser states and giving Prussia whatever she wanted was viable in the long run. He certainly did not care about the difficulties involved, even if he was aware of them. Whether he, or anyone else, could have successfully managed the necessary constitutional change from a federal to a unitary Germany must remain an open question.

The fact that Germany went to war with no clear vision of the settlement she might fashion if she won, and knowing that any division of the spoils of victory would prove difficult at best, reinforces the view that Germany lacked a coherent strategy. If anyone was supposed to articulate one and bring statesmen and generals together to execute it, that person was the Kaiser. Wilhelm II is often written off as a 'shadow Kaiser' who did little to determine the course of the First World War, whatever his role in starting it. His biographer, John Röhl, argues that his power evaporated 'almost over-night' as soon as the first shots were fired. He delegated the conduct of the war to his Chief of the General Staff and, according to Holger Afflerbach, only ever intervened directly in operational decisions rarely. The Kaiser himself complained that 'the General Staff tells me nothing and never asks my advice. If people in Germany think that I am the Supreme Commander they are grossly mistaken. I drink tea, saw wood and go for walks.' Most modern historians detect a further erosion of his power in August 1916 when Hindenburg and Ludendorff took over OHL. By offering the strategic leadership which Wilhelm had not, these two pushed the Kaiser even further to the margins. They forced out the Chancellor, Bethmann Hollweg, as well as other members of Wilhelm's entourage, and led Germany back into unrestricted submarine warfare. At the end, they almost sent the Kaiser off to meet a 'heroic' death in battle.[18]

The Kaiser was more important than this picture suggests, in three main ways. First, he retained significant power of his own, especially over appointments, and he was prepared to use it. Two examples show this clearly. In April 1918, after a routine visit to II Bavarian Corps, he insisted that its commander, General Otto von Stetten, be sacked. Whether he was correct that Stetten was exhausted or not, this constituted an insult to Bavaria, an infringement of her constitutional rights, and a disturbing intervention in day-to-day operations by a man whose qualifications to make such decisions were slight. Another case came up in Chapter 16, when Wilhelm II petulantly forbade an exchange of staffs between Fourth and Sixth Armies, designed to strengthen the command team likely to be hit by the next British Expeditionary Force (BEF) offensive in Flanders, because he wanted revenge on Rupprecht for sacking two corps commanders six months earlier who happened to be imperial favourites.[19]

Unpredictable meddling of this kind was a clear source of uncertainty. It was compounded by the second form of impact Wilhelm II had on his army. A leader sets the emotional tone for those under his command. Voltaire praised the Duke of Marlborough, for instance, for possessing 'that calm courage in the midst of tumult, that serenity of soul in danger, which is the greatest gift of nature for command'. A calm and resolute commander instils his staff and subordinates with confidence. The notorious emotional instability of Wilhelm II had exactly the opposite effect. Rupprecht had little respect for him, seeing him as a military dilettante who could not be bothered to listen to any briefing longer than twenty minutes. 'The Kaiser is an unstable character', he noted; 'on the one hand weak and soft, on the other at times...brutal'. On 25 May 1917 the Kaiser told a parade of his troops at Tournai to take no British prisoners. Rupprecht tried to hush it up, but within a couple of weeks it was in the English newspapers all the same. Rupprecht was exasperated:

> If only he would learn to keep control of his words. There's no hope in this regard. He often does not know himself what he is saying. He means no harm by what he says, however it sounds, he just loves striking a pose and this has got him in trouble several times before.

Childish behaviour set a poor example and left his subordinates wondering both where they stood with him and why they were fighting for such a man.[20]

The third way the Kaiser influenced command was less obviously under his own control, although it was important all the same. In much the same way as Thomas Ertman has argued that early modern states developed by imitating the models they had available to them, the power networks of the army had evolved by aping those of the imperial court. The Chief of the General Staff served entirely at His Majesty's whim (an especially appropriate word in the case of the Kaiser). Falkenhayn, throughout his tenure, was aware that he had not been a popular choice for the post and that influential voices were calling for his head. He was entirely beholden to Wilhelm II. At first, Ludendorff had rather more security by virtue of Hindenburg's popularity in the country at large. Nevertheless, he knew that even Hindenburg might not be able to save him if the capricious Kaiser wanted him gone, as indeed proved the case in October 1918. The command system was thus built on shaky foundations. Worse yet, at lower levels this monarch–courtier relationship was replicated, with subordinates so dependent on their superiors' goodwill that their independence was undermined. Men such as Tappen and Wetzell were no less dependent on the goodwill of Falkenhayn or Ludendorff than the Chiefs of the General Staff were on that of the Kaiser. We have already noted how influential cliques and personal relationships could be. An exception will prove this rule: when Ludendorff was temporarily too weak to object in September 1918, his Army Group commanders acted quickly to demand the break-up of his immediate cabal at OHL and infuse fresh blood.[21]

This instability within the army command meant that every time Falkenhayn or Ludendorff felt their position with the Kaiser threatened, their knee-jerk response was to suck power and decision-making back into OHL. Auftragstaktik had its place as a tactical measure at division level and below, but among the senior command ranks delegation was the exception rather than the rule. It flourished only briefly during Ludendorff's honeymoon period in autumn 1916. The default setting to which the army reverted when stress mounted involved centralization and increasing rigidity. This had two consequences. It made the job of operational commanders such as Rupprecht very tricky. They had to negotiate a shifting structure where responsibility and power flowed up, down, and around from day to day or minute to minute in unpredictable ways. In these circumstances, it was harder to make decisions and control compliance with orders than it needed to be. Further, enemy pressure and a politicized command hierarchy combined to bring poor reporting, an OHL ever more out of touch with reality, and worse decisions. This circle rapidly became vicious.

The German army between 1914 and 1918 was far from the well-oiled machine of myth. Instead, it was a deeply flawed institution which reached poor battlefield decisions and by doing so contributed significantly to Germany's defeat. The First World War was not just lost at the tactical and operational levels of war, however. Poor strategic and political decision-making also played a part, and it is to these that we now turn.

25

Rupprecht and Politics

In addition to his role as a military commander, Rupprecht saw himself, and was perceived, as the senior Bavarian on the Western Front. He thus represented Bavaria and, to some extent, German unity. This gave him political value above and beyond his military responsibilities. It also afforded him a measure of independence and protection from the worst excesses of army politics and offered him the opportunity to challenge prevailing orthodoxies on the strategic and political issues Germany faced as she fought. Rupprecht enjoyed another significant advantage, too. By dint of his position and status, he had access to a network of multiple sources of useful intelligence. Some of these were formal. The Bavarian government kept a representative at his headquarters: Leopold Krafft von Dellmensingen, a cousin of his first chief of staff. Together with the Bavarian military representatives at the Kaiser's General Headquarters, Leopold Krafft kept him in touch with gossip from Munich and the imperial court. Less formally, Rupprecht nurtured a wide range of contacts in the higher reaches of politics, business, and the military. Friends and like minds shared information and worked together from time to time. At no point did this form a definite group with a coherent agenda, however. Instead, informal coalitions came together opportunistically to try to influence policy on particular issues. The attempted coup against Falkenhayn is one obvious example, which we will come back to below. This chapter examines how far Rupprecht was able to exploit his independence to affect policy.[1]

Between 1914 and 1918 Germany faced a series of life-or-death decisions. The original choice to go to war was the first of these. As we saw in Chapter 1, neither Rupprecht nor any other Bavarian had any influence over that decision, which was taken in Berlin by the Kaiser and a small group of his closest advisers. There is no evidence that Rupprecht or his father opposed it, however, and one suspects they backed German expansion so long as Bavaria got her fair share. Once war had broken out, the questions became how violently the war should be fought and how it should be ended. The two were linked: the more unlimited the objectives, the more it made sense to escalate the violence. The resorts to poison gas and unrestricted submarine warfare were two controversial examples of the radicalization of war. As we saw in Chapters 7 and 14, at the time Rupprecht agreed with the use of both, whatever he sometimes said later. Rupprecht was broadly in line with the German consensus on how violently the war should be fought. Where he was out of step at times was when it came to how to end the war.

With the benefit of hindsight, it is clear that the French victory on the River Marne in early September 1914 marked the turning point of the war. Once the Schlieffen Plan had collapsed, Germany's hopes of a rapid victory evaporated. She became locked into exactly the kind of drawn-out war on multiple fronts she had desperately wanted to avoid. Should Germany accept a compromise peace ('Verständigungsfrieden')? Or fight on, win on the battlefield, and then impose the settlement she wanted ('Siegfrieden')? The idea that this was a choice open to Germany, however, was a mirage. She no longer had options. Once she had failed to snatch victory in a short war, she had no chance of winning a long one. Neither the German army nor the civil government was ready to see things this way, however. When Falkenhayn advised Bethmann Hollweg that military methods had failed and Germany must pursue a diplomatic solution in November 1914, he was denounced as defeatist. Rupprecht was one of those who did so, playing a leading role in the cabal which sought to force Falkenhayn from office. He then welcomed Falkenhayn's replacement by Hindenburg and Ludendorff. The two new men were firm believers in final military victory and intent on harnessing all Germany's strengths to achieve it. In retrospect, the switch of leadership clearly prolonged the war.

Rupprecht's faith in the Hindenburg/Ludendorff programme began to waver as his belief in the possibility of a war-winning offensive fell away. Where he had still been arguing for a single knock-out blow to decide the war in early 1916, by the time he had lived through Verdun and the Somme, his view had shifted. He came to believe that a major breakthrough was highly unlikely and that, even if there was one, no single battle was likely to yield victory. Rupprecht did not yet believe defeat was probable, much less inevitable, but from the end of 1916 onwards he recognized it as a possibility, even if he veered between optimism and pessimism at times. He was not alone in this view: indeed, of the chiefs of staff of the armies under his command, only one disagreed in January 1917. The next month, even Ludendorff and his staff seemed to accept that shortages of manpower, horses, transport, and ammunition left the army incapable of winning the war. They were relying on the U-boats instead. Neither Rupprecht nor any of the others followed this insight through to its logical conclusion, however, even when it became clear that submarine warfare was failing to deliver on the extravagant promises made for it. When, in July 1917, the Reichstag passed a resolution in favour of peace without annexations. Rupprecht's first instinct was to welcome it. This was not, however, because he was desperate for peace at any price. The 'peace resolution', which has often been represented as a pacifist rejection of war inspired by Bolshevik declarations in Russia, was nothing of the sort. Rather, it envisaged Germany retaining the territorial gains she had already made and marked an attempt to stiffen popular resolve. Although Rupprecht was aware of underlying problems with manpower and food supply and hoped for an end to the war in the autumn, the immediate situation seemed manageable.

Even as late as January 1918, emboldened by Russia's collapse, Rupprecht was still backing Ludendorff and thinking one major effort might yet win the war. His faith only began to drain away as his conviction grew that Ludendorff was butchering the execution of the spring offensives. On 19 February he warned the Kaiser that they represented Germany's last card, but Wilhelm II parroted Ludendorff's blithe confidence. He also expressed his concerns to members of the Kaiser's entourage such as Plessen and Lyncker. The next day he tried to explain the seriousness of the situation to his father, but was unable to deflate Ludwig's 'amazing optimism'. By this time Rupprecht had finally come round to the idea that the only way out of the war was to negotiate.[2]

As we saw in Chapter 21, it was only in May 1918, after the disappointments of MICHAEL and GEORGETTE, that Rupprecht finally accepted that Germany's situation was becoming hopeless. This set him at odds with Ludendorff who, despite wobbles in August and late September, remained capable of convincing himself that the western powers would collapse internally, as Russia had done, almost until the end. Rupprecht wrote to the Chancellor, Hertling, suggesting peace talks while Max von Baden talked to the Kaiser along the same lines. Hertling was old, tired, and little more than Oberste Heeresleitung's (OHL's) stooge by this time. He felt none of the urgency Rupprecht did and his reply was non-committal. An attempt to persuade Ludendorff face-to-face was no more successful.[3]

Rupprecht's efforts to convince the leadership that a negotiated peace was necessary took three forms. First, he continued to feed information to Max von Baden on the state of the army to use against those who even now wanted to prolong the war. Second, he tried to awaken his father to the dangers Bavaria and Germany faced. On 25 July he warned that the enemy had the advantage and every effort must be made for peace, even if it cost Germany. On 4 September, 'peace—as soon as possible and even at a great price—has become urgent', he wrote. Later that month he criticized OHL for refusing to accept that Germany was defenceless and must make peace at once, whatever the price. On 7 October he pointed out that military defeat might have broader political ramifications and suggested democratization: 'the failure of previous arrangements means the idea that the people should have a decisive voice in their fate has some legitimacy'. Rupprecht was beginning to despair: 'poor Bavaria, that you must pay so for Prussia's mistakes! Catastrophe can strike any day!' On 26 October, a new and even more ominous note entered Rupprecht's letters to Ludwig. Some Prussian officers had begun muttering that the removal of Ludendorff and Hindenburg would not go far enough. The Kaiser himself, and his dynasty, might also be ditched. 'That's how far we have come, already!' Worse, Rupprecht warned, there was a danger that other states might then follow the Prussian example. Finally, on 1 November, in the wake of press reports that the Hohenzollerns had become obstacles to peace, he begged his father to press the Kaiser to abdicate to enable an armistice. 'The situation', Rupprecht wrote, 'is extremely serious.... The [revolutionary and possibly separatist] movements which are getting ready in northern Germany and are already a fact in Austria could also transfer to Bavaria.'[4]

The King paid little attention to his son's warnings. Ludwig consistently under-estimated how far support for his regime was being weakened by food shortages, war-weariness, and his government's apparent failure to defend Bavarian interests against Prussia. As late as July 1918 he remained convinced that any peace treaty would result in German territorial expansion. Ludwig seems to have resented and feared his son's relative popularity. Remarkably, he felt that late October and early November 1918 was the perfect time to re-open an old argument about Rupprecht's home in Munich. In November 1916, after four years of bitter family dispute, it had been decided that Rupprecht should use the suite of rooms known as the Steinzimmer ('Stone Rooms') in the old palace known as the Residenz. Ludwig now overturned that agreement, deciding instead that Rupprecht should move into another building on the other side of the street. This triggered a new, unnecessary, and trivial row. Ludwig told Prime Minister Dandl to form a parliamentary government on 2 November, demonstrating how weak his grasp of the gravity of the situation was. It was too little and too late to satisfy the growing radicalism of his opponents. His last message to his son, sent on 7 November, while blithely asserting that he understood the seriousness of the situation, showed clearly that he did not: he hoped that 'after the Armistice it will be possible for you to come here soon'.[5]

The failure of indirect approaches drove Rupprecht to take more direct measures. He took a step he would never have dreamed of earlier in the war. On 21 September he wrote directly to Wilhelm II with a summary of the military situation and suggesting that Hertling had lost any value he had once had; he should be replaced as Chancellor. There is no evidence that Rupprecht ever received a reply. An appeal to the Kaiser in November, to be allowed to take over the defence of the Tirol against the Italians, proved equally unsuccessful.[6]

For all the advantages Rupprecht enjoyed, his ability to use them faced significant obstacles. First, there were considerable limits to his ability to assert his independence. His ultimate weapon was resignation, but the political consequences of threatening this were so great that he hesitated to use it. Any sign of disunity might encourage the enemy and weaken Bavarian influence further. Thus, as we saw above, he held back from resigning in protest at the 'scorched earth' order of March 1917. In private, he could be petulant: he seems to have mentioned resignation to members of his entourage at least six times during the war. The only occasion on which he formally threatened to resign, however, was carefully not on a general point of policy or principle. That might have laid him open to charges of disloyalty or irresponsibility. Instead the issue Rupprecht picked was Falkenhayn's undue interference in his command of Sixth Army. He never tried to use resignation to unseat his opponents, as Hindenburg and Ludendorff repeatedly did.[7]

Second, Rupprecht had no independent power. He was only heir to the throne, not sovereign. Therefore much depended on his ability to sell his ideas to others and work through them. Since one of his main routes to influence lay via his father, it was unfortunate that personal relations with Ludwig III were poor and widely known to be so. For instance, in January 1916, Rupprecht tried to persuade the King that Bavaria needed to stand firm against Prussian infringements of her rights, only to find that all his father wanted to discuss was uniforms. Rupprecht's ability to act as a channel to, or spokesman for, the Bavarian government was consequently limited. Ludwig's conservatism and poor political judgement only made matters worse and fed into a strange passivity on the part of the Bavarian government. Munich often lacked the confidence to demand a voice in imperial policy. In July 1917, for instance, Ludwig ignored warnings from his son that Prussian democratization might threaten the powers of the princely states and that 'the whole of Germany is watching and waiting for Bavaria to intervene! Much depends on this game, maybe everything!' Indeed, precisely because Bethmann Hollweg supported reforms which threatened the prerogatives of the princes, Ludwig made no effort to support him in his struggle with Ludendorff, despite Rupprecht's advice that Bethmann Hollweg offered a quicker end to the war and a better deal for Bavaria than any alternative Chancellor was likely to. Ludwig could not see, as Rupprecht could, that this inertia was undermining support for the monarchy. Bavaria's lack of a role in policy was not all the fault of the government in Munich, though. The Kaiser and those around him often gave scant consideration to Bavarian interests and concerns. When, for example, Hindenburg decided to set up a Supreme War Office ('Kriegsamt'), under the Prussian War Ministry, to coordinate industrial mobilization across the whole of Germany, he gave Munich only twenty-four hours' notice. Rupprecht complained of this 'typical Prussian lack of consideration. But it is a scandal, how badly we are bossed about by our allies in Berlin.'[8]

Rupprecht has sometimes been seen as sidelined politically because he was unfashionably downbeat about Germany's chances. As we have seen, however, Rupprecht was not a consistently negative voice within her councils of war. Indeed, pessimism finally triumphed over optimism and he gave up hope in victory only when the results of the spring 1918 offensives proved disappointing. Rupprecht was, however, a frequent and trenchant critic of Germany's conduct of the war. This was largely a function of frustration: one suspects he thought he could be making a better job of it. We have also seen how prickly he could be if he felt his rights or dignity, either personally or as a Bavarian, were threatened. This frustrated his superiors and diminished his influence. So did his tendency, shared with many born critics, to be better at identifying weak points in OHL's arguments than at finding constructive answers. When, for instance, he correctly identified that Falkenhayn's attritional approach could not deliver military victory, he could offer no realistic alternative. Later, he pressed Ludendorff for a compromise peace but could suggest no plan to deliver one. He was always coming up with problems, never solutions.[9]

Rupprecht's fallible judgement was another problem. To support Ludendorff over Falkenhayn was to choose a longer war. Similarly, as Chancellor, Bethmann Hollweg probably had a better chance of negotiating an end to the conflict than Rupprecht's candidate, Georg Hertling, who was seventy-three years old and never likely to be able to stand up to OHL. When Rupprecht observed the calls in Berlin for democratic reforms in July 1917, he spotted the threat this posed to Bavarian independence, and indeed the Hohenzollern dynasty, but failed to anticipate that pressure for constitutional change might spread to Munich, too.[10]

One of Rupprecht's most important judgements concerned ending the war. As we have seen, he realized that Germany could not hope for military victory, and needed to negotiate for peace, well before conservatives such as Ludendorff, Ludwig III, and the Kaiser. Nonetheless, he did not give up hope until April or May 1918. The interesting question is less why he lost faith in victory than why he carried on believing that Germany could win for as long as he did. Why did not Rupprecht, and the other warriors of the German Reich, see that any chance of victory had evaporated by the end of the Battle of the Marne?

Part of the explanation, no doubt, lies in a simple misjudgement about the balance of forces and willpower. The most common error in warfare is to under-estimate the enemy's capacity to resist. Faulty or inadequate intelligence can cause this. So also can the plain arrogance of assuming one's own troops are better than the enemy's—something we have seen the Germans were prone to—and wishful thinking. Even when one has managed to collate the right information, it remains easy to analyse it incorrectly, especially within an organization in which intellectual honesty sometimes took second place to politics.

A second explanation of the hard-liners' resistance to peace negotiations probably lay in their assumption that the Allies would be likely to drive a hard bargain. President Woodrow Wilson's Fourteen Points included demands that Germany evacuate Belgium and France, including the provinces of Alsace and Lorraine. These were hard for the Germans to swallow but were more moderate proposals than Germany was likely to be offered by some French statesmen, for example. To the German conservatives, there seemed no basis for compromise.

Linked to this was a third consideration. If Germany accepted the Fourteen Points as a basis for peace talks, she would effectively be admitting defeat. A war which had supposedly been fought to secure Germany from war for all time would have achieved less than nothing, at huge financial and human cost. The idea that she might end up with less territory than she had before 1871 was unthinkable. To accept defeat would be to value all the sacrifices of the last four years at nil and destroy the prestige of the army. Militaries are 'can-do' institutions. They pride themselves on their ability to find answers to complex problems, even when resources are limited, and in 1914 the Schlieffen Plan seemed to offer a military solution to Germany's political problems. To admit failure would shatter the army's self-image and so, since the military was one of the keystone imperial institutions, undermine also the legitimacy of the Reich itself. Already by 1918 demands for constitutional reform and a quick end to the war were growing. Once military and home-front morale began to collapse in the summer, the threat to the regime became increasingly obvious. The dissatisfaction of a war-weary public with a government which seemed unable to end the fighting fed back into frustration at those who had led Germany into a disastrous war and then lost it. Ludendorff saw this danger clearly and indeed shifted his priority to preserving the army intact as a bulwark against the socialist revolution he increasingly feared.

The German military mind thus had multiple reasons for the obstinacy with which it held out for final victory. Rupprecht possessed the temperament, and some of the independence of mind and position, to be intensely critical about aspects of how the German government and army were conducting the war. On the crucial question of ending it, however, it took him a long while to escape the orthodoxy of his heredity and upbringing. The fact that Rupprecht was able to do so proves that the militarist spell could be broken. That it took him so long, however, shows how deeply ingrained it had become as well as how seductive its ideas and glittering prizes were. In the self-destructive mentality of the imperial military lies Rupprecht's tragedy—and Germany's.[11]

26

Last Words

When I began writing this book, my first objective was to tell the sad story of how Rupprecht, proud Crown Prince of Bavaria and German army general, became plain Mr Landsberg, a fugitive surviving on the protection of strangers. In the course of doing so, however, Rupprecht has also offered us a handy lens through which to study broader themes about the First World War and to offer a new, German, perspective on a history which has too often been written exclusively from a British or Commonwealth point of view. This final chapter summarizes what we learn when we examine the First World War from this perspective.

First, the German army was far from the perfect instrument for waging war that it is often assumed to have been. It was neither rational meritocracy nor blessed with the most flexible of command systems, effortlessly delegating authority down the chain of command to the man best placed to make decisions. Command was highly personalized and the officer corps was riven with cliques and patronage. Auftragstaktik was very much the exception rather than the rule. The German army never managed to decide who should have control of the tactical defensive battle and especially of the counter-attack. Falkenhayn could not resist reaching far down the chain of command to micro-manage. At the operational level, the only time delegation was ever properly tried was in the autumn of 1916, when Ludendorff and Hindenburg took over Oberste Heeresleitung (OHL). As soon as things began to go wrong and Ludendorff started to feel the pressure, however, he began to exert central control once more. To some extent, this was dictated by the personalities of the men in charge. It was also, however, largely the default setting of German command during the First World War, reflecting the instability of a non-system built on the shaky foundations of the monarchy in general and Kaiser Wilhelm II in particular. To make imperial Germany function required the determination and skill of a Bismarck.[1]

Whether even he could have overcome the challenge of the First World War, we shall never know. What is certain, though, is that when Germany needed talents like his, her leaders fell short.

Centralizing operational decision-making in the hands of one man carried risks. First, there was the obvious danger of overload. Ludendorff broke down under the strain of trying to control the deployment of almost every single artillery battery. As one of his generals complained: 'he did not know how to delegate. Such centralization as he operated, only a Napoleon would have been up to, and Ludendorff was no Napoleon. He stubbornly carved his own course, with no view of reality, until a kind of military total insanity gripped him.'[2] A further, more insidious, danger existed, too. Information is never perfect on the battlefield, but the worse it is, the greater the chance of making bad decisions. Especially from 1917 onwards, the honesty of the reporting system was increasingly compromised as subordinates competed to tell their superiors what they wanted to hear. As Ludendorff grew ever more detached from reality, his grasp of the capabilities of not only the enemy but even his own forces faltered. During spring 1918 he under-estimated Allied resilience and over-extended his armies. In the autumn, he failed to understand the depth of the enemy's determination and exaggerated the ability of his men to hold on until it was all too late.

Poor information flow also affected the German army's ability to learn the lessons of, and adapt to, the challenges of modern warfare. When, from 1916 onwards, the Entente began to develop the material strength and battle-field know-how finally to pose a serious threat, the German army proved unable to keep up with the pace of innovation. There were two obstacles. The first, as just discussed, was that the mechanism for transmitting knowledge around the army broke down. Failure to analyse experience honestly led to the wrong problems being identified, the wrong lessons being learnt, and the wrong solutions being put forward.

The second factor inhibiting innovation was more conceptual. Throughout the First World War the German army sought to address operational, and sometimes even strategic, problems with tactical solutions. Thus, for example, it sought to answer Allied attritional attacks with a better scheme of defence. Similarly, in March 1918 infiltration was elevated from battlefield tactic to operational method, as Ludendorff looked to exploit weak spots wherever they were found, rather than fix objectives in advance. This was not because the Germans misdiagnosed the problem: they certainly understood the concept of operations. Rather, it was the result of a well-founded appreciation that when it came to strategic resources or operational scale, the balance lay strongly with the Entente, so Germany's comparative advantage lay at the tactical level of war. On the battlefield, German soldiers might be able to out-think and out-manoeuvre their enemies and offset enemy mass with agility. Since the alternative to believing this was to admit defeat, it is hardly surprising that they chose to believe. No amount of tactical innovation, however, could hold back the tide of strategic reality forever.

The German obsession with tactics led to two further tragedies. First, rather like the British in Blair's wars, the German army's confidence in its ability to solve problems outran its capability and led it to allow a probably unwinnable war to be fought. When Schlieffen and his successors pretended that they possessed a military solution to the problem of Germany's position in the centre of Europe, sandwiched between France and Russia, the first steps were taken on the road to disaster. Second, once war had begun, the Germans still kept looking for tactical answers when it would have been better for all to accept the strategic logic of the situation. This was especially the case on the battlefields of the First World War, where manoeuvre was so difficult and tactical brilliance traded at a discount. If there is a lesson for today, it is surely that the military needs to be ruthlessly honest, both with itself and with its politicians, about what it can and cannot achieve.

Third, Rupprecht forces us to revise long-cherished views about the armies of the Entente, too. Most obviously, his diary reminds us how important the French were. Not only were they the main enemy from August 1914 to the end of 1916 but even thereafter he still viewed the French army as a more dangerous opponent than the British Expeditionary Force (BEF). Rupprecht tended to look down upon the British, considering them brave enough most of the time but clumsily handled. Even into 1918 the BEF remained sometimes poor at coordinating attacks and exploiting any temporary success it managed to achieve. The main factor behind British success, Rupprecht thought, was weight of numbers, in men and especially in artillery. There is little evidence that Rupprecht was aware of, much less worried by, any British tactical improvement. He was less likely to note threatening British tactical innovations than instances of them repeating the same mistakes. The important exception was Plumer's artillery-heavy 'bite-and-hold' approach in late September 1917. This did cause concern but was too resource-intensive to be repeated often. Even in 1918, Rupprecht reckoned the average German soldier superior to a British one. This was a common view among German troops and officers during the First World

War and it is hard to know how much weight to give to such opinions. Were they an objective description of what German soldiers saw before them, or did they merely fit existing national stereotypes? It made obvious sense for the Germans to think this way about their enemy: there were clear morale benefits while the war went on and it offered a face-saving explanation of defeat once it was over. Better to have been overwhelmed than outfought, after all.

Fourth, Rupprecht enables us to view learning during the First World War in a fresh light. Over the last twenty-five years revisionist historians have painted a picture in which the BEF on the Western Front overcame the challenges of modern warfare one by one until it had built a 'weapons system' capable of beating the Germans in 1918. This useful corrective to the 'butchers and bunglers' stereotype had the benefit of capturing the central truth that the British army overcame daunting challenges to be much better at its job by 1918 than it had been earlier in the war. However, it also risked creating the impression that learning was a one-sided, British-only phenomenon and that the challenge of modern war was a largely static one. Finding the right solution, it suggested, was difficult, but possible: a single answer did exist, and once the BEF had worked it out, they could unlock the Western Front. The problem is often presented as rather like working out how to climb a fearsome mountain: far from easy; always dangerous; subject to numerous unpredictable variables, such as weather; but essentially a puzzle which, with time, thought, a lot of pluck, and a little bit of luck, could be unpicked.

Rupprecht shows us that there was more to learning than that. Learning was a front in the war, and contested just as fiercely as the others. It was a site of intense and dynamic competition between the combatants. Both sides took time to accept that they were now part of a new world but, once they had, measure clashed with counter-measure, was refined, tried again, parried once more, and so on, all in a never-ending and lethal race to a destination no-one knew. That the Germans lost this struggle, largely due to inherent institutional weaknesses within their army, does not diminish the achievement of the British and French in winning it. The fact that the learning environment was so much more complex and unforgiving than some historians have previously estimated only magnifies the respect the Entente armies are due. On both sides of the wire, ordinary men spent four years grappling with some of the most extraordinary and complex problems mankind has ever encountered. They did so under conditions of stress and danger which few of us today have ever encountered. That they adapted as well and as fast as they did testifies to human creativity even in the midst of the cruellest destruction.

Crown Prince Rupprecht of Bavaria was one of those men. Too proud to consider himself ordinary, he is not always an immediately sympathetic character to modern eyes. Like many royals, he could turn on easy-going charm when required, but just as smoothly behave with chilling reserve and ruthlessness. His social and political attitudes belonged to the nineteenth century. He could be short-tempered and prickly, especially when he thought he was not receiving the respect he was due. His moods swung rapidly from exhilaration to gloom. He was clearly a nuisance to command. He was, however, capable of inspiring loyalty and affection in those who worked for and alongside him. Some of them carried on fighting to defend his wartime record well into the 1930s, even after Rupprecht himself had sunk back into dignified silence. He was widely respected for his integrity, patriotism, and dedication. Rupprecht, to me at least, is not necessarily a very likeable man but he was a straight, honourable, and decent one, better perhaps as a business partner than a friend.

In 1914 some, as in Rupert Brooke's famous sonnet 'Peace', gladly turned from a world turned old and cold and weary and leapt into the cleanness of war. For them, the greys of peacetime resolved into blacks and whites. Here they found beauty among the horror, comradeship among the killing, and some even took delight in destruction.[3] Rupprecht was not one of these men. By temperament he was a professional, rather than a natural, warrior. He did what he must to execute his duty but derived little pleasure from it. He took his job seriously. The fact that he kept so full a diary is in itself evidence of that. He found release and relaxation in physical exercise, art, and hunting, not battle. He was highly sensitive to personal criticism. His paranoia was sometimes justified: some people, such as Falkenhayn, genuinely were trying to undermine him. Perhaps also, however, he was defensive out of a sense that he was not in his natural element and needed to work extra hard to prove, both to others and to himself, that he could handle the challenge of war. In this he was largely successful. He proved far from a figurehead, much less a dilettante. He set a high personal standard for his officers to follow: his army and, later, his Army Group, seem to have been well run and to have operated smoothly, at least until the army as a whole began to break down. His military judgement was generally good; he made sensible decisions; his troops were well prepared to fight; he oversaw an efficient logistics system which kept them equipped during combat; and he managed and directed the deployment of his reserves with care and skill. His ability was rewarded with extended responsibilities in August 1916 and he might even have been given command of the entire Western Front had it not been for the need to tip-toe around the Prussian Crown Prince. When he was bypassed by Ludendorff in 1918, this had little to do with his own performance. The same process was occurring all across the German army as Ludendorff struggled to keep control of a war he could feel slipping away from him.

Nonetheless, it would be silly to claim that Rupprecht was one of the great captains of history. The First World War did not produce many of those. It did shatter the reputations and careers of many, though, and Rupprecht was good enough to avoid such a fate. He made an uncertain start in 1914: Sixth Army failed first to tie down French forces in Lorraine and then to trap the BEF in Flanders. Nonetheless, for the next three years, despite days of disaster such as 25 September 1916 and 9 April 1917, his men were able to prevent Entente forces from achieving their objectives in seven major battles.[4] Only in 1918 was he clearly on the losing side in all the battles he fought. It could be argued that, being largely on the defensive, he had an easier job than his enemies. On the Western Front the outcome of single battles was less important than the cumulative effect of many, so the idea of victory and defeat is more complicated than it might have been for Napoleon or Julius Caesar. If we could look at individual battles in isolation, however, and define winning as achieving one's own objectives or preventing the enemy from gaining his, then Rupprecht won more than he lost. Not many generals in history can say that.

As time went on, he found it harder to deal with the pressures of war, both mentally and physically. He had trouble sleeping and his health began to weaken him. Of course, Rupprecht's sufferings were slight relative to those of his men. His daily life was comfortable. He slept under a roof and in a bed every night. His clothes were clean, his food always hot. He was rarely in personal danger, although he dealt with it well enough when he was. Most importantly, he survived the war sound in body and mind. Friends died but the only close family member he lost directly to the war was his cousin Heinrich, killed in Romania in 1916. The war had, however, torn him away from his two motherless sons and prevented Rupprecht from looking after, or even burying, one of them. The defeat and revolution of 1918 robbed him of his throne and his future. The war cost him much. Was

Rupprecht, however, to return to one of the questions raised in the Introduction, merely one of its victims? Was he, as I first thought, a man born too late, overwhelmed by the onrush of the modern world?

Without doubt, the circumstances Rupprecht had to handle were tough and eventually proved beyond him, as they proved beyond Germany herself. They brought catastrophe for Rupprecht, for Germany, and eventually for the whole world. The old certainties Rupprecht knew and fought to preserve were lost forever, sucked into the murderous whirlpool of the twentieth century. Inevitably, he did not have complete freedom of action. He lived and worked within structures, both institutional and conceptual, which constrained the decisions he took. As a general, he had to maintain the trust and respect of his subordinates while satisfying his superiors. In politics, he had always to work through others. His personality proved sometimes a help, sometimes a hindrance. Moreover, breeding and upbringing equipped him with the set of cultural and philosophical assumptions within which he operated. Eventually Rupprecht was able to see through the strategic group-think which gripped the senior ranks of the German military government. He saw that the war was hopeless when many others remain fixated on fighting on. He was more realistic than either his father or the Kaiser about the political consequences of defeat. Sadly, however, his conversion came too late: by 1918 the cumulative consequences of four years of poor decisions, made both individually by Rupprecht and collectively by Germany, were making themselves felt. Even then, he under-estimated the cost of failure and how radically his world was about to change. The paths Rupprecht took were not completely freely chosen, but neither were they entirely pre-determined. The more I studied Rupprecht, the more I realized that the choices he made, and indeed the decisions he did not make in time, affected what happened to him. We tend to describe any terrible accident as 'tragic', but Rupprecht's story is a tragedy in its original, ancient Greek, sense: a tale of human suffering brought about by the hero's weakness and mistakes.

There is another, possibly more important, way of looking at this question. Reading Rupprecht's diaries has shown me that he definitely saw himself as the subject of his own life, not just the object. A proud man with a strong sense of mission and responsibility, when Rupprecht looked in the shaving mirror every morning he surely saw himself as a man of action. The whole purpose of publishing his diary, after all, was to put forward his own account of his war in the face of criticism from the official historians. Rupprecht's diary thus contradicts the argument of the distinguished cultural historian Samuel Hynes, himself a combat veteran, that soldiers' tales are 'not concerned with *why*. War narratives are experience books; they are about what happened, and how it felt. *Why* is not a soldier's question.'[5] Many of the most powerful soldiers' tales from the First World War are stories of suffering. W. B. Yeats famously excluded poets such as Wilfred Owen, Siegfried Sassoon, and Isaac Rosenberg from his 1936 *Oxford Book of Modern Verse* on the grounds that 'passive suffering is not a theme for poetry'.[6] Between 1914 and 1918, it seemed, 'men no longer made war; war was made on men'.[7]

Rupprecht would never have shared such a view. He would have been repelled by the idea that he was no more than destiny's plaything. Rupprecht spoke in the active, not the passive, sense. Tempting as it may be to bucket together all the soldiers of the First World War as victims, when we do so we not only distort the historical record but also steal something of their sense of self from men who can no longer speak for themselves. This betrays their memory. It also conflicts with one of the primary purposes of history which surely is to let those whose voices have been stilled, by exclusion or death, speak again.

There is another wider point about the use of history in general, and the history of the twentieth century in particular, here. Before the First World War had even finished, those who saw themselves as its 'vanquished' began to harness victimhood to drive their agendas of vengeance and violence.[8] Mussolini and Hitler are only the two most obvious and chilling examples. Rupprecht, by never trying to exploit victimhood in that way, shows that there was nothing inevitable about doing so. Both the poets and the men of violence, for very different reasons and in very different ways, made a conscious choice to present themselves as pawns. We can see and feel the literary legacy of the Western Front around us still: due to the power of its appeal to empathy and emotion, it dominates the historical memory of the Great War and can be felt in much of how we remember and commemorate it today.

The consequences of the revanchists' myth of martyrdom were altogether more disastrous. Diabolic men led the world to the brink of a new Dark Age by the lights of their perverted history. Only after the Second World War had killed millions did they and their lies die in the flames of ruined Berlin. The final lesson we can learn from Rupprecht, perhaps, is that history is a powerful weapon which must be kept safe from those who would steal and twist it to their own evil ends.

Appendix: Note on Military Terminology

This note is designed to introduce some of the jargon used in the armies of the First World War and to explain their structure and hierarchy. In 1914 the British, French, and German armies were all set up along broadly similar lines, but organizations did change as the war went on. Here is a simplified version of the situation when war broke out. It reflects establishments on paper: practice on active service might deviate considerably, especially when casualties affected unit strength. As the war went on all armies tweaked the way they were organized. This note makes no attempt to keep up with all of these changes. Where they were important, they have already been identified in the text.

In 1914 the British army was manned entirely by long-serving regular soldiers, volunteers who had signed up for seven years' active service followed by five in the reserves. If war broke out, they could be called back to the colours. As the war went on, the original, regular British Expeditionary Force (BEF) was reinforced both by territorial units made up of part-time soldiers originally intended for home defence and by the wartime volunteers who famously signed up for Kitchener's New Armies. By 1916 Britain was running out of volunteers and turned to conscription, everywhere except Ireland. In Germany and France the system was different. There, conscripts formed the backbone of the army. After two or three years of active service, men became reservists until they reached the age of forty-five. After five years in the first-line reserves German men were transferred to the second-line Landwehr for ten years and thereafter to the Landsturm, where they might expect to serve mainly in rear areas. During the war the German army deployed active, Reserve, Ersatz, and Landwehr divisions in the front line. Apart from some minor differences in their orders of battle, there was increasingly little to choose between them. The same applied to the active, Reserve, and Territorial divisions of the French army, which employed a similar system of conscription and reservists.

British, German, or French, a new recruit arriving in the trenches to serve as an infantryman would be assigned to a section of 10–12 men. This was the team with which he would eat, sleep, and fight. Four sections made up a platoon; four platoons constituted a company; and four companies made up a battalion. In the German and French armies three battalions formed a regiment and fought together. Each division had four regiments. In the British army the regiment served a rather different function. It was an administrative, rather than a fighting, unit and the battalions of a regiment might never fight together. Different regiments had their own traditions and proud histories which served as a focus for esprit de corps. In the British army four battalions would be grouped into a brigade, and three brigades formed a division. In all three armies, therefore, the division comprised twelve infantry battalions. The division also included, as part of its permanent establishment, machine-guns, some cavalry, artillery, engineers, and medical units. In other words, the division was a combined arms formation capable of acting independently. It was also the building block used to construct higher commands on an 'as required' basis. Thus a corps in 1914 generally commanded two divisions, but by 1917–18 might have three or four attached. Four or five corps might be put together into an army, with a number of armies attached together in an Army Group, such as Rupprecht commanded.

The table below gives a (simplified) hierarchy of combat ranks within the British, French, and German armies and gives an idea of the job men at each rank might perform. The reality was considerably more complex. For instance, the British army distinguished between 'ranks' and 'appointments' and between substantive, brevet, temporary, and acting ranks. The practical effect of these distinctions was limited. Likewise, it makes little difference that what one line infantry regiment might call a 'private', the Guards would designate as a 'guardsman' and the Royal Engineers a 'sapper'. Or that a *Hauptmann* in the German infantry would be known as a *Rittmeister* in the cavalry. Unit strengths, of course, could vary dramatically, and casualties might mean that junior officers and non-commissioned officers (NCOs) found themselves temporarily in command one or even two levels above their normal station.

Rank	Command	Approximate number of men under command	German equivalent	French equivalent
Field Marshal	Army Group	2,000,000	Generalfeldmarschall	Maréchal de France
General	Army	300,000	Generaloberst	Général d'Armée
Lieutenant-General	Corps	60,000	General der Infanterie/Kavallerie/Artillerie	Général de Corps d'Armée
Major-General	Division	12,000	Generalleutnant	Général de Division
Brigadier-General	Brigade	3,500	Generalmajor	Général de Brigade
Colonel			Oberst	Colonel
Lieutenant-Colonel	Battalion commanding officer (CO)	1,000	Oberstleutnant	Lieutenant-Colonel
Major	Battalion second in command		Major	Commandant
Captain	Company	200	Hauptmann or Rittmeister	Capitaine
Lieutenant or Second Lieutenant	Platoon	50	Oberleutnant or Leutnant	Lieutenant or Sous-Lieutenant
Sergeant	Platoon second in command		Feldwebel or Sergeant	Sergent
Corporal or Lance Corporal	Section	12	Unteroffizier or Gefreiter	Caporal
Private	None	0	Soldat	Soldat

Notes

INTRODUCTION

1. See the Appendix for a note explaining ranks, units, and some other military details.
2. The passport is in the Geheimes Hausarchiv, Abteilung III, Bayerisches Hauptstaatsarchiv, Munich (GHA) Nachlaß (NL) Kronprinz Rupprecht (KPR) 255.
3. Early hagiographies in German include: Josef Breg, *Kronprinz Rupprecht von Bayern: Ein Lebensbild* (Munich: Max Kellerer, 1918); Otto Kolshorn, *Kronprinz Rupprecht von Bayern: Ein Lebens- und Charakterbild* (Munich: R. Piper & Co., 1918); Kurt Sendtner, *Rupprecht von Wittelsbach, Kronprinz von Bayern* (Munich: Richard Pflaum Verlag, 1954); Walter Wilhelm Goetz, *Rupprecht: Kronprinz von Bayern 1869–1955* (Munich: Bayerische Akademie für Wissenschaften, 1956). More modern, analytic treatments of Rupprecht's political career include: Dieter J. Weiß, *Kronprinz Rupprecht von Bayern: Eine politische Biografie* (Regensburg: Verlag Friedrich Pustet, 2007); Stefan März, *Das Haus Wittelsbach im Ersten Weltkrieg: Chance und Zusammenbruch monarchischer Herrschaft* (Regensburg: Friedrich Pustet, 2013). For the military side, see: Dieter Storz, 'Kronprinz Rupprecht von Bayern—dynastische Heeresführung im Massenkrieg', in Winfried Heinemann and Markus Pöhlmann (eds), *Monarchen und ihr Militär* (Potsdam: Militärgeschichtliches Forschungsamt, 2010), pp. 45–57; Holger Afflerbach, 'Kronprinz Rupprecht von Bayern im Ersten Weltkrieg', *Militärgeschichtliche Zeitschrift* 75:1 (May 2016), pp. 21–54.
4. For important and influential books on the First World War and modernity, see Paul Fussell, *The Great War and Modern Memory* (London: Oxford University Press, 1977) and Modris Eksteins, *The Rites of Spring: The Great War and the Birth of the Modern Age* (London: Bantam, 1989). They mean very specific things by 'modernity', involving the use of irony and the scope allowed to the individual. Here I use 'modern' in a more popular sense as a concept including senses of: a break from the traditional past; progress; speed; scale; the machine; urbanization.
5. Notable exceptions to this rule, by historians with a good feel for military realities, include: Hew Strachan, *The First World War* Volume I: *To Arms* (Oxford: Oxford University Press, 2001); David Stevenson, *1914–1918: The History of the First World War* (London: Allen Lane, 2004); Stevenson, *With Our Backs to the Wall* (London: Allen Lane, 2011), although all three works cover much more than just the Western Front.

6. Books on the former include: Martin Kitchen: *The Silent Dictatorship: The Politics of the German High Command under Hindenburg and Ludendorff, 1916–1918* (London: Croom Helm, 1976); Robert B. Asprey, *The German High Command at War: Hindenburg and Ludendorff Conduct World War I* (New York: William Morrow, 1991); better are: Holger Afflerbach, *Falkenhayn, Politisches Denken und Handeln im Kaiserreich* (Munich: R. Oldenbourg, 1994); Holger H. Herwig, *The First World War: Germany and Austria-Hungary 1914–1918* (London: Arnold, 1997); Annika Mombauer, *Helmuth von Moltke and the Origins of the First World War* (Cambridge: Cambridge University Press, 2001); Robert T. Foley, *German Strategy and the Path to Verdun: Erich von Falkenhayn and the Development of Attrition 1870– 1916* (Cambridge: Cambridge University Press, 2005); Alexander Watson, *Ring of Steel: Germany and Austria-Hungary at War, 1914–1918* (London: Allen Lane, 2014). For the latter, see: Benjamin Ziemann, *War Experiences in Rural Germany 1914– 1923* (Alex Skinner, trans.) (Oxford: Berg, 2007); Bernd Ulrich and Benjamin Ziemann (eds), *German Soldiers in the Great War: Letters and Eyewitness Accounts* (Barnsley: Pen and Sword, 2010); Jack Sheldon, *The Germany Army on the Somme 1916* (Barnsley: Leo Cooper, 2005); Sheldon, *The German Army at Passchendaele* (Barnsley: Pen & Sword, 2007); Sheldon, *The German Army on Vimy Ridge 1914– 1917* (Barnsley: Pen & Sword, 2008); Sheldon, *The German Army at Cambrai* (Barnsley: Pen & Sword, 2009); Sheldon, *The German Army At Ypres, 1914* (Barnsley: Pen & Sword, 2010) and others. There have also been excellent studies of individual battles, as well as useful overviews of the longer course of German military history: Dennis Showalter, *Tannenberg: Clash of Empires, 1914* (Hamden: Archon, 1991); Christopher Duffy, *Through German Eyes: The British and The Somme 1916* (London: Weidenfeld & Nicolson, 2006); David T. Zabecki, *The German 1918 Offensives: A Case Study in the Operational Level of War* (New York: Routledge, 2006); Robert M. Citino, *The German Way of War: From the Thirty Years' War to the Third Reich* (Lawrence, KS: University Press of Kansas, 2005). Robert Foley has published a useful series of specialist articles discussing innovation and the German army: Robert T. Foley, 'Learning War's Lessons: The Germany Army and the Battle of the Somme 1916', *Journal of Military History* 75 (April 2011), pp. 471–504; Foley, 'A Case Study in Horizontal Military Innovation: The German Army 1916–1918', *Journal of Strategic Studies* 35:6 (2012), pp. 799–827; Foley, 'Dumb Donkeys or Cunning Foxes? Learning in the British and German Armies during the Great War', *International Affairs* 90:2 (2014), pp. 279–98.

7. Although the Zentrum für Militärgeschichte und Sozialwissenschaften der Bundeswehr has produced an impressive array of work, such as: Christian Stachelbeck, *Militärische Effektivität im Ersten Weltkrieg: Die 11. Bayerische Infanteriedivision 1915 bis 1918* (Paderborn: Ferdinand Schöningh, 2010); Gerhard P. Groß, *Mythos und Wirklichkeit: Geschichte des operativen Denkens im deutschen Heer von Moltke d. Ä bis Heusinger* (Paderborn: Ferdinand Schöningh, 2012).

8. Examples of this school of thought include: Trevor N. Dupuy, *A Genius for War: The German Army and General Staff, 1807–1945* (London: Macdonald and Jane's,

1977); Timothy T. Lupfer, *The Dynamics of Doctrine: The Change in German Tactical Doctrine during the First World War* (Leavenworth Paper No. 4: Combat Studies Institute, U.S. Army Command and General Staff College, Fort Leavenworth, KS, 1981); Martin van Creveld, *Command in War* (Cambridge, MA: Harvard University Press, 1985); Allan R. Millett and Williamson Murray (eds), *Military Effectiveness*, 3 volumes (Boston, MA: Allen & Unwin, 1988); Martin Samuels, *Command or Control? Command, Training and Tactics in the British and German Armies, 1888–1918* (London: Frank Cass, 1995).

9. Winston S. Churchill, *The World Crisis*, 6 volumes (London: Thornton Butterworth, 1923–31); David Lloyd George, *War Memoirs*, 6 volumes (London: Nicholson & Watson, 1933–6); Basil Liddell Hart, *The Real War* (London, Faber & Faber, 1930; expanded and republished as *A History of the World War, 1914–1918* (1934) and as *History of the First World War* (1970)); Alan Clark, *The Donkeys* (London: Hutchinson, 1961); A. J. P. Taylor, *The First World War: An Illustrated History* (London: Hamish Hamilton, 1963); John Laffin, *British Butchers and Bunglers of World War One* (Stroud: Sutton, 1988).

10. Paddy Griffith, *Battle Tactics of the Western Front: The British Army's Art of Attack 1916–18* (New Haven, CT: Yale University Press, 1994); Gary Sheffield, *Forgotten Victory: The First World War: Myths and Realities* (London: Headline, 2001). See also, among many others, Bill Rawling, *Surviving Trench Warfare: Technology and the Canadian Corps 1914–1918* (Toronto: University of Toronto Press, 1992); Albert Palazzo, *Seeking Victory on the Western Front: The British Army and Chemical Warfare in World War I* (Lincoln, NE: University of Nebraska Press, 2000); Peter Simkins, *From the Somme to Victory: The British Army's Experience on the Western Front 1916–1918* (Barnsley: Pen & Sword, 2014).

11. Patrick Leigh Fermor, *A Time of Gifts: On Foot to Constantinople: From the Hook of Holland to the Middle Danube* (London: Penguin, 1988 [1978]); Leigh Fermor, *Between the Woods and the Water: On Foot to Constantinople from the Hook of Holland, the Middle Danube to the Iron Gates* (London: John Murray, 1986).

12. Author's note, Erich Maria Remarque, *All Quiet on the Western Front* (Brian Murdoch, trans.) (London: Vintage, 2005 [1994]), n.p. and p. 208; Wilfred Owen, 'Anthem for Doomed Youth', http://www.oucs.ox.ac.uk/ww1lit/collections/item/3290, accessed 7 January 2017; Stephane Audoin-Rouzeau and Annette Becker, *1914–1918: Understanding the Great War* (Catherine Temerson, trans.) (London: Profile, 2002), p. 2.

13. Paul Fussell's seminal *The Great War and Modern Memory* (Oxford: Oxford University Press, 2000 [1977]) is the most complete statement of the 'soldier as victim' hypothesis, but see the critique in Robin Prior and Trevor Wilson, 'Paul Fussell at War', *War in History* 1:1 (1994), pp. 63–80; also: Joanna Bourke, *Dismembering the Male: Men's Bodies, Britain and the Great War* (London: Reaktion, 1996); Bourke, *An Intimate History of Killing: Face-to-Face Killing in Twentieth Century Warfare* (London: Granta, 2000 [1999]), p. 375; Niall Ferguson, *The Pity of War* (London: Allen Lane, 1998), p. 357. For a more convincing exploration of some of the ways in which soldiers tried to assert agency over their situation

and environment, see Tony Ashworth, *Trench Warfare 1914–1918: The Live and Let Live System* (London: Macmillan, 1980) and, better still, Alexander Watson, 'Self-Deception and Survival: Mental Coping Strategies on the Western Front, 1914–18', *Journal of Contemporary History* 41:2 (2006), pp. 247–68.

14. Hans Binneveld, *From Shell Shock to Combat Stress: A Comparative History of Military Psychiatry* (Amsterdam: Amsterdam University Press, 1997), p. 57.

15. I am grateful to one of the anonymous readers of the first draft of this manuscript for suggesting this line of inquiry to me. As Holger Afflerbach points out, if it is hard to establish the precise significance in history of supreme commanders such as Wilhelm II or Hitler, it is even harder for those such as Rupprecht a level or two further down the ladder: Afflerbach, 'Kronprinz Rupprecht', p. 22.

16. The published version is Rupprecht, Kronprinz von Bayern (Eugen von Frauenholz, ed.), *Mein Kriegstagebuch* (Berlin: E. S. Mittler & Sohn, 3 volumes, 1929), abbreviated hereafter in these notes to Rupprecht, *Kriegstagebuch*. The manuscript version, which will be referred to as Rupprecht MS diary, is to be found in GHA NL KPR, 699–708. For ease of reference, wherever possible I have quoted from the former. Entry, 1 October 1917, Rupprecht MS diary, GHA NL KPR 707, pp. 2988–96. For an excellent discussion of the dispute between Rupprecht's detractors and supporters, see Markus Pöhlmann, *Kriegsgeschichte und Geschichtspolitik: Der Erste Weltkrieg: Die amtliche deutsche Militärgeschichtsschreibung 1914–1956* (Paderborn: Ferdinand Schöningh, 2002), pp. 284–321.

17. Bayerisches Kriegsarchiv, Abteilung IV, Bayerisches Hauptstaatsarchiv, Munich (BKA).

18. The German official history, *Der Weltkrieg 1914 bis 1918*, was published in fourteen volumes between 1925 and 1944, although the last volumes were not made public until 1956. The name of the institution producing it changed several times. For simplicity, it will here be referred to by GOH with the volume number. Similarly for the French (*Les Armées Françaises dans la Grande Guerre*) and British (*Military Operations France and Belgium*) official histories, with FOH and BOH respectively.

CHAPTER I

1. The details on Rupprecht's early life which follow are primarily drawn from Weiß, *Kronprinz Rupprecht* and Sendtner, *Rupprecht von Wittelsbach*. The Leuchtenberg Palace, in which he was born, stands on Odeonsplatz and now houses the Bavarian State's Ministry of Finance.

2. März, *Das Haus Wittelsbach*, pp. 62–9.

3. Statistics largely from tables in Volker R. Berghahn, *Imperial Germany, 1871–1914: Economy, Society, Culture, and Politics* (Providence, RI: Berghahn Books, 1994), pp. 294–339; Roger Chickering, *Imperial Germany and the Great War, 1914–1918* (2nd edn, Cambridge: Cambridge University Press, 2004): James Retallack (ed.), *Imperial Germany 1871–1918* (Oxford: Oxford University Press, 2008).

4. Breg, *Kronprinz Rupprecht*, p. 13; letter to author from Rupprecht's grandson, Herzog Franz von Bayern, 3 July 2015; Kolshorn, *Kronprinz Rupprecht*, pp. 47–8.
5. Quoted in Weiß, *Kronprinz Rupprecht*, p. 68.
6. März, *Das Haus Wittelsbach*, pp. 148–56.
7. Foreword, Rupprecht MS Diary, GHA NL KPR 699.
8. John Röhl, *Wilhelm II: Into the Abyss of War and Exile 1900–1941* (Sheila de Bellaigue and Roy Bridge, trans.) (Cambridge: Cambridge University Press, 2014), pp. 1092–3.

CHAPTER 2

1. Some of the numbers in this book are so large that they can be hard to visualize. Some comparisons might help: 250,000 people use Waterloo Station every day; Wembley Stadium holds 90,000 and Stamford Bridge a little over 40,000; the University of Birmingham has about 35,000 students; 10,000 soldiers marching four abreast would take about two hours to go past; a Northern Line tube train holds about 1,000 people.
2. Citino, *The German Way of War*, pp. 131, 150; Crown Prince William of Germany, *My War Experiences* (London: Hurst and Blackett, n.d.), p. 4.
3. Dieter Storz, '"Dieser Stellungs- und Festungskrieg ist scheußlich!" Zu den Kämpfen in Lothringen und in des Vogesen im Sommer 1914', in Hans Ehlert, Michael Epkenhans, and Gerhard P. Groß (eds), *Der Schlieffenplan: Analyse und Dokumente* (Paderborn: Ferdinand Schöningh, 2006), pp. 162–204, p. 166; entry, 31 July 1914, Krafft Diary, BKA NL Krafft 145; entry, 1–5 August 1914, Rupprecht MS Diary, GHA NL KPR 699, pp. 4–5.
4. Christian Stachelbeck, *Deutschlands Heer und Marine im Ersten Weltkrieg* (Munich: Oldenbourg, 2013), pp. 116–37; 'Aufmarschanweisung für Oberkommando der 6. Armee', 2 August 1914, GHA NL KPR 476, paras 38, 44.
5. Entries, 1–5 August and 9 September 1914, Rupprecht MS Diary, GHA NL KPR 699, pp. 4–5, 194; Ehlert, Epkenhans, and Groß (eds), *Der Schlieffenplan*, pp. 399–484; Krafft, 'Kurzer Überblick über die Vorgänge beim Oberkommando der 6. Armee im August 1914 bis zur Schlacht in Lothringen am 20.8.1914', GHA NL KPR 699, pp. 7–9; Robert Doughty, *Pyrrhic Victory: French Strategy and Operations in the Great War* (Cambridge, MA: Belknap Press, 2005), pp. 12–13; Rupprecht, 'Meine Teilnahme am Weltkrieg 1914–18', GHA NL KPR 716, p. 10.
6. Bayerisches Kriegsarchiv, *Die Bayern im Großen Kriege* (Munich: Verlag des Bayerischen Kriegsarchivs, 1923), pp. 5, 16; Holger H. Herwig, *The Marne, 1914: The Opening of World War I and the Battle that Changed the World* (New York: Random House, 2009), p. 46; GOH Volume I, p. 144. One corps consisted of 1,500 officers, 40,000 men, and 14,000 horses, most of them pulling 2,400 wagons for supplies and ammunition.
7. Krafft, 'Kurzer Überblick über die Vorgänge beim Oberkommando der 6. Armee im August 1914 bis zur Schlacht in Lothringen am 20.8.1914', GHA NL KPR 699, p. 2; 'Erste Beurteilung der Lage', Krafft Diary, BKA NL Krafft 145: Annex; Rupprecht, 'Meine Teilnahme am Weltkrieg 1914–18', GHA NL KPR 716, p. 13.

8. Entry, 6–9 August 1914, Rupprecht MS Diary, GHA NL KPR 699, p. 8.

9. Rupprecht, 'Meine Teilnahme am Weltkrieg 1914–18', GHA NL KPR 716, p. 15.

10. Sixth Army headquarters had no wireless and only one telephone in August 1914. Even once OHL moved to the Western Front, the one-way trip from there to Sixth Army could take nearly three hours by automobile: Rudolf von Xylander, *Deutsche Führung in Lothringen 1914: Wahrheit und Kriegsgeschichte* (Berlin: Junker und Dünnhaupt Verlag, 1935), p. 22; Rupprecht, *Kriegstagebuch* Volume I, footnote pp. 85–6; Krafft's note on entry, 2 September, Rupprecht MS Diary, GHA NL KPR 699, pp. 149–51.

11. Rupprecht, 'Meine Teilnahme am Weltkrieg 1914–18', GHA NL KPR 716, pp. 16–17; entry, 14 August 1914, Rupprecht MS Diary, GHA NL KPR 699, p. 16; GOH Volume I, pp. 644, 647–9.

12. Bayerisches Kriegsarchiv, *Die Bayern im Großen Kriege*, pp. 18–23; GOH Volume I, p. 174; Rupprecht, *Kriegstagebuch* Volume I, p. 10.

13. FOH I:1, pp. 161, 179–80, 230–5; Michel Goya, *La Chair et l'Acier: L'Invention de la Guerre Moderne (1914–1918)*, p. 181; Bayerisches Kriegsarchiv, *Die Bayern im Großen Kriege*, p. 24.

14. Rupprecht, *Kriegstagebuch* Volume I, p. 9; Krafft, 'Kurzer Überblick über die Vorgänge beim Oberkommando der 6. Armee im August 1914 bis zur Schlacht in Lothringen am 20.8.1914', GHA NL KPR 699, p. 14.

15. Krafft, 'Kurzer Überblick über die Vorgänge beim Oberkommando der 6. Armee im August 1914 bis zur Schlacht in Lothringen am 20.8.1914', GHA NL KPR 699, pp. 2, 11; entry, 17 August 1914, Rupprecht MS Diary, GHA NL KPR 699, p. 36; Rupprecht, *Kriegstagebuch* Volume I, pp. 6–21; Konrad Krafft von Dellmensingen, *Die Führung des Kronprinzen Rupprecht von Bayern auf dem linken deutschen Heeresflügel bis zur Schlacht in Lothringen im August 1914* (Berlin: E. S. Mittler & Sohn, 1925), pp. 17–21; GOH Volume I, p. 256. See also pp. 208, 210–11.

16. Instruction Générale No. 3, FOH Volume I:1 Annex 474, pp. 441–2; FOH Volume I:1, pp. 250–4; Elizabeth Greenhalgh, *Foch in Command: The Forging of a First World War General* (Cambridge: Cambridge University Press, 2011), pp. 14–19.

17. Entry, 20 August 1914, Rupprecht MS Diary, GHA NL KPR 699, p. 48; GOH Volume I, p. 451; Rupprecht, *Kriegstagebuch* Volume I, p. 30.

18. FOH Volume I:1, pp. 252–60; Rupprecht, *Kriegstagebuch* Volume I, pp. 36, 41.

19. Entry, 21 August 1914, 'Auszug aus einem am 6.6.1916 vom AOK 7 an die OHL eingereichten Bericht, AOK 7 Operations 3 August–16 September 1914', BKA Armeeoberkommando (AOK) 6 Vorl. 9; Ludwig von Gebsattel, *Von Nancy bis zum Camp des Romains 1914* (Oldenburg: Gerhard Stalling 1924), p. 14; Herwig, *The Marne, 1914*, p. 103; entry, 24 August 1914, Rupprecht MS Diary, GHA NL KPR 699, pp. 69, 72.

20. Entry, 27 August 1914, Rupprecht MS Diary, GHA NL KPR 699, pp. 110–28; entries, 24, 25 August 1914, BKA NL R. Xylander 12 Kriegstagebuch 1914/18 Volume I, pp. iv–v; Gebsattel, *Von Nancy bis zum Camp des Romains*, pp. 23,

22–36; John Horne and Alan Kramer, *German Atrocities 1914: A History of Denial* (New Haven, CT: Yale University Press, 2001), pp. 66–7; Fayolle cited in Michel Goya, *La Chair et l'Acier*, p. 183; Rupprecht, *Kriegstagebuch* Volume I, p. 53.

21. Rupprecht, *Kriegstagebuch* Volume I, p. 58.

CHAPTER 3

1. Rupprecht, *Kriegstagebuch* Volume I, p. 62; telegram, 30 August 1914, correspondence with King Ludwig III, GHA NL KPR 434; letter from Wenninger, 30 August 1914, in Bernd F. Schulte, 'Neue Dokumente zum Kriegsausbruch und Kriegsverlauf 1914', *Militärgeschichtliche Mitteilungen* 25:1 (1979), pp. 123–85: p. 159.

2. Storz, ' "Dieser Stellungs- und Festungskrieg ist scheußlich!" ', pp. 162–204: pp. 187–8; Herwig, *The Marne, 1914*, p. 231; Wenninger diary entry, 28–9 August and report, 1 September 1914, in Schulte, 'Neue Dokumente', pp. 158, 160.

3. Entry, 31 August 1914, 'Auszug aus einem am 6.6.1916 vom AOK 7 an die OHL eingereichten Bericht, AOK 7 Operations 3 August–16 September 1914', BKA AOK 6 Vorl. 9; Rupprecht, *Kriegstagebuch* Volume I, pp. 76–86.

4. Gebsattel, *Von Nancy bis zum Camp des Romains*, pp. 51–4.

5. Rupprecht, *Kriegstagebuch* Volume I, pp. 93–5, 99.

6. Rupprecht, *Kriegstagebuch* Volume I, pp. 103–7.

7. The post-war official German army medical report gave total losses (sick, wounded, dead, and missing) in Sixth and Seventh Armies in August and September as 127,496, of whom 38,875 were dead. The two armies had begun with 345,000 men between them: Heeres-Sanitätsinspektion des Reichskriegsministeriums, *Sanitätsbericht über das Deutsche Heer (Deutsches Feld- und Besatzungheer) im Weltkriege 1914/1918* Volume III: *Die Krankenbewegung bei dem Deutschen Feld- und Besatzungsheer im Weltkriege 1914/1918* (Berlin: E. S. Mittler & Sohn, 1934), pp. 36–9; Storz, ' "Dieser Stellungs- und Festungskrieg ist scheußlich!" ', pp. 162–204: p. 204; Gebsattel, *Von Nancy bis zum Camp des Romains*, p. 78, footnote to p. 87; Rupprecht, *Kriegstagebuch* Volume I, p. 118; Elizabeth Greenhalgh, *The French Army and the First World War* (Cambridge: Cambridge University Press, 2014), pp. 58–9.

8. Horne and Kramer, *German Atrocities 1914*, pp. 20, 22, 63–7.

9. Horne and Kramer, *German Atrocities 1914*, pp. 74–6, 95, 194–5, 349–50; Isabel V. Hull, *Absolute Destruction: Military Culture and the Practices of War in Imperial Germany* (Ithaca, NY: Cornell University Press, 2005), pp. 208–12; Hull, *A Scrap of Paper: Breaking and Making International Law during the Great War* (Ithaca, NY: Cornell University Press, 2014), pp. 51–60.

10. Letter to Krafft from the Supreme State Prosecutor, b.J. 353/20/12, 3 March 1923, Miscellaneous Documents regarding Crown Prince Rupprecht, BKA NL Krafft 196; Horne and Kramer, *German Atrocities 1914*, pp. 349–51.

11. Rupprecht, *Kriegstagebuch* Volume I, p. 34; entry 21 August 1914, Rupprecht MS Diary, GHA NL KPR 699, pp. 55–6.

12. Hull, *A Scrap of Paper*, p. 57 summarizes views she developed in *Absolute Destruction*.

13. Entry, 21 August 1914, Rupprecht MS Diary, GHA NL KPR 699, pp. 55–6; Army Order of the Day, 24 August 1914, Campaign 1914: Documents from Section Ic/d, BKA AOK 6 Vorl. 220; Special Order for 30 August 1914, Ic No. 11[29], 29 August 1914 and Special Proclamation, 9 September 1914, both in Special Orders, BKA AOK 6 Vorl. 206; Army Order of the Day for 19 September 1914, Army Orders of the Day, BKA AOK 6 Vorl. 611 and Campaign 1914: Documents from Section Ic/d Vorl. 221.

14. Rupprecht, *Kriegstagebuch* Volume I, pp. 65–6; Hull, *Absolute Destruction*, pp. 208–12; Hull, *A Scrap of Paper*, chapter 3; Röhl, *Wilhelm II: Into the Abyss*, pp. 77, 1129.

CHAPTER 4

1. Rupprecht, *Kriegstagebuch* Volume I, pp. 126–7; entry, 18 September 1914, Krafft diary, BKA NL Krafft 48, pp. 1a–2a; Foley, *German Strategy and the Path to Verdun*, pp. 99–102.

2. Rupprecht, *Kriegstagebuch* Volume I, p. 132; entries, 18, 21 September 1914, Krafft diary, BKA NL Krafft 48, pp. 1a–2a, 11a.

3. There had already been some sharp skirmishes in the area in August but the autumn fighting was on a different scale and more important: William Philpott, *Bloody Victory: The Sacrifice on the Somme and the Making of the Twentieth Century* (London: Little, Brown, 2009), pp. 18–19.

4. Entry, 27 September 1914, Krafft diary, BKA NL Krafft 48, pp. 33a, 35b; Rupprecht, *Kriegstagebuch* Volume I, p. 161.

5. Philpott, *Bloody Victory*, pp. 27–8; Rupprecht, *Kriegstagebuch* Volume I, p. 165. In fact, no British units were nearby. Sheldon, *The German Army on the Somme*, p. 34.

6. Entry, 2 October 1914, Rupprecht MS Diary, GHA NL KPR 700. This sentence is omitted from Rupprecht, *Kriegstagebuch* Volume I, p. 180.

7. Entries, 26, 28 September, 4 October 1914, Krafft diary, BKA NL Krafft 48, pp. 28a–b, 36b, 52a; entry, 2 October 1914, Rupprecht MS Diary, GHA NL KPR 700.

8. GOH Volume V, pp. 216–17.

CHAPTER 5

1. Rupprecht, *Kriegstagebuch* Volume I, p. 206. The sentences in italic feature only in the MS diary: entry, 14 October 1914, Rupprecht MS Diary, GHA NL KPR, 700. Entries, 13, 14 October 1914, Krafft diary, BKA NL Krafft 48, pp. 81b–82b, 84a–87a.

2. GOH Volume V, p. 286; entries 14, 15 October 1914, Krafft Diary, BKA NL Krafft 48, pp. 84a–87a, 91a; Rupprecht, *Kriegstagebuch* Volume I, p. 206.

3. Richard Holmes, *The Little Field Marshal: Sir John French* (London: Jonathan Cape, 1981), p. 244; Rupprecht, *Kriegstagebuch* Volume I, pp. 215, 221–2.

4. Rupprecht, *Kriegstagebuch* Volume I, p. 216; AOK 6 War Diary, BKA AOK 6 Bd 1 Vorl 1, p. 62; report to King, 30 October 1914, Correspondence with King Ludwig III, GHA NL KPR 428.

5. Armeetagesbefehl, 19 October 1914, Operations, GHA NL KPR 478; also reproduced in Rupprecht, *Kriegstagebuch* Volume III, pp. 57–8.

6. ' "Annihilate the English" ', *Daily Mail*, 2 November 1914, p. 4; 'Hatred of England', *The Times*, 29 October 1914, p. 8; 'National Hatred', *The Times*, 1 November 1914, p. 3; 'Germany's "most hated foe" ', *The Times*, 9 November 1914, p. 9; 'Rupprecht's Call for Help', *Daily Mail*, 29 September 1915, p. 5; 'Enemy Generals in the West', *Daily Mail*, 25 March 1918, p. 2; 'Shooting of British Prisoners', *Manchester Guardian*, 11 May 1915, p. 8; 'Murder of British Prisoners', *Daily Mail*, 11 May 1915, p. 6; 'House of Commons', *Manchester Guardian*, 12 May 1915, p. 4; *Hansard* HC Deb 19 May 1915 Volume 71 cc 2304–5; Rupprecht, *Kriegstagebuch* Volume I, p. 361. The allegations were a mixture of hearsay and first-person testimony made by German deserters to Dutch journalists. One of the stories was of forty British soldiers being burned alive in an aircraft hanger. Rupprecht and Krafft always denied any such order, and it is probably impossible to check the veracity of the reports of murders at this distance. See the discussion of this issue in Weiß, *Kronprinz Rupprecht*, pp. 174–8.

7. Rupprecht, *Kriegstagebuch* Volume I, pp. 227, 225.

8. One of the earliest official versions appears in German General Staff, *Ypres, 1914: An official account published by order of the German General Staff* (translation of *Die Schlacht an der Yser und bei Ypern im Herbst 1914* (Oldenburg: Gerhard Stalling, 1918) by G. C. W[ynne]), (Nashville, TN: Battery Press, 1994 [1919]), p. 43. See Ian F. W. Beckett, *Ypres: The First Battle, 1914* (Harlow: Pearson, 2004), pp. 46–8, 98–109, 237–40 for a good summary of the myth, which is more fully explored in Karl Unruh, *Langemarck: Legende und Wirklichkeit* (Koblenz: Bernard & Graefe, 1986); Bayerisches Kriegsarchiv, *Die Bayern im Großen Kriege*, p. 137.

9. Rupprecht, *Kriegstagebuch* Volume I, pp. 232–4; Diary entry 27 October 1914, MS Diary, GHA NL Kronprinz Rupprecht, 700, pp. 356–7. Sentence in italics only in MS diary.

10. [Wilhelm] Solger, 'Zur Ausarbeitung des Reichsarchivs "Die Erwägungen über einen Durchbruchs-Angriff gegen die westliche Stellungsfront von ende Februar bis 13. April 1915" ', dated 24 January–2 February 1930, pp. 7–8, Schemes for Breakthrough in the West, BKA NL Krafft 189; Bayerisches Kriegsarchiv, *Die Bayern im Großen Kriege*, pp. 139–40; 'Gedanken über die Führung der Operationen und Erfahrungen im Weltkriege', BKA, NL Krafft 324, p. 217a; GOH Volume V, p. 336; German General Staff, *Ypres, 1914*, p. 63.

11. Rupprecht, *Kriegstagebuch* Volume I, p. 236.

12. German General Staff, *Ypres, 1914*, p. 65.

13. First estimates were that Fabeck had lost 10,000, or one-third, of his men between 30 October and 2 November. The reality was even worse: 17,250. The 6th Bavarian Reserve Division suffered 40 per cent casualties in just five days. Fourth Army lost 39,000 dead and wounded with 13,000 missing, while Sixth Army, including Fabeck, suffered 27,000 dead and wounded with another 1,000 missing. Rupprecht, *Kriegstagebuch* Volume I, pp. 240, 244, 246; GOH Volume V,

pp. 346, 401; entries 3, 5 November 1914, Rupprecht MS Diary, GHA NL KPR 701, pp. 394, 402.

14. Holmes, *The Little Field Marshal*, pp. 248–9, 252–3; BOH 1914 Volume II, p. 383; entries, 4, 6 November 1914, War Diary, BKA AOK 6 Bd 1 Vorl No. 1, pp. 67, 73; Rupprecht, *Kriegstagebuch* Volume I, p. 245; Hermann Cron, *Imperial German Army 1914–18: Organisation, Structure, Orders-of-Battle* (C. F. Colton, trans.) (Solihull: Helion, 2002), footnote 17, p. 136.

15. GOH Volume V, p. 401; GOH Volume VI, pp. 1, 10, 15; Foley, *German Strategy and the Path to Verdun*, p. 103.

16. GOH Volume VI, p. 17.

17. Rupprecht, *Kriegstagebuch* Volume I, pp. 250–3; entry, 14 November 1914, War Diary, BKA AOK 6 Bund 1 Vorl No. 1, p. 75; GOH Volume VI, pp. 19–23, 371–2.

18. Of these, 7,960 were dead and 17,873 missing. The 'missing' fell into three groups: a few would have got lost somehow and rejoined their units later; many or most would be dead, their bodies in some way unrecoverable in No Man's Land; lastly, some others might have fallen into enemy hands as prisoners. In this case, slightly over 7,000 turned out to have been captured by the enemy: BOH 1914 Volume II, p. 383; Statistical Abstract of Information Regarding the Armies at Home and Abroad, No. 25, 1 October 1918, TNA WO 394/10, p. 137; War Office, *Statistics of the Military Effort of the British Empire during the Great War 1914–1920* (London: HMSO, 1922), p. 253.

19. Sixth Army lost 27,000 dead and wounded in the second half of October, plus a thousand missing. The figures for the first ten days of November seem to have been lost but 9,500 were killed or wounded, and another thousand went missing, between 10 and 18 November: Beckett, *Ypres*, pp. 225–6; GOH Volume V, p. 401; GOH Volume VI, p. 25.

20. 'Die Erwägungen über einen Durchbruchs-Angriff gegen die westliche Stellungsfront von ende Februar bis 13. April 1915', BKA NL Krafft 189, pp. 8–13 and Beilage 1, p. 2; entry, 9 November 1914, War Diary, BKA AOK 6 Bd 1 Vorl 1, p. 72.

21. BOH 1914 Volume II, pp. 464–5; J. P. Harris, *Sir Douglas Haig and the First World War* (Cambridge: Cambridge University Press, 2008), p. 377; Gary Sheffield, *The Chief: Douglas Haig and the British Army* (London: Aurum, 2011), pp. 98, 240; German General Staff, *Ypres, 1914*; GOH Volume V, p. 578; Foley, *German Strategy and the Path to Verdun*, pp. 100–1; entry 12 November 1914, Rupprecht MS Diary, GHA NL KPR, 701, p. 432.

22. Michael Howard, 'Men against Fire: Expectations of War in 1914', *International Security* 9:1 (Summer 1984), pp. 41–57.

23. Rupprecht, *Kriegstagebuch* Volume I, p. 10; Terence Zuber, *The Mons Myth: A Reassessment of the Battle* (Stroud: History Press, 2010), pp. 48–54; FOH Volume I:1, pp. 179–80; Goya, *La Chair et l'Acier*, p. 181; Joffre to army and corps commanders, 13 August 1914, Annexe 67, FOH I:2 Annex Volume I, pp. 62–3; Report, 1 October 1914, Operations File GHA NL KPR 477.

24. Report to Sixth Army, 1 October 1914, Operations, GHA NL KPR 477; First Army No. 1704, 11 September 1914, 'Instructions du général Dubail, commandant

la Iʳᵉ armée, au sujet des procédés de combat à employer vis-à-vis des Allemands',
Annexe 3258, FOH I:3 Annexe Volume 3, pp. 450–1; Krafft Diary, BKA NL
Krafft 145, p. 36b; Chef des Generalstabes des Feldheeres M.J. No. 6505,
11 October 1914, BKA AOK 6 Vorl. 587.

25. GQG No. 3565 'Note pour les commandants d'armée', 15 October 1914, Annexe
2864, FOH I:4 Annexe Volume III, pp. 573–5; entry, 22 October 1914, Krafft
Diary, BKA NL Krafft 145, p. 111a.

26. 'Aufmarschanweisung für Oberkommando der 6. Armee', 2 August 1914, para-
graph 21, GHA NL KPR 476; Rupprecht, *Kriegstagebuch* Volume I, pp. 71–2; III
Bayerische Armeekorps (BAK) Lessons Learnt Report, 31 August 1914, BKA
AOK 6, Vorl. 164.

27. AOK 6 Order, 11 December 1914, BKA AOK 6, Vorl. 164; AOK 6 J. No. 5118
26 December 1914, Operations, GHA NL KPR 481; 'Rundschreiben No. 6 der
7. Englischen Division vom 27.11.1914: "Lessons learnt in recent defensive
battles" ', BKA AOK 6 Vorl. 169; AOK 1 Ia No. 834 'Erfahrungen aus den französischen Angriffen gegen die Stellung des Gren. Rgts. 89 in der Zeit vom 21.
bis 25. Dezember, 31 December 1914', 4 January 1915, BKA AOK 6 Vorl. 164;
AOK 6 No. 5702, 7 January 1915, Operations, GHA NL KPR 481; Hermann
von Kuhl, *Der deutsche Generalstab in Vorbereitung und Durchführung des Weltkrieges*
(Berlin: E. S. Mittler & Sohn, 1920), pp. 187–8.

28. Michel Goya, *La Chair et L'Acier*, pp. 232–4; GQG Nos 1981 & 1982, 'Instruction
relative à l'emploi de l'artillerie', 9 November 1914, Annexes 4077–8, FOH I:4
Annexe Volume 4, pp. 742–5; Nikolas Gardner has argued that the learning
processes of the BEF worked effectively in the autumn of 1914, although the
conceptual limitations of senior commanders prevented them from learning
the correct lessons: 'The Beginning of the Learning Curve: British Officers and
the Advent of Trench Warfare, September–October 1914' (ESRI Working Papers:
Salford, 2003) and Gardner, *Trial by Fire: Command and the British Expeditionary
Force in 1914* (Westport, CT: Praeger, 2003).

29. Foley, 'A Case Study in Horizontal Military Innovation', pp. 799–827.

CHAPTER 6

1. Afflerbach, *Falkenhayn*, pp. 211–32; Foley, *German Strategy and the Path to Verdun*,
pp. 113–24; Rupprecht, *Kriegstagebuch* Volume I, pp. 306, 409; entries 2 March,
25 December 1915, Rupprecht MS Diary, GHA NL KPR, 702, pp. 634–4, 703,
1244–5.

2. Rupprecht, *Kriegstagebuch* Volume I, p. 265.

3. Rupprecht, *Kriegstagebuch* Volume I, pp. 253–4; entries, 29 November,
11 December 1914, War Diary, BKA AOK 6 Bund 1 Vorl No. 1, pp. 86, 91; entry,
25 November 1914, Rupprecht MS Diary, GHA NL KPR, 701, p. 463.

4. Goya, *La Chair et L'Acier*, pp. 255–6; BOH 1915 Volume I, p. 4; GOH Volume
VI, pp. 375–6; Bayerisches Kriegsarchiv, *Die Bayern im Großen Kriege*, p. 146.

5. BOH 1915 Volume I, pp. 17–19; entries, 14, 16 December 1914, War Diary, BKA
AOK 6 Bd 1 Vorl No. 1, pp. 92–4; Rupprecht, *Kriegstagebuch* Volume I, pp. 276–8.

6. Casualties in the four French divisions involved were 542 officers and 7,229 men. Doughty, *Pyrrhic Victory*, p. 127; FOH Volume II, pp. 171–9, 188–9.

7. Rupprecht, *Kriegstagebuch* Volume I, pp. 278–9; *BOH 1915* Volume I, pp. 20–2.

8. FOH Volume II, pp. 190–242, 410–81; entry 25 December 1914, Krafft diary, BKA NL Krafft 289, p. 900; entries 25, 26 December 1914, Rupprecht MS diary, GHA NL KPR 701, pp. 529–31; entry, 28 December 1914, War Diary, BKA AOK 6, Bd 1 Vorl No. 1 Kriegstagebuch, p. 98; Sheldon, *The German Army on Vimy Ridge 1914–1917*, pp. 37–8.

9. In August–November 1914, Sixth Army lost, on average, 37,630 men per month in combat. In December 1914 this fell to 15,799. GOH Volume VII, p. 56; Heeres-Sanitätsinspektion des Reichskriegsministeriums, *Sanitätsbericht* Volume II, pp. 342, 365, 396.

10. *BOH 1915* Volume I, pp. 69–154; G. C. Wynne, *If Germany Attacks: The Battle in Depth in the West* (Westport, CT: Greenwood Press, 1976 [1940]), pp. 19–41; GOH Volume VII, pp. 58–9; Robin Prior and Trevor Wilson, *Command on the Western Front: The Military Career of Sir Henry Rawlinson* (Barnsley: Pen & Sword 2004 [1992]), pp. 19–73.

11. Prior and Wilson, *Command on the Western Front*, p. 23; *BOH 1915* Volume I, p. 151.

12. Prior and Wilson, *Command on the Western Front*, pp. 23, 30–4; BOH 1915 Volume I, pp. 81–4, 91; Wynne, *If Germany Attacks*, pp. 22–4.

13. Quoted in Prior and Wilson, *Command on the Western Front*, p. 56; Sheffield, *The Chief*, p. 110.

14. Prior and Wilson, *Command on the Western Front*, pp. 59, 61; BOH 1915 Volume I, p. 128; Rupprecht, *Kriegstagebuch* Volume I, p. 310.

15. Entry 11 March 1915, Rupprecht MS diary, GHA NL KPR 702, p. 651.

16. Entry 11 March 1915, Rupprecht, *Kriegstagebuch* Volume I, pp. 310–12: see Krafft's comment, footnote, p. 312.

17. Entry 13 March 1915, Rupprecht, *Kriegstagebuch* Volume I, p. 314.

18. BOH 1915 Volume I, p. 149; Prior and Wilson, *Command on the Western Front*, pp. 77–80, 84–5; Paul Harris and Sanders Marble, 'The "Step-by-Step" Approach: British Military Thought and Operational Method on the Western Front, 1915–1917', *War in History* 15:1 (January 2008), pp. 17–42.

19. Mark Osborne Humphries and John Maker (eds), *Germany's Western Front: Translations from the German Official History of the Great War* Volume II: *1915* (Waterloo, Ontario: Wilfred Laurier University Press, 2010), pp. 384–7.

20. AOK 6 'Weisung für die nachsten Maßnahmen der Armeekorps', 29 November 1914; Rupprecht, *Kriegstagebuch* Volume III, pp. 58–63; GOH Volume VII, pp. 17–19; Humphries and Maker (eds), *Germany's Western Front* Volume II: *1915*, pp. 22–4; Rupprecht, *Kriegstagebuch* Volume I, p. 286.

21. Entry 13 March 1915, Rupprecht MS diary, GHA NL KPR 702, p. 654; Rupprecht, *Kriegstagebuch* Volume I, pp. 312–13; entry, 14 March 1915 War Diary, BKA AOK 6 Vorl. 2 Bd 1 Akt. 2, n.p.

22. Entry 16 March 1915, War Diary, BKA AOK 6 Vorl. 2 Bd 1 Akt. 2, n.p.; Rupprecht, *Kriegstagebuch* Volume I, p. 321 and Volume III, pp. 68–9; entry, 25 March 1915,

Rupprecht MS diary, GHA NL KPR 702, p. 678; BOH 1915 Volume 1, p. 151; GOH Volume VII, p. 59; entry 26 March, Krafft Diary, BKA NL Krafft 290, p. 1362.

CHAPTER 7

1. Humphries and Maker (eds), *Germany's Western Front* Volume II: *1915*, pp. 85–8.
2. Humphries and Maker (eds), *Germany's Western Front* Volume II: *1915*, pp. 89–94; see the 1930 report drawn up for the Reichsarchiv by Dr Wilhelm Solger, 'Zur Ausarbeitung des Reichsarchivs "Die Erwägungen über einen Durchbruchs-Angriff gegen die westliche Stellungsfront von ende Februar bis 13. April 1915"' and especially Beilage 2, 'Auszug der Stellen aus meinem Tagebuch über meinem Durchbruchs-Entwurf (u.a.) vom 2.3.1915', 'Erwägungen für einen Durchbruch im Westen', BKA NL Krafft 189.
3. Beilage 2, 'Auszug der Stellen aus meinem Tagebuch über meinem Durchbruchs-Entwurf (u.a.) vom 2.3.1915', pp. 4–5, 'Erwägungen für einen Durchbruch im Westen', BKA NL Krafft 189; entries 20, 26 November 1914, BKA NL Krafft 289, pp. 761, 784, and BKA NL Krafft 151, pp. 408–9; Rupprecht, *Kriegstagebuch* Volume I, p. 261; entry 18 March 1915, Rupprecht MS diary, GHA NL KPR 702, p. 667.
4. GOH Volume VIII, pp. 35–49; BOH 1915 Volume I, pp. 171–359. The German army lost about 35,000 men, the British nearly 60,000. German estimates that the French lost 18,000 on the first day alone seem exaggerated: only two divisions were directly affected.
5. Afflerbach, 'Kronprinz Rupprecht von Bayern', footnote 11, p. 24; Rupprecht, *Kriegstagebuch* I, pp. 305, 327; Rupprecht, 'Meine Teilnahme am Weltkrieg 1914–18', GHA NL KPR 716, pp. 33–4; entry 1 March 1915, Rupprecht MS diary, GHA NL KPR 701, pp. 636–8.
6. Rupprecht, *Kriegstagebuch* Volume I, pp. 333–6.
7. Rupprecht, *Kriegstagebuch* Volume I, pp. 326–7, 329; GOH Volume VIII, p. 57.
8. Rupprecht, *Kriegstagebuch* Volume I, pp. 336–7; entry, 9 May 1915, Xylander diary, BKA NL R. Xylander 12 Volume I, p. 301.
9. Adrian Bristow, *A Serious Disappointment: The Battle of Aubers Ridge and the Subsequent Munitions Scandal* (London: Leo Cooper, 2005), p. 80; Prior and Wilson, *Command on the Western Front*, p. 90; BOH 1915 Volume II, pp. 7–43.
10. BEF losses were finally calculated at 11,500. German casualties were probably fewer than 2,500. Bayerisches Kriegsarchiv, *Die Bayern im Großen Kriege*, pp. 231–2; GOH Volume VIII, pp. 58–9; BOH 1915 Volume II, pp. 7–43 (casualty statistics on p. 39); Bristow, *A Serious Disappointment, passim* and p. 172; entries, 10, 21 May 1915, Rupprecht MS diary, GHA NL KPR 702, pp. 759–60, 814; Harris, *Douglas Haig*, p. 141.
11. Harris, *Douglas Haig*, pp. 133–7; 142–4; BOH Volume II, p. 41; Prior and Wilson, *Command on the Western Front*, pp. 83–8, 91–3; Holmes, *The Little Field Marshal*, pp. 285–94; Sheffield, *Forgotten Victory*, p. 115.
12. Jonathan Krause, *Early Trench Tactics in the French Army: The Second Battle of Artois, May–June 1915* (Farnham: Ashgate, 2013), pp. 70, 19.

13. French maps marked the spot as Côte (Hill) 140. The British called it Hill 145. Today a stone memorial to the Moroccans stands near the huge Canadian monument.

14. Krause, *Early Trench Tactics*, pp. 70–3, 5–6; FOH Volume III, p. 43.

15. Bayerisches Kriegsarchiv, *Die Bayern im Großen Kriege*, pp. 227–8; Krause, *Early Trench Tactics*, pp. 70–2, 151–6; Sheldon, *The German Army on Vimy Ridge*, footnote 3, pp. 42–3; I Bayerische Reservekorps (BRK) Ia No. 3735.g. 'Erfahrungen aus den September-Kämpfen, verglichen mit dem Erfahrungen der 3. Armee in der Champagne', 22 January 1916, After-action Reports, BKA AOK 6 Vorl. 164, p. 3; entry 10 May 1915, Rupprecht MS diary, GHA NL KPR 702, pp. 759–62; Rupprecht, *Kriegstagebuch* Volume III, pp. 70–1.

16. Rupprecht, *Kriegstagebuch* Volume I, pp. 336–41.

17. Krause, *Early Trench Tactics*, pp. 77–9.

18. Krause, *Early Trench Tactics*, pp. 79, 105, 108; Rupprecht, *Kriegstagebuch* Volume I, pp. 345–7; Sheldon, *The German Army on Vimy Ridge*, p. 57; GOH Volume VIII, p. 66; Bayerisches Kriegsarchiv, *Die Bayern im Großen Kriege*, pp. 229–30. By the time the 5th Bavarian Reserve Division was finally pulled out of the line at Vimy during the night of 15/16 May, it had lost 184 officers and 6,600 men.

19. GOH Volume VIII, pp. 56, 64, 68, 72–3.

20. Entries, 13, 15 May 1915, Rupprecht MS diary, GHA NL KPR 702, pp. 789–90; entry, 12 May, Krafft diary, BKA NL Krafft 290, pp. 1615–16; entries, 13, 15 May, Xylander diary, BKA NL R. Xylander 12, pp. 308–9; Rupprecht, *Kriegstagebuch* Volume I, pp. 348–9, 354, 356–8.

21. Rupprecht's letter to the Kaiser, his reply, and Falkenhayn's apology to Rupprecht: see GHA NL KPR 495; Rupprecht, *Kriegstagebuch* Volume I, pp. 361–2; entry 19 May 1915, Krafft diary, BKA NL Krafft 290, pp. 1682–6; entry 19 May 1915, Rupprecht MS diary, GHA NL KPR 702, p. 808.

22. GOH Volume VIII, pp. 71–2; Wynne, *If Germany Attacks*, pp. 60–2; BOH 1915 Volume II, pp. 45–79. VII Corps lost 86 officers and 4,700 men in the period 9–20 May, but a proportion of these must have been lost on 9 May, when it suffered 1,100 wounded alone: entry 25 May 1915, War Diary, BKA AOK 6 Vorl. 2 Bd 1 Akt. 2, n.p.; entry 21 May, Rupprecht MS diary, GHA NL KPR 702, p. 814; Prior and Wilson, *Command on the Western Front*, pp. 94–9.

23. FOH Volume III, p. 58; Krause, *Early Trench Tactics*, pp. 106–9.

24. GOH Volume VIII, p. 198; Rupprecht, *Kriegstagebuch* Volume I, pp. 364–5; entries 4, 7, 11, and 15 June 1915, Rupprecht MS diary, GHA NL KPR 702, pp. 846, 853–4, 862, 870–1.

25. BOH 1915 Volume II, pp. 98–102; FOH III, pp. 99–100; Krause, *Early Trench Tactics*, pp. 132, 134–7.

26. Known to the Germans as the Gießler Heights and to the British, later, as The Pimple.

27. GOH Volume VIII, pp. 86–90; Rupprecht, *Kriegstagebuch* Volume I, pp. 366–8; entry 22 June 1915, GHA NL KPR 702, pp. 894–7; FOH III, pp. 71, 74–97; Krause, *Early Trench Tactics*, pp. 134–40.

28. In all, French Tenth Army lost 102,500 men between 9 May and 18 June. Of those, 16,703 were killed, 20,635 missing, and 65,162 wounded. British losses in the same period were some 32,000. Rupprecht's Sixth Army suffered casualties of 1,560 officers and 71,512 other ranks. FOH III, p. 100; BOH 1915 Volume 2, pp. 39, 76, 107; Humphries and Maker (eds), *Germany's Western Front* Volume II: *1915*, p. 210.

29. Foch to GPN, n.d. but 3 February 1915, Annexe 792, FOH II:2 Annexe Volume 2, pp. 24–9; GQG 923, 'Note pour les armées', 2 January 1915, Annexe 530, FOH II:2 Annexe Volume 1, pp. 746–8.

30. GQG Note 5779, 'But et conditions d'une action offensive d'ensemble', 16 April 1915, Annexe 52, FOH III Annexe Volume 1, pp. 94–108.

31. GQG 8192, 'Note sur les premiers enseignments à tirer des combats récents', 20 May 1915, Annexe 297; GQG 10379, 'Rectificatif à la note du 16 Avril 1915 sur les conditions d'une offensive d'ensemble', 26 May 1915, Annexe 368; GQG 7148, 'Annexe à la note du 16 Avril 1915 sur les buts et les conditions d'une offensive d'ensemble', 18 June 1915, Annexe 658; GQG 11286, Joffre to Foch 27 June 1915, Annexe 769: all in FOH III Annexe Volume 1, pp. 399–401, 490–1, 835–7, 992–4; GAN 1379/8, Foch to Joffre, 1 July 1915, Annexe 818, FOH III Annexe Volume 2, pp. 5–8; Krause, *Early Trench Tactics*, pp. 5–9, 140–1.

32. BOH 1915 Volume II, pp. vi–ix, 10–15, 77–9, 92–7, 393–9.

33. AOK 6 Ia J. No. 9690, 16 March 1915, and AOK 6 Ia No. 17105, 'Erfahrungen aus dem letzten Kämpfen', 28 June 1915; CGS M.J. No. 1740, 'Erfahrungen die sich im Laufe des Krieges für den Ausbau unserer Stellungen ergeben haben', 29 May 1915: all in BKA AOK 6 Vorl. 164; Humphries and Maker (eds), *Germany's Western Front* Volume II: *1915*, pp. 215–16.

CHAPTER 8

1. See Chapter 5.
2. 'My Job to Hold Joffre's Hosts, Says Rupprecht', *New York Times*, 29 June 1915, pp. 1–2.
3. Rupprecht, *Kriegstagebuch* Volume I, p. 375; entry 22 August 1915, Rupprecht MS diary, GHA NL KPR 703, p. 997.
4. Rupprecht, *Kriegstagebuch* Volume I, pp. 375–8; entries 28 August–14 September, Rupprecht MS diary, GHA NL KPR 703, pp. 1005–30; GOH Volume IX, pp. 21–2, 26–9.
5. BOH Volume II, pp. 135–8, 149–50; Prior and Wilson, *Command on the Western Front*, pp. 112–13.
6. Entry 22 September 1915, War Diary, BKA AOK 6 Vorl. 2 Bd 1 Akt. 2, n.p.; GOH Volume IX, pp. 29, 44–6.
7. GOH Volume IX, pp. 53–60; BOH Volume II, pp. 171–267; FOH III, pp. 433–42; Rupprecht, *Kriegstagebuch* Volume I, pp. 382–5.
8. Report of General Kunze, quoted in entry 1 November 1915, Rupprecht MS diary, GHA NL KPR 703, p. 1158; BOH Volume II, pp. 139–40, 308–335, 339, 341–5.

9. FOH III, pp. 442–50; Rupprecht, *Kriegstagebuch* Volume I, p. 387; GOH Volume IX, p. 74.

10. FOH III, pp. 457–60.

11. Entries 28–9 September 1915, Rupprecht MS Diary, GHA NL KPR 703, pp. 1077, 1082; entry 29 September 1915, Xylander diary, BKA NL R. Xylander 12, Volume II, p. 424; Rupprecht, *Kriegstagebuch* Volume I, p. 388; Rupprecht, 'Meine Teilnahme am Weltkrieg 1914–18', GHA NL KPR 716, p. 38.

12. Rupprecht, *Kriegstagebuch* Volume I, pp. 390.

13. Entry 12 October 1915, GHA NL KPR 703, p. 1116.

14. Nick Lloyd, *Loos 1915* (Stroud: History Press, 2008 [2006]), pp. 192–201.

15. BOH 1915 Volume II, p. 388; Lloyd, *Loos*, pp. 203–12.

16. The French lost 48,230 men in Artois, relatively few compared with the 143,567 casualties in Champagne. The British lost 50,380 men and the Germans 51,100: FOH III, p. 540; BOH 1915 Volume II, pp. 391–3; GOH Volume IX, pp. 89, 106–7.

17. GQG 11239, 'Instruction sur l'emploi de l'artillerie lourde', 20 November 1915; GQG 2481, 'Instruction sur le combat offensive des petites unités', 8 January 1916; GQG 9585, 'Instruction du 16 janvier 1916 visant le but et les conditions d'une action offensive d'ensemble', 16 January 1916; GQG 15350, 'Instruction sur le combat offensif des grandes unités', 26 January 1916: all in FOH IV:1, pp. 44–51; GQG 2641, 'Note pour les généraux commandants de GA', 5 December 1915, FOH III, pp. 560–3.

18. AOK 6 Ia No. 26525, 'Erfahrungen aus den letzten Kämpfen', 7 October 1915 and AOK 6 Ia No. 27516, 'Erfahrungen aus den letzten Kämpfen', 18 October 1915, both in BKA AOK 6 Vorl. 164; AOK 6 Ib No. 58385, 'Die Herbstschlacht bei La Bassée und Arras vom 25. September bis 13. Oktober 1915', 30 November 1915, Operations, GHA NL KPR 483; Humphries and Maker (eds), *Germany's Western Front* Volume II: *1915*, pp. 331–7; GOH Volume IX, pp. 99–107.

19. Rupprecht, *Kriegstagebuch* Volume I, p. 394.

20. Entries 1, 11 December 1915, Xylander diary, BKA NL R. Xylander 12, Volume II, pp. 472, 479.

CHAPTER 9

1. Groß, *Mythos und Wirlichkeit*, p. 123.

2. Foley, *German Strategy and the Path to Verdun*, pp. 178–208; Afflerbach, *Falkenhayn*, pp. 351–75, 543–5; entry 11 February 1916, Kuhl diary, Bundesarchiv-Militärarchiv (BAMA) RH 61/970, pp. 7–8; Rupprecht, *Kriegstagebuch* Volume I, p. 427; entry, 12 February 1916, Rupprecht MS diary, GHA NL KPR 703, pp. 1348–9.

3. Entries, 25, 27 December 1915, 10 January 1916, Rupprecht MS diary, GHA NL KPR 703, pp. 1244–5, 1247, 1269; Rupprecht, *Kriegstagebuch* Volume I, pp. 398, 409, 412.

4. Rupprecht, *Kriegstagebuch* Volume I, p. 427; entry, 12 February 1916, Rupprecht MS diary, GHA NL KPR 703, pp. 1348–9.

5. Foley, *German Strategy and the Path to Verdun*, pp. 197–200; AOK 6 No. 41494, 'Der Durchbruch', 26 February 1916, BKA AOK 6 Vorl. 417; Cron, *Imperial German Army 1914–18*, p. 145; entry 8 March, Rupprecht MS diary, GHA NL KPR 703, pp. 1397–9.

6. GOH Volume X, p. 271; Foley, *German Strategy and the Path to Verdun*, pp. 204–5, 217; entries 13 January, 2, 5 February 1916, Rupprecht MS diary, GHA NL KPR 703, pp. 1281, 1330, 1338; Rupprecht, *Kriegstagebuch* Volume I, p. 420.

7. Entries 28 February, 1 March 1916, Rupprecht, *Kriegstagebuch* Volume I, pp. 432–4.

8. Entry 27 March 1916, Kuhl diary, BAMA RH 61/970, p. 10; entry 29 April 1916, Rupprecht MS diary, GHA NL KPR 704, p. 1515; Rupprecht, *Kriegstagebuch* Volume I, pp. 438–9.

9. Rupprecht, *Kriegstagebuch* Volume I, pp. 459, 477; GOH Volume X, pp. 271–2, 275.

10. Rupprecht, *Kriegstagebuch* Volume I, pp. 415, 418, 424, 428, 431, 433–4, 454–6, 463, 465 and Volume III pp. 79–82, 84–7.

11. Rupprecht, *Kriegstagebuch* Volume I, p. 413; entries 9 January, 8 March, 20 June 1916, Rupprecht MS diary, GHA NL KPR 704, pp. 1268, 1400, 1681.

12. FOH IV:1, pp. 532–6.

13. Peter Chasseaud, 'Field Survey in the Salient: Cartography and Artillery Survey in the Flanders Operations in 1917', in Peter H. Liddle (ed.), *Passchendaele in Perspective: The Third Battle of Ypres* (Barnsley: Pen & Sword, 2013 [1997]), pp. 117–39: 117–21; Greenhalgh, *The French Army*, pp. 120–6; BOH 1915 Volume II, p. 19 footnote 2; Philpott, *Bloody Victory*, pp. 98–9, 113–15; Greenhalgh, *Foch in Command*, p. 146; entry, 8 April 1916, Rupprecht MS Diary, GHA NL KPR 704.

14. CGS No. 27956 op., 'Eininge Erfahrungen aus den Kämpfen im Maasgebiet (Februar und März 1916)', 15 May 1916, BKA AOK 6 Vorl. 164; Rupprecht, *Kriegstagebuch* Volume I, pp. 467–8.

15. One of the sources was described as Sir Ian Hamilton's 'sister'. Hamilton had only brothers. However, as Lady Hamilton's biographer Celia Lee has suggested, this may refer to his sister-in-law, Betty Moncrieffe. I am grateful to John and Celia Lee for discussing this with me; entries 15 May, 8, 14, 19 June 1916, Rupprecht MS diary, GHA NL KPR 704, pp. 1581, 1649, 1667, 1679; Rupprecht, 'Meine Teilnahme am Weltkrieg 1914–18', GHA NL KPR 716, p. 39; entries 1–22 June 1916, Kuhl diary, BAMA RH 61/970, pp. 14–16.

16. Rupprecht, *Kriegstagebuch* Volume I, pp. 481, 484–5, 496; GOH Volume X, pp. 318–20; BOH 1916 Volume I, pp. 316–19; entries 2 and 3 July 1916, Kuhl diary, BAMA RH 61/970, pp. 17–18; Duffy, *Through German Eyes*, p. 130.

CHAPTER 10

1. Sheffield, *The Chief*, p. 170; Prior and Wilson, *Command on the Western Front*, p. 185; BOH 1916 Volume I, p. 483.

2. Goya, *La Chair et L'Acier*, p. 265; Philpott, *Bloody Victory*, pp. 197–9; Prior and Wilson, *Command on the Western Front*, p. 184; Sheffield, *The Chief*, pp. 171–2.

3. Duffy, *Through German Eyes*, pp. 165–9.

4. Philpott, *Bloody Victory*, pp. 189–92, 204–8; Duffy, *Through German Eyes*, pp. 165–9; BOH 1916 Volume I, pp. vi–ix, 484–92; Travers, *The Killing Ground*, pp. 161–6; Prior and Wilson, *Command on the Western Front*, pp. 171–82; Sheffield, *The Somme*, pp. 135–40; Prior and Wilson, *The Somme*, pp. 112–18; J. P. Harris, *Douglas Haig and the First World War*, pp. 234–7.

5. GOH Volume X, pp. 382–3.

6. Jim Beach, *Haig's Intelligence: GHQ and the German Army, 1916–18* (Cambridge: Cambridge University Press, 2013), pp. 199–203; Philpott, *Bloody Victory*, pp. 219–43: p. 236; Prior and Wilson, *Command on the Western Front*, pp. 185–202: p. 189.

7. Duffy, *Through German Eyes*, p. 173.

8. Rupprecht had sent seven divisions to Verdun by the end of June. Rupprecht, *Kriegstagebuch* Volume I, pp. 499–501, 503; Philpott, *Bloody Victory*, p. 227; Reichsarchiv, GOH Volume X, pp. 355, 409–10, 407, 275.

9. Rupprecht, *Kriegstagebuch* Volume I, pp. 493–5, 503; Afflerbach, *Falkenhayn*, pp. 419–20; entries 3, 4 July 1916, Rupprecht MS diary, GHA NL KPR 704, pp. 1732–7.

10. Afflerbach, *Falkenhayn*, pp. 424–36; Foley, *German Strategy and the Path to Verdun*, pp. 256–8; entry 18 July 1916, Kuhl diary, BAMA RH 61/970, p. 19.

11. Rupprecht, *Kriegstagebuch* Volume I, pp. 494, 497–9, 501, 508; Rudolf von Valentini, *Kaiser und Kabinettschef* (Oldenburg: Gerhard Stalling, 1931), pp. 234–7; entry 9 July 1916, Rupprecht MS diary, GHA NL KPR 704, p. 1753.

12. Afflerbach, *Falkenhayn*, pp. 426–38; Afflerbach, *Kaiser Wilhelm II. als Oberster Kriegsherr im Ersten Weltkrieg: Quellen aus der militärischen Umbegung des Kaisers 1914–1918* (Munich: R. Oldenbourg, 2005), p. 49.

13. Afflerbach, *Falkenhayn*, pp. 436–44.

14. Rupprecht, *Kriegstagebuch* Volume I, pp. 520–1, 523–4; GOH Volume X, pp. 422–3.

15. Afflerbach, *Falkenhayn*, pp. 447–50.

16. Entry 29 August 1916, Kuhl diary, BAMA RH 61/970, p. 22.

17. 6 September 1916, Letter to King Ludwig III, GHA NL KPR 428.

CHAPTER 11

1. On the role of the staff, see David T. Zabecki (ed.), *Chief of Staff: The Principal Officers behind History's Great Commanders* Volume I: *Napoleonic Wars to World War I* (Annapolis, MD: Naval Institute Press, 2008); Thomas Müller, *Konrad Krafft von Dellmensingen (1862–1953): Porträt eines bayerischen Offiziers* (Munich: Kommission für bayerische Landesgeschichte, 2002), pp. 308–9; Foley, 'A Case Study in Horizontal Military Innovation', pp. 816–17; Foley, *German Strategy and the Path to Verdun*, p. 85; Groß, *Mythos und Wirklichkeit*, p. 116. More generally on the skill and flexibility of the German army, see Dupuy, *A Genius for War*; Lupfer, *The Dynamics of Doctrine*; Samuels, *Command or Control?* The most recent and comprehensive treatment of Auftragstaktik is Marco Sigg, *Der Unterführer als*

Feldherr im Taschenformat: Theorie und Praxis der Auftragstaktik im deutschen Heer 1869 bis 1945 (Paderborn: Ferdinand Schöningh, 2014).

2. Letter to author from Rupprecht's grandson, Herzog Franz von Bayern, 3 July 2015; Sendtner, *Rupprecht von Wittelsbach*, p. 129; entry, 26 October 1914, Krafft Diary, BKA NL Krafft 48, p. 124a; Harris, *Douglas Haig and the First World War*, p. 196; Gary Sheffield, *The Chief*, p. 136; Xylander Diary Volume II, BKA NL R. Xylander 12, pp. 455–6.

3. Rupprecht, 'Meine Teilnahme am Weltkrieg 1914–18', GHA NL KPR 716, p. 74; Sven Hedin, *With the German Armies in the West* (H. G. de Walterstorff, trans.) (London: John Lane, The Bodley Head, 1915), pp. 344–7.

4. Kuhl, *Der deutsche Generalstab*, p. 186.

5. Rupprecht, *Kriegstagebuch* Volume I, pp. 52–3; AOK 6 Order of Battle, 6 August 1914, Miscellaneous Orders, GHA NL KPR 476; HG KPR 'Vorläufige Stellenbesetzung', 19 September 1916, and 'Stellenbesetzung', 5 September 1918, both in Operations, GHA NL KPR 601; Cowan, 'Genius for War?', p. 187; Administrative Staff Miscellaneous Orders, BKA HG KPR 375. Today known as Chateau Gendebien, Chateau Hardenpont is an elegant mansion which has kept its military connection: it is the residence of the NATO Supreme Allied Commander Europe.

6. Administrative Staff Miscellaneous Orders, BKA HG KPR 375; entry, 26 January 1915, R. Xylander Diary Volume I, BKA NL R. Xylander 12, p. 212.

7. Entry 18 February 1915, Rupprecht MS Diary, GHA NL KPR 701, pp. 621–2; Krafft Diary, BKA NL Krafft 290, pp. 1522–4, 1557–60.

8. Rupprecht, *Kriegstagebuch* Volume II, p. 53; entry 27 October 1916, Rupprecht MS Diary, GHA NL KPR 705, pp. 2050–1, 2364–5. Within months, the Germans blew up Coucy-le-Chateau during their retreat to the Hindenburg Line. HG KPR IIb No. 12785 27 March 1917, BKA HG KPR 481; entries, 5 August, 24 December 1915, R. Xylander War Diary, BKA NL R. Xylander 12, Volume I, pp. 373–4 and Volume II, p. 488; letter, Rupprecht to Ludwig III, 27 December 1915, Correspondence with King, GHA NL KPR 428.

9. Müller, *Konrad Krafft von Dellmensingen*, pp. 308–9, 356–9; entry, 5 August 1914, Krafft Diary, BKA NL Krafft 145, p. 9; entry 18 November 1914, Krafft Diary, BKA NL Krafft 289, p. 753 and 48, p. 92b; entry, 27 September, Krafft Diary, BKA NL Krafft 48, pp. 33a, 71a; Krafft, 'Kurzer Überblick über die Vorgänge beim Oberkommando der 6. Armee im August 1914 bis zur Schlacht in Lothringen am 20.8.1914', 25 February 1916, Miscellaneous Orders, GHA NL KPR 476, p. 24; Pöhlmann, *Kriegsgeschichte und Geschichtspolitik*, pp. 284–321; Rupprecht, *Kriegstagebuch* Volume I, pp. 8–10, 20–3, 37–40, 80–1, 103–7, 169, 210–11; entries 28 August, 5 September, 14 October 1914, Rupprecht MS Diary, GHA NL KPR 699, pp. 110–11, 115, 172 and NL KPR 700, p. 308; entries, 14, 15 January 1915, Xylander Diary Volume I, BKA NL R. Xylander 12, pp. 196–7.

10. Rupprecht, *Kriegstagebuch* Volume I, p. 362; entries, 25 May, 8, 23, 25, 30 June, 3, 27 August, 29 September, 16 November 1915, Xylander Diary Volume I, BKA NL R. Xylander 12, pp. 319, 330, 344, 346, 350, 373, 383, 424, 461–2; entries,

24 June, 4 August, 19 October, 14, 16, 19, 22 November 1915, Rupprecht MS Diary, GHA NL KPR 702, p. 903 and 703, pp. 976, 1133–4, 1180–1, 1183, 1190, 1194; letter, Rupprecht to Nagel, 22 November 1915, Correspondence with Bavarian Military Representative at GHQ, GHA NL KPR 494.

11. Entry, 28 November 1915, Kuhl Diary, BA-MA RH 61/970, p. 4; entry, 1 December 1915, Xylander Diary Volume II, BKA NL R. Xylander 12, p. 472.

12. GOH Volume IV, pp. 533–7 and Volume I, pp. 187, 257–8; 'Aufmarschanweisung für Oberkommando der 6. Armee', 2 August 1914, Miscellaneous Orders, GHA NL KPR 476, paragraph 21; Mombauer, *Helmuth von Moltke*, pp. 254–5; Herwig, *The Marne, 1914*, pp. 171–2; Strachan, *The First World War* Volume I: *To Arms*, pp. 233–4; entry, 18 September 1914, Krafft Diary, BKA NL Krafft 48, p. 1a; Rupprecht, *Kriegstagebuch* Volume I, pp. 6–21, 37–61; Krafft, *Die Führung des Kronprinzen Rupprecht von Bayern*, pp. 17–21.

13. Rupprecht, *Kriegstagebuch* Volume I, pp. 126–7, 206, 232–6, 321, 348–52, 361–2, 369; entries 18, 23 September, 14 October 1914, Krafft Diary, BKA NL Krafft 48, pp 1a–2a, 15b–16b, 81b–82b, 84a–87a; entry, 5 March 1915, Krafft Diary Appendix 2, BKA NL Krafft 189; Foley, *German Strategy and the Path to Verdun*, pp. 99–102, 113–24; entries, 26 October 1914, 2 March, 15, 19 May, 15, 22, 25 June 1915, Rupprecht MS Diary, GHA NL KPR 701, pp. 356–7 and 702, pp. 643–4, 789–91, 808, 870–1, 894–7, 903–5; Afflerbach, *Falkenhayn* pp. 325–36. Note, however, that in his published diary Rupprecht seems to have played up the extent of his friction with Falkenhayn in an effort to distance himself from him. I am grateful to Holger Afflerbach for pointing this out: Afflerbach, 'Kronprinz Rupprecht', footnote 11, p. 24. Rupprecht, 'Meine Teilnahme am Weltkrieg 1914–18', GHA NL KPR 716, p. 33; letter, Minister Leopold Krafft von Dellmensingen to Privy Councillor Otto von Dandl, 25 May 1915, Dandl-Krafft Correspondence, GHA NL KPR 436.

14. Rupprecht, *Kriegstagebuch* Volume I, p. 521, Volume II, pp. 11–13, 15–16 and Volume III, pp. 108–11; entry, 26 August 1916, Rupprecht MS Diary, GHA NL KPR 704, pp. 1895–6; GOH Volume X, pp. 422–3 and Volume XI, pp. 106–9; Rupprecht, 'Meine Teilnahme am Weltkrieg 1914-18', GHA NL KPR 716, pp. 41–2.

15. Entry, 28 August 1914, Rupprecht MS Diary, GHA NL KPR 699, pp. 110–11; Gebsattel, *Von Nancy bis zum Camp des Romains 1914*, pp. 19–36, 59, 61–2.

CHAPTER 12

1. Heeresgruppe Kronprinz Rupprecht (HG KPR) Ic 'Liste des Einsatzes und der Verluste der Divisionen bei 1. und 2. Armee von Beginn der Somme-Schlacht bis 30.11.1916', n.d., GHA NL KPR 588; Rupprecht, *Kriegstagebuch* Volume II, pp. 4–6; entry 29 August 1916, Rupprecht MS diary, GHA NL KPR 704, pp. 1908; GOH Volume X, p. 384; GOH Volume XI, pp. 41–2.

2. One train could carry 26,800 rounds for the 77-mm field artillery cannon or 6,000 for heavy howitzers. GOH Volume X, pp. 360–1 and p. 219 footnote; GOH Volume XI, p. 16, especially footnote; Humphries and Maker (eds), *Germany's Western Front* Volume II: *1915*, pp. 150–3.

3. Rupprecht, *Kriegstagebuch* Volume II, pp. 3–8 and Volume III, pp. 94–6; entries 26, 29, 31 August 1916, Rupprecht MS diary, GHA NL KPR 704, pp. 1895–6, 1908, 1913; Duffy, *Through German Eyes*, p. 208.

4. Rupprecht, *Kriegstagebuch* Volume II, pp. 7–11.

5. Rupprecht, *Kriegstagebuch* Volume II, pp. 9–11; BOH 1916 Volume II, pp. 250–87; Philpott, *Bloody Victory*, pp. 347–9.

6. Rupprecht, *Kriegstagebuch* Volume II, pp. 9–13; Philpott, *Bloody Victory*, pp. 349–54; GOH Volume XI, pp. 59–62.

7. Rupprecht, *Kriegstagebuch* Volume II, pp. 6–7, 12, 18.

8. Rupprecht, *Kriegstagebuch* Volume II, pp. 14–16; entry 8 September 1916, Rupprecht MS diary, GHA NL KPR 704, p. 1940.

9. Watson, *Ring of Steel*, pp. 323–5; Rupprecht, *Kriegstagebuch* Volume II, pp. 13, 15, 17.

10. Greenhalgh, *Victory though Coalition*, p. 65; Philpott, *Bloody Victory*, pp. 354–5, 357–9.

11. Philpott, *Bloody Victory*, pp. 353–7; Rupprecht, *Kriegstagebuch* Volume II, pp. 18–28; entry 19 September 1916, Rupprecht MS diary, GHA NL KPR 704, p. 1970; GOH Volume XI, pp. 65–6, 73–4.

12. See discussion of this in Philpott, *Bloody Victory*, pp. 361–3, 368–9.

13. GOH Volume XI, pp. 68–70.

14. Rupprecht, *Kriegstagebuch* Volume II, pp. 21–2; GOH Volume XI, pp. 68–70; BOH Volume II, p. 354.

15. Rupprecht, *Kriegstagebuch* Volume II, p. 25.

16. Rupprecht, *Kriegstagebuch* Volume II, pp. 23–5 and Volume III, pp. 102, 104–5.

17. Rupprecht, *Kriegstagebuch* Volume II, pp. 24–6; entry, 23 September 1916, Rupprecht MS diary, GHA NL KPR 704, p. 1982; entries, 14, 21, 28 September, 4, 21, 26, 28 October 1916, Kuhl Diary, BAMA RH 61/970, pp. 24–8, 31, 34.

18. James S. Corum, 'Air War Over the Somme: The Evolution of British and German Air Operations', in Matthias Strohn (ed.), *The Battle of the Somme* (Oxford: Osprey, 2016), pp. 75–91; GOH Volume XI, p. 73; Rupprecht, *Kriegstagebuch* Volume II, pp. 27–9; entry 30 September 1916, Rupprecht MS diary, GHA NL KPR 705, p. 1997.

19. Rupprecht, *Kriegstagebuch* Volume II, p. 33; GOH Volume XI, pp. 75–7.

20. Duffy, *Through German Eyes*, pp. 236, 239–42; BOH 1916 Volume II, p. 354; Rupprecht, *Kriegstagebuch* Volume III, p. 111; Philpott, *Bloody Victory*, p. 377; Robin Prior and Trevor Wilson, *The Somme* (New Haven, CT: Yale University Press, 2005), pp. 259, 262–3; Christopher Pugsley, 'Trial and Error: The Dominion Forces on the Somme in 1916', in Strohn (ed.), *The Battle of the Somme*, pp. 113–29.

21. Rupprecht, *Kriegstagebuch* Volume II, pp. 34, 37; GOH Volume XI, p. 77; Jim Beach, *Haig's Intelligence*, pp. 214–15.

22. GOH Volume XI, pp. 77–9; Rupprecht, *Kriegstagebuch* Volume II, pp. 34, 36, 39–40; entry 30 September 1916, Rupprecht MS diary, GHA NL KPR 705, p. 1996; HG KPR Ic No. 694, Erfahrungen, 1 October 1916, GHA NL KPR 606.

23. HG KPR Ia No. 609, 'Betrifft die Lage an der Somme', 27 September 1916, reproduced in Rupprecht, *Kriegstagebuch* Volume III, pp. 106–11.

CHAPTER 13

1. See the useful collection of essays on British, French, and German tactics and operations in Matthias Strohn (ed.), *The Battle of the Somme* (Oxford: Osprey, 2016).

2. GOH Volume XI, pp. 62–3; Erich Ludendorff, *My War Memories: 1914–1918* Volume I (London: Hutchinson, 1919), pp. 265–74.

3. Rupprecht, *Kriegstagebuch* Volume II, p. 18.

4. Rupprecht, *Kriegstagebuch* Volume II, p. 26; Volume III, pp. 103–4 and HG KPR Ia No. 609, 'Betrifft die Lage an der Somme', 27 September 1916, reproduced pp. 106–11.

5. Philpott, *Bloody Victory*, pp. 374–5.

6. Philpott, *Bloody Victory*, pp. 386–92; BOH 1916 Volume II, pp. 457–8; Ian Malcolm Brown, *British Logistics on the Western Front 1914–1919* (Westport, CT: Praeger, 1998), pp. 109–38.

7. Rupprecht, *Kriegstagebuch* Volume II, pp. 42, 44, 61.

8. Rupprecht, *Kriegstagebuch* Volume II, pp. 39–40; entries 2, 4 October 1916, Kuhl Diary, BAMA RH 61/970, pp. 27–8.

9. Rupprecht, *Kriegstagebuch* Volume II, pp. 37, 40, 42, 44, 61; entry 8 October 1916, Kuhl Diary, BAMA RH 61/970, p. 28; GOH Volume XI, pp. 80–3; Philpott, *Bloody Victory*, pp. 395–400.

10. Entry, 13 October 1916, Kuhl Diary BAMA RH 61/970, p. 30; GOH Volume XI, p. 84.

11. BOH 1916 Volume II, pp. 440–3; Prior and Wilson, *Command on the Western Front*, pp. 252–4, 256–60; Gary Sheffield, *The Somme* (London: Cassell, 2004 [2003]), p. 142.

12. GOH Volume XI, pp. 87, 92; entries 30 October, 10 November 1916, Rupprecht, *Kriegstagebuch* Volume II, pp. 54, 63, 95, 111.

13. Rupprecht, *Kriegstagebuch* Volume II, pp. 44, 47, 49, 53–4, 56, 58, 62.

14. Prior and Wilson, *The Somme*, pp. 296–7.

15. BOH 1916 Volume II, pp. xii–xvii; GOH Volume XI, p. 186; Sheffield, *The Somme*, pp. 151–2 and *The Chief*, p. 432, footnote 92; Prior and Wilson, *The Somme*, pp. 300–1; James McRandle and James Quirk, 'The Blood Test Revisited: A New Look at German Casualty Counts in World War I', *Journal of Military History* 70 (2006), pp. 667–702; Philpott, *Bloody Victory*, pp. 600–3; Watson, *Ring of Steel*, p. 324.

16. J. H. Boraston, (ed.), *Sir Douglas Haig's Despatches (December 1915–April 1919)* (London: J. M. Dent and Sons, 1919).

17. Rupprecht, *Kriegstagebuch* Volume I, p. 438.

18. Philpott, *Bloody Victory*, p. 447; Watson, *Ring of Steel*, p. 323.

19. Sheffield, *The Chief*, pp. 165–9, 194–8; Rupprecht, *Kriegstagebuch* Volume II, p. 34; letter to King Ludwig III, 25 October 1916, Correspondence, GHA Munich NL KPR 428; Alexander Watson, *Enduring the Great War: Combat, Morale and Collapse in the German and British Armies, 1914–1918* (Cambridge: Cambridge University Press, 2008), pp. 165–8.

20. Rupprecht, *Kriegstagebuch* Volume I, p. 493 and Volume II, p. 63; IV Armeekorps (AK) Ic No. 185 31 July 1916, Operations File Lessons Learnt Reports, August–October 1916, BKA NL KPR 216; 56 Infanteriedivision (ID) Ia No. 2497, 15 September 1916, Operations File Lessons Learnt Reports, August–October 1916, BKA NL KPR 216; Hauptmann Grimm, im (sachs.) Inf. Rgt. No. 133 'Bericht auf befehl der OHL gem. B.K.O. 416 I v. 12.9.' 17 September 1916, BKA AOK 6 Vorl. 164 Lessons Learnt 1914–1917.

21. Philpott, *Bloody Victory*, pp. 454–63; Rupprecht, *Kriegstagebuch* Volume II, pp. 69–70.

CHAPTER 14

1. GOH Volume XII, p. 1; Watson, *Ring of Steel*, pp. 378–84; Rupprecht, *Kriegstagebuch* Volume II, pp. 76, 91.

2. Rupprecht, *Kriegstagebuch* Volume I, pp. 453–4, 463 and Volume II, pp. 81–2, 104–5; Afflerbach, 'Kronprinz Rupprecht', pp. 43–4; Afflerbach, *Kaiser Wilhelm II. als Oberster Kriegsherr*, pp. 23–5; GOH Volume XII, pp. 4–9, 52–9; Anthony Cowan, 'Genius for War? German Operational Command on the Western Front in Early 1917' (unpublished PhD thesis, King's College London, 2016), chapter 8.

3. GOH Volume XII, pp. 26–32; GOH Volume X, pp. 382–9.

4. GOH Volume XI, pp. 107–16; GOH Volume XII, pp. 32–7; CGS Ia/II No. 175, 'Erfahrungen der Somme-Schlacht and Lehren', 25 September 1916, Lessons Learnt, BKA HG KPR 216; HG KPR Ia No. 609, 'Betrifft die Lage an der Somme', 27 September 1916: Rupprecht, *Kriegstagebuch* Volume III, pp. 106–11; Lessons Learnt, BKA HG KPR 215–17; Foley, 'Learning War's Lessons', pp. 471–504.

5. Max Bauer, *Der große Krieg in Feld und Heimat* (Tübingen: Osiander'sche Buchhandlung, 1922), pp. 118–19; GOH Volume XII, pp. 38–51.

6. I am grateful to Dr Tony Cowan for his help with these publications. GOH Volume XII, pp. 50–1; AOK1 Ia No. 2122, 'Erfahrungen der 1. Armee in der Sommeschlacht', 30 January 1917, Operations, GHA NL KPR 581; Foley, 'Learning War's Lessons', pp. 502–3.

7. Rupprecht, *Kriegstagebuch* Volume II, p. 100; GOH Volume XII, pp. 34, 52–60; HG KPR Ic 10103, 19 February 1917, Lessons Learnt, BKA HG KPR 220.

8. Rupprecht, *Kriegstagebuch* Volume II, pp. 76–8, 83–6; HG KPR Ia No. 2026 'Vorschlag für die Operationen auf dem französischen Kriegsschauplatz im Früjahr 1917', 15 January 1917, Operations: Alberich, October 1916–March 1917, GHA NL KPR 586; Kuhl Diary, BAMA RH 61/970, p. 39.

9. Rupprecht, *Kriegstagebuch* Volume III, p. 126 and Volume I, p. 70. Also HG KPR Id No. 1496, 2 November 1916, Operations: Siegfried Stellung, October 1916–February 1917, GHA NL KPR 585; Rupprecht, *Kriegstagebuch* Volume II, p. 70.

10. Kuhl Diary, BAMA RH 61/970, p. 39; Rupprecht, *Kriegstagebuch* Volume II, pp. 83–4.

11. Kuhl Diary, BAMA RH 61/970, pp. 40–6; Rupprecht, *Kriegstagebuch* Volume II, pp. 13, 17, 22, 30, 88–94 and Volume III, pp. 133–4; entry, 4 February 1917,

Rupprecht MS Diary, GHA NL KPR 705, p. 2248; Kuhl Diary, BAMA RH 61/970, pp. 35–6, 45; HG KPR Id 'Vergleich zwischen jetziger Front und Siegfried', 16 February 1917, and HG KPR to OHL Iad No. 2104 'Ausnützung der großen rückw. Stellungen im Frühjahr 1917: die augenblickliche Lage', 28 January 1917, both in Operations: Siegfried Stellung, October 1916–February 1917, GHA NL KPR 585; Rupprecht, 'Meine Teilnahme am Weltkrieg 1914–18', GHA NL KPR 716, pp. 45–6.

12. Rupprecht, *Kriegstagebuch* Volume II, pp. 22, 33, 46, 98, 115–16; entries, 17 October 1916, 5 March 1917, Rupprecht MS Diary, GHA NL KPR 705, pp. 2031–2, 2312; Rupprecht, 'Meine Teilnahme am Weltkrieg 1914-18', GHA NL KPR 716, pp. 45–6; GOH Volume XII, pp. 121–33.

13. BOH 1917 Volume I, p. 93.

14. Rupprecht, *Kriegstagebuch* Volume II, pp. 105, 110–18, 122–5; GOH Volume XII, pp. 133–45; BOH 1917 Volume I, pp. 89–94, 129, 169–70; Beach, *Haig's Intelligence*, pp. 224–32.

15. GOH Volume XII, pp. 145–6; Beach, *Haig's Intelligence*, p. 233; BOH 1917 Volume I, pp. 171–2.

16. GOH Volume XII, pp. 81–7, 184–203; Rupprecht, *Kriegstagebuch* Volume II, pp. 103, 125–31.

17. GOH Volume XII, p. 34.

18. Goya, *La Chair et L'Acier*, pp. 261–9; Greenhalgh, *The French Army and the First World War*, pp. 162–9, 176–7; FOH Volume V:1, pp. 161–3, 175–6; GQG 'Instruction visant le but et les conditions d'une action offensive d'ensemble' summarized in GQG 24141, 'Note pour les groupes d'armées, les armées d'attaque et autres armées', 28 December 1916, Annexe 358, in Annexes Volume I (1932), pp. 587–8.

19. IV Armee-Korps Ic No. 185, 'Beurteilung der englischen Truppen während der Kämpfe an der Somme', 31 July 1916, Lessons Learnt, BKA HG KPR 216; Paddy Griffith, *Battle Tactics of the Western Front*, pp. 55–60, 76–9; John Lee, 'Some Lessons of the Somme: The British Infantry in 1917', in Brian Bond (ed.), *'Look to Your Front': Studies in the First World War by The British Commission for Military History* (Staplehurst: Spellmount, 1999), pp. 79–88; Jim Beach, 'Issued by the General Staff: Doctrine Writing at British GHQ, 1917–18', *War in History* 19:4 (2012), pp. 464–91.

20. Simon Robbins, *British Generalship on the Western Front 1914–18: Defeat into Victory* (London: Routledge, 2005), pp. 94–7; Peter Simkins, *From the Somme to Victory*, pp. 46–9; Lee, 'Some Lessons of the Somme', pp. 80–6.

21. John Lee, 'Some Lessons of the Somme', pp. 86–7; SS 135, 'Instructions for the Training of Divisions for Offensive Action', IWM EPH 1553, pp. 9–10.

22. Jonathan Boff, *Winning and Losing on the Western Front: The British Third Army and the Defeat of Germany in 1918* (Cambridge: Cambridge University Press, 2012), pp. 59–63.

CHAPTER 15

1. BOH 1917 Volume I, pp. 180–6, 201, 302–6, 312–16.
2. GOH Volume XII, pp. 210–12.
3. GOH Volume XII, pp. 212–21; Rupprecht, *Kriegstagebuch* Volume II, pp. 135–6; HGr KPR to OHL, Ia No. 2857, Preliminary Report on 9 April, dated 21 April 1917, Operations File Arras April 1917 GHA NL KPR 587; BOH 1917 Volume I, sketch 11 (facing p. 241); Sheldon, *The German Army on Vimy Ridge*, p. 302.
4. Rupprecht, *Kriegstagebuch* Volume II, p. 136.
5. Rupprecht, *Kriegstagebuch* Volume II, pp. 138–41; GOH Volume XII, pp. 224–32; BOH 1917 Volume I, pp. 244–81, 340–56.
6. BOH 1917 Volume I, pp. 201, 273–6; GOH Volume XII, p. 234.
7. Extract from letter, General von Hartz (Bavarian Military Representative at GHQ), 15 April 1917, GHA NL KPR 587; letters, Councillor Leopold Krafft von Dellmensingen to Prime Minister Otto von Dandl, 14, 19, 24 April 1917, Correspondence, GHA NL KPR 436; Rupprecht, *Kriegstagebuch* Volume II, pp. 140–1, 149.
8. HG KPR Iac No. 2774 to OHL, 12 April 1917; HG KPR Ia No. 2857 to OHL, 21 April 1917; I BRK No. 15290, 12 April; 1st Bavarian Reserve Division (BRD) I No. 2710, 12 April; 1st Bavarian Reserve Infantry Brigade (BRIB) No. 7752, 13 April; 17th Reserve Division (RD) I No. 910, 14 April; 14th Bavarian Infantry Division (BID) No. 5340/Ia, 15 April 1917; all in BKA HG KPR 221; see Cowan, 'Genius for War?', pp. 217–27, for a less negative view of the German after-action process at Arras. I am grateful to Dr Cowan for directing my attention to this passage.
9. BOH 1917 Volume I, pp. 239–41, 552–3.
10. GOH Volume XII, pp. 235–9; HG KPR Ia No. 2583, 'Erfahrungen und Folgerungen aus den Kämpfen bei Arras am 9.4.17', 21 April 1917, BKA HG KPR 221; Franz Behrmann, *Die Osterschlacht bei Arras 1917* Part I: *Zwischen Lens und Scarpe* (Gerhard Stalling: Oldenburg, 1929), pp. 95–6, 112, 121.
11. Gary Sheffield, *Command and Morale: The British Army on the Western Front, 1914–1918* (Barnsley: Pen & Sword, 2014), chapter 7.
12. BOH 1917 Volume I, p. 280.
13. BOH 1917 Volume I, pp. 282–4, 378; Harris, *Douglas Haig and the First World War*, pp. 314–18; Sheffield, *The Chief*, pp. 216–18.
14. Greenhalgh, *The French Army and the First World War*, pp. 175–99; Rupprecht, *Kriegstagebuch* Volume II, pp. 145, 147; Harris, *Douglas Haig and the First World War*, pp. 319–21.
15. Rupprecht, *Kriegstagebuch* Volume II, pp. 144, 148, 150–1, 154; BOH 1917 Volume I, pp. 378–402, 412–26; GOH Volume XII, pp. 248–53; HG KPR Ic No. 2910, 28 April 1917, BKA HG KPR 221.
16. Rupprecht, *Kriegstagebuch* Volume II, pp. 159–62, 164; GOH Volume XII, pp. 257–60; BOH 1917 Volume I, pp. 427–54.

17. In April and May 1917, the British suffered nearly 158,660 casualties, 29,505 of them dead with another 20,876 missing. German losses were 85,000 at Arras versus 158,000 on the Aisne and in Champagne, where French casualties may have been as high as 271,000. OAD 258, GHQ to army commanders, 2 January 1917, BOH 1917 Volume I, Appendix 6 and pp. 556–61, 535; GOH Volume XII, pp. 277–8, 403 and Appendix 27; Cowan, 'Genius for War?', p. 245.

18. Fayolle quoted in William Philpott, *War of Attrition: Fighting the First World War* (New York: Overlook Press, 2014), p. 290; BOH 1917 Volume I, pp. 294–7, 544–52.

19. Beach, *Haig's Intelligence*, pp. 232–8; AOK 6 CoS No. 730, 13 May 1917; HG KPR Ic No. 3023, 13 May 1917: both in BKA HG KPR 222.

20. HG KPR 1c No. 15818, 3 May 1917, BKA HG KPR 222.

21. CGS I No. 54448, 4 May 1917; OHL Ia No. 3124, 7 May 1917; HG KPR Ic 16261, 8 May 1917; AOK 2 report for CGS 11 May 1917; all in BKA HG KPR 222.

22. AOK 6 Ia/Ie No. 9000, Armeebefehl, 1 May 1917, Lessons Learnt, BKA HG KPR 222.

23. AOK 6 Ia/Ie No. 9000, 1 May 1917, BKA HG KPR 222; entry, 12 May 1917, Rupprecht MS Diary GHA NL KPR 706, p. 2494; Rupprecht, *Kriegstagebuch* Volume II, p. 164.

CHAPTER 16

1. BOH 1917 Volume I, pp. 428–30; Rupprecht, *Kriegstagebuch* Volume II, p. 165.

2. GOH Volume XII, pp. 429–36, 438–42; Rupprecht, *Kriegstagebuch* Volume II, pp. 167, 169, 172–4, 177–8, 182–4; Kuhl Diary, BA-MA RH 61/970, pp. 65–6, 67–9.

3. GOH Volume XII, pp. 425–7, 448–52; BOH 1917 Volume, pp. 41, 44–9; Rupprecht MS Diary, GHA NL KPR 706, pp. 2604–5.

4. GOH Volume XII, pp. 453–4; Rupprecht MS Diary, GHA NL KPR 706, pp. 2604–5; 35 ID Ia No. 1756 12 June 1917, Lessons Learnt, BKA HG KPR 235; Rupprecht, *Kriegstagebuch* Volume III, pp. 165–70.

5. GOH Volume XII, pp. 454–61; BOH 1917 Volume II, pp. 32–95; Rupprecht, *Kriegstagebuch* Volume III, pp. 165–70; 35 ID Ia No. 1756, 12 June 1917, Lessons Learnt, BKA HG KPR 235; Wynne, *If Germany Attacks*, pp. 272–81; Robin Prior and Trevor Wilson, *Passchendaele: The Untold Story* (New Haven, CT: Yale University Press, 1996), pp. 61–6.

6. Rupprecht, *Kriegstagebuch* Volume II, pp. 187–95 and Volume III, pp. 163–5; Rupprecht MS Diary, GHA NL KPR 706, pp. 2588–9, 2592, 2604–5; Kuhl Diary, BA-MA RH 61/970, pp. 70–1.

7. GOH Volume XII, p. 471; BOH 1917 Volume II, p. 87; Rupprecht, *Kriegstagebuch* Volume II, pp. 191–3.

8. Kuhl Diary, BA-MA RH 61/970, pp. 71–4; entries, 25 January, 12 June, 6 August, 3 September 1917, Rupprecht MS Diary, GHA NL KPR 705, p. 2221 and 706, pp. 2610, 2782, 2893; Rupprecht, *Kriegstagebuch* Volume II, p. 257.

9. Rupprecht, *Kriegstagebuch* Volume II, pp. 198, 204–9, 213–20, 229–30; entries 19, 30 July, Rupprecht MS Diary, GHA NL KPR 706, pp. 2743, 2760; GOH Volume XII, Beilage 27 and Volume XIII, pp. 41, 56–7, Beilage 28b; BOH 1917 Volume II, p. 134; Prior and Wilson, *Passchendaele*, pp. 71–3.

10. BOH 1917 Volume II, p. 138 footnote 2; GOH Volume XIII, pp. 60–3.

11. Rupprecht, *Kriegstagebuch* Volume II, pp. 231–2.

12. Prior and Wilson, *Passchendaele*, pp. 86–96; GOH Volume XIII, pp. 64–5, 96, Beilage 28b; BOH 1917 Volume II, pp. 164–79.

13. Rupprecht, *Kriegstagebuch* Volume II, pp. 232, 211; Kuhl Diary, BA-MA RH 61/970, p. 84.

14. Entry, 2 August 1917, Rupprecht MS Diary, GHA NL PR 706, p. 2770; Fusilier Regiment 73 B No. 4733, 9 August 1917; 111th ID I No. 1149, 11 August 1917; Lehr Infantry Regiment (no number or date); 3rd Guards Division (GD) I No. 7142, 9 August 1917: all in Lessons Learnt, BKA HG KPR 236; OHL Liaison Officer with AOK 4 to HG KPR, 6 August 1917, Lessons Learnt, BKA HG KPR 225.

15. Rupprecht, *Kriegstagebuch* Volume II, pp. 235–6; entry, 4 August 1917, Kuhl Diary, BA-MA RH 61/970, p. 84.

16. BOH 1917 Volume II, pp. 208–10; Rupprecht, *Kriegstagebuch* Volume II, pp. 244–9, 257, 259–60; 26th ID Ia No. 7074, 6 September 1917, Lessons Learnt, BKA HG KPR 236; AOK 4, 29 August 1917, Lessons Learnt, BKA HG KPR 244; Strength and Casualty Returns, BKA HG KPR 438; entries, 21 August and 5 September 1917, War Diary, BKA HG KPR 8; GOH Volume XIII, Beilage 28b and pp. 70–1; entry, 20 August 1917, Kuhl Diary, BA-MA RH 61/970, p. 86.

17. Rupprecht, *Kriegstagebuch* Volume II, pp. 259–62; GOH Volume XIII, p. 71.

CHAPTER 17

1. BOH 1917 Volume II, pp. 237–44, 250–79; HG KPR Ic No. 31500, 30 October 1917, Lessons Learnt, BKA HG KPR 217; 2nd GRD Ia 281/9, 24 September 1917 and 9th RD, 23 September 1917, both in Lessons Learnt BKA HG KPR 244; Prior and Wilson, *Passchendaele*, pp. 113–23; GOH Volume XIII, pp. 74–6.

2. GOH Volume XIII, p. 76; BOH 1917 Volume II, pp. 280–95.

3. GOH Volume XIII, pp. 77–8, Appendix 28b.

4. The Germans lost 38,500 men against 36,000 for the British. GOH Volume XIII, p. 76; Prior and Wilson, *Passchendaele*, pp. 125–6, 131.

5. Rupprecht, *Kriegstagebuch* Volume II, pp. 264–5 and Volume III, pp. 173–4.

6. Entries, 26, 27, 29 September, 1, 2 October 1917, Rupprecht MS Diary, GHA NL KPR 707, pp. 2979–80, 2983–6, 2989, 2997; entries 30 September, 3 October 1917 Kuhl Diary, BA-MA RH 61/970, p. 90; OHL Iac No. 3996, 28 September 1917, War Diary, BKA HG KPR 8; AOK4 Ia/g No. 791/Sept., 30 September 1917, Lessons Learnt, BKA HG KPR 244.

7. GOH Volume XIII, pp. 78–80; 4th GD report in Rupprecht, *Kriegstagebuch* Volume III, pp. 179–81; Rupprecht MS Diary, GHA NL KPR 707, pp. 3001,

3003–5, 3010; BOH 1917 Volume II, pp. 296–322; Prior and Wilson, *Passchendaele*, pp. 133–9; OHL Ia No. 4071, 7 October 1917, War Diary, BKA HG KPR 8; AOK 4 Ia/g 276. Oktober, 7 October 1917, Lessons Learnt, BKA HG KPR 244.

8. GOH Volume XIII, pp. 77–8; Matthias Strohn, *The German Army and the Defence of the Reich: Military Doctrine and the Conduct of the Defensive Battle 1918–39* (Cambridge: Cambridge University Press, 2010).

9. GOH Volume XIII, pp. 77–8, Appendix 28b; Strohn, *The German Army and the Defence of the Reich*; 4th GD and 195th ID reports in Rupprecht, *Kriegstagebuch* Volume III, pp. 179–81 and 174–6 respectively; see also entry 5 October 1917, Volume II, pp. 267–8; 6th Bavarian Infantry Division Ia No. 7660, 15 October 1917; 119th Infantry Division Ia No. 2027, n.d.; 233rd Infantry Division Ia No. 4045, 21 October 1917, all in Lessons Learnt, BKA HG KPR 236; Rupprecht MS Diary, GHA NL KPR 707, pp. 3001, 3003–4.

10. OHL Iab No. 4153, 14 Oct 1917, War Diary, BKA HG KPR 8; entries, 2, 5, 9 October 1917, Rupprecht MS Diary, GHA NL KPR 707, pp. 2997–8, 3003–4, 3022; Rupprecht, *Kriegstagebuch* Volume II, pp. 269–70 and Volume III, p. 174; entries 3, 5 October 1917, Kuhl Diary, BA-MA RH 61/970, p. 90.

11. BOH 1917 Volume II, pp. 323–38; Prior and Wilson, *Passchendaele: The Untold Story*, pp. 159–65; AOK 4 Ia/g No. 420/Okt, 11 October 1917, Operations, GHA NL KPR 589; GOH Volume XIII, pp. 82–3; Rupprecht, *Kriegstagebuch* Volume II, p. 270; Strength and Casualty Returns, BKA HG KPR 438; entries, 11 and 13 October 1917, Rupprecht MS Diary, GHA NL KPR 707, pp. 3029, 3032–3; entries 6, 8, 10 October 1917, Kuhl Diary, BA-MA RH 61/970, pp. 91–2.

12. GOH Volume XIII, pp. 83–5; BOH 1917 Volume II, pp. 339–45; Prior and Wilson, *Passchendaele*, pp. 165–9; Strength and Casualty Returns, BKA HG KPR 438; Rupprecht, *Kriegstagebuch* Volume III, pp. 174–9; 22nd RD I No. 10303, Lessons Learnt, BKA HG KPR 236.

13. Rupprecht, *Kriegstagebuch* Volume II, pp. 271–3; entry, 13 October 1917, Rupprecht MS Diary, GHA NL KPR 707, pp. 3032–3; Albrecht von Thaer (Siegfried A. Kaehler, ed.), *Generalstabsdienst an der Front und in der O.H.L.* (Göttingen: Vandenhoeck & Ruprecht, 1958), pp. 137–9, 142–5.

14. BOH 1917 Volume II, pp. 345–60; Rupprecht, *Kriegstagebuch* Volume II, pp. 277–83; entries, 31 October, 7 November 1917, Rupprecht MS Diary, GHA NL KPR 707, pp. 3127, 3164–5.

15. Rupprecht, *Kriegstagebuch* Volume II, p. 287; GOH Volume XIII, Appendix 28b.

16. GOH Volume XIII, pp. 95–9; BOH 1917 Volume II, pp. 360–5; Greenhalgh, *The French Army and the First World War*, p. 235; Stevenson, *With Our Backs to the Wall*, p. 27; Ludendorff, *War Memories*, Volume II, pp. 491–2; Bayerisches Kriegsarchiv, *Die Bayern im Großen Kriege*, p. 410.

17. BOH 1917 Volume II, pp. xii–xv, 366–87.

18. Entry 5 December 1917, War Diary, BKA HG KPR 8; GOH Volume XIII, pp. 32, 95–9, 146, Appendix 28b; GOH Volume XI, pp. 186–7; Watson, *Enduring the Great War*, pp. 164–7, 153–5; Rupprecht, *Kriegstagebuch* Volume II, pp. 281, 284–8; entry, 11 November 1917, Rupprecht MS Diary, GHA NL KPR 707, p. 3181.

19. Sheffield, *The Chief*, pp. 247–8; Harris, *Douglas Haig and the First World War*, pp. 381–2; Greenhalgh, *The French Army and the First World War*, pp. 201–16; Beach, *Haig's Intelligence*, pp. 239–61.

20. Prior and Wilson, *Passchendaele*, p. 199; entry, 16 November 1917, Rupprecht MS Diary, GHA NL KPR 707, p. 3194.

21. Prior and Wilson, *Passchendaele*, pp. 171–81, 200.

22. Stevenson, *With Our Backs to the Wall*, p. 29.

CHAPTER 18

1. Rupprecht, *Kriegstagebuch* Volume II, pp. 288, 290; Rupprecht MS diary, GHA KPR 707, pp. 3208–9; GOH Volume XIII, pp. 124–6. The best modern account is Bryn Hammond, *Cambrai 1917: The Myth of the First Great Tank Battle* (London: Weidenfeld & Nicolson, 2008).

2. BOH 1917 Volume III, pp. 1–49.

3. Rupprecht, *Kriegstagebuch* Volume II, pp. 291–2; Rupprecht MS diary, GHA KPR 707, p. 3211.

4. 'Victory Peals at St Paul's', *The Times*, 24 November 1917, p. 7; Hammond, *Cambrai*, pp. 429–37.

5. HG KPR Ic No. 4561 24 November 1917, Lessons Learnt BKA HG KPR 244; HG KPR Ic No. 4703, 4 December 1917, Lessons Learnt, BKA HG KPR 234; entry 22 November 1917, Kuhl Diary, BA-MA RH 61/970, p. 97; Rupprecht, *Kriegstagebuch* Volume II, pp. 291–2; Rupprecht MS diary, GHA KPR 707, p. 3211.

6. BOH 1917 Volume III, pp. 120–61; Sheffield, *The Chief*, pp. 248–57.

7. Rupprecht, *Kriegstagebuch* Volume II, pp. 295–6; Kuhl Diary, BA-MA RH 61/970, pp. 97–8.

8. Rupprecht, *Kriegstagebuch* Volume II, pp. 294–8, 301; Rupprecht MS diary, GHA KPR 707, p. 3250; GOH Volume XIII, pp. 133–42.

9. Rupprecht, *Kriegstagebuch* Volume III, pp. 192–222; Hammond, *Cambrai*, pp. 371–7; BOH 1917 Volume III, pp. 257–61.

10. BOH 1917 Volume III, pp. 273–5; GOH Volume XIII, pp. 143–5; Rupprecht, *Kriegstagebuch* Volume II, p. 299.

11. BOH 1917 Volume III, pp. v, 165–6, 168, 294–305; Hammond, *Cambrai*, pp. 437–40; Beach, *Haig's Intelligence*, pp. 262–72: p. 265.

12. Ludendorff, *War Memories* Volume II, p. 497; Rupprecht, *Kriegstagebuch* Volume II, pp. 294–8; Rupprecht MS Diary, GHA NL KPR 707, p. 3275; Rupprecht, *Kriegstagebuch* Volume III, pp. 190, 192–222.

13. BOH 1917 Volume III, p. iii.

14. HG KPR Ia No. 4692, 4 December 1917, Rupprecht, *Kriegstagebuch* Volume III, pp. 188–9; HG KPR Ibd No. 4781, 11 December 1917, Lessons Learnt, BKA HG KPR 245.

15. HG KPR Ia No. 4692, 'Erfahrungen beim Angriff am 30. November', 4 December 1917; HG KPR Iad No. 4812, 'Erfahrungen aus den Angriffskämpfen bei Cambrai für die "Angriffsschlacht"', 14 December 1917; '1. Fortsetzung zu

Erfahrungen aus den Angriffskämpfen bei Cambrai für die "Angriffsschlacht"',
18 December 1917; '2. Fortsetzung zu Erfahrungen aus den Angriffskämpfen
bei Cambrai für die "Angriffsschlacht"', 24 December 1917: all in Rupprecht,
Kriegstagebuch Volume III, pp. 188–9, 192–222.

16. Bruce I. Gudmundsson, *Stormtroop Tactics: Innovation in the German Army, 1914–
1918* (New York: Praeger, 1989), pp. 148–51; Samuels, *Command or Control?*,
pp. 241–5; GOH Volume XIV, pp. 43–50; CGS Ia/II No. 6608, 16 February 1918,
Lessons Learnt, BKA HG KPR 244; Rupprecht, *Kriegstagebuch* Volume II,
pp. 317–19 and Volume III, pp. 263, 282–3; entries, 18–23 January 1918, War
Diary, BKA HG KPR 9.

CHAPTER 19

1. Stevenson, *With Our Backs to the Wall*, pp. 31–4; Zabecki, *The German 1918
Offensives*, pp. 93–6.

2. Entry, 24 October 1917, Kuhl Diary, BA-MA RH 61/970, pp. 92–3; Rupprecht,
Kriegstagebuch Volume II, pp. 274–5, 278–9; GOH Volume XIV, pp. 50–1.

3. GOH Volume XIV, pp. 53–5; Kuhl Diary, BA-MA RH 61/970, pp. 94–5;
Rupprecht, *Kriegstagebuch* Volume II, pp. 284–7; Rupprecht MS Diary, GHA
NL KPR 707, p. 3181; Zabecki, *The German 1918 Offensives*, pp. 97–100.

4. GOH Volume XIV, pp. 55–8; HG KPR Ia 4501, 20 November 1917, Rupprecht,
Kriegstagebuch Volume III, pp. 222–38, also in Operations, GHA NL KPR 591.

5. GOH Volume XIV, pp. 58–67; HG KPR Ia No. 4835, 15 December and HG
KPR Ia No. 4877, 19 December 1917, GHA NL KPR 591; the former is repro-
duced also in Rupprecht, *Kriegstagebuch* Volume III, pp. 238–45; entry, 19
December 1917, Kuhl Diary, BA-MA RH 61/970, pp. 100–1; Zabecki, *The
German 1918 Offensives*, pp. 101–7.

6. GOH Volume XIV, pp. 67–9; Rupprecht, *Kriegstagebuch* Volume II, pp. 304–11;
BOH 1918 Volume I, pp. 95–7; Beach, *Haig's Intelligence*, pp. 283–4; entry
4 September 1917, Rupprecht MS Diary, GHA NL KPR 706, p. 2893; entry 29
December 1917, Rupprecht MS Diary, GHA NL KPR 707, pp. 3309–10; Kuhl
Diary, BA-MA RH 61/970, p. 102.

7. Rupprecht, *Kriegstagebuch* Volume II, pp. 305–9.

8. HG KPR Iaf No. 5002, 3 January 1918, War Diary, BKA HG KPR 8; Georg
Mayer (ed.), *Generalfeldmarschall Wilhelm Ritter von Leeb: Tagebuchaufzeichnungen
und Lagebeurteilungen aus zwei Weltkriegen* (Stuttgart: Deutsche Verlags-Anstalt,
1976), p. 103; Rupprecht, *Kriegstagebuch* Volume II, pp. 313–14 and Volume III,
pp. 248–59.

9. GOH Volume XIV, pp. 72–9; Rupprecht, *Kriegstagebuch* Volume II, pp. 317–24
and Volume III, pp. 263–4; entry, 22 January 1918, Kuhl Diary, BA-MA RH
61/970, pp. 105–7; entry 23 January 1918, War Diary, BKA HG KPR 9;
Rupprecht, 'Meine Teilnahme am Weltkrieg 1914-18', GHA NL KPR 716,
pp. 51–2; Ludendorff, *War Memories* Volume II, pp. 590–2; Zabecki, *The
German 1918 Offensives*, pp. 101–7.

10. HG KPR Ia No. 5423, 26 January 1918, Operations, GHA NL KPR 591; entry, 3 February 1918, War Diary, BKA HG KPR 9; Rupprecht, *Kriegstagebuch* Volume III, pp. 277–8, 282–3; Zabecki, *The German 1918 Offensives*, pp. 113–16; minutes of meeting, 21 January 1918, BA-MA PH 5 I/45; Ludendorff, *War Memories* Volume II, pp. 590–2.

11. Rupprecht, *Kriegstagebuch* Volume II, pp. 326, 330–2, 336; Correspondence with King Ludwig III, GHA NL KPR 428; entries, 6, 8 February 1918, Kuhl Diary, BA-MA RH 61/970, pp. 109–11.

12. Rupprecht, *Kriegstagebuch* Volume II, pp. 326, 330–2, 336; Correspondence with King Ludwig III, GHA NL KPR 428; entry, 6 February 1918, entries 6, 8 February 1918, Kuhl Diary, BA-MA RH 61/970, pp. 109–11; GOH Volume XIV, pp. 92–3.

13. HG KPR Ia No. 6702 and AOK2 Ia No. 532, both 6 March 1918, Operations, GHA NL KPR 593; GOH Volume XIV, pp. 82–4; Zabecki, *The German 1918 Offensives*, pp. 116–18; Rupprecht, *Kriegstagebuch* Volume II, p. 335.

14. OHL Ia No. 7070, 10 March 1918 and HG KPR Ia No. 6263, 16 March 1918, both in Operations, GHA NL KPR 593; see also Rupprecht, *Kriegstagebuch* Volume III, pp. 299–302 and Volume II, pp. 337–43; GOH Volume XIV, pp. 84–7.

15. Rupprecht, *Kriegstagebuch* Volume II, pp. 343; Rupprecht, 'Meine Teilnahme am Weltkrieg 1914–18', GHA NL KPR 716, p. 53.

CHAPTER 20

1. GOH Volume XIV, p. 104.

2. Rupprecht, *Kriegstagebuch* Volume II, pp. 344–5; GOH Volume XIV, pp. 105–32.

3. BOH 1918 Volume I, pp. 166–217, 240–59; GOH Volume XIV, pp. 105–32; Zabecki, *The German 1918 Offensives*, pp. 138–42.

4. BOH 1918 Volume I, pp. 264–326; GOH Volume XIV, pp. 132–47; Zabecki, *The German 1918 Offensives*, pp. 142–3.

5. Rupprecht, *Kriegstagebuch* Volume III, pp. 305–6 and Volume II, pp. 346–50.

6. BOH 1918 Volume I, pp. 327–98; GOH Volume XIV, pp. 147–60, 162–9; Zabecki, *The German 1918 Offensives*, pp. 143–5; Rupprecht, *Kriegstagebuch* Volume II, pp. 350–1.

7. BOH 1918 Volume I, pp. 399–495; GOH Volume XIV, pp. 169–89; Zabecki, *The German 1918 Offensives*, pp. 145–9; Rupprecht, *Kriegstagebuch* Volume II, pp. 353–5; HG KPR Ia No. 6427, 25 March 1918, Operations, GHA NL KPR 593.

8. Douglas Haig, *War Diaries and Letters 1914–18* (Gary Sheffield and John Bourne, eds), (London: Phoenix, 2006 [2005]), pp. 392–3; Harris, *Douglas Haig and the First World War*, pp. 453–6; Sheffield, *The Chief*, pp. 272–6; Greenhalgh, *The French Army and the First World War*, pp. 274–6; Greenhalgh, 'Myth and Memory: Sir Douglas Haig and the Imposition of Allied Unified Command in March 1918', *Journal of Military History* 68:2 (2004), pp. 771–820; Zabecki, *The German 1918 Offensives*, pp. 148–9; BOH 1918 Volume I, pp. 538–44; Stevenson, *With Our Backs to the Wall*, pp. 62–5.

9. Rupprecht, *Kriegstagebuch* Volume II, pp. 355–60; Zabecki, *The German 1918 Offensives*, pp. 149–54; BOH 1918 Volume I, pp. 496–536 and Volume II, pp. 12–41; GOH Volume XIV, pp. 189–202, 206–13; entries 25 and 27 March 1918, Kuhl Diary, BA-MA RH 61/970, pp. 115–16; HG KPR Ia No. 6438, 26 March 1918, Operations, GHA NL KPR 593.

10. GOH Volume XIV, pp. 206–13; Rupprecht, *Kriegstagebuch* Volume II, pp. 358–61; Zabecki, *The German 1918 Offensives*, pp. 153–5.

11. GOH Volume XIV, pp. 213–29; Rupprecht, *Kriegstagebuch* Volume II, pp. 360–2; entry, 6 April 1918, Kuhl Diary, BA-MA RH 61/970, pp. 128–9; HG KPR Ia No. 6468, HG KPR Ia No. 6478 and OHL Ia 7380, all 28 March 1918, Operations, GHA NL KPR 593.

12. GOH Volume XIV, pp. 224–36; Rupprecht, *Kriegstagebuch* Volume II, pp. 362–5; Kuhl Diary, BA-MA RH 61/970, p. 119; Rupprecht MS Diary, GHA NL KPR 707, pp. 3595–6; Mayer (ed.), *Generalfeldmarschall Wilhelm Ritter von Leeb*, p. 112.

13. GOH Volume XIV, pp. 236–41; Rupprecht, *Kriegstagebuch* Volume II, pp. 367–9.

14. GOH Volume XIV, pp. 241–54; Zabecki, *The German 1918 Offensives*, pp. 157–9.

15. GOH Volume XIV, pp. 254–9; BOH 1918 Volume II, pp. 113, 456–93; Zabecki, *The German 1918 Offensives*, pp. 160–73.

CHAPTER 21

1. GOH Volume XIV, pp. 270–1.

2. Rupprecht, *Kriegstagebuch* Volume II, p. 372; entries 4, 6 April, Kuhl Diary, BA-MA RH 61/970, pp. 125, 128–9; Georg Mayer (ed.), *Generalfeldmarschall Wilhelm Ritter von Leeb*, p. 113; Untersuchungsausschuss der Deutschen Verfassunggebenden Nationalversammlung und des Deutschen Reichstages 1919–26, *Die Ursachen des Deutschen Zusammenbruchs im Jahre 1918*, Volume III (Berlin: Deutsche Verlagsgesellschaft für Politik und Geschichte, 1925), pp. 156–7; Hermann von Kuhl, *Der Weltkrieg 1914–1918* Volume II (Berlin: Tradition Wilhelm Kolk, 1929), p. 331; GOH Volume XIV, pp. 265–71.

3. Rupprecht, *Kriegstagebuch* Volume II, pp. 375–9; BOH 1918 Volume II, pp. 156–283, 512; Zabecki, *The German 1918 Offensives*, pp. 186–90; GOH Volume XIV, pp. 53, 272–80; entry, 6 May 1918, Rupprecht MS Diary, GHA NL KPR 708, p. 3728.

4. Rupprecht, *Kriegstagebuch* Volume II, pp. 381–7; entry, 15 April 1918, Rupprecht MS Diary, GHA NL KPR 707, pp. 3662–4; entries 2, 13, 15 April, 11 June 1918, Kuhl Diary, BA-MA RH 61/970, pp. 124–5, 138–41, 152.

5. Rupprecht, *Kriegstagebuch* Volume II, pp. 381–7, 393; entry, 15 April, Rupprecht MS Diary, GHA NL KPR 707, pp. 3662–4; BOH 1918 Volume II, pp. 284–455; GOH Volume XIV, pp. 280–98, 301–10; Zabecki, *The German 1918 Offensives*, pp. 190–8.

6. 325,800 German and 328,304 allied soldiers were dead, wounded, or missing. British casualties were 236,300 and French 92,004. GOH Volume XIV, pp. 299–301; BOH 1918 Volume II, pp. 488–93; Zabecki, *The German 1918 Offensives*, pp. 198–205.

7. FOH VI:1, pp. 521–4; BOH 1918 Volume III, pp. 4–5.

8. Zabecki, *The German 1918 Offensives*, pp. 206–17, 280–7; OHL Ia No. 7960, 2 May 1918, Operations, GHA NL KPR 594.

9. CGS Ia/II No. 7745 'Angriffserfahrungen', 17 April 1918, Operations, GHA NL KPR 593; 6 BID Ia No. 2500, 24 April 1918, Lessons Learnt, BKA HG KPR 236; HG KPR Iaf No. 7454 'Einzelerfahrungen', 28 May 1918, Operations, GHA NL KPR 594; Gerhard P. Groß, 'Das Dogma der Beweglichkeit: Überlegungen zur Genese der deutschen Heerestaktik im Zeitalter der Weltkriege', in Bruno Thoß and Hans-Erich Volkmann (eds), *Erster Weltkrieg, Zweiter Weltkrieg: Ein Vergleich: Krieg, Kriegserlebnis, Kriegserfahrung in Deutschland* (Paderborn: Ferdinand Schöningh, 2002), pp. 151–3; Rupprecht, *Kriegstagebuch* Volume II, p. 396; Thaer, *Generalstabsdienst*, pp. 187–8.

10. Rupprecht, *Kriegstagebuch* Volume II, pp. 395–8, 401 and Volume III, pp. 318, 321; report, 7 May 1918, Correspondence with King Ludwig III, GHA NL KPR 428.

11. Rupprecht, *Kriegstagebuch* Volume II, pp. 399–401; Lothar Machtan, *Prinz Max von Baden: Der letzte Kanzler des Kaisers: Eine Biografie* (Berlin: Suhrkamp, 2013), pp. 347–61; Rupprecht MS Diary, GHA NL KPR 708, p. 3765.

12. Entry, 21 May 1918, Kuhl Diary, BA-MA RH 61/970, p. 152; Rupprecht, *Kriegstagebuch* Volume III, p. 321; Rupprecht MS Diary, GHA NL KPR 708, p. 3760.

13. Zabecki, *The German 1918 Offensives*, pp. 206–32; Rupprecht, *Kriegstagebuch* Volume II, pp. 402–4.

14. Zabecki, *The German 1918 Offensives*, pp. 287–301; Rupprecht, *Kriegstagebuch* Volume III, pp. 327, 331–2; entry, 9 June 1918, Rupprecht MS Diary, GHA NL KPR 708, p. 3807; entry, 11 June 1918, Kuhl Diary, BA-MA RH 61/970, pp. 158–9.

15. BOH 1918 Volume III, pp. 194–213; Rupprecht, *Kriegstagebuch* Volume II, pp. 406, 409, 414, 418.

16. OHL Ia/II No. 9135, 6 July 1918, Operations, GHA NL KPR 596; Rupprecht, *Kriegstagebuch* Volume II, pp. 419–20; Heeres-Sanitätsinspektion, *Sanitätsbericht über das Deutsche Heer* Volume III, pp. 122–3.

17. Rupprecht, *Kriegstagebuch* Volume II, pp. 415–17; entry, 2 July 1918, War Diary, BKA HG KPR 9; H. A. Jones, *The War in the Air: Being the Story of the Part Played in the Great War by the Royal Air Force* Volume VI (Oxford: Clarendon, 1937), pp. 409–10. The raids were suspended after a week, having proved that air power did not yet possess the accuracy to cut railways by day or night.

18. Zabecki, *The German 1918 Offensives*, pp. 246–79, 302–7; Michael S. Neiberg, *The Second Battle of the Marne* (Bloomington, IN: Indiana University Press, 2008); entry 20 July 1918, Kuhl Diary, BA-MA RH 61/970, pp. 169–70; HG KPR Ia No. 8528 and No. 8542, 20 July 1918, Operations, GHA NL KPR 596; OHL Ia 9388, 20 July 1918, BKA HG KPR 105; GOH Volume XIV, pp. 531–5; Fritz von Loßberg, *Meine Tätigkeit im Weltkriege 1914–1918* (Berlin: E. S. Mittler & Sohn, 1939), p. 352.

CHAPTER 22

1. Rupprecht, *Kriegstagebuch* Volume II, pp. 426–30; entry, 3 August 1918, Rupprecht MS Diary, GHA NL KPR 708, pp. 3955–6; entry, 4 August 1918, Kuhl Diary, BA-MA RH 61/970, p. 175.

2. BOH 1918 Volume IV, pp. 16–92; GOH Volume XIV, pp. 549–57; Thilo von Bose, *Die Katastrophe des 8. August 1918* (Berlin: Gerhard Stalling, 1930), p. 196; entry, 8 August 1918, Kuhl Diary, BA-MA RH 61/970, p. 176; Rupprecht, *Kriegstagebuch* Volume III, p. 346; entry, 9 August 1918, Rupprecht MS Diary, GHA NL KPR 708, p. 3970.

3. Entry, 9 August 1918, Rupprecht MS Diary, GHA NL KPR 708, pp. 3976–7; entries, 10–11 August 1918, Kuhl Diary, BA-MA RH 61/970, pp. 176–8; BOH 1918 Volume IV, pp. 93–162; GOH Volume XIV, pp. 557–67. Good modern treatments of Amiens can be found in Charles Messenger, *The Day We Won the War: Turning Point at Amiens, 8 August 1918* (London: Weidenfeld & Nicolson, 2008); Nick Lloyd, *Hundred Days: The End of the Great War* (London: Viking, 2013), pp. 28–70, and J. P. Harris with Niall Barr, *Amiens to the Armistice: The BEF in the Hundred Days Campaign, 8 August–11 November 1918* (London: Brassey's, 1998), pp. 59–117.

4. Bose, *Die Katastrophe des 8. August 1918*, pp. 196–8; Ludendorff, *War Memories: 1914–1918* Volume II, pp. 679, 684; Nebelin, *Ludendorff*, pp. 444–5, 451; Rupprecht, *Kriegstagebuch* Volume II, p. 435.

5. Rupprecht, *Kriegstagebuch* Volume II, p. 438; Rupprecht MS Diary, GHA NL KPR 708, pp. 3990–4001; Herbert Michaelis and Ernst Schraepler (eds), *Ursachen und Folgen vom deutschen Zusammenbruch 1918 and 1945 bis zur staatlichen Neuordnung Deutschlands in der Gegenwart* Volume II: *Der militärische Zusammenbruch und das Ende des Kaiserreichs* (Berlin: Herbert Wendler & Co., n.d.), pp. 283–4.

6. Beach, *Haig's Intelligence*, pp. 307–16; entry, 23 August 1918, Kuhl Diary, BA-MA RH 61/970, pp. 182–4.

7. Entry, 2 September 1918, Rupprecht MS Diary, GHA NL KPR 708, p. 4001; entries, 27–8 August 1918, Kuhl Diary, BA-MA RH 61/970, pp. 186–7; Ludendorff, *War Memories* Volume II, p. 696; Nebelin, *Ludendorff*, p. 452; report, 4 September 1918, Correspondence with King Ludwig III, GHA NL KPR 428.

8. 'Zusammenstellung der Gesamtverpflegung-Stärken der Armeen 19 September 1916–30 October 1918', BKA HG KPR 438; GHQ AG War Diary, TNA WO 95/26; Rupprecht, *Kriegstagebuch* Volume II, p. 441. For contrasting views on morale, compare Watson, *Enduring the Great War*, pp. 184–232 with Boff, *Winning and Losing on the Western Front*, pp. 92–122.

9. Rupprecht, *Kriegstagebuch* Volume II, p. 442; entry, 6 September 1918, Kuhl Diary, BA-MA RH 61/970, pp. 190–2; Loßberg, *Meine Tätigkeit im Weltkriege*, p. 357; 3rd Marine Division Ia No. 806, 6 September 1918, Lessons Learnt, BKA HG KPR 236.

10. Boff, *Winning and Losing on the Western Front*, pp. 45–53, 165–78; OHL II No. 10162, 4 September 1918, BKA 16 BID, Bd 10/7; GOH Volume XIV, pp. 607–8; entries, 13, 17 September 1918, Rupprecht MS Diary, GHA NL KPR 708, pp. 4040, 4056; Rupprecht, *Kriegstagebuch* Volume II, p. 356.

11. Nebelin, *Ludendorff*, pp. 453–6; entry, 6 September, Kuhl Diary, BA-MA RH 61/970, p. 191; entries, 9, 27 September 1918, Rupprecht MS Diary, GHA NL KPR 708, pp. 4028–9, 4083; GOH Volume XIV, footnote 1, pp. 594–5.

12. Entry, 9 September 1918, Rupprecht MS Diary, GHA NL KPR 708, pp. 4028–9; diary entries 11, 13–14, 17–20 September 1918, War Diary, BKA HG KPR 9; Rupprecht, *Kriegstagebuch* Volume II, p. 446; entry 14 September 1918, Kuhl Diary, BA-MA RH 61/970, p. 192; GOH Volume XIV, pp. 606–7.

13. Greenhalgh, *The French Army and the First World War*, pp. 336–41.

14. Rupprecht, *Kriegstagebuch* Volume II, p. 452 and Volume III, p. 358; OHL No. 10552, 30 September 1918, BKA HG KPR 99/101; report and letter, 30 September 1918, Correspondence with King Ludwig III, GHA NL KPR 428; Mayer (ed.), *Generalfeldmarschall Wilhelm Ritter von Leeb*, p. 138; entry, 30 September 1918, Kuhl Diary, BA-MA RH 61/970, pp. 193–4.

15. Ludendorff, *War Memories* Volume I, pp. 719–22; Thaer, *Generalstabsdienst*, p. 234; entry, 5 October 1918, Kuhl Diary, BA-MA RH 61/970, p. 195; Rupprecht, *Kriegstagebuch* Volume II, p. 455; Rupprecht MS Diary, GHA NL KPR 708, pp. 4102–3; Stevenson, *With Our Backs to the Wall*, pp. 510–5; Watson, *Ring of Steel*, pp. 533–5.

16. Rupprecht, *Kriegstagebuch* Volume II, p. 456; entry, 11 October 1918, War Diary, BKA HG KPR 5.

17. Heeresgruppe Boehn (HB) Ia No. 1620, 3 October 1918, HB War Diary, BA-MA PH 5 I/47; entry, 11 October 1918, Kuhl Diary, BA-MA RH 61/970, p. 196; entry, 11 October 1918, Rupprecht MS Diary, GHA NL KPR 708, p. 4113; Rupprecht, *Kriegstagebuch* Volume II, p. 458.

18. Wilhelm Deist, 'The Military Collapse of the German Empire: The Reality Behind the Stab-in-the-Back Myth' (E. J. Feuchtwanger, trans.), *War in History* 3:2 (April 1996), pp. 186–207; Christoph Jahr, *Gewöhnliche Soldaten: Desertion under Deserteure im deutschen und britischen Heer 1914–1918* (Göttingen: Vandenhoeck & Ruprecht, 1998), pp. 150–76; Watson, *Enduring the Great War*, pp. 186–230; Scott Stephenson, *The Final Battle: Soldiers of the Western Front and the German Revolution of 1918* (Cambridge: Cambridge University Press, 2009), chapters 1 and 2; Boff, *Winning and Losing on the Western Front*, pp. 92–122.

19. Stevenson, *With Our Backs to the Wall*, pp. 519–20; Watson, *Ring of Steel*, pp. 549–51; Lloyd, *Hundred Days*, pp. 234–7; entries, 27–31 October 1918, Kuhl Diary, BA-MA RH 61/970, pp. 198–9; entry, 27 October 1918, Rupprecht MS Diary, GHA NL KPR 708, p. 4165.

20. Mayer (ed.), *Generalfeldmarschall Wilhelm Ritter von Leeb*, p. 149; HKR Ia No. 10606, 5 November, BKA HKR Bd 99/101.

21. März, *Das Haus Wittelsbach im Ersten Weltkrieg*, pp. 492–500.

22. Mayer (ed.), *Generalfeldmarschall Wilhelm Ritter von Leeb*, p. 154; Rupprecht, *Kriegstagebuch* Volume II, pp. 472–6 and Volume III, pp. 368–71; entries, 2, 5 November 1918, Rupprecht MS Diary, GHA NL KPR 708, pp. 4182–91; entry, 4 November 1918, Rupprecht MS Diary, GHA NL KPR 709, n.p.; Mayer (ed.), *Generalfeldmarschall Wilhelm Ritter von Leeb*, p. 154.

CHAPTER 23

1. Passport for the party of Marquis de Villalobar, Correspondence, GHA NL KPR 255.
2. Letter to Krafft from the Supreme State Prosecutor, b.J. 353/20/12, 3 March 1923, Miscellaneous Documents regarding Crown Prince Rupprecht, BKA NL Krafft 196; Horne and Kramer, *German Atrocities 1914*, pp. 63–70, 329–55; Heather Jones, *Violence against Prisoners of War: Britain, France and Germany, 1914–20* (Cambridge: Cambridge University Press, 2011), p. 78.
3. Weiß, *Kronprinz Rupprecht von Bayern*, pp. 223–4.
4. Reiner Pommerin, 'Die Ausweisung von "Ostjuden" aus Bayern 1923. Ein Beitrag zum Krisenjahr der Weimarer Republik', *Vierteljahrhefte für Zeitgeschichte* 34:3 (July 1986), pp. 311–40; Weiß, *Kronprinz Rupprecht von Bayern*, pp. 211–22.
5. Weiß, *Kronprinz Rupprecht von Bayern*, pp. 211–22; März, *Das Haus Wittelsbach*, p. 530.
6. Weiß, *Kronprinz Rupprecht von Bayern*, pp. 263–72.
7. This school was apparently also well known at the time as good at handling free-spirited young ladies. I am grateful to Mr Charles Messenger for this information.

CHAPTER 24

1. Rupprecht, *Kriegstagebuch* Volume II, pp. 33, 38; entry, 8 October 1916, Kuhl Diary, BA-MA RH 61/970, p. 29.
2. Entries 12, 14, 16 April 1917, Kuhl Diary, BA-MA RH 61/970, pp. 55–6; entry 16 April 1917, Rupprecht MS Diary, GHA NL KPR 706, pp. 2425–6; Gebsattel quoted in Ulrich and Ziemann (eds), *German Soldiers in the Great War*, pp. 170–1.
3. Rupprecht, *Kriegstagebuch* Volume II, pp. 164, 211; entries, 12, 21 May, 2 July 1917, Rupprecht MS Diary, GHA NL KPR 706, pp. 2494, 2520, 2669; entries, 1–2 July 1917, Kuhl Diary, BA-MA RH 61/970, p. 79.
4. Entries, 27 September 1917, 2, 9 October, Rupprecht MS Diary, GHA NL KPR 707, pp. 2980, 2998–9, 3022; Thaer, *Generalstabsdienst*, pp. 187–8; Rupprecht, *Kriegstagebuch* Volume II, pp. 269–70.
5. Entries, 13–15 April, 9 June, 10, 24–30 August 1918, Kuhl Diary, BA-MA RH 61/970, pp. 138–42, 158, 177, 184–7.
6. Entries, 24 November, 25 December 1915, 21 February 1917, Rupprecht MS Diary, GHA NL KPR 703, p. 1195 and 705, pp. 2150–2, 2281–2; entries, 24 November, 1,

2, 11 December 1915, Xylander Diary Volume II, BKA NL R. Xylander 12, pp. 466, 472–3, 479; Kuhl Diary, BA-MA RH 61/970, pp. 19–20; Rupprecht, 'Meine Teilnahme am Weltkrieg 1914–18', GHA NL KPR 716, pp. 38–41; Kuhl, *Der deutsche Generalstab*, p. 191; Rupprecht, *Kriegstagebuch* Volume II, p. 266, 439.

7. See Markus Pöhlmann's discussion of this in his *Kriegsgeschichte und Geschichtspolitik: Der Erste Weltkrieg: Die amtliche deutsche Militärgeschichtsschreibung 1914–1956* (Paderborn: Ferdinand Schöningh, 2002), pp. 249–51.

8. Entries, 28 June, 1, 4, 6, 7, 14, 15 July, 16, 26 August, 1 September 1917, Kuhl Diary, BA-MA RH 61/970, pp. 78–87; entry, 7 July 1917, Rupprecht MS diary, GHA NL KPR 706, p. 2686; Thaer, *Generalstabsdienst*, p. 126.

9. März, *Das Haus Wittelsbach im Ersten Weltkrieg*, pp. 56–61.

10. März, *Das Haus Wittelsbach im Ersten Weltkrieg*, p. 58; Weiß, *Kronprinz Rupprecht von Bayern*, p. 34.

11. Weiß, *Kronprinz Rupprecht von Bayern*, pp. 88–96; Rupprecht, 'Meine Teilnahme am Weltkrieg 1914-18', GHA NL KPR 716, p. 10; Afflerbach, 'Kronprinz Rupprecht von Bayern im Ersten Weltkrieg', p. 29.

12. Rupprecht, *Kriegstagebuch* Volume I, pp. 356, 462–3, 469, 473, 503–5 and Volume II, pp. 55, 142; letters, Rupprecht to War Minister General Otto Kreß von Kreßenstein, 25 May and 3 October 1915, Correspondence with War Minister, GHA NL KPR 430.

13. Telegram, Kaiser Wilhelm II to Crown Prince Rupprecht, 13 August 1914, GHA NL KPR 419; Rupprecht, 'Meine Teilnahme am Weltkrieg 1914–18', GHA NL KPR 716, p. 22; entries, 8 September, 21, 22, 25 October 1916, Kuhl Diary, BA-MA RH 61/970, pp. 24, 33; letter, Counsellor Leopold Krafft von Dellmensingen to Prime Minister Dandl, 24 October 1916, Correspondence, GHA NL KPR 436; Rupprecht, *Kriegstagebuch* Volume II, p. 116; Benjamin Ziemann, *Front und Heimat: Ländliche Kriegserfahrungen im südlichen Bayern 1914–1923* (Essen: Klartext, 1997), p. 68.

14. Entries 27 September, 19 October 1914, Krafft Diary, BKA NL Krafft 48, pp. 33a, 100a; entries 9 December 1916, 21 February 1917, Rupprecht MS Diary, GHA NL KPR 705, pp. 2116–7, 2281–2; Wenninger, letter, 6 September 1914, quoted in Schulte, 'Neue Dokumente zu Kriegsausbruch und Kriegsverlauf 1914', p. 168. For further detail, see Tony Cowan, 'A Picture of German Unity? Federal Contingents in the German Army, 1916–17', in Jonathan Krause, *The Greater War: Other Combatants and Other Fronts* (Basingstoke: Palgrave Macmillan, 2014), pp. 141–60.

15. Entries 21 December 1916, 19 January 1917, Rupprecht MS Diary, GHA NL KPR 705, pp. 2141–2, 2210.

16. Letters from Ludwig III to Rupprecht, 22 November, 7 December 1914, 28 September 1915 and letters from Rupprecht to Ludwig III, 21 July, 2 August 1915: all in Correspondence with King, GHA NL KPR 427 and 428; Rupprecht, *Kriegstagebuch* Volume I, pp. 285, 405, 475–6.

17. Rupprecht, *Kriegstagebuch* Volume II, p. 302: entries 19 December 1917, 12, 16 May 1918, Rupprecht MS diary, GHA NL KPR 707, p. 2191 and 708, pp. 3743,

3748; report to Ludwig III, 31 March 1918, Correspondence with King, GHA NL KPR 428.

18. Afflerbach, *Kaiser Wilhelm II. als Oberster Kriegsherr*, pp. 1–91; Röhl, *Wilhelm II: Into the Abyss of War and Exile, 1900–41*, p. 1108; Walter Görlitz (ed.), *The Kaiser and his Court: The Diaries, Note Books and Letters of Admiral Georg Alexander von Müller, Chief of the Naval Cabinet, 1914–1918* (London: Macdonald, 1961), pp. 42, 181; Holger Afflerbach, 'Wilhelm II as Supreme Warlord', Isabel V. Hull, 'Military Culture, Wilhelm II, and the End of the Monarchy in the First World War', Matthew Stibbe, 'Germany's "Last Card": Wilhelm II and the Decision in Favour of Unrestricted Submarine Warfare in January 1917', all in Annika Mombauer and Wilhelm Deist (eds), *The Kaiser: New Research on Wilhelm II's Role in Imperial Germany* (Cambridge: Cambridge University Press, 2003), pp. 195–217 (quotation from p. 210), 219–34, 235–58.

19. Afflerbach, *Kaiser Wilhelm II. als Oberster Kriegsherr im Ersten Weltkrieg*, p. 17; entries 13, 15 April 1918, Kuhl Diary, BA-MA RH 61/970, pp. 138–41.

20. Voltaire quoted in Archibald Wavell, *Generals and Generalship* (Harmondsworth: Penguin, 1941), p. 20; entries, 5 September 1914, 18 March 1915, 10 August 1916, 25 May and 6 June 1917, Rupprecht MS Diary, GHA NL KPR 699, p. 172, NL KPR 702, p. 667, NL KPR 704, p. 1851; Rupprecht, 'Meine Teilnahme am Weltkrieg 1914–18', GHA NL KPR 716, p. 39.

21. Thomas Ertman, *Birth of Leviathan: Building States and Regimes in Medieval and Early Modern Europe* (Cambridge: Cambridge University Press, 1997), p. 317; Manfred Nebelin, *Ludendorff: Diktator im Ersten Weltkrieg* (Munich: Siedler, 2010), pp. 453–4; Wilhelm Heye, Lebenserinnerungen des Generaloberst W. Heye: Teil II: 'Wie ich den Weltkrieg erlebte', NL Generaloberst W. Heye, BA-MA N 18/4, pp. 66–8.

CHAPTER 25

1. März, *Das Haus Wittelsbach im Ersten Weltkrieg*, p. 172.

2. Entry, 12 February 1916, Rupprecht MS Diary, GHA NL KPR 703, pp. 1348–9; Rupprecht, *Mein Kriegstagebuch* Volume II, pp. 76, 103, 219–29, 305–9, 321–6, 329–32; entry, 22 January 1918, Kuhl Diary, BA-MA RH 61/970, pp. 105–7; Watson, *Ring of Steel*, pp. 458–60.

3. Entry, 14 May 1918, Rupprecht MS diary, GHA NL KPR 708, p. 3745; Rupprecht, *Mein Kriegstagebuch* Volume II, p. 399; Karl Hertling, *Ein Jahr in der Reichskanzlei: Erinnerungen an die Kanzlerschaft meines Vaters* (Freiburg: Hedersche Verlagshandlung, 1919), pp. 139–41; Watson, *Ring of Steel*, pp. 533–5, 547–51; März, *Das Haus Wittelsbach*, pp. 461–3.

4. Letters from Rupprecht, 15 August, 18 October 1918, Prince Max von Baden Correspondence, GHA NL KPR 650–1; Letters and Reports from Rupprecht, 25 July, 4, 30 September, 7, 14, 15, 26 October, 1 November 1918, King Ludwig III Correspondence, GHA NL KPR 428.

5. März, *Das Haus Wittelsbach im Ersten Weltkrieg*, pp. 461–85; entry, 2 November 1918, Rupprecht MS Diary, GHA NL KPR 708, p. 4182; Letter to Rupprecht, 7 November 1918, King Ludwig III Correspondence, GHA NL KPR 435.
6. Rupprecht, *Kriegstagebuch* Volume II, pp. 448–9, 473.
7. This occurred in May 1915. The other occasions were October 1914, May and July 1916, February and June 1917.
8. März, *Das Haus Wittelsbach im Ersten Weltkrieg*, pp. 401–9; entry, 10 January 1916, Rupprecht MS diary, GHA NL KPR 703, pp. 1274–6; letter from Rupprecht, 13 July 1917, King Ludwig III Correspondence, GHA NL KPR 428; entry, 13 July 1917, Rupprecht MS diary, GHA NL KPR 706, p. 2707; Weiß, *Kronprinz Rupprecht*, pp. 126–34, 143–5; entry, 19 January 1917, Rupprecht MS diary, GHA NL KPR 705, p. 2210.
9. Ludendorff, *War Memories* Volume I, p. 275.
10. Entries, 31 May, 11, 13 July, 1917, Rupprecht MS Diary, GHA NL KPR 706, pp. 2557, 2698, 2707; letter, Leopold Krafft von Dellmensingen to Otto Dandl, 1 June 1917, GHA NL KPR 436; letter from Rupprecht, 13 July 1917, King Ludwig III Correspondence, GHA NL KPR 428; Machtan, *Max von Baden*, pp. 355–66; Weiß, *Kronprinz Rupprecht*, pp. 148–9; März, *Das Haus Wittelsbach*, pp. 373–6; 404–10.
11. März, *Das Haus Wittelsbach*, pp. 390, 440–8, 456–65; Dieter Storz, ' "Aber was hätte anders geschehen sollen?" Die deutschen Offensiven an der Westfront', in Jörg Duppler and Gerhard Groß (eds), *Kriegsende 1918: Ereignis, Wirkung, Nachwirkung*, pp. 51–95; Watson, *Ring of Steel*, pp. 523–37, 547–55.

CHAPTER 26

1. Jonathan Steinberg argues that Bismarck deliberately arranged power to this end: *Bismarck: A Life* (Oxford: Oxford University Press, 2011).
2. Hans von Below memoir, 27 February 1919, Nachlass Otto von Below, BA-MA N 87/2, p. 14.
3. Rupert Brooke, 'Peace' at: http://projects.oucs.ox.ac.uk/jtap/tutorials/intro/brooke/ipeace.html#peace, accessed 10 February 2017; J. Glenn Gray, *The Warriors: Reflections on Men in Battle* (New York: Harper & Row, 1967 [1959]), pp. 28–52.
4. Three battles of Artois in 1915; the Somme in 1916; Artois, Flanders, and Cambrai in 1917.
5. Samuel Hynes, *The Soldier's Tale: Bearing Witness to Modern War* (London: Pimlico, 1998), p. 11.
6. W. B. Yeats, *The Oxford Book of Modern Verse* (Oxford: Oxford University Press, 1936), p. xxxiv.
7. Eksteins, *Rites of Spring*, p. 184.
8. See Robert Gerwarth, *The Vanquished: Why the First World War Failed to End* (London: Allen Lane, 2016).

Bibliography

UNPUBLISHED PRIMARY MATERIAL

Geheimes Hausarchiv, Abteilung III, Bayerisches Hauptstaatsarchiv, Munich (GHA)

Nachlass Kronprinz Rupprecht (NL KPR)

17, 41:	correspondence, family
140:	correspondence, miscellaneous
164–7:	correspondence, Pappenheim
251, 255:	correspondence, miscellaneous
393, 416, 427–8, 434–5:	correspondence, King Ludwig III
419, 495:	correspondence, Kaiser Wilhelm II
430, 614:	correspondence, War Minister
436:	correspondence, Leopold Krafft von Dellmensingen with Dandl
476–93, 561, 578–601, 606–10:	military operations
494:	correspondence, Bavarian military representative
602–3:	correspondence, Generals 1917–18
626:	correspondence, wartime
639, 647:	correspondence, miscellaneous
650–1:	correspondence, political
699–709:	manuscript diary
716:	memoir
723:	correspondence, Konrad Krafft von Dellmensingen, 1920–51

Bayerisches Kriegsarchiv, Abteilung IV, Bayerisches Hauptstaatsarchiv, Munich (BKA)

Armeeoberkommando 6 (AOK 6): war diary, orders, operations and after-action reports

Vorl. 1–2, 6, 9, 11–12, 24–5, 34, 61, 164, 169, 206, 220–1, 270–1, 417, 419–20, 587, 611, 653, 774

Heeresgruppe Kronprinz Rupprecht (HG KPR)

1–12:	war diary and annexes
178, 198, 286, 375, 381, 391–2:	miscellaneous

214–63:	after-action reports
438–44:	strength returns and replacements
477:	morale
478–82:	miscellaneous

Nachlass Frauenholz

| 1: | memoirs |

Nachlass Krafft von Dellmensingen

70–4:	notebooks
145–52, 290:	diary
183, 186–9, 196, 202, 391:	post-1918 correspondence regarding the war
260:	letters to wife
288–9, 324:	operations

Nachlass R. Xylander

| 12: | diary |
| 16: | Lorraine |

Bundesarchiv-Militärarchiv, Freiburg-im-Breisgau (BAMA)

N 18/4, 6	Nachlass Generaloberst W. Heye
N 46/129, 157	Nachlass Wilhelm Groener
N 87/2, 65	Nachlass Otto von Below
PH 5 I/42	Heeresgruppe Kronprinz Rupprecht war diary
PH 5 I/47–8	Heeresgruppe Boehn war diary
PH 5 II/124–7	Armeeoberkommando 2 war diary
RH 61/970	Hermann von Kuhl diary

OFFICIAL PRINTED SOURCES

Bayerisches Kriegsarchiv, *Die Bayern im Großen Kriege* (Munich: Verlag des Bayerischen Kriegsarchivs, 1923)

Beach, James (intro.), *The German Army Handbook of 1918* (Barnsley: Frontline, 2008 [1918])

Behrmann, Franz, *Die Osterschlacht bei Arras 1917* Part I: *Zwischen Lens und Scarpe* (Oldenburg: Gerhard Stalling, 1929)

Behrmann, Franz, *Die Osterschlacht bei Arras 1917* Part II: *Zwischen Scarpe und Bullecourt* (Oldenburg: Gerhard Stalling, 1929)

Beumelburg, Werner, *Loretto* (Oldenburg: Gerhard Stalling, 1927)

Beumelburg, Werner, *Flandern 1917* (Oldenburg: Gerhard Stalling, 1928)

Bose, Thilo von, *Die Katastrophe des 8. August 1918* (Berlin: Gerhard Stalling, 1930)

Cron, Hermann, *Imperial German Army 1914–18: Organisation, Structure, Orders-of-Battle* (C. F. Colton, trans.) (Solihull: Helion, 2002 [original published in German, 1937])

Edmonds, James E. (ed.), *Military Operations, France and Belgium*, 14 volumes (London: HMSO and Macmillan & Co., 1922–48)

Gebsattel, Ludwig von, *Von Nancy bis zum Camp des Romains 1914* (Oldenburg: Gerhard Stalling, 1924)

German General Staff, *Ypres, 1914: An Official Account Published by Order of the German General Staff* (translation of *Die Schlacht an der Yser und bei Ypern im Herbst 1914* (Oldenburg: Gerhard Stalling, 1918) by G. C. W[ynne]) (Nashville, TN: Battery Press, 1994 [1919])

Heeres-Sanitätsinspektion des Reichskriegsministeriums, *Sanitätsbericht über das Deutsche Heer (Deutsches Feld- und Besatzungheer) im Weltkriege 1914/1918*, 3 volumes (Berlin: E. S. Mittler & Sohn, 1934–8)

Humphries, Mark Osborne and Maker, John (eds), *Germany's Western Front: Translations from the German Official History of the Great War* Volume II: *1915* (Waterloo, Ontario: Wilfred Laurier University Press, 2010)

Raleigh, Sir Walter and Jones, H. A., *The War in the Air: Being the Story of the Part Played in the Great War by the Royal Air Force*, 6 volumes (Oxford: Clarendon, 1922–37)

Reichsarchiv, *Der Weltkrieg 1914 bis 1918*, 14 volumes (Berlin: E. S. Mittler & Sohn, 1925–56)

Service Historique, État-Major de l'Armée, Ministère de la Guerre, *Les Armées Françaises dans la Grande Guerre*, 11 volumes (Paris: Imprimerie Nationale, 1922–36)

Stosch, Albrecht von, *Somme-Nord*, 2 volumes (Oldenburg: Gerhard Stalling, 1927)

Strutz, Georg, *Die Tankschlacht bei Cambrai 20–29 November 1917* (Oldenburg: Gerhard Stalling, 1929)

Untersuchungsausschuss der Deutschen Verfassunggebenden Nationalversammlung und des Deutschen Reichstages 1919–26, *Die Ursachen des Deutschen Zusammenbruchs im Jahre 1918*, Volume III (Berlin: Deutsche Verlagsgesellchaft für Politik und Geschichte, 1925)

War Office, *Statistics of the Military Effort of the British Empire during the Great War 1914–1920* (London: HMSO, 1922)

PRIMARY PUBLISHED SOURCES

Balck, W., *Entwicklung der Taktik im Weltkriege* (Berlin: R. Eisenschmidt, 1922)

Bauer, Max, *Der große Krieg in Feld und Heimat* (Tübingen: Osiander'sche Buchhandlung, 1922)

Boraston, J. H. (ed.), *Sir Douglas Haig's Despatches (December 1915–April 1919)* (London: J. M. Dent and Sons, 1919)

Brooke, A. F., 'The Evolution of Artillery in the Great War', *The Journal of the Royal Artillery* Volume LI (1924), pp. 250–68, 359–72; Volume LII (1925–6), pp. 37–51, 369–87; Volume LIII (1927), pp. 76–93, 233–51, 320–39, 469–82

Churchill, Winston S., *The World Crisis*, 6 volumes (London: Thornton Butterworth, 1923–31)

Condell, Bruce and Zabecki, David T. (eds and trans.), *On the German Art of War: Truppenführung* (Boulder, CO: Lynne Rienner, 2001)

Deuringer, Karl, *Die Schlacht in Lothringen und in des Vogesen 1914: Die Feuertaufe der Bayerischen Armee*, 2 volumes (Munich: Max Schick, 1929)

Foch, Ferdinand, *The Memoirs of Marshal Foch* (T. Bentley Mott, trans.) (London: William Heinemann, 1931)

Görlitz, Walter (ed.), *The Kaiser and his Court: The Diaries, Note Books and Letters of Admiral Georg Alexander von Müller, Chief of the Naval Cabinet, 1914–1918* (London: Macdonald, 1961)

Groener, Wilhelm, *Der Felherr wider Willen: Operative Studien über den Weltkrieg* (Berlin: E. S. Mittler & Sohn, 1931)

Haig, Douglas (Gary Sheffield and John Bourne, eds), *War Diaries and Letters 1914–18* (London: Phoenix, 2006 [2005])

Hedin, Sven, *With the German Armies in the West* (H. G. de Walterstorff, trans.) (London: John Lane, The Bodley Head, 1915)

Hertling, Karl, *Ein Jahr in der Reichskanzlei: Erinnerungen an die Kanzlerschaft meines Vaters* (Freiburg: Hedersche Verlagshandlung, 1919)

Hoeppner, Ernst von, *Deutschlands Krieg in der Luft* (Leipzig: K. F. Koehler, 1921)

Krafft von Dellmensingen, Konrad, *Die Führung des Kronprinzen Rupprecht von Bayern auf dem linken deutschen Heeresflügel bis zur Schlacht in Lothringen im August 1914* (Berlin: E. S. Mittler & Sohn, 1925)

Krafft von Dellmensingen, Konrad, *Das Oberkommando in den Reichslanden im Sommer 1914* (Munich: Max Schick, 1931)

Kuhl, Hermann von, *Der deutsche Generalstab in Vorbereitung und Durchführung des Weltkrieges* (Berlin: E. S. Mittler & Sohn, 1920)

Kuhl, Hermann von, *Der Weltkrieg 1914–1918*, 2 volumes (Berlin: Tradition Wilhelm Kolk, 1929)

Leeb, Wilhelm von (Georg Mayer, ed.), *Generalfeldmarschall Wilhelm Ritter von Leeb: Tagebuchaufzeichnungen und Lagebeurteilungen aus zwei Weltkriegen* (Stuttgart: Deutsche Verlags-Anstalt, 1976)

Lloyd George, David, *War Memoirs*, 6 volumes (London: Nicholson & Watson, 1933–6)

Loßberg, Fritz von, *Meine Tätigkeit im Weltkriege 1914–1918* (Berlin: E. S. Mittler & Sohn, 1939)

Ludendorff, Erich, *My War Memories: 1914–1918*, 2 volumes (London: Hutchinson, 1919)

Ludendorff, Erich, *Urkunden der Obersten Heeresleitung über ihre Tätigkeit 1916/18* (Berlin: Ernst Siegfried Mittler und Sohn, 1920)

Marwitz, Georg von der (Erich von Tschischwitz, ed.), *General von der Marwitz: Weltkriegsbriefe* (Berlin: Ernst Steiniger, 1940)

Morgen, Curt von, *Meiner Truppen Heldenkämpfe* (Berlin: Ernst Siegfried Mittler und Sohn, 1920)

Rupprecht, Kronprinz von Bayern (Eugen von Frauenholz, ed.), *Mein Kriegstagebuch*, 3 volumes (Berlin: E. S. Mittler & Sohn, 1929)

Schulte, Bernd F., 'Neue Dokumente zum Kriegsausbruch und Kriegsverlauf 1914', *Militärgeschichtliche Mitteilungen* 25:1 (1979), pp. 123–85

Thaer, Albrecht von (Siegfried A. Kaehler, ed.), *Generalstabsdienst an der Front und in der O.H.L.* (Göttingen: Vandenhoeck & Ruprecht, 1958)

William, Crown Prince of Germany, *My War Experiences* (London: Hurst and Blackett, n.d.)

Xylander, Rudolf von, *Deutsche Führung in Lothringen 1914: Wahrheit und Kriegsgeschichte* (Berlin: Junker und Dünnhaupt Verlag, 1935)

SECONDARY ARTICLES AND BOOKS

Afflerbach, Holger, *Falkenhayn, Politisches Denken und Handeln im Kaiserreich* (Munich: R. Oldenbourg, 1994)

Afflerbach, Holger, *Kaiser Wilhelm II. als Oberster Kriegsherr im Ersten Weltkrieg: Quellen aus der militärischen Umbegung des Kaisers 1914–1918* (Munich: R. Oldenbourg, 2005)

Afflerbach, Holger, 'Kronprinz Rupprecht von Bayern im Ersten Weltkrieg', *Militärgeschichtliche Zeitschrift* 75:1 (May 2016), pp. 21–54

Ashworth, Tony, *Trench Warfare 1914–1918: The Live and Let Live System* (London: Macmillan, 1980)

Asprey, Robert B., *The German High Command at War: Hindenburg and Ludendorff Conduct World War I* (New York: William Morrow, 1991)

Audoin-Rouzeau, Stephane and Becker, Annette, *1914–1918: Understanding the Great War* (Catherine Temerson, trans.) (London: Profile, 2002)

Bailey, Jonathan, *The First World War and the Birth of the Modern Style of Warfare*, Strategic and Combat Studies Institute Occasional Paper No. 22 (SCSI: Camberley, 1996)

Bailey, Jonathan B. A., 'The First World War and the Birth of Modern Warfare', in MacGregor Knox and Williamson Murray (eds), *The Dynamics of Military Revolution 1300–2050* (Cambridge: Cambridge University Press, 2001), pp. 132–53

Beach, Jim, *Haig's Intelligence: GHQ and the German Army, 1916–18* (Cambridge: Cambridge University Press, 2013)

Beckett, Ian F. W., *Ypres: The First Battle, 1914* (Harlow: Pearson, 2004)

Beckett, Ian F. W. and Corvi, Steven J. (eds), *Haig's Generals* (Barnsley: Pen & Sword, 2006)

Berghahn, Volker R., *Imperial Germany, 1871–1914: Economy, Society, Culture, and Politics* (Providence, RI: Berghahn Books, 1994)

Bernhardi, Friedrich von, *Deutschlands Heldenkampf 1914–1918* (Munich: J. F. Lehmann, 1922)

Biddle, Stephen, *Military Power: Explaining Victory and Defeat in Modern Battle* (Princeton, NJ: Princeton University Press, 2004)

Bidwell, Shelford and Graham, Dominick, *Fire-Power: British Army Weapons and Theories of War 1904–1945* (London: George Allen and Unwin, 1982)

Binneveld, Hans, *From Shell Shock to Combat Stress: A Comparative History of Military Psychiatry* (Amsterdam: Amsterdam University Press, 1997)

Boff, Jonathan, *Winning and Losing on the Western Front: The British Third Army and the Defeat of Germany in 1918* (Cambridge: Cambridge University Press, 2012)

Bond, Brian and Cave, Nigel (eds), *Haig: A Reappraisal 70 Years On* (Barnsley: Leo Cooper, 1999)

Bourke, Joanna, *Dismembering the Male: Men's Bodies, Britain and the Great War* (London: Reaktion, 1996)

Bourke, Joanna, *An Intimate History of Killing: Face-to-Face Killing in Twentieth-Century Warfare* (London: Granta, 2000 [1999])

Breg, Josef, *Kronprinz Rupprecht von Bayern: Ein Lebensbild* (Munich: Max Kellerer, 1918)

Bristow, Adrian, *A Serious Disappointment: The Battle of Aubers Ridge and the Subsequent Munitions Scandal* (London: Leo Cooper, 2005)

British Commission for Military History, *'Look to your Front': Studies in the First World War* (Staplehurst: Spellmount, 1999)

Brose, Eric Dorn, *The Kaiser's Army: The Politics of Military Technology in Germany during the Machine Age, 1870–1918* (Oxford: Oxford University Press, 2001)

Brown, Ian M., 'Not Glamorous, But Effective: The Canadian Corps and the Set-Piece Attack, 1917–1918', *Journal of Military History* 58 (July 1994), pp. 421–44

Brown, Ian M., *British Logistics on the Western Front 1914–1919* (Westport, CT: Praeger, 1998)

Campbell, Frederick Francis, 'The Bavarian Army 1870–1918: The Constitutional and Structural Relations with the Prussian Military Establishment' (unpublished PhD thesis, Ohio State University, 1972)

Chasseaud, Peter, 'Field Survey in the Salient: Cartography and Artillery Survey in the Flanders Operations in 1917', in Peter H. Liddle (ed.), *Passchendaele in Perspective: The Third Battle of Ypres* (Barnsley: Pen & Sword, 2013 [1997]), pp. 117–39

Chickering, Roger, *Imperial Germany and the Great War, 1914–1918* (2nd edn, Cambridge: Cambridge University Press, 2004)

Citino, Robert M., *The German Way of War: From the Thirty Years' War to the Third Reich* (Lawrence, KS: University Press of Kansas, 2005)

Clark, Alan, *The Donkeys* (London: Hutchinson, 1961)

Clark, Christopher, *Kaiser Wilhelm II: A Life in Power* (London: Penguin, 2009)

Clayton, Anthony, *Paths of Glory: The French Army 1914–18* (London: Cassell, 2005 [2003])

Corrigan, Gordon, *Sepoys in the Trenches: The Indian Corps on the Western Front 1914–1915* (Staplehurst: Spellmount, 1999)

Corum, James S., 'Air War over the Somme: The Evolution of British and German Air Operations', in Matthias Strohn (ed.), *The Battle of the Somme* (Oxford: Osprey, 2016), pp. 75–91

Cowan, Anthony, 'Genius for War? German Operational Command on the Western Front in Early 1917' (unpublished PhD thesis: King's College London, 2016)

Creveld, Martin van, *Fighting Power: German and U.S. Army Performance, 1939–1945* (Westport, CT: Greenwood Press, 1982)

Creveld, Martin van, *Command in War* (Cambridge, MA: Harvard University Press, 1985)

Creveld, Martin van, *Supplying War: Logistics from Wallenstein to Patton* (Cambridge: Cambridge University Press, 2004 [1977])

Deist, Wilhelm, *Militär und Innenpolitik im Weltkrieg 1914–1918*, 2 volumes (Dusseldorf: Droste, 1990)

Deist, Wilhelm, 'Verdeckter Militärstreik im Kriegsjahr 1918?', in Wolfram Wette (ed.), *Der Krieg des kleinen Mannes: Eine Militärgeschichte von unten* (Munich: Piper, 1992), pp. 146–67

Deist, Wilhelm, 'The Military Collapse of the German Empire: The Reality Behind the Stab-in-the-Back Myth' (E. J. Feuchtwanger, trans.), *War in History* 3:2 (April 1996), pp. 186–207

Dennis, Peter and Grey, Jeffrey (eds), *1918: Defining Victory: Proceedings of the Chief of Army's History Conference held at the National Convention Centre, Canberra 29 September 1998* (Canberra: Army History Unit, Department of Defence, 1999)

Doughty, Robert, *Pyrrhic Victory: French Strategy and Operations in the Great War* (Cambridge, MA: Belknap Press, 2005)

Duffy, Christopher, *Through German Eyes: The British and The Somme 1916* (London: Weidenfeld & Nicolson, 2006)

Dupuy, Trevor N., *A Genius for War: The German Army and General Staff, 1807–1945* (London: Macdonald and Jane's, 1977)

Echevarria II, Antulio J., *After Clausewitz: German Military Thinkers before the Great War* (Lawrence, KS: University of Kansas Press, 2000)

Ehlert, Hans, Epkenhans, Michael and Groß, Gerhard P. (eds), *Der Schlieffenplan: Analyse und Dokumente* (Paderborn: Ferdinand Schöningh, 2006)

Einem, Karl von (Junius Alter, ed.), *Ein Armeeführer erlebte den Weltkrieg* (Leipzig: Von Hase & Koehler, 1938)

Ekins, Ashley (ed.), *1918 Year of Victory: The End of the Great War and the Shaping of History* (Auckland: Exisle Publishing, 2010)

Eksteins, Modris, *The Rites of Spring: The Great War and the Birth of the Modern Age* (London: Bantam, 1989)

Erdmann, Karl Dietrich, *Der Erste Weltkrieg* (Munich: Deutscher Taschenbuch, 1980)

Ertman, Thomas, *Birth of Leviathan: Building States and Regimes in Medieval and Early Modern Europe* (Cambridge: Cambridge University Press, 1997)

Ferguson, Niall, *The Pity of War* (London: Allen Lane, 1998)

Foley, Robert T., *German Strategy and the Path to Verdun: Erich von Falkenhayn and the Development of Attrition 1870–1916* (Cambridge: Cambridge University Press, 2005)

Foley, Robert T., 'Learning War's Lessons: The German Army and the Battle of the Somme 1916', *Journal of Military History* 75 (April 2011), pp. 471–504

Foley, Robert T., 'A Case Study in Horizontal Military Innovation: The German Army 1916–1918', *Journal of Strategic Studies* 35:6 (2012), pp. 799–827

Foley, Robert T., 'Dumb Donkeys or Cunning Foxes? Learning in the British and German Armies during the Great War', *International Affairs* 90:2 (2014), pp. 279–98

Fox-Godden, Aimée, ' "Putting Knowledge in Power": Learning and Innovation in the British Army of the First World War' (unpublished PhD thesis, University of Birmingham, 2015)

Fox-Godden, Aimée, 'Beyond the Western Front: The Practice of Inter-Theatre Learning in the British Army during the First World War', *War in History* 23:2 (2016), pp. 190–209

French, David, *Raising Churchill's Army: The British Army and the War against Germany 1919–1945* (Oxford: Oxford University Press, 2000)

French, David, 'Doctrine and Organisation in the British Army, 1919–32', *Historical Journal* 44 (2001), pp. 497–515

French, David, *Military Identities: The Regimental System, the British Army, and the British People, c. 1870–2000* (Oxford: Oxford University Press, 2005)

Fussell, Paul, *The Great War and Modern Memory* (London: Oxford University Press, 1977)

Gardner, Nikolas, 'The Beginning of the Learning Curve: British Officers and the Advent of Trench Warfare, September–October 1914' (ESRI Working Papers: Salford, 2003)

Gardner, Nikolas, *Trial by Fire: Command and the British Expeditionary Force in 1914* (Westport, CT: Praeger, 2003)

Geddes, Alistair, 'Solly-Flood, GHQ, and Tactical Training in the BEF, 1916–1918' (unpublished MA dissertation, University of Birmingham, 2007)

Gerwarth, Robert, *The Vanquished: Why the First World War Failed to End* (London: Allen Lane, 2016)

Geyer, Michael, 'Insurrectionary Warfare: The German Debate about a Levée en Masse in October 1918', *Journal of Modern History* 73:3 (September 2001), pp. 459–527

Goetz, Walter Wilhelm, *Rupprecht: Kronprinz von Bayern 1869–1955* (Munich: Bayerische Akademie für Wissenschaften, 1956)

Goya, Michel, *La Chair et l'Acier: L'Invention de la Guerre Moderne (1914–1918)* (Paris: Tallandier, 2004)

Greenhalgh, Elizabeth, 'Myth and Memory: Sir Douglas Haig and the Imposition of Allied Unified Command in March 1918', *Journal of Military History* 68:2 (2004), pp. 771–820

Greenhalgh, Elizabeth, *Foch in Command: The Forging of a First World War General* (Cambridge: Cambridge University Press, 2011)

Greenhalgh, Elizabeth, *The French Army and the First World War* (Cambridge: Cambridge University Press, 2014)

Griffith, Paddy, *Battle Tactics of the Western Front: The British Army's Art of Attack 1916–18* (New Haven, CT: Yale University Press, 1994)

Griffith, Paddy (ed.), *British Fighting Methods in the Great War* (London: Frank Cass, 1996)

Groß, Gerhard P., 'Das Dogma der Beweglichkeit: Überlegungen zur Genese der deutschen Heerestaktik im Zeitalter der Weltkriege', in Bruno Thoß and Hans-Erich Volkmann (eds), *Erster Weltkrieg, Zweiter Weltkrieg: Ein Vergleich: Krieg,*

Kriegserlebnis, Kriegserfahrung in Deutschland (Paderborn: Ferdinand Schöningh, 2002), pp. 143–66

Groß, Gerhard P., *Mythos und Wirklichkeit: Geschichte des operativen Denkens im deutschen Heer von Moltke d.Ä bis Heusinger* (Paderborn: Ferdinand Schöningh, 2012)

Gudmundsson, Bruce I., *Stormtroop Tactics: Innovation in the German Army, 1914–1918* (New York: Praeger, 1989)

Gudmundsson, Bruce I., *On Artillery* (Westport, CT: Praeger, 1993)

Hammond, Bryn, *Cambrai 1917: The Myth of the First Great Tank Battle* (London: Weidenfeld & Nicolson, 2008)

Harris, J. P., *Men, Ideas and Tanks: British Military Thought and Armoured Forces, 1903–1939* (Manchester: Manchester University Press, 1995)

Harris, J. P., *Sir Douglas Haig and the First World War* (Cambridge: Cambridge University Press, 2008)

Harris, J. P. with Barr, Niall, *Amiens to the Armistice: The BEF in the Hundred Days Campaign, 8 August–11 November 1918* (London: Brassey's, 1998)

Harris, Paul and Marble, Sanders, 'The "Step-by-Step" Approach: British Military Thought and Operational Method on the Western Front, 1915–1917', *War in History* 15:1 (January 2008), pp. 17–42

Hartcup, Guy, *The War of Invention: Scientific Developments, 1914–18* (London: Brassey's, 1988)

Herwig, Holger H., *The First World War: Germany and Austria-Hungary 1914–1918* (London: Arnold, 1997)

Herwig, Holger H., *The Marne, 1914: The Opening of World War I and the Battle that Changed the World* (New York: Random House, 2009)

Heyck, Thomas William, 'Myths and Meanings of Intellectuals in Twentieth-Century British National Identity', *Journal of British Studies* 37:2 (April 1998), pp. 192–221

Hirschfeld, G., Krumeich G., and Renz, I. (eds) *Die Deutschen an der Somme 1914–1918* (Essen: Klartext, 2006)

Holmes, Richard, *The Little Field-Marshal: Sir John French* (London: Jonathan Cape, 1981)

Horne, John and Kramer, Alan, *German Atrocities 1914: A History of Denial* (New Haven, CT: Yale University Press, 2001)

Howard, Michael, 'Men against Fire: Expectations of War in 1914', *International Security* 9:1 (Summer 1984), pp. 41–57

Hughes, Matthew and Seligmann, Matthew (eds), *Leadership in Conflict 1914–1918* (Barnsley: Leo Cooper, 2000)

Hull, Isabel V., *The Entourage of Kaiser Wilhelm II 1888–1918* (Cambridge: Cambridge University Press, 1982)

Hull, Isabel V., *Absolute Destruction: Military Culture and the Practices of War in Imperial Germany* (Ithaca, NY: Cornell University Press, 2005)

Hull, Isabel V., *A Scrap of Paper: Breaking and Making International Law during the Great War* (Ithaca, NY: Cornell University Press, 2014)

Hynes, Samuel, *A War Imagined: The First World War and English Culture* (London: Pimlico, 1992 [1990])

Hynes, Samuel, *The Soldier's Tale: Bearing Witness to Modern War* (London: Pimlico, 1998)

Jahr, Christoph, *Gewöhnliche Soldaten: Desertion und Deserteure im deutschen und britischen Heer 1914–1918* (Göttingen:Vandenhoeck & Ruprecht, 1998)

Johnson, Hubert C., *Breakthrough! Tactics, Technology and the Search for Victory on the Western Front in World War I* (Novato, CA: Presidio, 1994)

Jones, Heather, *Violence against Prisoners of War: Britain, France and Germany, 1914–20* (Cambridge: Cambridge University Press, 2011)

Kirke, Charles, *Red Coat, Green Machine: Continuity in Change in the British Army 1700 to 2000* (London: Continuum, 2009)

Kitchen, Martin, *The German Officer Corps 1890–1914* (Oxford: Clarendon Press, 1968)

Kitchen, Martin, *The Silent Dictatorship: The Politics of the German High Command under Hindenburg and Ludendorff, 1916–1918* (London: Croom Helm, 1976)

Kolshorn, Otto, *Kronprinz Rupprecht von Bayern: Ein Lebens- und Charakterbild* (Munich: R. Piper & Co., 1918)

Krause, Jonathan, *Early Trench Tactics in the French Army: The Second Battle of Artois, May–June 1915* (Farnham: Ashgate, 2013)

Krause, Jonathan, 'The French Battle for Vimy Ridge, Spring 1915', *Journal of Military History* 77 (January 2013), pp. 91–113

Laffin, John, *British Butchers and Bunglers of World War One* (Stroud: Sutton, 1988)

Liddell Hart, Basil, *The Real War* (London: Faber & Faber, 1930)

Lloyd, Nick, *Loos 1915* (Stroud: History Press, 2008 [2006])

Lloyd, Nick, *Hundred Days: The End of the Great War* (London:Viking, 2013)

Lupfer, Timothy T., *The Dynamics of Doctrine: The Change in German Tactical Doctrine during the First World War* (Leavenworth Paper No. 4: Combat Studies Institute, U.S.Army Command and General Staff College, Fort Leavenworth, Kansas, 1981)

Luvaas, Jay, *The Education of an Army: British Military Thought, 1815–1940* (London: Cassell, 1965)

Machtan, Lothar, *Prinz Max von Baden: Der letzte Kanzler des Kaisers: Eine Biografie* (Berlin: Suhrkamp, 2013)

McRandle, James and Quirk, James, 'The Blood Test Revisited: A New Look at German Casualty Counts in World War I', *Journal of Military History* 70 (2006), pp. 667–702

März, Stefan, *Das Haus Wittelsbach im Ersten Weltkrieg: Chance und Zusammenbruch monarchischer Herrschaft* (Regensburg: Friedrich Pustet, 2013)

Messenger, Charles, *Call to Arms: The British Army 1914–18* (London: Weidenfeld & Nicolson, 2005)

Messenger, Charles, *The Day We Won the War: Turning Point at Amiens, 8 August 1918* (London: Weidenfeld & Nicolson, 2008)

Michaelis, Herbert and Schraepler, Ernst (eds), *Ursachen und Folgen vom deutschen Zusammenbruch 1918 and 1945 bis zur staatlichen Neuordnung Deutschlands in der Gegenwart* Volume II: *Der militärische Zusammenbruch und das Ende des Kaiserreichs* (Berlin: Herbert Wendler & Co., n.d.)

Millett, Allan R. and Murray, Williamson (eds), *Military Effectiveness*, 3 volumes (Boston, MA: Allen & Unwin, 1988)

Mombauer, Annika, *Helmuth von Moltke and the Origins of the First World War* (Cambridge: Cambridge University Press, 2001)

Mombauer, Annika and Deist, Wilhelm (eds), *The Kaiser: New Research on Wilhelm II's Role in Imperial Germany* (Cambridge: Cambridge University Press, 2003)

Müller, Thomas, *Konrad Krafft von Dellmensingen (1862–1953): Porträt eines bayerischen Offiziers* (Munich: Kommission für bayerische Landesgeschichte, 2002)

Murray, Williamson, *Military Adaptation in War: With Fear of Change* (Cambridge: Cambridge University Press, 2011)

Nebelin, Manfred, *Ludendorff: Diktator im Ersten Weltkrieg* (Munich: Siedler, 2010)

Neiberg, Michael S., *The Second Battle of the Marne* (Bloomington, IN: Indiana University Press, 2008)

Palazzo, Albert, 'The British Army's Counter Battery Staff Office and Control of the Enemy in World War I', *Journal of Military History* 63 (January 1999), pp. 55–74

Palazzo, Albert, *Seeking Victory on the Western Front: The British Army and Chemical Warfare in World War I* (Lincoln, NE: University of Nebraska Press, 2000)

Philpott, William, *Bloody Victory: The Sacrifice on the Somme and the Making of the Twentieth Century* (London: Little, Brown, 2009)

Philpott, William, *War of Attrition: Fighting the First World War* (New York: Overlook Press, 2014)

Pöhlmann, Markus, *Kriegsgeschichte und Geschichtspolitik: Der Erste Weltkrieg: Die amtliche deutsche Militärgeschichtsschreibung 1914–1956* (Paderborn: Ferdinand Schöningh, 2002)

Pöhlmann, Markus, 'Yesterday's Battles and Future War: The German Official Military History, 1918–1939', in Roger Chickering and Stig Förster (eds), *The Shadows of Total War: Europe, East Asia, and the United States, 1919–1939* (Cambridge: Cambridge University Press, 2003), pp. 223–38

Pommerin, Reiner, 'Die Ausweisung von "Ostjuden" aus Bayern 1923: Ein Beitrag zum Krisenjahr der Weimarer Republik', *Vierteljahrhefte für Zeitgeschichte* 34:3 (July 1986), pp. 311–40

Prior, Robin and Wilson, Trevor, 'Paul Fussell at War', *War in History* 1:1 (1994), pp. 63–80

Prior, Robin and Wilson, Trevor, *Passchendaele: The Untold Story* (New Haven, CT: Yale University Press, 1996)

Prior, Robin and Wilson, Trevor, *Command on the Western Front: The Military Career of Sir Henry Rawlinson* (Barnsley: Pen & Sword, 2004 [1992])

Prior, Robin and Wilson, Trevor, *The Somme* (New Haven, CT: Yale University Press, 2005)

Pugsley, Christopher, 'Trial and Error: the Dominion forces on the Somme in 1916', in Matthias Strohn (ed.), *The Battle of the Somme* (Oxford: Osprey, 2016), pp. 113–29

Pyta, Wolfram, *Hindenburg: Herrschaft zwischen Hohenzollern und Hitler* (Munich: Siedler, 2007)

Rawling, Bill, *Surviving Trench Warfare: Technology and the Canadian Corps 1914–1918* (Toronto: University of Toronto Press, 1992)

Retallack, James (ed.), *Imperial Germany 1871–1918* (Oxford: Oxford University Press, 2008)

Ritter, Gerhard, *The Sword and the Sceptre: The Problem of Militarism in Germany*, 4 volumes (Heinz Norden, trans.) (London: Allen Lane, 1973)

Robbins, Simon, *British Generalship on the Western Front 1914–18: Defeat into Victory* (London: Frank Cass, 2005)

Röhl, John C. G., *The Kaiser and his Court: Wilhelm II and the Government of Germany* (Terence F. Cole, trans.) (Cambridge: Cambridge University Press, 1994)

Röhl, John C. G., *Wilhelm II: Into the Abyss of War and Exile 1900–1941* (Sheila de Bellaigue and Roy Bridge, trans.) (Cambridge: Cambridge University Press, 2014)

Samuels, Martin, *Doctrine and Dogma: German and British Infantry Tactics in the First World War* (Westport, CT: Greenwood Press, 1992)

Samuels, Martin, *Command or Control? Command, Training and Tactics in the British and German Armies, 1888–1918* (London: Frank Cass, 1995)

Sendtner, Kurt, *Rupprecht von Wittelsbach, Kronprinz von Bayern* (Munich: Richard Pflaum Verlag, 1954)

Sheffield, Gary, *Forgotten Victory: The First World War: Myths and Realities* (London: Headline, 2001)

Sheffield, Gary, *The Somme* (London: Cassell, 2004 [2003])

Sheffield, Gary, *The Chief: Douglas Haig and the British Army* (London: Aurum, 2011)

Sheffield, Gary, *Command and Morale: The British Army on the Western Front, 1914–1918* (Barnsley: Pen & Sword, 2014)

Sheffield, Gary and Gray, Peter, *Changing War: The British Army, the Hundred Days Campaign and the Birth of the Royal Air Force, 1918* (London: Bloomsbury, 2013)

Sheffield, Gary and Todman, Dan (eds), *Command and Control on the Western Front: The British Army's Experience 1914–1918* (Staplehurst: Spellmount, 2004)

Sheldon, Jack, *The Germany Army on the Somme 1916* (Barnsley: Leo Cooper, 2005)

Sheldon, Jack, *The German Army at Passchendaele* (Barnsley: Pen & Sword, 2007)

Sheldon, Jack, *The German Army on Vimy Ridge 1914–1917* (Barnsley: Pen & Sword, 2008)

Sheldon, Jack, *The German Army at Cambrai* (Barnsley: Pen & Sword, 2009)

Sheldon, Jack, *The German Army At Ypres, 1914* (Barnsley: Pen & Sword, 2010)

Showalter, Dennis, *Tannenberg: Clash of Empires, 1914* (Hamden: Archon, 1991)

Sigg, Marco, *Der Unterführer als Feldherr im Taschenformat: Theorie und Praxis der Auftragstaktik im deutschen Heer 1869 bis 1945* (Paderborn: Ferdinand Schöningh, 2014)

Simkins, Peter, *From the Somme to Victory: The British Army's Experience on the Western Front 1916–1918* (Barnsley: Pen & Sword, 2014)

Simpson, Andy, *Directing Operations: British Corps Command on the Western Front 1914–18* (Stroud: Spellmount, 2006)

Stachelbeck, Christian, *Militärische Effektivität im Ersten Weltkrieg: Die 11. Bayerische Infanteriedivision 1915 bis 1918* (Paderborn: Ferdinand Schöningh, 2010)

Stachelbeck, Christian, *Deutschlands Heer und Marine im Ersten Weltkrieg* (Munich: Oldenbourg, 2013)

Stephenson, Scott, *The Final Battle: Soldiers of the Western Front and the German Revolution of 1918* (Cambridge: Cambridge University Press, 2009)

Stevenson, David, *1914–1918: The History of the First World War* (London: Allen Lane, 2004)

Stevenson, David, *With Our Backs to the Wall: Victory and Defeat in 1918* (London: Allen Lane, 2011)

Storz, Dieter, ' "Aber was hätte anders geschehen sollen?" Die deutschen Offensiven an der Westfront', in Jörg Duppler and Gerhard Groß (eds), *Kriegsende 1918: Ereignis, Wirkung, Nachwirkung* (Munich: R. Oldenbourg, 1999), pp. 51–95

Storz, Dieter, ' "Dieser Stellungs- und Festungskrieg ist scheußlich!" Zu den Kämpfen in Lothringen und in den Vogesen im Sommer 1914', in Hans Ehlert, Michael Epkenhans, and Gerhard P. Groß (eds), *Der Schlieffenplan: Analyse und Dokumente* (Paderborn: Ferdinand Schöningh, 2006), pp. 162–204

Storz, Dieter, 'Kronprinz Rupprecht von Bayern—dynastische Heeresführung im Massenkrieg', in Winfried Heinemann and Markus Pöhlmann (eds), *Monarchen und ihr Militär* (Potsdam: Militärgeschichtliches Forschungsamt, 2010), pp. 45–57

Strachan, Hew, 'The Morale of the German Army 1917–18', in Hugh Cecil and Peter Liddle (eds), *Facing Armageddon: The First World War Experienced* (London: Leo Cooper, 1996), pp. 383–98

Strachan, Hew, *The First World War Volume I: To Arms* (Oxford: Oxford University Press, 2001)

Strohn, Matthias, *The German Army and the Defence of the Reich: Military Doctrine and the Conduct of the Defensive Battle 1918–39* (Cambridge: Cambridge University Press, 2010)

Strohn, Matthias (ed.), *The Battle of the Somme* (Oxford: Osprey, 2016)

Strong, Paul and Marble, Sanders, *Artillery in the Great War* (Barnsley: Pen & Sword Military, 2011)

Taylor, A. J. P., *The First World War: An Illustrated History* (London: Hamish Hamilton, 1963)

Terraine, John, *To Win a War: 1918 The Year of Victory* (London: Sidgwick and Jackson, 1978)

Terraine, John, *White Heat: The New Warfare 1914–18* (London: Leo Cooper, 1992 [1982])

Thoß, Bruno and Volkmann, Hans-Erich, *Erster Weltkrieg, Zweiter Weltkrieg: Ein Vergleich: Krieg, Kriegserlebnis, Kriegserfahrung in Deutschland* (Paderborn: Ferdinand Schöningh, 2002)

Travers, T. H. E., 'The Offensive and the Problem of Innovation in British Military Thought, 1870–1915', *Journal of Contemporary History* 13 (1978), pp. 531–53

Travers, Tim, 'The Hidden Army: Structural Problems in the British Officer Corps, 1900–1918', *Journal of Contemporary History* 17:3 (July 1982), pp. 523–44

Travers, Tim, *The Killing Ground: The British Army, the Western Front and the Emergence of Modern Warfare 1900–1918* (London: Allen & Unwin, 1987)

Travers, Tim, *How the War Was Won: Command and Technology in the British Army on the Western Front, 1917–1918* (London: Routledge, 1992)

Uhle-Wettler, Franz, *Erich Ludendorff in seiner Zeit: Soldat—Stratege—Revolutionär—Eine Neubewertung* (Berg: Kurt Vowinckel, 1995)

Ulrich, Bernd and Ziemann, Benjamin (eds), *German Soldiers in the Great War: Letters and Eyewitness Accounts* (Barnsley: Pen and Sword, 2010)

Unruh, Karl, *Langemarck: Legende und Wirklichkeit* (Koblenz: Bernard & Graefe, 1986)

Valentini, Rudolf von, *Kaiser und Kabinettschef* (Oldenburg: Gerhard Stalling, 1931)

Venohr, Wolfgang, *Ludendorff: Legende und Wirchlichkeit* (Berlin: Ullstein, 1993)

Watson, Alexander, 'Self-Deception and Survival: Mental Coping Strategies on the Western Front, 1914–18', *Journal of Contemporary History* 41:2 (2006), pp. 247–68

Watson, Alexander, *Enduring the Great War: Combat, Morale and Collapse in the German and British Armies, 1914–1918* (Cambridge: Cambridge University Press, 2008)

Watson, Alexander, *Ring of Steel: Germany and Austria-Hungary at War, 1914–1918* (London: Allen Lane, 2014)

Wavell, Archibald, *Generals and Generalship* (Harmondsworth: Penguin, 1941)

Weiß, Dieter J., *Kronprinz Rupprecht von Bayern: Eine politische Biografie* (Regensburg: Verlag Friedrich Pustet, 2007)

Winter, Denis, *Haig's Command: A Reassessment* (London: Viking, 1991)

Wynne, G. C., *If Germany Attacks: The Battle in Depth in the West* (Westport, CT: Greenwood Press, 1976 [1940])

Zabecki, David T., *The German 1918 Offensives: A Case Study in the Operational Level of War* (New York: Routledge, 2006)

Zabecki, David T. (ed.), *Chief of Staff: The Principal Officers behind History's Great Commanders* Volume I: *Napoleonic Wars to World War I* (Annapolis, MD: Naval Institute Press, 2008)

Ziemann, Benjamin, *Front und Heimat: Ländliche Kriegserfahrungen im südlichen Bayern 1914–1923* (Essen: Klartext, 1997)

Ziemann, Benjamin, *War Experiences in Rural Germany 1914–1923* (Alex Skinner, trans.) (Oxford: Berg, 2007)

Zuber, Terence, *The Mons Myth: A Reassessment of the Battle* (Stroud: History Press, 2010)

Picture Acknowledgements

Note: BayHStA = Bayerisches Hauptstaatsarchiv; GHA = Geheimes Hausarchiv;
W.B. = Wittelsbacher Bildersammlung; AWM = Australian War Memorial

Frontispiece	AWM H12371
2.1	BayHStA, GHA, W.B. 249/242e
5.1	Bayerisches Hauptstaatsarchiv (BayHStA), Geheimes Hausarchiv (GHA), Wittelsbacher Bildersammlung (W.B.) III 3/229a
8.1	BayHStA, GHA, W.B. 149/151a
11.1	BayHStA, GHA, W.B. 243/245d (author: Franz Grainer)
12.1	BayHStA, GHA, W.B. 112/114e
13.1	AWM H12354
14.1	BayHStA, GHA, W.B. 2996
15.1	AWM H11990
20.1	AWM H13220
22.1	Bayerische Staatsbibliothek München/Bildarchiv
23.1	BayHStA, GHA, W.B. 67/68 (author: Franz Grainer)

Index